Teacher Edition

American
LITERATURE

ENCOURAGING THOUGHTFUL CHRISTIANS TO BE WORLD CHANGERS

By James P. Stobaugh

10-Digit ISBN: 0805458999
13-Digit ISBN: 9780805458992

Published by Broadman & Holman Publishers
Nashville, Tennessee

DEWEY: 810
SUBHD: AMERICAN LITERATURE

Unless otherwise noted, scripture text is from The Holy Bible, *Holman Christian Standard Bible* ®,
Copyright © 1999, 2000, 2001, 2002, 2003 by Holman Bible Publishers. Other "Credits, Permissions,
and Sources" are listed at the back of the book.

Cover and interior design by Paul T. Gant, Art & Design — Nashville, TN

1 2 3 4 5   09 08 07 06 05

This Book is gratefully dedicated to
Karen
and
our four children:
Rachel, Jessica, Timothy, and Peter.

He has given us a ministry of reconciliation . . .
2 Corinthians 5:18

Students, to you 'tis given to scan the heights
Above, to traverse the ethereal space,
And mark the systems of revolving worlds.
Still more, ye sons of science ye receive
The blissful news by messengers from heav'n,
How Jesus blood for your redemption flows . . .

—Phillis Wheatley

ACKNOWLEDGMENTS

From the Broadman and Holman Home Education Division, I wish to thank Sheila Moss, whose editorial assistance and encouragement have been greatly appreciated; Matt Stewart, whose vision and perseverance have made this project possible; and Paul Gant and Mark Grover for their work with graphics and the DVD. Likewise, I thank my four children and my distance learning students who so graciously allowed me to use their essays. Finally, and most of all, I want to thank my best friend and lifelong editor, my wife, Karen. "Come, let us glorify the Lord and praise His name forever . . . ." (Psalm 34:3)

Contents

*Provided in the student textbook.

It is strongly suggested that students read most of the following books during the summer before taking this course:

Augustine, *Confessions*

Dostoevsky, *Crime and Punishment*

Goethe, *Tragedy of Foust*

Homer, *Iliad*

Homer, *Odyssey*

Paton, *Cry the Beloved Country*

Tolstoy, *War and Peace*

Virgil, *Aeneid*

Preface

The heart of these American, British, and World Literature courses is the notion of *rhetoric*, which is the ability to communicate effectively through the written and spoken word. *Written* and *spoken* are the crucial concepts of understanding rhetoric. We can communicate well enough by sending a photograph of something or a CD with music describing something, or painting a picture of something, but that is not rhetoric. Rhetoric is a discipline demanding that a writer dutifully follow laws of grammar, logic, and communication to explain and to describe something.

Quality rhetoric is important and necessary. I agree with Greek philosophers that a democracy demands a responsible, well-considered rhetoric. It is absolutely necessary that we participate in legitimate conversation about important issues. Rhetoric will help us do that.

Rhetoric demands that we reclaim the use of *metaphor*. A metaphor is a word picture. It describes one thing with a dissimilar thing. It demands discipline and control. A four-year-old cannot understand predestination, for instance, unless the communicator pulls out experiences and images that are familiar to the four-year-old. To describe predestination from the perspective of a seminary professor might be accurate, but it is not rhetoric for a four-year-old. We can take a picture of a sunset and send it to millions of people via e-mail, but that is not rhetoric either. *Rhetoric is the attempt to communicate [a sunset] by the use of the spoken or written word.* Thus, metaphor is at the heart of rhetoric, and rhetoric is at the heart of classical education.

Rhetoric is also at the heart of *apologetics*, a systematic argumentative discourse in defense of Christianity. It is my prayer that these courses will ultimately prepare your students to think apologetically.

To ignore rhetoric is to invite ourselves on a dangerous search for truth. Our mindless search for relevance and literalness has gotten us pretty lost in the cosmos. When something we seek is so easily obtained by computer chip or digital photograph, then we lazily refuse to engage ourselves in the discipline of metaphor, or even of thinking. For example, love is not easily photographed. Only the metaphor does it justice. Question: if we lose the written metaphor, will we also lose love? How can we understand 1 Corinthians 13 without first understanding metaphor? Metaphor, or comparison between two ostensibly dissimilar phenomena, is absolutely critical to understanding abstract theological concepts, and, for that matter, it is critical to creative problem solving.

The problems of this age demand a kind of thinking that is promoted and encouraged by rhetoric. The problems of this age will "literally" remain unsolved. However, rhetoric, through the power of metaphor, will invite this generation to look for more creative solutions. Immorality, for instance, will not be removed unless we look to the written Word, that is, the Bible, for answers. Nothing in our experience offers a solution. We will not understand the Bible unless we can employ metaphorical thinking. How else will we apply the Savior's ethical teachings spoken 2000 years ago? Metaphor, along with other mysteries, has become victim of 20th century pretension, pomposity, and obsequious thinking.

Loss of metaphor is only the beginning of the problem. Could it be that great literary works are no longer read—and if they are—there are no rules for interpreting them? In philosophy, indeed in all communication, truth and reality are considered relative. Without rules the rhetorician is invited to come to any kind of conclusion and is on shaky ground. At times it seems that evangelical Christians, who believe in a personal relationship with God, as well as non-Christians, have both sold out to modernity. We have both embraced a sort of existential faith instead of a confessional faith: if it feels good do it and believe it. Unless evangelicals participate in serious apologetics, God will be "weightless."

The rise of relativism has had disastrous results. Rhetoric ferrets out truth. If there is no truth, can there be any sense of authority? And can a society survive if there is no authority? Without a legitimate, honest, well-considered rhetoric, will history be reduced to the "pleasure principle"?

As I mentioned in the Introduction, in some ways American Evangelical Christianity's loss of rhetorical skills—and I think rhetoric is akin to apologetics—has presaged disaster in many arenas. Without rhetoric, we Christians have no tools to engage modern culture. In some ways we have lost mainline denominations to neo-orthodoxy, and we have lost universities to liberals. Where is a modern Jonathan Edwards? A modern C. S. Lewis? Good thinking and good talking may redeem the Church from both the Overzealous and the Skeptic. Rhetorical skills may help us regain the intellectual and spiritual high ground we so grievously surrendered without a fight. WE Christians have conceded much of American culture to modernism by our inability to merge thought and communication in cogency and inspiration. We fail to persuade the modernist culture. Without the main tool to do battle—rhetoric—evangelicals allow orthodoxy to be sacrificed on the altar of relativism. Basically, *Encouraging Thoughtful Christians to be World Changers: Skills for Literary Analysis, Rhetoric, American Literature, British Literature,* and *World Literature* are more than five challenging English courses; they are an attempt to equip this generation of students to participate in apologetics.

DESCRIPTION OF THE COURSE

Toward equipping this generation in apologetics, the *American, World,* and *British Literature* courses are rhetoric level courses that presume a certain level of writing skills.

The *American, British,* and *World Literature* books are content-based. Each literary work is treated individually, much like a unit study. Each author or work, therefore, can be studied independently from the other.

These Literature Critical Thinking courses are primarily essay-based. Each lesson contains several critical thinking questions. Most students will write two or three essays per week. Students may answer the other questions orally or may outline their answers. Since the literature courses are *whole-book/whole-piece,* the entire book/literary piece must be read before the lesson begins. Finally, when writing essays, context is as important as content. In other words, *how* a writer says something is as important as *what* he says.

Literature is defined by Webster's Dictionary as "writings in prose or verse; especially: writings having excellence of form or expression and expressing ideas of permanent or universal interest."

The person who examines, interprets, and analyzes literature is a *critic*. A critic is a guide to the reader; he is not a prophet; he is not a therapist. While it is the critic's right to express preferences and to influence others, telling the reader what to like or not like is not the task of the literary critic. However, the critic is a helper, a guide helping the reader better understand the author's intention and art.

In fact, the critic is concerned about the structure, sound, and meaning of the literary piece. These structures are described as genres: prose, poetry, essays, drama.

Literary analysis or criticism is a method of talking about literature. Literary analysis is a way to better understand literature. If we really want to understand something, we need to have a common language with everyone else. In discussing football, for instance, we need to know and use certain terminology when describing the game. Not knowing what a tackle is would certainly limit communication about the game! Not knowing what the referee means when he says, "first and ten!" would certainly limit enjoyment in watching a game Literary analysis employs a common language to take apart and to discuss literary works. The following is part of a student's literary critical paper concerning the main character in the modern American novel *A Separate Peace,* by John Knowles.

John Knowles was a master at creating internal struggles with his characters. In *A Separate Peace* Gene, the protagonist and perfect student struggles with his feelings about his best friend Finny and Gene's alter-ego antagonist. Knowles skillfully shows how Gene feels both love and hatred toward Finny.

Gene and Finny are two extremes. Gene is excellent at scholarly activities. He has the best grades in Devon. Finny, however, is the best athlete. He breaks records and plays nearly every sport Devon has to offer. Often Gene is in trouble for things that Finny escapes. Finny is able to talk his way out of almost everything. Thus, Finny and Gene are opposites.

In spite of these substantial differences, Gene loves Finny and is his best friend. Gene struggles with these two conflicting thoughts, and his ambivalent feelings toward Finny cause Gene to shake Finney out of the tree. (Peter Stobaugh)

One final word: every lesson will include at least one literary criticism question. Literary criticism papers are more frequently assigned than any other high school or college writing assignment. Therefore, students will do well to develop this craft and continue to refine it throughout their writing careers.

Grammar concepts are incorporated in these courses when students are expected to apply something they may not be familiar with. Knowing grammar *before* beginning the courses is optimal. However, for those parent/educators and students who wish to continue studies in grammar, mechanics, punctuation, spelling and diction, effective sentences, and the larger elements of composition, teaching these elements during a separate period of the day is a feasible option. Perhaps identifying areas of writing difficulties within student compositions and providing worksheet interventions will help satisfy those troublesome areas. It is common even for advanced students to need refinement with writing concepts.

This course uses the cognitive-developmental approach: it facilitates learning stages based on B.S.Bloom's taxonomy theories (*A Taxonomy of Educational Objectives: Handbook I: Cognitive Domain*, N.Y. David McKay, 1956).

An underlying assumption in a cognitive-developmental course is the notion that people learn in stages. They do not move to another stage unless they are thinking well at the previous stage. Inevitably, too, students will not progress to higher thinking without dissonance or conflict. They must be dissatisfied with their previous thinking so that they might progress to more profound thinking. Students move from simple thinking and problem solving to more complicated, difficult problem solving/thinking.

Thus, this course implements mostly higher-level thinking exercises: application, analysis, synthesis, and evaluation; however, there will be a few knowledge, comprehension, and application questions on the tests.

> BLOOM'S TAXONOMY
>
> KNOWLEDGE: Remembering the material without understanding, using, or changing the material.
>
> COMPREHENSION: Understanding the material being given without comparing it to anything else.
>
> APPLICATION: Using a general concept to solve a problem.
>
> ANALYSIS: Taking something apart.
>
> SYNTHESIS: Creating something new by putting different ideas together to make a new whole.
>
> EVALUATION: Judging the value of material.

WHAT DOES IT MEAN "TO THINK CRITICALLY"?

If I show you a truck I am giving you knowledge of the truck. If I show you the parts of the truck, tell you their names, let you sit in the driver's seat and even play with the radio, I am increasing your comprehension of the truck. However, I have not allowed you to drive the truck yet. You know a lot about the truck, perhaps you even have pretended to drive it. You can now tell someone else the names of all the parts, and perhaps you learned how to work the radio. However, you haven't learned to drive it yet. You have passed from the knowledge phase, to the comprehension phase, and are now ready for the application phase. You know a lot about the truck, and you may even know something about how to drive it. However, the fact is you have not driven it yet.

Then, if I allow you to drive the truck I am helping you apply your understanding about the truck to a specific task. Now all that you have learned is being used. It is at this point that this course begins. The student has learned information and hopefully understands it well. Now he needs to learn how to use this information.

Finally, if I wish you to know more about the truck, I could suggest that you take the truck apart, analyze each part, and discover how each part works together. You would be analyzing the truck at this point.

You would know the parts of the truck; you would know more about how to fix the truck if it breaks down. You could take the truck apart, put it back together again, and, what is more exciting, you could decide that you don't want a truck anymore. You could even build different things with the truck parts because you know what the truck parts are and do. This step is called synthesis.

Finally, you can decide if this is a good truck after all. Now that you know all about this truck, you can ask yourself, "Is this a good truck?" and "Can I make a better truck?" At this phase of knowledge acquisition, you are evaluating the truck.

This is a crude analogy, and no doubt the metaphor breaks down at times, but you get the point. This course teaches students how to apply knowledge, how to analyze knowledge, how to synthesize knowledge, and finally how to evaluate knowledge.

All of the painstaking thinking is for one glorious purpose: to encourage our thoughtful students to be world changers for Christ.

GOALS AND OBJECTIVES

Typically, the parent/educator will seek to inculcate several goals/objectives. Usually, these include
   cognitive or learning goals,
   spiritual or affective goals,
   behavioral goals.

Cognitive goals usually relate to the understanding of (a) concept(s) and/or the understanding or acceptance of a generalization. A concept is something understood from evidence or other information. It is an abstract or generic idea generalized from particular instances. The understanding of several concepts may lead to the acceptance and understanding of a generalization. A generalization is the act or process whereby a response is made to a stimulus similar to but not identical with a reference stimulus. A generalization will have application far beyond the original concept(s) introduced. For instance, a concept that students will study in American Literature Lesson 1 is "Puritanism." After the students read several literary pieces by and about Puritans, they should consider and hopefully accept this generalization: "Puritans were not dry, lifeless people as they are depicted in Hollywood films."

Writing literary criticism, thinking critically, reflecting on biblical dilemmas, and pondering challenge/enrichment questions will never be easy. Students will have to commit themselves to a year long, indeed, lifelong, discipline of learning.

Also, students will be able to evaluate the worldview of each author. This is a critical step. Students will also evaluate the world view of each author and compare it to their own worldview.

As a result of this course students will understand, appreciate, and analyze American literature, and will be able to articulate their worldview and identify the worldview(s) of several authors.

How will the parent/educator know when these goals have been fulfilled? When the student is able to write cogent, inspired essays with minimal errors and to discuss the concepts with others.

Every lesson will include a suggested planning paradigm/format that the parent/educator may find helpful. For example:

Goals/Objectives: What is the purpose of this lesson?	Strategies to meet these goals: How will I obtain these goals/objectives?	Evaluation: How will I know when I have met these goals/objectives?
Concept: literary technique (cognitive goal)	In open discussion students will be able to articulate the reasoning behind this particular narrative technique in this particular literary work.	Students will be able to read any book or watch any movie and discuss in an informed way a particular literary technique.
Concept: analysis (cognitive goal)	Write an essay: Choose a Critical Thinking Essay, a Biblical Application Essay, and/or an Enrichment Essay.	With minimal errors students will clearly answer the assigned questions.
Concept: worldview of the author; comparison of worldviews (spiritual/affective goal)	In class or at dinner time students will verbally explain the worldview of the lesson's literary work and compare it to their own. Students will discuss the worldview of a current television program.	Students will state clearly the worldview of the author and other cultural influences encountered during this week.

Goals/Objectives: What is the purpose of this lesson?	Strategies to meet these goals: How will I obtain these goals/objectives?	Evaluation: How will I know when I have met these goals/objectives?
Concept: writing an essay (cognitive goal)	Write an essay discussing a particular concept.	With minimal errors students will clearly answer the assigned questions.
Concept: truth in generalization (cognitive goal)	Write an essay discussing a particular concept.	With minimal errors students will clearly answer the assigned questions.
Concept: working in a group setting (behavioral goal)	In a class, in a co-op experience, or during dinnertime, students will participate in a group discussion of the book.	Students will exhibit practical listening skills and will manifest understanding of opposing world-views.

NOTE: Completing a planning strategy for each lesson is optimum.

SUGGESTED

Weekly *Implementation*

DAY 1	DAY 2	DAY 3	DAY 4	DAY 5
Teacher and students will decide on required essays for this lesson, choosing two or three essays.

The rest of the essays can be outlined, answered with shorter answers, or skipped.

Teacher may want to discuss assigned reading(s) with students.

Review all readings for Assigned Lesson. | Review reading(s) from next lesson.

Outline essays due at the end of the week.

Per teacher instructions, students may answer orally in a group setting some of the essays that are not assigned as formal essays. | Write rough drafts of all assigned essays.

The teacher and/or a peer evaluator may correct rough drafts. | Re-write corrected copies of essays due tomorrow. | Essays are due.

Take Lesson 1 test.

Reading ahead: This memo will give you a reminder of what to be reading for future lessons.

Guide: These questions will guide your thinking and study as you read for the next lesson. |

SPIRITUAL DEVELOPMENT OF THE STUDENT

The parent/educator should consciously stimulate spiritual/faith development in the student. Gone are the days, if they ever existed, that moral development can be separated from knowledge acquisition. Moral decisions are made by

1. Factual information and
2. Values and loyalties.

Other insights about morality include:

1. Morality is manifested in human relationships.
2. Moral/faith growth only occurs when there is dissonance.
3. One goal is to participate in unselfish acts under authority of the Word of God in relationship with God (see Romans 12).
4. Risk is involved in moral/faith.
5. Learning to think critically *can* accelerate moral/faith development but does not guarantee its growth.

Students will mature in these approximate stages:

Age 0-4. Child decides what is sacred and important, usually determined by what the parent finds important.

Age 5-12. Family is primary but understands that "Johnny" has different beliefs; many children commit their lives to Christ at this age

Age 12-17. Child understands faith, racial, and social classification.

Age 19-Adult. Indigenous values inculcated in the young person are no longer accepted without question.

Adulthood. Individual learns from other individuals or knowledge bases and willingly changes.

Adulthood. Person is a living example of Galatians 2: 20—I have been crucified with Christ and I no longer live, but Christ lives in me. The life I live in the body, I live by faith in the Son of God, who loved me and gave himself for me. (Roughly based on thoughts by Dr. James Fowler)

SPECIAL NEEDS STRATEGIES

The *Encouraging Thoughtful Christians to be World Changers* courses are perfect courses to use with students who learn differently.

1. The unit studies format lends itself well because the parent/educator can choose which literary works and lessons most apply to the student's needs. Each unit stands alone. The parent/educator is free to spend as much time on each unit as needed.

2. There are several options for dealing with very long or very difficult reading selections: besides the ability to skip very long or difficult works, the learning challenged student and parent/educator may also choose which question(s) to answer verbally and which to answer in writing. For example, parent and student will decide on the number of required essays for each lesson, typically choosing one to three essays. Choices can be from the Critical Thinking questions, the Biblical Application questions, and the Enrichment Question with the option to write essays, speak/discuss essays, and even outline essays. In some cases abridged editions or editions in large print ease the accomplishment of the task and at the same time provide the more difficult content that might otherwise be skipped due to length.

3. Additionally, the parent/educator may want to help the student read the more difficult readings by providing unabridged book tapes of the assigned text. Book tapes of most works can be obtained from www.forsuchatimeasthis.com.

4. Another strategy in working with students who learn differently is to *share the reading*: students and parents enjoy the literature by alternately reading to each other in a comfortable setting. This method is highly recommended by scholars who work with students who learn differently.

PARENT/EDUCATORS' ROLES AND RESPONSIBILITIES

It is the parent/educator's responsibility to:

1. Make sure the student has read the assigned, whole literary piece sometime before the first assignment which begins the lesson. The parent/educator should also encourage the student to read ahead for future lessons. (Student editions of this series include an Assignment Memo in a text box on each lesson's front page.)

2. Read the assigned text or a thorough summary of the text. The parent/educator should not hesitate to read an abridged help such as "Cliff Notes"®. However, the student should read the unabridged version if at all possible. There will be many lessons where the whole unabridged book will be over 600 pages. Parents and students should decide on the edition most appropriate for the student. Typically, the parent/educator is free to choose the unabridged translation/version of the text he desires. These lessons are unit studies—they stand alone. Students do not have to do *all* the lessons: some lessons may be skipped if you wish, depending on the level of accomplishment you and your student opt.

3. Discuss the goal of the lesson found on the first page of each lesson and in the Suggested Weekly Implementation table at the end of the Student text and in the middle of the Teacher text.

4. Alert students to future reading assignments and pique their interest with the guide questions.

5. Discuss the background material.

6. Choose the Assignments/Activities the student will complete during the assignment period. Assignment choices include these three types of questions: Literary Criticism, Biblical Application, and Enrichment. Most students will write two or three 1-2 page essays per week. Typically, the student should alter writing short essays (300 to 500 words) with longer essays (500-2000 words). In this series the most difficult essay is typically found in the Enrichment challenges.

7. Evaluate essays. There are many methods for evaluating essays. Two samples are provided for you in the Appendices. Please note that how and when you evaluate each essay help determine writing development and set the stage not only for writing progress but for student attitudes toward writing. Appropriate evaluation of essays is fundamental to student growth as a writer. If they repeat common errors essay after essay, these errors get more firmly entrenched in their writing and become more difficult to overcome.

8. Credit the Course. Whatever evaluation technique the teacher/educator may choose, this course is at least a one year/one credit course when it is *satisfactorily completed*.

NOTE: If students decide to faithfully respond to the Biblical Application questions every week and keep the Prayer Journal daily, *in addition to* the Critical Thinking or Enrichment Questions, they may earn an additional high school 1/2 elective credit. If students choose this option, a separate Biblical Application Portfolio can show evidence of the course work.

9. Oversee other activities the student will complete during the assignment period. These activities include **vocabulary card** completion. Students will be assigned particular works to read during this course; however, as time allows, students should read books from the enclosed supplemental book list (Appendix). Students should read most of the books on the enclosed list before graduating from high school. After reading a literary work, for this course or for any other reason, students should complete a **book checkup** (Appendices) as a record of high school reading. The book list in the Appendix is not meant to be exhaustive but is intended as a guide to good reading. Students should read 35-50 pages per night (or 200 pages per week). This amount includes reading the books for this course. Part of the reason students are asked to read so many challenging literary works is for increasing their functional vocabulary. Studies show that within 24 hours most students forget new words given to them to learn every week if they are not read in context. The best means of increasing your students' vocabulary is through having them read a vast amount of classical, well-written literary works. While reading these works, students should harvest as many unknown words as possible. One way to have students remember vocabulary words is to have them *use five new words in each essay they write*.

Have students create three-by-five vocabulary cards.

How many vocabulary cards students create can be determined by how many new words they encounter in their reading. By the end of this course students will have collected between 350-500 vocabulary cards.

Students may find this process tedious and frustrating, but the method is a valuable tool for learning. To decrease frustration, buy copies of the books and allow students to highlight unknown words which will be used on vocabulary cards.

10. Other activities include the Enrichment Resources/Activities and Supplemental Resources. Teachers may use these resources at their discretion.

11. Complete literary check-ups. As I mentioned, students need to read about 200 pages of new material every week. This page count can include other literary works besides those assigned in this course. Students should complete a literary check-up (see Appendix) every time they finish a literary work. They can use the suggested list in the Appendix or merely complete literary check-ups on readings in other required courses.

12. Make sure students are ready for the Final Portfolio: a collection of corrected essays, literary checkups, vocabulary cards, pictures or artifacts from field trips, and other pertinent material. Ideally, this Portfolio will be presented orally to peers, siblings, and/or co-op groups.

13. Finally, the parent/educator should <u>obtain the requisite literary material</u> for students. See the scope and sequence of this course below.

SCOPE AND SEQUENCE
AMERICAN LITERATURE

LESSON	PERIOD/WORLDVIEW AUTHORS/ TEXTS
1	**The New Land to 1750: Puritanism and Native American Voices** *The History of Plimoth Plantation*, William Bradford.* *The Navajo Origin Legend;* Navajo Tribe, from *The Iroquois Constitution* Iroquois Tribe
2	**Worldview Formation and Discernment** No Readings Required
3	**The New Land to 1750: Puritanism** *Religious Affections*, Jonathan Edwards; "Diary Entries,"* Esther Edwards; Poems* by Anne Bradstreet
4	**The Revolutionary Period, 1750-1800 (Part 1)** *The Autobiography of Benjamin Franklin*, Benjamin Franklin
5	**The Revolutionary Period, 1750-1800 (Part 2)** Poems* by Phillis Wheatley; *Speech in the Virginia Convention,** Patrick Henry; *The Declaration of Independence,** Thomas Jefferson; *Letter to Her Daughter from the* *New White House,** Abigail Adams
6	**A Growing Nation, 1800-1840: National Period (Part 1)** "Thanatopsis,"* William Cullen Bryant; "The Devil and Tom Walker,"* Washington Irving
7	**A Growing Nation, 1800-1840: National Period (Part 2)** "The Fall of the House of Usher,"*and "The Tell Tale Heart,"* Edgar Allan Poe
8	**Romanticism: New England Renaissance, 1840-1855 (Part 1)** *The Scarlet Letter* and "Birthmark,"* Nathaniel Hawthorne
9	**Romanticism: New England Renaissance, 1840-1855 (Part 2)** Poems* by Henry Wadsworth Longfellow, Oliver Wendell Holmes, James Russell Lowell, John Greenleaf Whittier, and Emily Dickinson.
10	**Romanticism: New England Renaissance, 1840-1855 (Part 3)** Selected Poems,* Ralph Waldo Emerson
11	**Romanticism: New England Renaissance, 1840-1855 (Part 4)** *Walden*, Henry David Thoreau
12	**Romanticism: New England Renaissance, 1840-1855 (Part 5)** *Billy Budd*, Herman Melville

*Provided in the student textbook.

13	**Division, War, and Reconciliation, 1855-1865 (Part 1)**
	"O Captain, My Captain!"* Walt Whitman;
	"Go Down Moses,"* "Deep River,"* Roll Jordan, Roll,"*
	"Swing Low, Sweet Chariot;"* Negro Spirituals;
	"The Gettysburg Address,"* Abraham Lincoln;
	"I will Fight No More Forever,"* Chief Joseph
14	**Division, War, and Reconciliation, 1855-1865 (Part 2)**
	Narrative of the Life of Frederick Douglass, Frederick Douglass
15	**Realism, Naturalism, and The Frontier, 1865-1915 (Part 1)**
	The Adventures of Huckleberry Finn, Mark Twain
16	**Realism, Naturalism, and The Frontier, 1865-1915 (Part 2)**
	The Adventures of Huckleberry Finn, Mark Twain
17	**Realism, Naturalism, and The Frontier, 1865-1915 (Part 3)**
	Red Badge of Courage, Stephen Crane
18	**Realism, Naturalism, and The Frontier, 1865-1915 (Part 4)**
	Red Badge of Courage, Stephen Crane
19	**Realism, Naturalism, and The Frontier, 1865-1915 (Part 5)**
	"The Outcasts of Poker Flat, "* Bret Harte;
	"The Story of an Hour,"* Kate Chopin;
	"Richard Cory,"* Edwin Arlington Robinson;
	"Lucinda Matlock,"* Edgar Lee Masters
20	**The Modern Age, 1915-1946: Late Romanticism/ Naturalism (Part 1)**
	Ethan Frome, Edith Wharton
21	**The Modern Age, 1915-1946: Late Romanticism/ Naturalism (Part 2)**
	20th Century Poetry
22	**The Modern Age, 1915-1946: Late Romanticism/ Naturalism (Part 3)**
	A Farewell to Arms, Ernest Hemingway
23	**The Modern Age, 1915-1946: Late Romanticism/ Naturalism (Part 4)**
	Their Eyes Were Watching God, Zora Neale Hurston
24	**The Modern Age, 1915-1946: Late Romanticism/ Naturalism (Part 5)**
	The Unvanquished, William Faulkner
25	**The Modern Age, 1915-1946: Late Romanticism/ Naturalism (Part 6)**
	The Pearl, John Steinbeck
26	**The Modern Age, 1946-1960: Late Romanticism/ Naturalism (Part 1)**
	20th Century Drama: *The Emperor Jones*, Eugene Gladstone O'Neill

*Provided in the student textbook.

27	**The Modern Age, 1946-1960: Realism/ Naturalism (Part 2)** 20th Century Drama: *The Little Foxes*, Lillian Hellman.
28	**The Modern Age, 1946-1960: Realism/ Naturalism (Part 3)** 20th Century Drama: *The Glass Menagerie*, Tennessee Williams
29	**The Modern Age, 1946-1960: Realism/ Naturalism (Part 4)** 20th Century Drama: *The Glass Menagerie*, Tennessee Williams
30	**The Modern Age, 1946-1960: Realism/Naturalism (Part 5)** *The Crucible*, Arthur Miller
31	**Contemporary Writers, 1960-Present (Part 1)** *A Separate Peace*, John Knowles
32	**Contemporary Writers, 1960-Present: The Southern Renaissance: (Part 2)** "Everything That Rises Must Converge"* Flannery O'Connor; "A Worn Path"* Eudora Welty; "The Jilting of Granny Weatherall"* Katherine Anne Porter
33	**Contemporary Writers, 1960-Present (Part 3)** *Cold Sassy Tree*, Olive Ann Burns
34	**Contemporary Writers, 1960-Present (Part 4)** *The Chosen*, Chiam Potok

*Provided in the student textbook.

Audio presentations of most of the readings in the book may be obtained from Blackstoneaudio.com

American Literature Reading List

Additional texts, not included within the study, needed for this program:

Religious Affections by Jonathan Edwards

The Autobiography of Benjamin Franklin by Benjamin Franklin

Walden by Henry David Thoreau

Billy Budd by Herman Melville

Narrative of the Life of Frederick Douglass by Frederick Douglass

The Adventures of Huckleberry Finn by Mark Twain

Red Badge of Courage by Stephen Crane

Ethan Frome by Edith Wharton

A Farewell to Arms by Ernest Hemingway

Their Eyes Were Watching God by Zora Neale Hurston

The Unvanquished by William Faulkner

The Pearl by John Steinbeck

The Emperor Jones by Eugene Gladstone O'Neill

The Little Foxes by Lillian Hellman

The Glass Menagerie by Tennessee Williams

The Crucible by Arthur Miller

Cold Sassy Tree by Olive Ann Burns

The Chosen by Chiam Potok

My prayer for you is

"For this reason I bow my knees before the Father from whom every family in heaven and on earth is named. I pray that He may grant you, according to the riches of His glory, to be strengthened with power through His Spirit in the inner man, and that the Messiah may dwell in your hearts through faith. I pray that you, being rooted and firmly established in love, may be able to comprehend with all the saints what is the length and width, height and depth of God's love, and to know the Messiah's love that surpasses knowledge, so you may be filled with all the fullness of God. Now to Him who is able to do above and beyond all that we ask or think — according to the power that works in you — to Him be glory in the church and in Christ Jesus to all generations, forever and ever. Amen."
(Ephs. 3:14-21)

James Stobaugh

From the Editor

Developing appropriate curricula for a specific audience is a major and intricate endeavor. Doing so for the homeschool and Christian communities is perhaps even more difficult: homeschool approaches, methodology, and content are as diverse as traditional educational trends have ever dared to be. Homeschooling is complex—from unschooling to the Classical approach, there are myriads of opinions of what to teach, when to teach it, and how to teach it to whom at what age and at what level of development. Perhaps you struggle with choices between a *whole-book* approach to literature study or a more traditional and inclusive canon. Perhaps you are still wading through myriads of questions associated with homeschooling teenagers. However, perhaps your decision is final and you merely need a solid literature-and-writing-based English curriculum. Keep reading.

In one-year literature/writing-based courses, including all the quality literature that has ever been published is impossible—there is simply too much good literature and not enough space to include it; neither is there time enough to read it all. Regrettably, many selections of quality literature have not been included in this course—not because they are unworthy, but because they all cannot fit into the designated framework. The author and I have done our best to include whole-book or whole-work selections from the major genres of literature (prose, poetry, and drama). In the *Literary Analysis, Rhetoric,* and *American, British,* and *World Literature* courses in this series, literary selections incorporate many ethnicities from both male and female writers. We believe our selections inform the purpose of the curricula: *Encouraging Thoughtful Christians to be World Changers.*

According to a well-known author, homeschool conference speaker, and long-time homeschooling mom, two of the greatest needs in the homeschool community reside in curricula for high school and for special needs. These English curricula consider those needs; they were conceived in prayer, deliberated through educational experience, and nurtured with inspiration. We are providing unique five-year curricula for required English studies for the multifarious Christian community. Canonical and Classical literature is emphasized; students are meticulously guided through carefully honed steps of *critical thinking, biblical challenge for spiritual growth,* and even additional *enrichment* motivators. A major key to the successful completion of these courses falls in the statements, "Teachers and students will decide on required essays for this lesson, choosing two or three essays. All other essays may be outlined, discussed, or omitted." These statements, repeated in every lesson, allow tremendous flexibility for various levels of student maturity and interests. Since each lesson may offer 10-15 essays, choosing essays each week is vital.

In any literature course offered to Christian audiences there will be differences in opinions regarding acceptable and appropriate content, authors, poets, and playwrights. Some educators may object to specific works or specific authors, poets, or playwrights included in these curricula *even though we have been very conscientious with selections.* For that reason we highly encourage educators and students to confab—choose units according to students' maturity, ability, age, sensitivity, interests, educational intentions, and according to family goals. Educators decide how much they want to shelter their students or to sanction certain works or authors, poets, and playwrights.

On a broader note, our goal in this series is to provide parent educators and Christian schools with educationally sound, rigorous literature courses that equip students

1. to think critically about their world and their participation in it;

2. to write their thoughts, primarily through essays;

3. to articulate their thoughts through small group discussions with peers, families, broader communities, and through occasional formal speeches;

4. to enhance vocabulary through reading and studying quality literature;

5. to converse about the major worldviews of authors of literature, past and present;

6. to develop and refine their own worldviews through participating in biblical application and Christian principles in weekly studies.

Additionally, we provide educators with an instructional CD in the back of each teacher edition. Narrated by the author, the CD is designed to provide extra commentary on the unit studies.

Ideally, students will complete these entire curricula; however, parent educators and teachers are free to choose literary selections that best fit their goals with students. Regardless of the choices, I pray that students come away from studying *Skills for Literary Analysis*, *Skills for Rhetoric*, *American Literature*, *British Literature*, and *World Literature* not only highly educated but also equipped to participate in and contribute to their earthly home while preparing for their heavenly home.

Enjoy!
Sheila Moss

Introduction

I am profoundly enthusiastic about the future. Not only do I trust in our Mighty God, I am greatly encouraged by what I see in this generation. God is doing great things in the midst of students.

There is much need in our physical world. In his seminal work *The Dust of Death* (Downers Grove, Illinois: Intervarsity Press, 1973), social critic Os Guinness prophetically argues that "western culture is marked . . . by a distinct slowing of momentum . . . a decline in purposefulness. . . ." Guinness implies that ideals and traditions that have been central to American civilization are losing their compelling cultural authority. In short, there is no corpus of universally accepted morality that Americans follow. As Dallas Willard in *The Divine Conspiracy* (San Francisco: HarperCollins Publishers, 1997) states, ". . . there is no recognized moral knowledge upon which projects of fostering moral development could be based."

In his poem "The Second Coming" William Butler Yeats writes

The best lack all conviction, while the worst
Are full of passionate intensity
Turning and turning in the widening gyre;
The falcon cannot hear the falconer.

In the beginning of the twenty-first century, America is spinning out of control. She is stretching her wings adventurously but is drifting farther away from her God. America is in trouble. How do we know?

You are America's first generation to grow up when wholesale murder is legal; the first generation to access 130 channels and at the same time to access almost nothing of value. In 1993 in their book *The Day America Told the Truth* (NY: Simon & Schuster Publishers, Inc.), James Patterson and Peter Kim warned that 87% of Americans do not believe that the Ten Commandments should be obeyed and 91% of them tell at least one lie a day. Unfortunately, I doubt things are any better today than they were over 10 years ago. The challenge, the bad news, is that this is a time when outrage is dead. Whatever needs to be done, you and your friends are probably going to have to do it.

I think the good news is that we are turning a corner. I believe that in the near future Americans will be looking to places of stability and strength for direction. Besides, by default, those people whose lives are in reasonably good shape, who have some reason to live beyond the next paycheck, will have an almost inexorable appeal. Those who walk in the Light will draw others into the very-same Light. My prayer is that these curricula will help you walk in the Light in a modest way.

I believe that God is raising a mighty generation at the very time that many twenty-first century Americans are searching for truth—at the very time they are hungry for things of the Lord. You will be the culture-creators of the next century. You are a special generation, a special people.

Young people, I strongly believe that you are the generation God has called *for such a time as this* to bring a Spirit-inspired revival. God is stirring the water again at the beginning of this century. He is offering a new beginning for a new nation. I believe you are the personification of that new beginning.

You are part of one of the most critical generations in the history of Western culture. Indeed, only Augustine's generation comes close in importance to your generation. In both cases—today and during the life of Augustine, Bishop of Hippo—civilizations were in decline. Young Augustine lived through the decline of the Roman world; you are living through the decline of American cultural superiority. Even though the barbarians conquered Rome, the Christians conquered the barbarians.

Similar to Anne Bradstreet and other young Puritans who settled in 1630 Boston, you will need to replace this old, reprobate culture with a new God-centered, God-breathed society, or our nation may not survive another century.

While I was a graduate student at Harvard University in the mid-1970s, I attended a chapel service where the presenter self-righteously proclaimed that we Harvard students were the next generation of culture creators. Indeed. Perhaps he was right—look at the moral mess my generation created!

Evangelical scholars Nathan Hatch and George Marsden argue, and I think persuasively, that you young people will be the next generation of elites: important politicians, inspired playwrights, and presidents of Fortune 500 companies.

I profoundly believe and fervently hope that you young people will also be the new elite of culture creators. I define "elitism" as the ability and propensity of an individual or a group to assume leadership and culture-creation in a given society. In his essay "Blessed Are the History-Makers," theologian Walter Bruggemann reminds us that culture is created and history is made by those who are radically committed to obeying God at all costs.

Will you be counted among those who are radically committed—being smart, but above all, loving, worshipping, and being obedient to the Word of God? In your generation and for the first time in 300 years of American cultural history, the marriage of smart minds and born-again hearts is becoming visible. This combination is potent indeed and has revolutionary implications for twenty-first century cultural America. Now, as in the Puritan era, a spirit-filled elite with all its ramifications is exciting to behold.

This book is dedicated to the ambitious goal of preparing you to be a twenty-first century world changer for the Christ whom John Milton in *Paradise Lost* called "the countenance too severe to be beheld" (VI, 825).

James Stobaugh

LESSON 1

NEW LAND TO 1750:
PURITANISM AND NATIVE AMERICAN VOICES

Readings Due For This Lesson: *The History of Plimoth Plantation,* William Bradford or excerpt in book. *A Quest for Godliness,* J. I. Packer (optional). Navajo: from *The Navajo Origin Legend;* Iroquois: from *The Iroquois Constitution.*

Reading Ahead: Readings from John Smith and William Bradford are provided in Lesson 2. While reading Lesson 2, students will ask themselves, "What does the word worldview mean? What is your worldview? What worldviews do you encounter in the world around you?"

Goal: Students will analyze Puritan literature and 2 Native American voices.

Goals/Objectives: What is the purpose of this lesson?	Strategies to meet these goals: How will I obtain these goals/objectives?	Evaluation: How will I know when I have met these goals/objectives?
As a result of this lesson students should experience the dissonance that the Puritans no doubt felt when they settled in the New World (affective goal) and students will have to create an original essay based on the same format/genre of a personal journal similar to *The History of Plimoth Plantation.* (cognitive goal) Students will learn how to write a descriptive essay. (cognitive goal) Students will practice writing a summary and a thesis statement.(cognitive goal) Students will increase their vocabulary.(cognitive goal)	Students will write a 1 page descriptive essay on the following topic: Pretend that you are part of an expedition to Mars. What similarities do you find between your expedition and that presented in *The History of Plimoth Plantation.* (Critical Thinking A)? Students will collect at least five new vocabulary words from their reading and use these words in their essays.	Students, with minimal errors, will clearly answer the assigned question in a 1 page essay. Students will use five vocabulary words in conversation during the week as well as use the words in their essays.

Goals/Objectives: What is the purpose of this lesson?	Strategies to meet these goals: How will I obtain these goals/objectives?	Evaluation: How will I know when I have met these goals/objectives?
Students will consider the generalization that the Puritan view of nature is theistic and orthodox and will value this view. (spiritual/affective/cognitive goal)	Students will write an essay on the following topic: What was William Bradford's view of nature? (Critical Thinking B)	Students, with minimal errors, will clearly answer the assigned question in a 1-2 page essay.
Students will understand the concept *allusion* and will see how it is employed in *Of Plimoth Plantation* (cognitive goal) Students will learn how to write an illustrative essay. (cognitive goal)	Students will write an essay on the following topic: An allusion is a brief, often indirect reference to a person, place, event or artistic work which the author assumes the reader will recognize. To that end, Bradford uses many biblical allusions. Find two examples and in a 1 page illustrative essay show how Bradford uses them. (Critical Thinking, C).	Students, with minimal errors, will clearly answer the assigned question in a 1-2 page essay.
Students will exhibit higher level thinking as they analyze *A Quest for Godliness: The Puritan Vision of the Christian Life*, J. I. Packer. (cognitive goal) Students will value Puritan theology and consider the generalization that Christians should build their worldviews on confession (i.e., the Word of God), not on emotion. (i.e., existentialism). (affective goal)	Write an essay on the following topic: Write a 1 page essay agreeing or disagreeing with Packer's thesis. (Enrichment)	Students, with minimal errors, will clearly answer the assigned questions in a 1 page essay. Students will value, even emulate, some of the behavior of the Puritans. (behavioral goal)
Students will understand this concept: Navajo Creation Legend. (cognitive goal)	Compare the above creation legend with Genesis 1-2. (Biblical Application A) Based on this text, compare Native American views of mankind with Biblical views. (Biblical Application B)	Students, with minimal errors, will clearly answer the assigned question in a 1-2 page essay.
Students will understand this concept: benevolent despotism vs. democracy. (cognitive goal)	Normally Native People governments were benevolent despotisms. Yet, the Iroquois Confederacy made a great effort to be democratic. Why? Offer evidence from the text. (Critical Thinking)	Students, with minimal errors, will clearly answer the assigned question in a 1-2 page essay.

Goals/Objectives: What is the purpose of this lesson?	Strategies to meet these goals: How will I obtain these goals/objectives?	Evaluation: How will I know when I have met these goals/ objectives?
Students will consider the generalization that ethnic genocide of Native American peoples was both immoral and unnecessary. (affective goal)	History shows that early colonial efforts to create a European society to the exclusion of Native Americans resulted in an ethnic cleansing which eliminated almost the entire Native population in the early 19th century. First, discuss the moral implications of this action. Secondly, offer an alternative solution. (Enrichment)	Students, with minimal errors, will clearly answer the assigned question in a 1-2 page essay.
Students will work in a group setting. (behavioral goal)	In a class, in a co-op experience, or during a family discussion, students will answer the following question: What were the strengths and weaknesses of the Puritan vision?	Students will exhibit practical listening skills and will manifest understanding of opposing worldviews.
Students will understand the following concept: Metaphysical poet. (cognitive goal) Students will be able to discern spirituality that is not Christ-centered. (affective goal) Students will exhibit higher thinking—specifically comparison and contrast skills. (cognitive goal) Students will compare Taylor's poetry with English metaphysical poets (e.g., George Herbert)	Students will write an essay on the following topic: Edward Taylor's poetry displays the influence of English metaphysical poets. Research the metaphysical poets in England and compare and contrast their writings with Taylor's. (Enrichment B)	Students, with minimal errors, will clearly answer the assigned question in a 1-2 page essay.
Students will be able to recall the information taught in the lesson. (cognitive goal)	Lesson 1 Test	Students will take the test at the end of this lesson and score at least 80%.
Students will experience reflective writing (affective/spiritual goal).	Using the Journal Guide Questions in the Appendices, students will record at least three entries this week. Suggested Scriptures: Psalm 23	Students will show evidence that they have reflected on this issue, including informed discussions and written responses.

SUGGESTED
Weekly *Implementation*

DAY 1	DAY 2	DAY 3	DAY 4	DAY 5
Prayer journal.	**Prayer journal.**	**Prayer journal.**	**Prayer journal.**	**Prayer journal.**
Students review the required reading(s) before the assigned lesson begins.	Student should review reading(s) from next lesson.	Students should write rough drafts of all assigned essays.	Student will re-write corrected copies of essays due tomorrow.	Essays are due.
Teacher may want to discuss assigned reading(s) with students.	Student should outline essays due at the end of the week.	The teacher or a peer evaluator may correct rough drafts.		Students should take the Lesson 1 test.
Teacher will discuss with students the number of essays to be assigned for this lesson. They may choose two or three essays. The rest of the essays can be outlined, answered with shorter answers, or skipped.	Per teacher instructions, students may answer orally in a group setting some of the essays that are not assigned as formal essays.			Reading ahead: No readings are necessary for Lesson 2. Students should review *Religious Affections*, Jonathan Edwards for Lesson 3.
Students should review all readings for Lesson 1.				Guide: What does the word "worldview" mean? What is your worldview? What worldviews do you encounter in the world around you?

Note: References to sources are in student edition.

ENRICHMENT ACTIVITIES/PROJECTS

Students should research the Puritans. How accurately does Hollywood portray the Puritans?

Students should pretend that they were on the Mayflower and they should write 2-4 entries.

SUPPLEMENTAL RESOURCES

Bennet, Arthur (Editor), *The Valley of Vision: A Collection of Puritan Prayers and Devotions.*

Bennet understands that the Puritans were men and women of God who were devoutly spiritual in their worship and fervently sincere in their faith. The reader will find these 17th century devotions to be surprisingly contemporary.

Bradford, William. *Mourt's Relation: A Journal of the Pilgrims at Plymouth.*

A wonderful primary source with description of the Plimoth pilgrims.

Davies, Horton. *The Worship of the English Puritans.*

Davis shows that Puritan worship was not the lifeless, colorless experience that many suppose.

Delbanco, Andrew. *The Puritan Ordeal.*

This book is about the experience of becoming American in the seventeenth century. It emphasizes what Delbanco calls renewal and risk. This book is a distinctive of American history.

Edmund, Morgan. *The Puritan Dilemma: The Story of John Winthrop.*

Morgan correctly argues that Winthrop and the Puritans were 17th century radicals.

Graham, Judith S. *Puritan Family Life: The Diary of Samuel Sewall.*

This book takes a close look at Judge Samuel Sewall, using his diary as an example of Puritan family life. Sewall's experiences directly contradict the common understanding of the repressive and joyless Puritan household. His diaries show the reader that Puritans had a loving, vital relationship with their children.

Middlekauff, Robert. *The Mathers: Three Generations of Puritan Intellectuals, 1596-1728.*

Robert Middlekauff traces the evolution of Puritan thought and theology in America. He focuses on three generations of intellectual ministers—Richard, Increase, and Cotton Mather—in order to challenge the traditional telling of the secularization of Puritanism, a story of faith transformed by reason, science, and business.

Miller, Perry. *The American Puritans.*

Without a doubt Perry Miller is the undisputed scholar in Puritan studies.

Miller, Perry. *The New England Mind: The Seventeenth Century.*

Schmidt, Gary D. *William Bradford: Plymouth's Faithful Pilgrim.*

In very descriptive language Schmidt tells the reader about the horrible first winter in Plimoth and how the believing Pilgrims correctly conceptualized their ordeal in Christian concepts.

Notes:

CRITICAL THINKING

Pretend you are part of an expedition to Mars. Write a one-page descriptive essay about your surroundings. What similarities do you find between your expedition and that in Bradford's diary?

Write a one-paragraph summary of what you find.

Write a one-sentence summary.

ANSWER: *Answers will vary, but all observations will be conceptualized by what the students' former experience has been. Such was the case with William Bradford. Bradford's understanding of history was unapologetically subjective—his experience tells him that God is alive, faithful, and ever-present in the lives of people. Subjectivity, at least in this case, is an asset. Bradford was able to see through the eyes of faith that brought the true story to his readers, which does not to imply that Bradford was inaccurate. On the contrary, his attention to detail combined with his acute sense of providence, evidence his skillful historical methods. The writing of history is the selection of information and the synthesis of this information into a narrative that will stand the critical eye of time. History, though, is never static. One never creates the definitive theory of an historical event. History invites each generation to re-examine its own story and to reinterpret past events in light of present circumstance. In this case, it was William Bradford's turn.*

The creation of this story is more difficult than it seems. From the beginning the historian is forced to decide what sort of human motivations matter most: Economic? Political? Religious?

While the historian knows that he can never be completely neutral about history, scholarly historical inquiry demands that he implement the following principles:

The historian must evaluate the veracity of sources. There must be a hierarchy of historical sources.

The historian must be committed to telling both sides of the historical story. He may choose to lobby for one view over the other, but the historian must fairly present all theories.

He must avoid stereotypes and archetypes. He must overcome personal prejudices and dispassionately view history in ruthlessly objective terms.

He must be committed to the truth no matter where his scholarship leads him. At times the historian will discover unflattering information about his nation/state. He must not hesitate to accept and then to tell the truth.

Finally, the Christian historian believes that real, abiding, and eternal history ultimately is made only by people who obey God at all costs.

B. What was William Bradford's view of nature?

ANSWER: *To William Bradford, nature was only an extension of God's creation. It was not alive; it was not even ubiquitous. It was not friendly or unfriendly. God was alive. God was in control, and God loved Bradford very much—a fact of which Bradford was acutely aware. It is from this secure base that Bradford created his history. William Bradford, an English Separatist, was forced to reckon with awful conditions—1/2 of his Plymouth Pilgrims died the first winter. Nevertheless, Bradford continued to affirm God's basic goodness* *in the face of horrible conditions. William Bradford's state of mind was not dependent upon circumstances. Listen to Bradford's own words:*

> *But here I cannot but stay and make a pause, and stand half amazed at this poor people's present condition; and so I think will the reader too, when he well considers the same. Being thus passed the vast ocean, and a sea of troubles before in their preparation (as may be remembered by that which went before), they had now no friends to welcome them, nor inns to entertain or refresh their weather-beaten bodies, no houses or much less towns to repair to, to seek for succor. It is recorded in scripture as a mercy to the apostle and his shipwrecked company, that the barbarians showed no small kindness in refreshing them, but these savage barbarians, when they met with them (as after will appear) were readier to fill their sides full of arrows then otherwise. And for the season it was winter, and they that know the winters of that country know them to be sharp and violent and subject to cruel and fierce storms, dangerous to travel to known places, much more to search an unknown coast. Besides, what could they see but a hideous and desolate wilderness, full of wild beasts and wild men? and what multitudes there might be of them they knew not. Neither could they, as it were, go up to the top of Pisgah, to view from this wilderness a more goodly country to feed their hopes; for which way soever they turned their eyes (save upward to the heavens) they could have little solace or content in respect of any outward objects. For summer being done, all things stand upon them with a weather-beaten face; and the whole country, full of woods and thickets, represented a wild and savage hew. If they looked behind them, there was the mighty ocean which they had passed, and was now as a main bar and gulf to separate them from all the civil parts of the world. If it be said they had a ship to succor them, it is true; but what heard they daily from the master and company? But that with speed they should look out a place with their shallop, where they would be at some near distance; for the season was such as he would not stir from thence till a safe harbor was discovered by them where they would be, and he might go without danger; and that victuals consumed apace, but he must and would keep sufficient for themselves and their return. Yea, it was muttered by some, that if they got not a place in time, they would turn them and their goods ashore and leave them. Let it also be considered what weak hopes of supply and succor they left behind them, that might bear up their minds in this sad condition and trials they were under; and they could not but be very small. It is true, indeed, the affections and love of their brethren at Leyden was cordial and entire towards them, but they had little power to help them, or themselves; and how the case stood between them and the merchants at their coming away, hath already been declared. What could now sustain them but the spirit of God and his grace? Say not and ought not the children of these fathers rightly say: 'Our fathers were Englishmen which came*

over this great ocean, and were ready to perish in this wilderness; but they cried unto the Lord, and he heard their voice, and looked on their adversity, etc. Let them therefore praise the Lord, because he is good, and his mercies endure forever. Yea, let them which have been redeemed of the Lord, show how he hath delivered them from the hand of the oppressor. When they wandered in the desert wilderness out of the way, and found no city to dwell in, both hungry, and thirsty, their soul was overwhelmed in them. Let them confess before the Lord his loving kindness, and his wonderful works before the sons of men.' (Of Plimoth Plantation, William Bradford).

C. An allusion is a brief, often indirect reference to a person, place, event, or artistic work which the author assumes the reader will recognize. To that end, Bradford uses many Biblical allusions. Find two examples and in a one-page illustrative essay show how Bradford uses them.

ANSWER: *There are several. For instance, on September 6, Bradford compares the Pilgrim's landing on Plymouth Rock to Paul's shipwreck on Malta in Acts 28:2: "And the natives showed us unusual kindness, for they kindled a fire and welcomed us all, because it had begun to rain and was cold."*

ENRICHMENT

Read J. I. Packer, *A Quest For Godliness: The Puritan Vision of the Christian Life* (Wheaton, Ill: Crossway Books, Inc., 1990). Packer argues that the depth and breadth of Puritan spiritual life stands in stark contrast to the facile and deadness of modern Western Christianity. He concludes that the main difference between the Puritans and us is spiritual maturity—the Puritans had it, and we simply do not. The Puritans believed in an omnipotent God. They were not grouchy, legalistic, colorless settlers but wore bright colors and enjoyed life. They had a passion for righteousness; they had a passion for God. In a one-page essay, agree or disagree with Packer's thesis.

ANSWER: *My favorite quote is "Puritans were not wild men, fierce and freaky, religious fanatics and social extremists, but sober, conscientious, and cultured citizens: persons of principle, devoted, determined, and disciplined, excelling in the domestic virtues, and with no obvious shortcomings save a tendency to run to words when saying anything important, whether to God or to man...They were great souls serving a great God. In them clear-headed passion and warm-hearted compassion combined." This quote gives evidence of why I wholeheartedly agree with Packer.*

FINAL PROJECT

Students should correct and rewrite all essays and place them in their Final Portfolio.

Native American Voices

BIBLICAL APPLICATION

A. Compare the story of Native American creation with Genesis 1-2.

ANSWER: *There is no mention of a Sovereign, omnipotent God in the Navajo creation story. The world more or less evolves out of nothing into something. There is no divine purpose or design.*

B. Based on this text, compare Native American views of mankind with Biblical views.

ANSWER: *Again, mankind appears out of nothing with no suggestion that he is created in the image of God.*

CRITICAL THINKING

Normally Native People governments were *benevolent despotisms*. Yet, the Iroquois Confederacy made a great effort to be *democratic*. Why? Offer evidence from the text.

ANSWER: *In the selection of their leaders and in the conduct of business, the Iroquois consciously tried to include as many divergent parts of the confederation as possible. The idea was that groups, not individuals, would rule. This design was in direct conflict with leadership paradigms of other Native American people but much like the United States Constitution (1789).*

ENRICHMENT

Generally, European Americans made no effort either to live side-by-side with Native Americans or to assimilate Native Americans into their lives. Native Americans were treated as aliens and subversives. As General Sheridan observed two centuries later, the only good Indian was a dead Indian. Therefore, the American military employed a systematic form of genocide unparalleled in American history. History shows that early colonial efforts to create a European society to the exclusion of Native Americans resulted in an ethnic cleansing which eliminated almost the entire Native population in the early 19th century.

First, discuss the moral implications of this action. Next, offer an alternative solution.

ANSWER: *This is a very difficult question. On one hand it is important that one people group respect and honor the customs and culture of another people group. However, how can the people be left alone and also proselytized? William Penn and the Quakers came closest to keeping these tensions in perspective when they settled the colony of Pennsylvania. Colonists who settled in this colony were obligated to treat the Native Americans fairly.*

LESSON I TEST

OBJECTIVE TEST (15 POINTS)

Answer each question with *true* or *false*.

_____The Boston Puritans loved the Church of England and only wished to "purify" it.

_____The Pilgrims were a special type of Puritan.

_____The Pilgrims lived in Northern Ireland before they traveled to America.

_____The Pilgrims' landing in Cape Cod was really a mistake.

_____The Puritans' main motivation to traveling to America was to make money.

DISCUSSION QUESTION (30 POINTS)

Explain what these quotes from *The History of Plimoth Plantation* mean and give their historical context:

A. The one side (the Reformers) laboured to have ye* right worship of God & discipline of Christ established in ye church, according to ye simplicitie of ye gospell, without the mixture of mens inventions, and to have & to be ruled by ye laws of Gods word, dispensed in those offices, & by those officers of Pastors, Teachers, & Elders, according to ye Scripturs. The other partie (the Church of England), though under many colours & pretences, endevored to have ye episcopall dignitie (affter ye popish maner) with their large power & jurisdiction still retained; with all those courts, cannons, & ceremonies, togeather with all such livings, revenues, & subordinate officers, with other such means as formerly upheld their antichristian greatnes, and enabled them with lordly & tyranous power to persecute ye poore servants of God.

B. Being thus arived in a good harbor and brought safe to land, they fell upon their knees & blessed ye God of heaven, who had brought them over ye vast & furious ocean, and delivered them from all ye periles & miseries therof, againe to set their feete on ye firme and stable earth, their proper elemente. And no marvell if they were thus joyefull, seeing wise Seneca was so affected with sailing a few miles on ye coast of his owne Italy; as he affirmed, that he had rather remaine twentie years on his way by land, then pass by sea to any place in a short time; so tedious & dreadfull was ye same unto him. But hear I cannot but stay and make a pause, and stand half amased at this poore peoples presente condition; and so I thinke will the reader too, when he well considered ye same. Being thus passed ye vast ocean, and a sea of troubles before in their preparation (as may be remembred by yt which wente before), they had now no friends to wellcome them, nor inns to entertaine or refresh their weather-beaten bodys, no houses or much less townes to repaire too, to seeke for succoure. ... Let it also be considred what weake hopes of supply & succoure they left behinde them, yt might bear up their minds in this sade condition and trialls they were under; and they could not but be very smale. It is true, indeed, ye affections & love of their brethren at Leyden was cordiall & entire towards them, but they had litle power to help them, or them selves; and how ye case stode betweene them & ye marchants at their coming away, hath already been declared. What could not sustaine them but ye spirite of God & his grace? May not & ought not the children of these fathers rightly say : "Our faithers were Englishmen which came over this great ocean, and were ready to perish in this willdernes; but they cried unto ye Lord, and he heard their voyce, and looked on their adversitie . . ."

C. They begane now to gather in ye small harvest they had, and to fitte up their houses and dwellings against winter, being all well recovered in health & strenght, and had all things in good plenty; fFor as some were thus imployed in affairs abroad, others were excersised in fishing, aboute codd, & bass, & other fish, of which yey tooke good store, of which every family had their portion. All ye somer ther was no want. And now begane to come in store of foule, as winter approached, of which this place did abound when they came first (but afterward decreased by degrees). And besids water foule, ther was great store of wild Turkies, of which they tooke many, besids venison, Besids, they had about a peck a meale a weeke to a person, or now since harvest, Indean corn to yt proportion. Which made many afterwards write so largly of their plenty hear to their freinds in England, which were not fained, but true reports.

*This "y" in Old English stood for "the."

SHORT ANSWER (55 POINTS)

Answer these questions in *75 words or less.*

A. Compare William Bradford with a contemporary political or religious figure.

   (10 points)

B. Explain what the historian Perry Miller meant when he said, "Without some understanding of Puritanism. . . there is no understanding of America." (15 points)

C. Even though *Of Plimoth Plantation* is a nonfiction work, in many ways this book has more action than fiction novels. In that vein, discuss the literary plot of this book. In other words, identify the rising action, climax, and falling action. (10 points)

D. Is (are) there antagonist(s) in *Of Plimoth*? Who? Why?(10 points)

E. Explain why the Bible was so important to the Puritans. (10 points)

LESSON I TEST ANSWERS

OBJECTIVE QUESTIONS (15 POINTS)

Answer each question true or false.

ANSWER:

T—The Boston Puritans loved the Church of England and only wished to "purify" it. *The Separatist Puritans at Plymouth, MA, sought to separate from the Church of England; the Puritans who settled in Boston wished merely to purify the Church of England.*

F—The Pilgrims were a special type of Puritan. *The Pilgrims included Separatist Puritans and secular settlers who immigrated to Plymouth, MA, in 1620.*

F—The Pilgrims lived in Northern Ireland before they traveled to America. *They stayed in Holland.*

T—The Pilgrims' landing in Cape Cod was really a mistake. *They meant to settle in Virginia.*

F—The Puritans' main motivation in traveling to America was to make money.

DISCUSSION QUESTIONS (30 POINTS)

Explain what these quotes from *The History of Plymouth Plantation* mean and give their historical context:

A. ANSWER: *Bradford is attacking the Church of England's "petences" and "tyranous power to persecute."*

B. ANSWER: *This passage illustrates in broad relief the landing of the Pilgrims at Plymouth, MA and how completely they conceptualized it as an act of God.*

C. ANSWER: *This is the story of the first Thanksgiving.*

SHORT ANSWER (55 POINTS)

Answer these questions in 75 words or less.

A. ANSWER: *Answers will vary. Bradford was a very godly man who lived out his convictions!*

B. ANSWER: *The Puritans were the intellectual and spiritual epicenter of the American civilization for 150 years.*

C. ANSWER: *The trip over on the Mayflower certainly piques the reader's interest (rising action). The climax would be the first winter when over half died. The falling action would be Thanksgiving. Of course answers will vary.*

D. ANSWER: *It is insightful that nature is not the enemy (Naturalism) and neither is the Native American. The enemy is the Devil. In that sense, he is the antagonist. However, this is a nonfiction piece as contrasted with a fictional novel.*

E. ANSWER: *To the Puritans the Bible was the inerrant, inspired Word of God. It was the basis for everything they did—the guidebook for life itself.*

LESSON 2
WORLDVIEW FORMATION AND DISCERNMENT

Readings Due For This Lesson: All readings are provided for the student.

Reading Ahead: Jonathan Edwards, *Religious Affections: A Christian's Character Before God* (provided in Lesson 3) and *Sinners in the Hands of An Angry God* (provided in Lesson 3). Why was Jonathan Edwards so effective in his preaching during the 18th century?

Goal: Students will articulate their own worldview as they evaluate the veracity of other worldviews.

Goals/Objectives: What is the purpose of this lesson?	Strategies to meet these goals: How will I obtain these goals/objectives?	Evaluation: How will I know when I have met these goals/ objectives?
As a result of this lesson, students should understand and recognize different worldviews. (cognitive goal) Students will value Christian Theism above all worldviews. (affective goal) Students will learn how to write a comparative essay. (cognitive goal)	Students will write a 2 page comparative essay analyzing several worldviews. (Critical Thinking A)	Students, with minimal errors, will clearly answer the assigned question in a 2 page essay.
Students will increase their vocabulary. (cognitive goal)	Students will collect at least five new vocabulary words from their reading and use these words in their essays.	Students will use five vocabulary words in conversation during the week as well as use the words in their essays.
Students will consider the generalization that the Puritan view of nature is Theistic and orthodox and will value this view. (spiritual/ affective/cognitive goal) Students will learn how to write a comparative essay. (cognitive goal)	Students will write an essay on the following topic: Compare the worldviews represented in the next two passages. Which worldview is obviously Christian? From these descriptions what generalizations can you draw about the Virginia and Plymouth settlements? (Critical Thinking B)	Students, with minimal errors, will clearly answer the assigned question in a 1-2 page essay.

Goals/Objectives: What is the purpose of this lesson?	Strategies to meet these goals: How will I obtain these goals/objectives?	Evaluation: How will I know when I have met these goals/ objectives?
Students will gain new insights into Old Testament Law. (cognitive goal) Students will consider the generalization that while the Old Testament is literally the inspired, inerrant Word of God and the law is still important to culture (e.g., the Ten Commandments), some Old Testament laws should not be enforced literally. (affective goal)	Students will write an essay on the following topic: The Puritans based their society on Old Testament law. For instance, the Connecticut Code, 1650 stated: " If any man have a stubborn and rebellious son of sufficient years and understanding . . . which will not obey the voice of his father or mother . . . but lives in sundry notorious crimes, such a son shall be put to death." Why should/should not Old Testament law have literal application to today's society? (Biblical Application)	Students, with minimal errors, will clearly answer the assigned question in a 1-2 page essay.
Students will exhibit higher level thinking as they analyze several different advertisements and movies. (cognitive goal)	Write an essay on the following topic: Most Americans obtain their worldview from the television. The following advertisements represent a particular worldview(s). What is(are) it (they)? (Enrichment A) If your parents will allow you to do so, watch the following movies and discuss in an essay the worldview of each of them: *Star Wars*, *The Lion King*, *True Grit*, *Ice Age*, and *Hoosiers*. (Enrichment B)	Students, with minimal errors, will clearly answer the assigned questions in a one-page essay.
Students will work in a group setting. (behavioral goal)	In a class, in a co-op experience, or during a family discussion, students will answer the following question: What are the different worldviews that you see in your environment? Should Theistic students only participate in artistic experiences that are Theistic?	Students will exhibit practical listening skills and will manifest understanding of opposing worldviews.
Students will be able to recall the information taught in the lesson. (cognitive goal)	Lesson 2 Test	Students will take the test at the end of this lesson and score at least 80%.
Students will experience reflective writing. (affective/spiritual goal)	Using the Journal Guide Questions in the Appendices, students will record at least three entries this week. Suggested Scriptures: Romans 4 & 6.	Students will show evidence that they have reflected on this issue, including informed discussions and written responses.

SUGGESTED
Weekly *Implementation*

DAY 1	DAY 2	DAY 3	DAY 4	DAY 5
Prayer journal. Review the required reading(s) before the assigned lesson begins. Teacher may want to discuss assigned reading(s) with students. Teacher and students will decide on the number of required essays. The rest of the essays can be outlined, answered with shorter answers, or skipped. Students will review all readings for Lesson 2.	**Prayer journal.** Review reading(s) from next lesson. Student should outline essays due at the end of the week. Per teacher instructions, students may answer orally in a group setting some of the essays that are not assigned as formal essays.	**Prayer journal.** Write rough drafts of all assigned essays. The teacher or a peer evaluator may correct rough drafts.	**Prayer journal.** Student will re-write corrected copies of essays due tomorrow.	**Prayer journal.** Essays are due. Students should take the Lesson 2 test. Reading ahead: Students should review *Religious Affections*, Jonathan. Guide: Why was Jonathan Edwards so effective in his preaching during the 18th century?

Note: References to sources are in student edition.

ENRICHMENT ACTIVITIES/PROJECTS

Watch the *Star Wars* trilogy and discuss its worldview.

During the next year, for family devotions, use *A Fire that Burns: Devotions for Growing Christians* (Hollsopple, PA: For Such A Time As This, 2003), by James P. Stobaugh.

The whole family could play a tic-tac-toe world-view game. Each participant has a card with seven worldviews on it. During a road trip, participants will identify different worldviews. The object of the game is to identify worldviews as they are manifested on billboards, on radio programs, or other venues. When a confirmed worldview is discovered, the participant is allowed to place an X on his card in the corresponding square. The first one to fill his card completely wins the game!

Deism	Existentialism	Romanticism
Christian Theism	Free Square	Naturalism
Realism	Absurdism	Theism

The following is an example of the Stobaugh Family mission statement:

The Stobaugh Family WorldView Statement

We are called to live radical Christian lives as if we belong to God and not to ourselves (Gals. 2:20). Therefore, we will seek the Lord with all our heart—knowing He will be found. We will have a heart for the Lost. He has given us the ministry of reconciliation; indeed, our family is an image of this reconciliation (Romans 8; 2 Cor. 5) Whatever the cost to us personally: We will be His ambassadors. We are called to advance the Kingdom. We want to be world changers. The job(s) to which God has called us requires all we have, and it is worthy of our best and total efforts.

Our Family: We will be world changers for Christ.

Our Jobs: Pastoring, Writing, Lecturing, Teaching, Learning—All are related to the abovementioned mission statement.

Henceforth, the Stobaughs shall make decisions based on this mission statement—not on circumstances. Every new job or activity must further this mission statement or be rejected.

After obtaining parental permission, students could watch the following movies and discuss the worldview of each of them: *Star Wars*, *The Lion King*, *True Grit*, *Ice Age*, and *Hoosiers*.

The whole family should write a family mission statement.

SUPPLEMENTAL RESOURCES

Chang, Curtis. *Engaging Unbelief: A Captivating Strategy from Augustine and Aquinas.*

Chang, Inter-varsity Christian Fellowship chaplain at Tufts, M.I.T. and Harvard, urges the church to convert the post-Christian (1990 and beyond) world in the tradition of the theologians Augustine and Aquinas, whom he contends were missionary works—Augustine to the pagan culture and Aquinas to the Islamic world. Both theologians were comfortable in the larger cultures of their audiences, able to draw non-Christian readers into the Gospel story by using their own familiar cultural authorities. Once they had engaged their audience, Augustine and Aquinas showed where their readers' cultures fell short, pointing to Christ as the answer. A must read for all students planning to attend secular universities.

Davis, John Jefferson. *Evangelical Ethics.*

A comprehensive, readable overview of evangelical ethical positions concerning such important issues as abortion, euthanasia, and population control.

Guinness, Os. *Fit Bodies, Fat Minds: Why Evangelicals Don't Think and What to Do about It.*
The title tells it all.

Guinness, Os. *Long Journey Home: A Guide to Your Search for the Meaning of Life.*
The Christian scholar Os Guinness invites the student to articulate his own world view. Excellent!

Guinness, Os. *Steering through Chaos: Vice and Virtue in an Age of Moral Confusion.*
One of the best anthologies of worldview analysis on the market. Using anecdotes and case studies, Guinness challenges Evangelical Christians to take seriously their moral positions.

Noll, Mark A. *The Scandal of the Evangelical Mind.*
Noll takes aim at lightweight Christians, stating that the scandal of the Evangelical mind is that they do not have a mind! In spite of this caustic comment, Noll makes some timely points.

Noebel, David. *Thinking Like a Christian: Understanding and Living a Biblical Worldview.*
Dr. Noebel is the undisputed champion of a socio-political theory of worldviews. His paradigm is accurate and very helpful, but different from the worldview paradigm in this book (i.e., cultural paradigm). For example, Dr. Noebel would call a proponent of Existentialism a "cosmic humanist." Be sure to view the accompanying video.

Numbers, Ronald L. *The Creationists: The Evolution of Scientific Creationism.*

This reader appreciates Number's discussion of Creationism. Numbers believes in a literal flood and a relatively short life span for the earth (about 10,000 years). The rejection of Creationism teaching, Numbers believes, is at the heart of modernity and Post-Christian heresy.

Wells, David F. *God in the Wasteland: The reality of Truth in a World of Fading Dreams.*

Wells challenges the contemporary Evangelical community to examine honestly its effect on the 21st century secular world. Wells is convinced that Modernity is now the Tempter seducing human pride to betray itself through a pawn-like participation in "an ironic recapitulation of the first dislocation in which God's creatures replaced their Creator and exiled Him from His own world."

Notes:

CRITICAL THINKING: CHALLENGE QUESTION

A. In a two page essay, compare the worldviews of each of the following passages.

So God created man in His own image, in the image of God.

ANSWER: *Of course this biblical passage is a Christian Theistic statement.*

Gatsby believed . . . tomorrow we will run faster, stretch out our arms farther . . . And one fine morning—So we beat on, boats against the current, borne back ceaselessly into the past (Fitzgerald, *The Great Gatsby*, Charles Scribner's Sons, 1925, p. 182)

ANSWER: *The author F. Scott Fitzgerald had strong Romantic and Naturalist tendencies that are reflected in this passage. "So we beat on, boats against the current, bore ceaselessly into the past." The implication is that people are captured in a beautiful, perhaps altruistic, but ubiquitous Nature. However, this Nature is in total control, and it sometimes bores "people ceaselessly into the past" when they might not want to go there. By the way, if you think Romantic Naturalist is an oxymoron, you are correct. One of the ironies of all worldviews, except Christian Theism, is the fact that they readily exist together in the same artistic piece with other worldviews, even opposing worldviews. Christian Theism, on the other hand, cannot co-exist with any other worldview. It ipso facto claims superiority over all other worldviews. The God of Theism will not share His rule with any other worldview.*

For mere improvement is not redemption . . . God became man to turn creatures into sons: not simply to produce better men of the old kind but to produce a new kind of man (Lewis, *Mere Christianity*, A Touchstone Book, 1980, p. 183).

ANSWER: *This Christian Theistic worldview shows something that makes it remarkably unique and appealing: it offers redemption for those who adhere to this worldview. No other worldview makes that claim. Romanticism argues for a "heightened consciousness," but it does not offer salvation like Christian Theism does.*

If it feels good do it!—The world is totally insane, out of control, stupid!

ANSWER: *This Absurdist worldview, popular among many contemporary artists, invites the participant to embrace a mindless nihilism that releases participants from all responsibilities for their actions. This is typical evidence for Absurdism (and Existentialism).*

All my friends do it, so it must be ok.

ANSWER: *This subjective worldview has elements of Romanticism—subjective decisions are appropriate—but in the final analysis is more an Existentialist worldview that promises the participants that it is ok to do what feels good, particularly if it is universally embraced.*

B. What generalizations can you draw about the worldviews of the Virginia and Plymouth settlements?

ANSWER: *While both passages are Theistic, Bradford's faith is stronger than Smith's. Smith begins, "left to our fortunes." Can you imagine Bradford talking about "fortune" or "luck?" Bradford refers to "a special act of God's Providence."*

BIBLICAL APPLICATION

The Puritans based their society on Old Testament law. For instance, the Connecticut Code, 1650 stated: " If any man have a stubborn and rebellious son of sufficient years and understanding . . . which will not obey the voice of his father of mother . . . but lives in sundry notorious crimes, such a son shall be put to death." Why should/should not Old Testament law have literal application to today's society?

ANSWER: *The Word of God has immutable, universal application; however, certain laws (e.g., stoning children for disobeying their parents) should no doubt be mitigated by grace. The law was fulfilled by Christ in the New Testament. This does not, however, forgive blatant disregard for laws. People must not sin so that grace will abound. (Romans 4 & 6)*

ENRICHMENT

A. Most Americans obtain their worldview from the television. The following advertisements represent a particular worldview(s). What is(are) it (they)?

ANSWER: *Picture A celebrates the innocence of youth which invites the consumer to buy a particular product to create a "sunny meal." While there are some wholesome, perhaps Theistic implications to this advertisement, it also has a decidedly Romantic edge too. Notice the flowers. There is also evidence of Existentialism: the viewer cannot quite make out the faces of the children. They, therefore, have a universalist view and even appear a little surreal.*

Picture B is clearly an existentialist invitation. Its stoicism invites the reader to indulge nothing other than his appetite.

Picture C is a 19th century advertisement whose primary appeal is Theistic. Theism does not have much commercial appeal to 21st century America.

FINAL PROJECT

Students should correct and rewrite all essays and place them in their Final Portfolio.

LESSON 2 TEST

OVERVIEW CHART (80 POINTS)

Write responses to these statements according to each worldview.

Worldview	Christian Theism	Romanticism/ Transcendentalism	Naturalism/ Realism	Absurdism/ Existentialism
Jesus Christ is Lord.				
The world was created by God in six literal 24-hour days.				
If it feels good, do it.				
People would just be better off if society left them alone.				
Everyone will be saved as long as they are good people.				
I am not going to worry about the future; when my time is up, it is up.				
An animal is merely a person in animal garb.				
All I want to do is help people.				
God has a plan for us.				

DISCUSSION QUESTION (20 POINTS)

Imagine that you have finished playing in a soccer game. You are walking across the field. Create conversations among players, parents, and spectators that exhibit at least four different worldviews.

LESSON 2 TEST ANSWERS

OVERVIEW CHART (80 POINTS)

Write responses to these statements according to each worldview below.

ANSWER: WorldView	Christian Theism	Romanticism/ Transcendentalism	Naturalism/ Realism	Absurdism/ Existentialism
Jesus Christ is Lord.	*Yes, He is.*	*Yes, and so are Buddha and the others.*	*He is not.*	*That statement has no meaning.*
The world was created by God in six days.	*Absolutely!*	*I guess so—and didn't He do a great job. Nature is so beautiful!*	*No, that is religion. Science tells us that the world was created in a big bang.*	*Who cares?*
If it feels good do it.	*Whether it feels good or not, the wages of sin is death. Obedience to God and His Word is life.*	*Yes, and the more natural the feeling, the more spontaneous the response, the better.*	*Absolutely! Let it all hang out!*	*Yes and if it feels bad, do it too—who really cares what you do anyway? Leave me alone!*
People would just be better off if society left them alone.	*People will never be better off until they are in right relation-ship with God.*	*Surely that is true.*	*Yes, they may be better off for a while but sooner or later some rock will fall on their head or something bad will happen.*	*They will be better off if they stop pretending there is any reason to live.*
Everyone will be saved as long as they are good people.	*No, they will be saved only if they commit their lives to Jesus Christ.*	*Salvation occurs when people are in complete concert with nature.*	*There is no salvation; we all are doomed.*	*There is no future but nothingness.*
I am not going to worry about the future; when my time is up, it is up.	*If I don't worry about the future it is because my future is in the hands of the Lord.*	*Death is only a natural extension of life.*	*You got that right! There is nothing we can do about the future except duck when it comes our way!*	*Our future is not even planned yet. It merely happens in a disorganized fashion.*
An animal is merely a person in animal garb.	*No, mankind is created in the image of God. Nothing else is.*	*No, that is not true. Although, I wish mankind acted more like animals—innocent and free.*	*Yes, makes sense to me.*	*Who really cares?*
All I want to do is help people.	*Nice idea; through God's love a person can help another person.*	*Nice idea.*	*Why?*	*What will you get out of it?*
God has a plan for us.	*Absolutely, and everything works for good for those called by His name to His purposes.*	*Absolutely. He wants you to return to nature.*	*Absolutely. He means for you to be miserable.*	*If there was a God, and there really isn't, what makes you think He cares one iota about you?*

DISCUSSION QUESTION (20 POINTS)

Imagine that you have finished playing in a soccer game. You are walking across the field. Create conversations among players, parents, and spectators that exhibit at least four different worldviews.

ANSWER: *"Good game!" I say to an opposing team member.*

"Who really cares." He answers (Absurdism)

"God does—and He loves you!" I answer (Christian Theism)

"If there is a God, He must hate me," a bystander replies (Naturalism)

"How can He hate you? Just feel this grass, look at that sun!" another bystander retorts (Romanticism)

LESSON 3

THE NEW LAND TO 1750: PURITANISM

Readings Due For This Lesson: All readings are provided for the student. Students should review *Religious Affections*, Jonathan Edwards and "Diary Entries," Esther Edwards, and Poems by Anne Bradstreet.

Reading Ahead: Students should read *The Autobiography of Benjamin Franklin*, Benjamin Franklin. What was Franklin's faith? Was it a Christian faith or was it a sort of "good works" civil faith?

Goals: Students will write their own worldview and learn about Puritan worldviews in this lesson.

Goals/Objectives: What is the purpose of this lesson?	Strategies to meet these goals: How will I obtain these goals/objectives?	Evaluation: How will I know when I have met these goals/objectives?
As a result of this lesson, students will understand what Winthrop meant when he called for his community to be a "City on a Hill." (cognitive) Students will value Christian Theism above all worldviews. (affective goal) Students will learn how to write an analysis essay. (cognitive)	Students will write a two-page essay on the following topic: In his book *A Modell of Christian Charity* (1630), John Winthrop, first governor of the Puritan Massachusetts Bay Colony, wrote: The Lord will take our name a praise and glory, so that men shall say of succeeding plantations: The Lord make it like that of New England. For we must consider that we shall be like a City upon a Hill; the eyes of all people are on us. What does Winthrop mean "a City upon a Hill?" Why does/does not this statement seem a little presumptuous on his part? (Critical Thinking, A)	Students, with minimal errors, will clearly answer the assigned question in a two-page essay.

Goals/Objectives: What is the purpose of this lesson?	Strategies to meet these goals: How will I obtain these goals/objectives?	Evaluation: How will I know when I have met these goals/objectives?
Students will increase their vocabulary. (cognitive)	Students will collect at least five new vocabulary words from their reading and use these words in their essays.	Students will use five vocabulary words in conversation during the week as well as use the words in their essays.
Students will consider the generalization that Christian Theism is making great progress in capturing the elite culture of the United States. (spiritual/ affective/cognitive goal)

Students will learn how to write an evaluation essay. (cognitive goal) | Students will write an essay on the following topic: Is there hope that born-again Christians will regain the high ground in culture and thought? (Critical Thinking, B) | Students, with minimal errors, will clearly answer the assigned question in a one or two page essay. |
| Students will analyze the evolution of the American hero and speculate upon future developments. (cognitive) | Students will write an essay on the following topic: How will the American hero evolve in the next 20 years? (Critical Thinking C) | Students, with minimal errors, will clearly answer the assigned question in a one or two page essay. |
| Students will understand this concept: Edward's *Religious' Affections.* *(cognitive)*

Students will accept the generalization that Christian behavior is intentional and important. (affective goal) | Students will write an essay on the following topic: Describe Edwards' religious affections and explain how they are evidences of true religion. (Biblical Application A) | Students, with minimal errors, will clearly answer the assigned question in a one or two page essay. |
| Students will exhibit higher level thinking as they write a comparison paper. (cognitive) | Students will write an essay on the following topic: Compare and contrast the image we see of Jonathan Edwards through his sermon and the way Esther saw him. (Biblical Application B) | Students, with minimal errors, will clearly answer the assigned questions in a one or two page essay. |
| Students will exhibit higher level thinking as they write a comparison paper. (cognitive) | Students will write an essay on the following topic: Describe your dad (or another parent or guardian) using the techniques Esther used to describe her dad. In what ways has the Lord used your father (or another adult) in your life? Compare your dad (or another adult) with King David, Joseph, or another dad in the Bible. (Biblical Application C) | Students, with minimal errors, will clearly answer the assigned questions in a one or two page essay. |

Goals/Objectives: What is the purpose of this lesson?	Strategies to meet these goals: How will I obtain these goals/objectives?	Evaluation: How will I know when I have met these goals/objectives?
Students will consider the generalization that Christians should forgive those who offend them. (behavioral objective)	Students will answer the following question: When you were disappointed, how did you keep from becoming bitter? Many Christian thinkers are calling brothers and sisters to forgiveness: forgiveness helps the person wronged more than the person who committed the wrong. Find scriptural evidence that commands you to forgive those who have wronged you. (Biblical Application D)	Students, with minimal errors, will clearly answer the assigned questions in a one or two page essay.
Students will articulate their positions on important ethical issues. (affective/cognitive goals)	Students should answer the following essay question: Read *Evangelical Ethics*, by Professor John Jefferson Davis, Ph.D., Gordon Conwell Seminary, South Hamilton, MA. After reading Dr. Davis' book, state your position on these ethical issues: euthanasia, abortion, capital punishment, and others. (Enrichment A)	Students, with minimal errors, will clearly answer the assigned questions in a one or two page essay.
Students will understand this concept: summary. (cognitive)	Students should answer the following question: Summarize what Edwards says about the youth of his town in a passage from "A Faithful Narrative of the Surprising Work of God." Next, compare these youth to the youth in your church. (Enrichment B)	Students, with minimal errors, will clearly answer the assigned questions in a one or two page essay.
Students will exhibit higher level thinking as they write a synthesis essay of future revivalism. (cognitive)	Students should answer the following question: Research recent church history and speculate upon the form and nature of future revivalism. Will it be like the mass rallies in the past or will revivalism look a lot different? (Enrichment C)	Students, with minimal errors, will clearly answer the assigned questions in a one or two page essay.

Goals/Objectives: What is the purpose of this lesson?	Strategies to meet these goals: How will I obtain these goals/objectives?	Evaluation: How will I know when I have met these goals/ objectives?
Students will exhibit higher level thinking as they compare "Eleanor Rigby" by Paul McCartney and John Lennon with Anne Bradstreet's "Upon the Burning of Our House." (cognitive goal) Students will understand these concepts: theme, tone, plot, and use of figurative language. (cognitive goal)	Compare "Eleanor Rigby" by Paul McCartney and John Lennon with Anne Bradstreet's "Upon the Burning of Our House." Identify differences in theme, tone, plot, and use of figurative language. (Critical Thinking A)	Students, with minimal errors, will clearly answer the assigned question in a 1-2 page essay.
Students will consider the generalization that only in accepting Christ as Savior is there redemption. (affective/cognitive goal) Students will exhibit higher level thinking as they learn how to write a comparative essay. (cognitive goal)	Students will write an essay on the following topic: Compare Eleanor Rigby with the woman caught in adultery. (John 8:2-11). (Biblical Application)	Students, with minimal errors, will clearly answer the assigned question in a 1-2 page essay.
Students will exhibit higher level thinking as they evaluate the beginnings of Puritan historiography. (cognitive goal)	Students will write an essay on the following topic: Modern Americans accuse the Puritans of being colorless and legalistic. Typically, to be "Puritan" means "to hide one's feelings." Yet, when reading Anne Bradstreet, one is struck by the power of Puritan emotion! She never hesitated to share her heart with her reader. Explore the genesis of the notion that Puritans were emotionless, colorless people. Which historian/writer first advanced that idea? (Enrichment A)?	Students, with minimal errors, will clearly answer the assigned question in a 1-2 page essay.
Students will work in a group setting. (behavioral goal)	In a class, in a co-op experience, or during a family discussion, students will discuss the following ethical issues: abortion and euthanasia.	Students will exhibit practical listening skills and will manifest understanding of opposing worldviews.
Students will be able to recall the information taught in the lesson. (cognitive goal)	Lesson 3 Test	Students will take the test at the end of this lesson and score at least 80%.

Goals/Objectives: What is the purpose of this lesson?	Strategies to meet these goals: How will I obtain these goals/objectives?	Evaluation: How will I know when I have met these goals/objectives?
Students will experience reflective writing. (affective/spiritual goal)	Using the Journal Guide Questions in the Appendices, students will record at least three entries this week. Suggested Scriptures: Luke 24	Students will show evidence that they have reflected on this issue, including informed discussions and written responses.

SUGGESTED
Weekly *Implementation*

DAY 1	DAY 2	DAY 3	DAY 4	DAY 5
Prayer journal. Students should review the required reading(s) *before* the assigned lesson begins. Teacher and students will discuss the number of required essays for this week, choosing two or three essays. The rest of the essays can be outlined, answered with shorter answers, or skipped. Students will review all readings for Lesson 3.	**Prayer journal.** Students should review reading(s) from next lesson. Students should outline essays due at the end of the week. Per teacher instructions, students may answer orally in a group setting some of the essays that are not assigned as formal essays.	**Prayer journal.** Students should write rough drafts of all assigned essays. The teacher or a peer evaluator may correct rough drafts.	**Prayer journal.** Students will re-write corrected copies of essays due tomorrow.	**Prayer journal.** Essays are due. Students should take the Lesson 3 test. Reading ahead: Students should review *The Autobiography of Benjamin Franklin*, Benjamin Franklin. Guide: What was Franklin's faith? Was it a Christian faith? Or a sort of "good works" civil faith?

Note: References to sources are in student edition.

ENRICHMENT ACTIVITIES/PROJECTS

Students should ask their mom and/or dad to sing "Eleanor Rigby."

Students should ask their parents what they were doing during Woodstock. (1970)

CRITICAL THINKING

A. In his book *A Modell of Christian Charity* (1630), John Winthrop, first governor of the Puritan Massachusetts Bay Colony, wrote:

The Lord will make our name a praise and glory, so that men shall say of succeeding plantations: The Lord make it like that of New England. For we must consider that we shall be like a City upon a Hill; the eyes of all people are on us.
http://history.hanover.edu/texts/winthmod.html

What does Winthrop mean "a City upon a Hill?" Why does/does not this statement seem a little presumptuous on his part?

ANSWER: *Probably Winthrop is borrowing a metaphor from Augustine's* City of God. *The call to be salt and light to an unsaved people is certainly a biblical notion and in that sense it is not presumptuous. On the contrary, one would hope that the Puritan Christian civilization would be a like a "City upon a Hill."*

B. Puritans effectively combined sound scholarship and profound spirituality. They led American society in education and science for a century. They founded most of the universities in New England. Some modern Evangelical scholars lament that this combination has been lost. Professor Mark Noll, professor at Wheaton College, argues that "the scandal of the evangelical mind is that there is not much of an evangelical mind." Noll is speaking of a comprehensive ability to think theologically across a broad spectrum of life (e.g., politics, arts, culture, and economics). Evangelicals, he argue, have a propensity for shallow analysis of complex cultural issues (See Mark A. Noll, *The Scandal of the Evangelical Mind*, Grand Rapids, MI: Eerdmans Publishing Company, 1994). This is a view held by other scholars as well. (See David F. Wells, *God in the Wasteland: The Reality of Truth in a World of Fading Dreams*, Eerdmans). "Surely the God who is rendered 'weightless' by modern culture (especially evangelical Christians) is quite different from the living God." Do you agree with Noll and Wells? Is there hope that born-again Christians will regain the high ground in culture and thought?

ANSWER: *All answers are opinions. As it was in the Puritan epoch, there certainly is hope that Christians will again assume leadership in American culture.*

C. In American culture the concept of "hero" has changed considerably over the last 50 years.

1940s "classical" Theism
John Wayne: Do the Right Thing the Right Way.

1970s "nostalgic" Theism
Star Wars: Do the Right Thing For the Downtrodden.

1980s "nostalgic" Theism
Clint Eastwood: Do The Right Thing even if you have to do the Wrong Thing to Get there.

1990s Absurdism
Toy Story Character: Do The Right Thing The Old Fashioned Way—But Toys can do it Better.

2000 Existentialism/Romanticism revivalism
Tom Cruise: Doing the Right Thing is What is Right For Me.

How will the American hero evolve in the next 20 years?

ANSWER: *All answers are opinions. One opinion is that the American hero will become more and more Theistic, if not Christian Theistic. Americans are becoming hungry for heroes who are honorable and moral. Some scholars, like Os Guinness, argue that American hunger for art that has transcendent value is growing.*

BIBLICAL APPLICATION

In about one page students should answer biblical applications in essay form; they should include biblical references.

A. Describe Edwards' religious affections and explain how they are evidences of true religion.

ANSWER: *There are two kinds of true religion (p. 16): Love for Christ, Joy in Christ. Both grow out of suffering. Holy affections are evidence of a deeper piety and, to Edwards, personal piety is never so personal that it is not open to scrutiny* *by larger society. Edwards would be horrified with modern notions (i.e., Existentialism) that emphasize privatism and the notion that "it is acceptable to do whatever pleases a person as long as it does not harm others."*

B. Read the following passage from Esther Edwards' diary entitled "...The Awful Sweetness of Walking With God." Esther, by the way, had a famous son, Aaron Burr.

Though father is usually taciturn or preoccupied—my mother will call these large words—even when he takes one of us children with him, today he discoursed to me of the awful sweetness of walking with God in Nature. He seems to feel God in the woods, the sky, and the grand sweep of the river which winds so majestically through the woody silences here. (Written in Northhampton, MA, 1741.)

("Esther Edwards" in James Miller, Robert O'Neal, and Robert Hayden, *The American Literary Tradition*, NY: Scott, Foresman, and Company, 1973, 36-37)

Compare and contrast the image we see of Jonathan Edwards through his sermon and the way Esther saw him. (If you are unfamiliar with writing comparison and contrast papers, refer to a writing manual.)

ANSWER: *Jonathan Edwards was a man of prayer and a very stern preacher. Ironically, he did not like people much—he much preferred to study the Word alone in his library. In fact, to many, he appeared cold. However, to his family he was a warm, compassionate, vulnerable man—in an 18th century sort of way. He managed to be a great scholar, accomplished preacher, and devoted father and husband. Perhaps that is why he was so effective for God's kingdom. Unfortunately, those attributes were not valued by his congregation—who wished for Edwards to do more visitation—and Edwards was dismissed from his position.*

C. Describe your dad (or another parent or guardian) using Esther's method of description of her dad. In what ways has the Lord used your father (or another adult) in your life? Compare your dad/adult with King David, Joseph, or another dad in the Bible.

ANSWER: *Answers will have to be opinions.*

D. Have you ever been disappointed? How did you keep from being bitter? Many Christian thinkers are calling brothers and sisters to forgiveness: forgiveness helps the person wronged more than the person who committed the wrong. Find scriptural evidence that commands you to forgive those who have wronged you.

50

Jonathan Edwards gave his whole life to the Northhampton Church and was fired anyway. The following is his farewell sermon. Does he show any sign of bitterness?

EDWARDS' FAREWELL SERMON:

I have just now said that I have had a peculiar concern for the young people, and in so saying I did not intend to exclude you. You are in youth, and in the most early youth. Therefore I have been sensible that if those that were young had a precious opportunity for their souls' good, you who are very young had, in many respects, a peculiarly precious opportunity. And accordingly I have not neglected you. I have endeavored to do the part of a faithful shepherd, in feeding the lambs as well as the sheep. Christ did once commit the care of your souls to me as your minister; and you know, dear children, how I have instructed you, and warned you from time to time. You know how I have often called you together for that end, and some of you, sometimes, have seemed to be affected with what I have said to you. But I am afraid it has had no saving effect as to many of you, but that you remain still in an unconverted condition, without any real saving work wrought in your souls, convincing you thoroughly of your sin and misery, causing you to see the great evil of sin, and to mourn for it, and hate it above all things, and giving you a sense of the excellency of the Lord Jesus Christ, bringing you with all your hearts to cleave to him as your Savior, weaning your hearts from the world, and causing you to love God above all, and to delight in holiness more than in all the pleasant things of this earth. And I must now leave you in a miserable condition, having no interest in Christ, and so under the awful displeasure and anger of God, and in danger of going down to the pit of eternal misery. — Now I must bid you farewell. I must leave you in the hands of God. I can do no more for you than to pray for you. Only I desire you not to forget, but often think of the counsels and warnings I have given you, and the endeavors I have used, that your souls might be saved from everlasting destruction.

Dear children, I leave you in an evil world that is full of snares and temptations. God only knows what will become of you. This, the Scripture, has told us that there are but few saved, and we have abundant confirmation of it from what we see. This we see, that children die as well as others. Multitudes die before they grow up, and of those that grow up, comparatively few ever give good evidence of saving conversion to

God. I pray God to pity you, and take care of you, and provide for you the best means for the good of your souls, and that God himself would undertake for you to be your heavenly Father, and the mighty Redeemer of your immortal souls. Do not neglect to pray for yourselves. Take heed you be not of the number of those who cast off fear, and restrain prayer before God. Constantly pray to God in secret, and often remember that great day when you must appear before the judgment seat of Christ, and meet your minister there, who has so often counseled and warned you. http://www.jonathanedwards.com/sermons.htm

ANSWER: *Edwards knew that forgiveness is paramount in Christian doctrine. (Matthew 6)*

ENRICHMENT ACTIVITIES/PROJECTS

Students should write worldview statements for a popular actor (actress), for an active politician, and for a local clergyperson.

Students should discuss the worldviews of advertising signs along roads. They should also discuss worldviews found in the local newspaper. How does a particular worldview influence the way a current event is presented?

A. Read *Evangelical Ethics,* by Professor John Jefferson Davis, Ph.D., Gordon Conwell Seminary, South Hamilton, MA. After reading Dr. Davis' book, students should state their position on these ethical issues: euthanasia, abortion, capital punishment, and others.

ANSWER: *Answers will have to be opinions.*

B. Summarize what Edwards says about the youth of his town in this passage from "A Faithful Narrative of the Surprising Work of God." Next, students should compare these youth to the youth in their church.

ANSWER: *Edwards was experiencing problems with his youth. They were not showing the degree of commitment that he wished to see.*

Excerpt from "A Faithful Narrative of the Surprising Work of God"

The people of the country, in general, I suppose, are as sober, orderly, and good sort of people, as in any part of New England; and I believe they have been preserved the freest by far of any part of the country, from error, and variety of sects and opinions. Our being so far within the land, at a distance from sea-ports, and in a corner of the country, has doubtless been one reason why we have not been so much corrupted with vice, as most other parts. But without question, the religion and good order of the county, and purity in doctrine, has, under God, been very much owing to the great abilities, and eminent piety of my venerable and honored grandfather Stoddard. I suppose we have been the freest of any part of the land from unhappy divisions and quarrels in our ecclesiastical and religious affairs, till the late lamentable Springfield contention. (The Springfield Contention relates to the settlement of a minister there, which occasioned too warm debates between some, both pastors and people, that were for it, and others that were against it, on account of their different apprehensions about his principles, and about some steps that were taken to procure his ordination.)

Being much separated from other parts of the province and having comparatively but little intercourse with them, we have always managed our ecclesiastical affairs within ourselves. It is the way in which the country, from its infancy, has gone on, by the practical agreement of all; and the way in which our peace and good order has hitherto been maintained.

The town of Northampton is of about 82 years standing, and has now about 200 families; which mostly dwell more compactly together than any town of such a size in these parts of the country. This probably has been an occasion, that both our corruptions and reformations have been, from time to time, the more swiftly propagated from one to another through the town. Take the town in general, and so far as I can judge, they are as rational and intelligent a people as most I have been acquainted with. Many of them have been noted for religion; and particularly remarkable for their distinct knowledge in things that relate to heart religion, and Christian experience, and their great regards thereto.

I am the third minister who has been settled in the town. The Rev. Mr. Eleazer Mather, who was the first, was ordained in July, 1669. He was one whose heart was much in his work, and abundant in labors for the good of precious souls. He had the high esteem and great love for his people, and was blessed with no small success. The Rev. Mr. Stoddard who succeeded him, came first to the town the November after his death; but was not ordained till September 11, 1672, and died February 11, 1728-9. So that he continued in the work of the ministry here, from his first coming to town, near 60 years. And as he was eminent and renowned for his gifts and grace; so he was blessed, from the beginning, with extraordinary success in his ministry, in the conversion of many souls. He had five harvests, as he called them. The first was about 57 years ago; the second about 53; the third about 40; the fourth about 24; the fifth and last about 18 years ago. Some of these times were much more remarkable than others, and the ingathering of souls more plentiful. Those about 53, and 40, and 24 years ago, were much greater than either the first or the last: but in each of them, I have heard my grandfather say, the greater part of the young people in the town, seemed to be mainly concerned for their eternal salvation.

After the last of these, came a far more degenerate time (at least among the young people), I suppose, than ever before. Mr. Stoddard, indeed, had the comfort, before he died, of seeing a time where there were no small appearances of a divine work among some, and a considerable ingathering of souls, even after I was settled with him in the ministry, which was about two years before his death; and I have reason to bless God for the great advantage I had by it. In these two years there were nearly twenty that Mr. Stoddard hoped to be savingly converted; but there was nothing of any general awakening. The greater part seemed to be at that time very insensible of the things of religion, and engaged in other cares and pursuits. Just after my grandfather's death, it seemed to be a time of extraordinary dullness in religion. Licentiousness for some years prevailed among the youth of the town; there were many of them very much addicted to night-walking, and frequenting the tavern, and lewd practices, wherein some, by their example, exceedingly corrupted others. It was their manner very frequently to get together, in conventions of both sexes for mirth and jollity, which they called frolics; and they would often spend the greater part of the night in them, without regard to any order in the families they belonged to: and indeed family government did too much fail in the town. It was become very customary with many of our young people to be indecent in their carriage at meeting, which doubtless would not have prevailed in such a degree, had it not been that my grandfather, through his great age (though he retained his powers surprisingly to the last), was not so able to observe them. There had also long prevailed in the town a spirit of contention between two parties, into which they had for many years been divided; by which they maintained a jealousy one of the other, and were prepared to oppose one another in all public affairs.

But in two or three years after Mr. Stoddard's death, there began to be a sensible amendment to these evils. The young people showed more of a disposition to hearken to counsel, and by degrees left off their frolics; they grew observably more decent in their attendance on the public worship, and there were more who manifested a religious concern than there used to be.

C. In America, religion has more or less embraced revivalism as a mode of church expansion, growth, and influence. According to historian D. E. Dieter, "Revivalism is the movement within the Christian tradition which emphasizes the appeal of religion to the emotional and affectional nature of individuals as well as to their intellectual and rational nature. It believes that vital Christianity begins with a response of the whole being to the gospel's call for repentance and spiritual rebirth by faith in Jesus Christ. This experience results in a personal relationship with God. Some have sought to make revivalism a purely American and even a predominantly frontier phenomenon." Historian Geoff Waugh writes, "Revival must of necessity make an impact on the community and this is one means by which we may distinguish it from the more usual operations of the Holy Spirit." Roy Hession notes that the outward forms of revivals do, of course, differ considerably, but the inward and permanent content of them is always the same: a new experience of conviction of sin among the saints; a new vision of the Cross and of Jesus and of redemption; a new willingness on man's part for brokenness, repentance, confession, and restitution; a joyful experience of the power of the blood of Jesus to cleanse fully from sin and restore and heal all that sin has lost and broken; a new entering into the fullness of the Holy Spirit and of His power to do His own work through His people; and a new gathering in of the lost ones to Jesus.

Research recent church history and speculate upon the form and nature of future revivalism. Will it be like the mass rallies in the past or will revivalism look a lot different?

ANSWER: *All answers are opinions. Perhaps revivals will be more empathic, less confessional, and often tied to the arts. If so, this news is both good and bad. The good news is that heretofore untouched aspects of culture could be touched (e.g., the arts). The challenge is to be empathic in an orthodox, confessional way.*

D. Write a worldview for yourself. Use the following questions to guide you.

> When you write your worldview, consider these three essential questions:
>
> A. What is the priority of the spiritual world?
>
> B. What is the essential uniqueness of man?
>
> C. What is the objective character of truth and goodness?—*Toward a Recovery of Christian Belief,* Carl F. H. Henry

What is the priority of the spiritual world?

Authority: Is the Bible important to you? Do you obey God and other authority, your parents, officials of the court, etc. even when it is uncomfortable to do so?

Pleasure: What do you really enjoy doing? Does it please God?

What is the essential uniqueness of man?

Fate: What/who really determines your life? Chance? Circumstances? God?

What is the objective character of truth and goodness?

Justice: What are the consequences of your actions? Is there some sort of judgment? Do bad people suffer? Why do good people suffer?

ANSWER: *The following is a worldview position paper*

Sample Worldview Essay:

Isaac Watts' famous hymn, "When I Survey the Wondrous Cross," is the best summation of my worldview:

"When I survey the wondrous cross on which the Prince of Glory died,/My richest gain I count but loss, And pour contempt on all my pride . . ." As the theologian Dietrich Bonhoeffer mused a few weeks before his death in a Nazi prison in late World War II, so I profess: Christ is at once my boundary and my rediscovered center. In my Resurrected Lord I see the faithfulness of gracious God encountering sinful humankind.

How we need the grace of God! We are a lonely, separated, broken people desperately in need of a Savior. All humankind, good and bad alike, rich and poor, are in the wrong before God, and we all fall under God's judgment. In spite of our sincere intentions, we systematically, inevitably shatter our virtuous dreams by allowing self-interest and hostility to motivate our lives. Without the resurrected Lord at the center of our

being, we are, as the Christian poet T. S. Eliot hauntingly reflects, "paralyzed force, gesture without motion." Yes, we all deserve the wrath of God. As the theologian Karl Barth explains, "The judgment of God is the righteousness of God without Jesus Christ." However, God, out of His great love for us all, gave us His Son to be our Savior. Yes, with Christ as the center of our lives, we have hope. I am unequivocal in my confession that a decision for Christ is the only way to health, happiness, wholeness, and eternal security.

"Were the whole realm of nature mine, that were a present far too small;/Love so amazing, so divine, Demands my soul, my life, my all." God's love is so amazing that He sent His only Begotten Son to die for me. Therefore, He has a right to demand all of me in return!

Likewise, I am not ambivalent in my confession that "There is no Jew or Greek, slave or free, male or female; for you are all one in Christ Jesus. (Galatians 3:28.) In the areas of social justice, equality between the sexes and races, ministry to the poor and to the homeless, peacemaking, the church must be prophetic. "For in as much as you helped the least of these, you helped me . . ."

Equally important is my responsibility to create and to support wholesome family life. The Christian family remains the single most important channel that God has chosen to inculcate in humankind His nurturing principles of fulfilled living. Solid, healthy Christian family life is a primary goal for my time on this earth. Recognizing the pressures of economics and time, I must nonetheless obtain the knowledge and skills necessary to keep Jesus Christ in the center of my home. (James P. Stobaugh)

CRITICAL THINKING

Compare "Eleanor Rigby" by Paul McCartney and John Lennon with Anne Bradstreet's "Upon the Burning of Our House." Identify differences in theme, tone, plot, and use of figurative language.

ANSWER: *Bradstreet invites us to believe in a loving God. The Beatles exhibit the self-serving, subjectivity of the 1960s. On the surface, however, the Beatles appeared harmless, and in light of what followed (e.g., heavy metal bands) they appear mild indeed. However, to their age, they were certainly radical. They also were the first of their genre. "Ah, look at all the lonely people..." Many people would recognize this line as the beginning of the song "Eleanor Rigby" written by the Beatles. It continues, "Eleanor Rigby picks up the rice in the* church where a wedding has been, lives in a dream, waits at the window wearing the face that she keeps in a jar by the door. Who is it for?" Then comes the chorus, a continual, unanswered question: "All the lonely people, where do they all come from? All the lonely people, where do they all belong?"

This song stands in stark contrast to the poem, "Upon the Burning of Our House," by Anne Bradstreet, a seventeenth century poet. What is striking in her poem is not the story of the fire but the peace and even the joy with which she was enabled by her God to face the calamity.

Bradstreet's poem is more hopeful than "Eleanor Rigby" because, though she lost her home and precious possessions to fire, she knew that as a Christian she had "an house on high erect" which "stands permanent tho' this be fled." When her home was gone, it only reminded her that she had a home above that was unshakeable. Though her possessions were destroyed, she did not complain; she said, "The world no longer let me love, my hope and treasure lies above." She had her hope in God even in earthly despair.

In contrast, Eleanor Rigby and Father McKenzie are completely trapped and controlled by their circumstances. When Eleanor's fruitless life ends without the fulfillment of her dream of love, there is no further hope; she is "buried along with her name" and sinks into oblivion. Father McKenzie works hard, but for no purpose – "no one sees" and "no one is saved."

BIBLICAL APPLICATION

Compare Eleanor Rigby with the woman caught in adultery. (John 8:2-11)

ANSWER: *Poor Eleanor needed Christ, not the empty cultic worship she found in this dreary poem. Rigby is captured in the hopeless web of Naturalism (i.e., Nihilism and an impersonal god) and existentialism (i.e., experience). Both Eleanor and the adulterous woman were lonely, guilty, and rejected. Only one found Christ.*

ENRICHMENT

A. Modern Americans accuse the Puritans of being colorless and legalistic. Typically, to be "Puritan" means "to hide one's feelings." Yet, to read Anne Bradstreet, one is struck by the power of Puritan emotion! She never hesitated to share her heart with her reader.

To My Dear And Loving Husband

If ever two were one, then surely we.

If ever man were lov'd by wife, then thee.
If ever wife was happy in a man,
Compare with me, ye women, if you can.
I prize thy love more than whole Mines of gold
Or all the riches that the East doth hold.
My love is such that Rivers cannot quench,
Nor ought but love from thee give recompense.
Thy love is such I can no way repay.
The heavens reward thee manifold, I pray.
Then while we live, in love let's so persevere
That when we live no more, we may live ever.
http://eirlibrary.utotonto.ca/rpo/display/poet27.html

Explore the genesis of the notion that Puritans were emotionless, colorless people. Which historian/writer first advanced that idea?

ANSWER: *During the middle of the 19th century, several historians (e.g., Beard) advanced the notion that Puritans were unhappy, bigoted people. This particular viewpoint appealed a great deal to liberal, Romantic 19th century historians. The Harvard historians (e.g., Perry Miller, Douglas Edward Leech, and Samuel Morison) reclaimed the Puritans as our spiritual ancestors.*

B. Do you agree or disagree with Puritan Cotton Mather's rendition of what a good school is?

A Good School deserves to be call'd, the very Salt of the Town, that hath it: And the Pastors of every Town are under peculiar obligations to make this a part of their Pastoral Care, That they may have a Good School, in their Neighbourhood. A woeful putrefaction threatens the Rising Generation; Barbarous Ignorance, and the unavoidable consequence of it, Outrageous Wickedness will make the Rising Generation Loathsome, if it have not Schools to preserve it.

But Schools, wherein the Youth may by able Masters be Taught the Things that are necessary to qualify them for future Serviceableness, and have their Manners therewithal well-formed under a Laudable Discipline, and be over and above Well-Catechised in the principles of Religion, Those would be a Glory of our Land, and the preservatives of all other Glory . . . When the Reformation began in Europe an hundred and fourscore years ago, to Erect Schools everywhere was one principal concern of the Glorious and Heroic Reformers; and it was a common thing even for Little Villages of Twenty or Thirty Families, in the midst of all their Charges, and their Dangers, to maintain one of them. The Colonies of New England were planted on the Design of pursuing that Holy Reformation; and now the Devil cannot give a greater Blow to the Reformation among us, than by causing Schools to Languish under Discouragements. If our General Courts decline to contrive and provide Laws for the Support of Schools; or if particular Towns Employ their Wits, for Cheats to Elude the wholesome Laws; little do they consider how much they expose themselves to that Rebuke of God, Thou hast destroyed thyself, O New England.

And the first Instance of their Barbarity will be, that they will be undone for want of men, but not see and own what it was that undid them. You will therefore pardon my Freedom with you, if I Address you, in the words of Luther: "If ever there be any Considerable Blow given to the Devil's Kingdom, it must be, by Youth Excellently Educated. It is a serious Thing, a weighty Thing, and a thing that hath much of the Interest of Christ, and of Christianity in it, that Youth be well-trained up, and that Schools, and School-Masters be maintained. Learning is an unwelcome guest to the Devil, and therefore he would fain starve it out." But the Freedom with which this Address is made unto you, is not so great as the Fervour that has animated it. My Fathers and Brethren, If you have any Love to God and Christ and Posterity; let (Godly) Schools be more Encouraged. (Cotton Mather)

ANSWER: *To separate education from religion would be unthinkable. Morality and faith were intricately connected to freedom, justice, and democracy.*

FINAL PROJECT

Students should correct and rewrite all essays and place them in their Final Portfolio.

SUPPLEMENTAL RESOURCES

Davis, John Jefferson. *The Victorious Kingdom of Christ.*

Post-millennialism offers a theological rubric that is important for serious Christian apologetics, Christian missions in particular. Optimism based on the Word of God—not on 17th century Enlightenment—is sorely needed in the Christian community as well as American society at large.

Dawn, Marva J. (a pseudonym), *Reaching Out Without Dumbing Down: A Theology of Worship for the Turn-of-the-Century Culture.*

Dr. Dawn uses the expression "dumbing down" to describe the status of most contemporary worship services—informal and formal, low and high, charismatic and traditional. Dawn draws many of her views about dumbing down from Jane Healey's book *Endangered Minds* (p. 6). It argues persuasively that many cultural forces are at work to sabotage people's abilities to think (p. 7).

Marsden, George. *The Soul of the University.*

Marsden traces the regrettable loss of influence that the Evangelical community once had on American Universities.

McGrath, Alistair. *Evangelicalism and the Future of Christianity.*

The idea of an established church situated in a friendly society is over. We need to rethink our evangelism strategies in that light. McGrath calls us back to the 1st Century and Jonathan Edwards—in the same book!

Murray, Ian. *Jonathan Edwards: A New Biography.*

A wonderful historic narrative of the life of Jonathan Edwards.

Noll, Mark A. *America's God: From Jonathan Edwards to Abraham Lincoln.*

A powerful, but readable story of how American views of God and the world have changed over the last 350 years.

Pelikan, Jaroslav. *The Idea of the University.*

Pelikan insists that intelligent discussion of the university requires an analysis of its most basic nature and a discussion of the role it can and should play among other institutions and communities within the local, national, and international community.

Notes:

LESSON 3 TEST

DISCUSSION QUESTION (100 POINTS)

A. Define "religious affection" and discuss the religious affection Edwards highlights in this passage from *Religious Affections*: (25 points)

Gracious affections are attended with evangelical humiliation. Evangelical humiliation is a sense that a Christian has of his own utter insufficiency, despicableness, and odiousnesss, with an answerable frame of heart. There is a distinction to be made between a legal and evangelical humiliation. The former is what men may be the subjects of, while they are yet in a state of nature, and have no gracious affections; the latter is peculiar to true saints: the former is from the common influence of the Spirit of God, assisting natural principles, and especially natural conscience; the latter is from the special influences of the Spirit of God, implanting and exercising supernatural and divine principles: the former is from the mind's being assisted to a greater sense of the things of religion, as to their natural properties and qualities, and particularly of the natural perfections of God, such as his greatness, terrible majesty, which were manifested to the congregation of Israel, in giving the law at mount Sinai; the latter is from a sense of the transcendent beauty of divine things in their moral qualities: in the former, a sense of the awful greatness, and natural perfections of God, and of the strictness of his law, convinces men that they are exceeding sinful, and guilty, and exposed to the wrath of God, as it will wicked men and devils at the day of judgment; but they do not see their own odiousness on the account of sin; they do not see the hateful nature of sin; a sense of this is given in evangelical humiliation, by a discovery of the beauty of God's holiness and moral perfection. In a legal humiliation, men are made sensible that they are little and nothing before the great and terrible God, and that they are undone, and wholly insufficient to help themselves; as wicked men will be at the day of judgment: but they have not an answerable frame of heart, consisting in a disposition to abase themselves, and exalt God alone; this disposition is given only in evangelical humiliation, by overcoming the heart, and changing its inclination, by a discovery of God's holy beauty: in a legal humiliation, the conscience is convinced; as the consciences of all will be most perfectly at the day of judgment; but because there is no spiritual understanding, the will is not bowed, nor the inclination altered: this is done only in evangelical humiliation. In legal humiliation, men are brought to despair of helping themselves; in evangelical, they are brought voluntarily to deny and renounce themselves: in the former, they are subdued and forced to the ground; in the latter, they are brought sweetly to yield, and freely and with delight to prostrate themselves at the feet of God. Legal humiliation has in it no spiritual good, nothing of the nature of true virtue; whereas evangelical humiliation is that wherein the excellent beauty of Christian grace does very much consist. Legal humiliation is useful, as a means in order to evangelical; as a common knowledge of the things of religion is a means requisite in order to spiritual knowledge. Men may be legally humbled and have no humility: as the wicked at the day of judgment will be thoroughly convinced that they have no righteousness, but are altogether sinful, and exceedingly guilty, and justly exposed to eternal damnation, and be fully sensible of their own helplessness, without the least mortification of the pride of their hearts: but the essence of evangelical humiliation consists in such humility, as becomes a creature, in itself exceeding sinful, under a dispensation of grace; consisting in a mean esteem of himself, as in himself nothing, and altogether contemptible and odious; attended with a mortification of a disposition to exalt himself, and a free renunciation of his own glory.

This is a great and most essential thing in true religion. The whole frame of the gospel, and everything appertaining to the new covenant, and all God's dispensations towards fallen man, are calculated to bring to pass this effect in the hearts of men. They that are destitute of this, have no true religion, whatever profession they may make, and how high soever their religious affections may be: Heb. 2:4, "Look, his ego is inflated; he is without integrity. But the righteous one will live by his faith." i.e., he shall live by his faith on God's righteousness and grace, and not his own goodness and excellency. God has abundantly manifested in his word, that this is what he has a peculiar respect to in his saints, and that nothing is acceptable to him without it. Psalm 34:18, "The Lord is near the brokenhearted; He saves those crushed in spirit." Psalm 51:17, "The sacrifice pleasing to God is a broken spirit. God, You will not despise a broken and humbled heart." Psalm 138:6, "Though the Lord is exalted, He takes note of the humble." Prov. 3:34, "He mocks those who mock, but gives grace to the humble." Isa. 57:15, "For the High and Exalted One who lives forever, whose name is Holy says this: "I live in a high and holy place, and with the oppressed and lowly of spirit, to revive the spirit of the lowly and revive the heart of the oppressed." Isa. 66:1, 2, "This is what the Lord says: Heaven is My throne, and earth is My footstool. What house could you possibly build for Me? And what place could be My home? My hand made all these things, and so they all came into being. [This is] the Lord's declaration. I will look favorably on this kind of person: one who is humble, submissive broken in spirit, and who trembles at My word." Micah 6:8, "He has told you men what is good and what it is the Lord requires of you: Only to act justly, to love faithfulness, and to walk humbly with your God." Matt. 5:3, "Blessed are the poor in spirit, because the kingdom of heaven is theirs." Matt. 18:3, 4, "I assure you," He said, "unless you are converted Or are turned around and become like children, you will never enter the kingdom of heaven. Therefore, whoever humbles himself like this child—this one is the greatest in the kingdom of heaven." Mark 10:15, "I assure you: Whoever does not welcome the kingdom of God like a little child will never enter it." The centurion, that we have an account of, Luke 7, acknowledged that he was not worthy that Christ should enter under his roof, and that he was not worthy to come to him. See the manner of the woman's coming to Christ, that was a sinner, Luke 7:37: "And a woman in the town who was a sinner found out that Jesus was reclining at the table in the Pharisee's house. She brought an alabaster flask of fragrant oil and stood behind Him at His feet, weeping, and began to wash His feet with her tears. She wiped His feet with the hair of her head, kissing them and anointing them with the fragrant oil. " She did not think the hair of her head, which is the natural crown and glory of a woman (1 Cor. 11:15), too good to wipe the feet of Christ withal. Jesus most graciously accepted her, and says to her, "thy faith hath saved thee, go in peace." He answered, "It isn't right to take the children's bread and throw it to their dogs." "Yes, Lord," she said, "yet even the dogs eat the crumbs that fall from their masters' table!" Then Jesus replied to her, "Woman, your faith is great. Let it be done for you as you want."" Matt. 15:26, 27, 28. The prodigal son said, "I'll get up, go to my father, and say to him, Father, I have sinned against heaven and in your sight. I'm no longer worthy to be called your son. Make me like one of your hired hands." Luke 15:18. See also Luke 18:9: "He also told this parable to some who trusted in themselves that they were righteous and looked down on everyone else. But the tax collector, standing far off, would not even raise his eyes to heaven but kept striking his chest mourning and saying, 'God, turn Your wrath from me—a sinner!' I tell you, this one went

down to his house justified rather than the other; because everyone who exalts himself will be humbled, but the one who humbles himself will be exalted." Matt. 28:9, "Just then Jesus met them and said, "Good morning!" They came up, took hold of His feet, and worshiped Him." Col. 3:12, "Therefore, God's chosen ones, put on heartfelt humility." Ezek. 20:41, 42, "When I bring you from the peoples and gather you from the countries where you have been scattered, I will accept you as a pleasing aroma. And I will demonstrate My holiness through you in the sight of the nations. When I lead you into the land of Israel, the land I swore to give your fathers, you will know that I am the Lord." Chap. 36:26, 27, 31, "I will give you a new heart and put a new spirit within you; I will remove your heart of stone and give you a heart of flesh. I will place My Spirit within you and cause you to follow My statutes and carefully observe My ordinances. Then you will remember your evil ways and your deeds that were not good, and you will loathe yourselves for your iniquities and abominations." Chap. 16:63, "you will remember and be ashamed, and never open your mouth again because of your disgrace." this is the declaration of the Lord God." Job 42:6, "Therefore I take back and repent in dust and ashes."

As we would therefore make the holy Scriptures our rule in judging of the nature of true religion, and judging of our own religious qualifications and state, it concerns us greatly to look at this humiliation, as one of the most essential things pertaining to true Christianity. This is the principal part of the great Christian duty of self-denial. That duty consists in two things, viz., first, in a man's denying his worldly inclinations, and in forsaking and renouncing all worldly objects and enjoyments; and, secondly, in denying his natural self-exaltation, and renouncing his own dignity and glory and in being emptied of himself; so that he does freely and from his very heart, as it were renounce himself, and annihilate himself. Thus the Christian doth in evangelical humiliation. And this latter is the greatest and most difficult part of self-denial: although they always go together, and one never truly is, where the other is not; yet natural men can come much nearer to the former than the latter. Many Anchorites and Recluses have abandoned (though without any true mortification) the wealth, and pleasures, and common enjoyments of the world, who were far from renouncing their own dignity and righteousness; they never denied themselves for Christ, but only sold one lust to feed another, sold a beastly lust to pamper a devilish one; and so were never the better, but their latter end was worse than their beginning; they turned out one black devil, to let in seven white ones, that were worse than the first, though of a fairer countenance. It is inexpressible, and almost inconceivable, how strong a self-righteous, self-exalting disposition is naturally in man; and what he will not do and suffer to feed and gratify it: and what lengths have been gone in a seeming self-denial in other respects, by Essenes and Pharisees among the Jews, and by Papists, many sects of heretics, and enthusiasts, among professing Christians; and by many Mahometans; and by Pythagorean philosophers, and others among the Heathen; and all to do sacrifice to this Moloch of spiritual pride or self-righteousness; and that they may have something wherein to exalt themselves before God, and above their fellow creatures.

B. Outline a sermon that Edwards might preach. Include his text, a title, and three points he might make. (25 Points)

C. Paraphrase the following Bradstreet poem: (50 Points)

What is its rhyme scheme in lines 1-20? (10 Points)
Identify four examples of figurative language. (10 Points)
To what animal(s) does she compare her children? (10 Points)
Explain what lines 75-77 mean. (10 Points)
What did Anne try to do for her children? (lines 88-90) (10 Points)

In Reference to Her Children, 23 June 1659
Anne Bradstreet

I had eight birds hatcht in one nest,
2 Four Cocks were there, and Hens the rest.
3 I nurst them up with pain and care,
4 No cost nor labour did I spare
5 Till at the last they felt their wing,
6 Mounted the Trees and learned to sing.
7 Chief of the Brood then took his flight
8 To Regions far and left me quite.
9 My mournful chirps I after send
10 Till he return, or I do end.
11 Leave not thy nest, thy Dame and Sire,
12 Fly back and sing amidst this Quire.
13 My second bird did take her flight
14 And with her mate flew out of sight.
15 *Southward* they both their course did bend,
16 And Seasons twain they there did spend,
17 Till after blown by *Southern* gales
18 They *Norward* steer'd with filled sails.

19 A prettier bird was no where seen,
20 Along the Beach, among the treen.
21 I have a third of colour white
22 On whom I plac'd no small delight,
23 Coupled with mate loving and true,
24 Hath also bid her Dame adieu.
25 And where *Aurora* first appears,
26 She now hath percht to spend her years.
27 One to the Academy flew
28 To chat among that learned crew.
29 Ambition moves still in his breast
30 That he might chant above the rest,
31 Striving for more than to do well,
32 That nightingales he might excell.
33 My fifth, whose down is yet scarce gone,
34 Is 'mongst the shrubs and bushes flown
35 And as his wings increase in strength
36 On higher boughs he'll perch at length.
37 My other three still with me nest,
38 Until they're grown, then as the rest,
39 Or here or there, they'll take their flight,
40 As is ordain'd, so shall they light.
41 If birds could weep, then would my tears
42 Let others know what are my fears
43 Lest this my brood some harm should catch
44 And be surpris'd for want of watch
45 Whilst pecking corn and void of care
46 They fall un'wares in Fowler's snare;
47 Or whilst on trees they sit and sing
48 Some untoward boy at them do fling,
49 Or whilst allur'd with bell and glass
50 The net be spread and caught, alas;
51 Or lest by Lime-twigs they be foil'd;
52 Or by some greedy hawks be spoil'd.
53 O would, my young, ye saw my breast
54 And knew what thoughts there sadly rest.
55 Great was my pain when I you bred,
56 Great was my care when I you fed.
57 Long did I keep you soft and warm
58 And with my wings kept off all harm.
59 My cares are more, and fears, than ever,
60 My throbs such now as 'fore were never.
61 Alas, my birds, you wisdom want
62 Of perils you are ignorant.
63 Oft times in grass, on trees, in flight,
64 Sore accidents on you may light.
65 O to your safety have an eye,
66 So happy may you live and die.
67 Mean while, my days in tunes I'll spend
68 Till my weak lays with me shall end.
69 In shady woods I'll sit and sing

70 And things that past, to mind I'll bring.
71 Once young and pleasant, as are you,
72 But former toys. (no joys) adieu!
73 My age I will not once lament
74 But sing, my time so near is spent,
75 And from the top bough take my flight
76 Into a country beyond sight
77 Where old ones instantly grow young
78 And there with seraphims set song.
79 No seasons cold, nor storms they see
80 But spring lasts to eternity.
81 When each of you shall in your nest
82 Among your young ones take your rest,

83 In chirping languages oft them tell
84 You had a Dame that lov'd you well,
85 That did what could be done for young
86 And nurst you up till you were strong
87 And 'fore she once would let you fly
88 She shew'd you joy and misery,
89 Taught what was good, and what was ill,
90 What would save life, and what would kill.
91 Thus gone, amongst you I may live,
92 And dead, yet speak and counsel give.
93 Farewell, my birds, farewell, adieu,
94 I happy am, if well with you.

LESSON 3 TEST ANSWERS

DISCUSSION QUESTION (100 POINTS)

A. Define "religious affection" and discuss the religious affection Edwards highlights in this passage from *Religious Affections*: (25 Points)

ANSWER: *The religious affection Edwards described is humility. "True religion" is to be like Christ: to be humble like Christ. To Edwards the distinction between the natural mind and the evangelical or redeemed mind is great. He was not ready, however, to denigrate the natural mind.*

B. Outline a sermon that Edwards might preach. Include his text, a title, and three points he might make. (25 Points)

ANSWER:
Romans 8
I. More than Conquerors
II. We are predestined
III. We need to respond in faith to God's grace.

C. **ANSWER:**

Paraphrase Bradstreet's poem (50 Points total)
Answer: Bradstreet takes each child and describes him/her as a type of bird. As she describes the life cycle of each bird, she is describing each child. She ends the poem by celebrating her future—which will be the satisfaction of rearing her children properly and then soaring to heaven!

What is its rhyme scheme in lines 1-20? (10 Points)
Answer: It is aa, bb, cc, dd, and so on.

Identify four examples of figurative language (10 Points)

To what animal(s) does she compare her children? (10 Points)
Answer: Birds.

Explain what lines 75-77 mean. (10 Points)

75 And from the top bough take my flight
76 Into a country beyond sight
77 Where old ones instantly grow young

Answer: Someday the mother will be going to heaven.

What did Anne try to do for her children? (lines 88-90) (10 Points)

88 She shew'd you joy and misery,
89 Taught what was good, and what was ill,
90 What would save life, and what would kill.

Answer: To prepare them for all of life—good and bad.

LESSON 4
THE REVOLUTIONARY PERIOD, *1750-1800 (Part 1)*

Readings Due For This Lesson: Students should review *The Autobiography of Benjamin Franklin*, Benjamin Franklin.

Reading Ahead: Students should review Poems by Phillis Wheatley, *Speech in the Virginia Convention*, Patrick Henry; *The Declaration of Independence*, Thomas Jefferson; *Letter to Her Daughter from the New White House*, Abigail Adams.

Guide Question: In the midst of slavery and fear, how can this poet write with such optimism?

Goals: Students will analyze *Autobiography of Benjamin Franklin*, Benjamin Franklin.

Goals/Objectives: What is the purpose of this lesson?	Strategies to meet these goals: How will I obtain these goals/objectives?	Evaluation: How will I know when I have met these goals/ objectives?
	Students will answer the following question: What are the definitions of the underlined words? (Critical Thinking A)	
Students will increase their vocabulary. (cognitive goal)	Students will collect at least five new vocabulary words from their reading and use these words in their essays.	Students will use five vocabulary words in conversation during the week as well as use the words in their essays.
Students will understand the following concept: word definitions from context. (cognitive goal)	Students will answer the following question: What are the definitions of the underlined words? (Critical Thinking A)	
Students will understand this concept: Franklin's writing style. (cognitive goal)	Students will answer this essay question: What is the writing style that Franklin employs? (Critical Thinking B)	Students, with minimal errors, will clearly answer the assigned question in a 1-2 page essay.

Goals/Objectives: What is the purpose of this lesson?	Strategies to meet these goals: How will I obtain these goals/objectives?	Evaluation: How will I know when I have met these goals/objectives?
Students will understand the following concept: Franklin's faith journey. (cognitive goal)	Students will answer the following essay question: Describe Franklin's faith journey. (Biblical Application)	Students, with minimal errors, will clearly answer the assigned question in a 1-2 page essay.
Students will exhibit higher-level thinking skills as they discuss whether or not this story is an egotistical story. (cognitive goal)	Was the *Autobiography* a "rags to riches" story or was it a self-serving, egotistical story of a man's self-absorption? (Enrichment)	Students, with minimal errors, will clearly answer the assigned question in a 1-2 page essay.
Students will work in a group setting. (behavioral goal)	In a class, in a co-op experience, or during a family discussion, students will answer the following question: Was Franklin a believer?	Students will exhibit practical listening skills and will manifest understanding of opposing worldviews.
Students will be able to recall the information taught in the lesson. (cognitive goal)	Lesson 4 Test	Students will take the test at the end of this lesson and score at least 80%.
Students will experience reflective writing. (affective/spiritual goal)	Using the Journal Guide Questions in the Appendices, students will record at least three entries this week. Suggested Scriptures: John 8	Students will show evidence that they have reflected on this issue, including informed discussions and written responses.

SUGGESTED
Weekly *Implementation*

DAY 1	DAY 2	DAY 3	DAY 4	DAY 5
Prayer journal.	**Prayer journal.**	**Prayer journal.**	**Prayer journal.**	**Prayer journal.**
Students review the required reading(s) *before* the assigned lesson begins.	Student should review reading(s) from next lesson.	Students should write rough drafts of all assigned essays.	Student will re-write corrected copies of essays due tomorrow.	Essays are due.
Teacher may want to discuss assigned reading(s) with students.	Student should outline essays due at the end of the week.	The teacher and/or a peer evaluator may correct rough drafts.		Students should take the Lesson 4 test.
Teacher and students will decide on the number of essays to be required for this lesson, choosing two or three essays.	Per teacher instructions, students may answer orally in a group setting some of the essays that are not assigned as formal essays.			Reading ahead: Students should review Poems by Phillis Wheatley; *Speech in the Virginia Convention*, Patrick Henry; *The Declaration of Independence*, Thomas Jefferson; *Letter to Her Daughter from the New White House*, Abigail Adams.
The rest of the essays can be outlined, answered with shorter answers, or skipped.				Guide: In the midst of slavery and fear, how can Wheatley write with such optimism?
Students will review all readings for Lesson 4.				

Note: References to sources are in student edition

SUPPLEMENTAL RESOURCES

Isaacson, Walter. *Benjamin Franklin: An American Life.*
    Isaacson gives an earthy, real-life picture of the Founding Father.

Morgan, Edmund S. *Benjamin Franklin.*
    The standard biography of Franklin from which all others are judged.

Notes:

CRITICAL THINKING

A. What writing style does Franklin employ?

    Answer: *Franklin wrote in a simple style for his age, even though what he said was profound. He used subtle humor to give the reader insights into himself and his 18th century contemporaries.*

B. What are the definitions of the underlined words? http://etext.lib.virginia.edu/

    Having emerged from the poverty and <u>obscurity</u> (anonymity) in which I was born and bred, to a state of affluence (prosperity) and some degree of reputation in the world, and having gone so far through life with a considerable share of felicity (great happiness), the conducing (contributing) means I made use of, which with the blessing of God so well succeeded, my posterity (descendants) may like to know, as they may find some of them suitable to their own situations, and therefore fit to be imitated (Part I).

It was written in 1675, in the home-spun verse of that time and people, and addressed to those then concerned in the government there. It was in favor of liberty of conscience, and in behalf of the Baptists, Quakers, and other sectaries that had been under persecution, ascribing the Indian wars, and other distresses that had befallen the country, to that persecution, as so many judgments of God to punish so heinous (terrible) an offense, and exhorting (strongly urging) a repeal of those uncharitable (unjust; ungenerous) laws (Part I).

At his table he liked to have, as often as he could, some sensible friend or neighbor to converse with, and always took care to start some ingenious (original) or useful topic for discourse (conversation), which might tend to improve the minds of his children (Part I).

I continu'd this method some few years, but gradually left it, retaining only the habit of expressing myself in terms of modest diffidence (shyness) (Part II).

In 1751, Dr. Thomas Bond, a particular friend of mine, conceived the idea of establishing a hospital in Philadelphia a very beneficent (beneficial; advantageous) design, which has been ascrib'd to me, but was originally his), for the reception and cure of poor sick persons, whether inhabitants of the province or strangers. He was zealous (enthusiastic) and active in endeavoring to procure (obtain) subscriptions for it, but the proposal being a novelty (new thing) in America, and at first not well understood, he met with but small success (Part IV).

BIBLICAL APPLICATION

Describe Franklin's faith journey using this quote and other passages: "Before I enter upon my public appearance in business, it may be well to let you know the then state of my mind with regard to my principles and morals, that you may see how far those influenc'd the future events of my life. My parents had early given me religious impressions, and brought me through my childhood piously in the Dissenting way. But I was scarce fifteen, when, after doubting by turns of several points, as I found them disputed in the different books I read, I began to doubt of Revelation itself. Some books against Deism fell into my hands; they were said to be the substance of sermons preached at Boyle's Lectures. It happened that they wrought an effect on me quite contrary to what was intended by them; for the arguments of the Deists, which were quoted to be refuted, appeared to me much stronger than the refutations; in short, I soon became a thorough Deist. My arguments perverted some others, particularly Collins and Ralph; but, each of them having afterwards wrong'd me greatly without the least compunction, and recollecting Keith's conduct towards me (who was another freethinker), and my own towards Vernon and Miss Read, which at times gave me great trouble, I began to suspect that this doctrine, tho' it might be true, was not very useful." http://etext.lib.virginia.edu/

Answer: *While Franklin was not an active church member and never indicates that he was a Christian believer, he nonetheless exhibited strong moral fiber. By his own admission he was a Deist (someone who does not believe that God is active in human affairs). Of course, this book only discusses Franklin's life until 1752. There is evidence that he became far more "religious" later. Let's hope so.*

ENRICHMENT

Is the *Autobiography* a "rags to riches" story or is it a self-serving, egotistical story of a man's self-absorption?

Answer:
Answers will very but perhaps it is unfair to suggest that Franklin had any hidden agenda. He was an intensely secure, confident man, but it is probably not fair to say that he was egotistical.

FINAL PROJECT

Students should correct and rewrite all essays and place them in their Final Portfolio.

LESSON 4 TEST

OBJECTIVE TEST (50 POINTS)

1._____Franklin was the first American (A) to express openly his discontent with England (B) to be considered an equal to European scientists (C) to send a telegraph message to England.

2._____Franklin did not enter the ministry because (A) he did not feel called (B) he preferred to be a lawyer (C) after considering the paltry salary that ministers made, his father made him work at his shop.

3._____At age 12 Franklin (A) was apprenticed to his brother James (B) traveled to Georgia (C) invented the Franklin Stove.

4._____Franklin founded (A) the *Philadelphia Enquirer* (B) the *Pennsylvania Gazette* (C) the Spectator Society.

5._____In 1732 he published (A) his memoirs (B) *Poor Richard's Almanac* (C) a book of verse.

ESSAY (50 POINTS)

In what ways does Franklin change throughout his life?

LESSON 4 TEST ANSWERS

OBJECTIVE TEST (50 POINTS)

1. ___B___, 2. ___C___, 3. ___A___, 4. ___B___, 5. ___B___

ESSAY (50 POINTS)

In what ways does Franklin change throughout his life?

ANSWER: *As the book progresses Franklin can be seen growing more pensive and religious.*

LESSON 5
THE REVOLUTIONARY PERIOD 1750-1800 (Part 2)

Readings Due For This Lesson: Before this lesson begins, students should have read poems by Phillis Wheatley and the background narrative material on slavery. All poems and readings are provided in the text.

Reading Ahead: Read all narrative background and selections from 19th century poetry (Lesson Six). All poems are provided in the text.

Students should also review Nathaniel Hawthorne's, *The Scarlet Letter* (Lesson 7).

Goal: Students will read and analyze poems by Phillis Wheatley.

Goals/Objectives: What is the purpose of this lesson?	Strategies to meet these goals: How will I obtain these goals/objectives?	Evaluation: How will I know when I have met these goals/objectives?
Students will write a descriptive two page essay about colonial women—both white and black, colonist and Native American or slave. (cognitive goal)	Students will write a descriptive two page essay about colonial women—both white and black, colonist and Native American or slave. (Critical Thinking A)	With minimal errors, students will clearly answer the assigned question in a two-page essay.
Students will review how to write a descriptive essay. (cognitive goal)		
Students will increase their vocabulary. (cognitive goal)	Students will collect at least five new vocabulary words from their reading and use these words in their essays.	Students will use five vocabulary words in conversation during the week as well as use the words in their essays.
Students will agree or disagree with the following statement: Some scholars feel that Wheatley seemed too willing to accept her station in life. Do you agree? State your position and defend it in a one-page persuasive essay. (cognitive goal)	Students will agree or disagree with the following statement: Some scholars feel that Wheatley seemed too willing to accept her station in life. Do you agree? State your position and defend it in a one-page persuasive essay. (Literary Criticism B)	With minimal errors, students will clearly answer the assigned question in a one-page essay.
Students will learn how to write a persuasive essay. (cognitive goal)		

Goals/Objectives: What is the purpose of this lesson?	Strategies to meet these goals: How will I obtain these goals/objectives?	Evaluation: How will I know when I have met these goals/objectives?
Students will research the Jamestown, VA, settlement. (cognitive goal) Students will practice writing a comparison essay. (cognitive goal)	Students will write an essay on the following topic: Research the Jamestown, VA, settlement. Contrast this settlement (1607) with the Pilgrim settlement (1620) and Puritan experiment (1630). (Enrichment A)	With minimal errors, students will clearly answer the assigned question in a one or two-page essay.
Students will exhibit higher thinking—specifically evaluation skills. (cognitive goal)	Students will write an essay on the following topic: Describe how it might have felt to be a member of the Lenape Native American tribe. Your name is Mary White Feather. You are a mother of three children. Your husband is an average Native American brave. You are watching these strange people in their big ships land at Jamestown. Describe your fears and hopes. (Enrichment B)	With minimal errors, students will clearly answer the assigned question in a one or two-page essay.
Students will exhibit higher thinking—specifically evaluation skills. (cognitive goal)	Students will write an essay on the following topic: Describe how you would feel if you were an Englishman named Ebenezer Davis. It is 1619. You have survived a long horrowing sea voyage and are now a settler in Jamestown. You have left your family behind in Yorkshire, England. You have never seen anything like America, much less a Lenape Native American! What are your fears and expectations? (Enrichment C)	With minimal errors students will clearly answer the assigned question in a one or two-page essay.

Goals/Objectives: What is the purpose of this lesson?	Strategies to meet these goals: How will I obtain these goals/objectives?	Evaluation: How will I know when I have met these goals/objectives?
Students will exhibit higher thinking—specifically evaluation skills. (cognitive goal)	Students will write an essay on the following topic: Notwithstanding the somewhat fictionalized Disney version, Pocahontas was a real person. Research your history books and find out about this Native American princess! (Enrichment E)	Students, with minimal errors, will clearly answer the assigned question in a 1-2 page essay.
Students will understand this concept: Rhetorical devices that Patrick Henry uses to persuade his audience. (cognitive goal)	Students will write an essay on the following topic: What rhetorical devices does Patrick Henry employ to persuade his audience? (Critical Thinking)	Students, with minimal errors, will clearly answer the assigned question in a 1-2 page essay.
Students will exhibit higher-level thinking as they consider if/when a Christian should rebel against authority. (cognitive goal)	Students will write an essay on the following topic: At what point, if ever, should a Christian rebel against authority? Does Thomas Jefferson offer sufficient arguments to justify a revolution? (Biblical Application)	Students, with minimal errors, will clearly answer the assigned question in a 1-2 page essay.
Students will exhibit higher-level thinking as they discuss whether historical events make people or if people make history. (cognitive goal)	Students will write an essay on the following topic: Does history make people, or do people make history? In other words, were these famous Americans the product of their age, or did they actually create the events that unfolded in their age? (Enrichment)	Students, with minimal errors, will clearly answer the assigned question in a 1-2 page essay.
Students will work in a group setting. (behavioral goal)	In a class, in a co-op experience, or during a family discussion, students will answer the following question: In light of the social situation in colonial America, was slavery justified?	Students will exhibit practical listening skills and will manifest understanding of opposing worldviews.
Students will be able to recall the information taught in the lesson. (cognitive goal)	Lesson 5 Test	Students will take the test at the end of this lesson and score at least 80%.
Students will experience reflective writing. (affective/spiritual goal)	Using the Journal Guide Questions in the Appendices, students will record at least three entries this week. Suggested Scriptures: James	Students will show evidence that they have reflected on this issue, including informed discussions and written responses.

SUGGESTED
Weekly *Implementation*

DAY 1	DAY 2	DAY 3	DAY 4	DAY 5
Prayer journal.	**Prayer journal.**	**Prayer journal.**	**Prayer journal.**	**Prayer journal.**
Students should review the required reading(s) *before* the assigned lesson begins.	Students should review reading(s) from next lesson.	Students should write rough drafts of all assigned essays.	Students will re-write corrected copies of essays due tomorrow.	Essays are due.
Teacher may want to discuss assigned reading(s) with students.	Students should outline essays due at the end of the week.	The teacher or a peer evaluator may correct rough drafts.		Students should take Lesson 5 test.
Teacher and students will decide the number of required essays for this lesson, choosing two or three essays.	Per teacher instructions, students may answer orally in a group setting some of the essays that are not assigned as formal essays.			Reading ahead: Students should read 18th and 19th century poetry provided in the text (Lesson 6).
The rest of the essays can be outlined, answered with shorter answers, or skipped.				Guide: What is (are) the worldview battle(s) being waged in 18th and 19th century poetry?
Students will review all readings for Lesson 5.				

ENRICHMENT ACTIVITIES/PROJECTS

Students should watch several movies about the Puritan and Jamestown settlements and compare them to the actual historical occurrences.

SUPPLEMENTAL RESOURCES

Asante, Molefi K. and Mark T. Mattson. *Historical and Cultural Atlas of African-Americans.*
The single best resource of the African-American experience in America. It is full of pictures, graphs, and timely articles.

Bellah, Robert N. and Frederick E. Greenspahn. *Uncivil Religion: Interreligious Hostility in America.*
Bellah and Greenspahn are gifted sociologists who employ their skills to analyze cross-racial religious controversy in America—one of the most lamentable chapters in our history.

Billingsley, Andrew. *Black Families in White America.*
A scholarly book that nonetheless is important to

this area. Billingsley argues that the African-American family is the key to the slave's survival and the maintenance of African-American culture.

Blankenhorn, Jr., David. *Fatherless America: Confronting Our Most Urgent Social Problem.*

A scathing criticism of the American social welfare system. David Blankenhorn, in his revolutionary work of cultural criticism, asks an anti-modern, almost heretical question: "So the question is not, *What do men want?* but rather, *What do men do?*" Blankenhorn goes where very few social historians have dared to go before: he argues that men should be, quite simply, good fathers—no matter how hard it is or how foolish it may seem. "In a larger sense, the fatherhood story is the irreplaceable basis of a culture's most urgent imperative: the socialization of males." (p. 65). American children need fathers. American society needs fathers.

Blassingame, John W. *The Slave Community.*

Blassingame, like Billingsley, argues for the efficacy of the African-American slave family.

Bryan, Ashley. *Sing to the Sun, The Story of Lightning and Thunder, Climbing Jacob's Ladder: Heroes of the Bible in African-American Spirituals, Turtle Knows Your Name,* and *All Night, All Day: A Child's First Book of African-American Spirituals.*

The foremost African-American cultural historian in America. Using children's books as a vehicle, Bryan inspires his reader with fresh insights of African-American culture.

Dawson, John. *Healing America's Wounds.*

Dawson explores the consequences of racism on American society and offers biblical solutions.

Fogel, Robert William, and Stanley L. Engerman. *Time on the Cross: The economics of American Negro Slavery.*

Fogel and Engerman argue persuasively that slavery was very profitable—which assured its duration.

Stampp, Kenneth M. *The Peculiar Institution: Slavery in the Ante-Bellum South.*

A seminal work on African-American history. The serious historian starts here.

Notes:

CRITICAL THINKING

A. Read the following two poems written by Phillis Wheatley. Historians have marveled at the fact that Phillis Wheatley, brought from Africa at the age of eight and enslaved nearly all her life, was able to acquire literary and scholastic acumen. Her avocation was certainly atypical of most colonial women of any race. Explore your own history texts and materials from your home and public libraries for accounts of the status of slaves and that of women in colonial America. Write a descriptive two page essay about colonial women—both white and black, colonist and Native American or slave.

ANSWER: *Colonial women had no spare time. With limited hygiene knowledge and minimal medical care, women often died in childbirth by age 30—long before their husbands died of other causes. They had no actual rights apart from or with their fathers and husbands. White and African-American women were similarly without property and power. However, Bradstreet and Wheatley inspire us all. Native American women, depending on the tribe, had more authority and power. Generally, however, families at this time were patriarchal.*

B. Read the two poems below. Some critics—especially of African American descent—have been critical of Phillis Wheatley. While they respect her achievements and writing ability, they wish that she had used her talents to lead a slave revolt or to perform a Harriet Tubman-like role, at least not to extol the whites. She seemed too willing to accept her station in life. Do you agree or disagree? State your position and defend it in a one-page persuasive essay.

ANSWER: *Because of her positive attitude in the face of her negative circumstances, Phillis Wheatley refused to give in to the anger, hatred, and unforgiveness which she could have justified feeling. She is to be commended and honored for her Christian witness. Phillis Wheatley was the first African-American writer of consequence in America, and her life was an inspiring example to generations of Americans of all races. Abolitionists recognized this fact and reprinted her poetry. The powerful ideas contained in her deeply moving verse stood indirectly against the institution of slavery. Why would abolitionists publish an author's poetry if that author were not opposed to slavery? Clearly, Wheatley opposed slavery but saw God's sovereignty in her life in this place of adversity. She is to be applauded and imitated—not castigated—for such faith.*

Descriptive essays describe. Using as many details as possible, bring the idea, object, or place alive to your reader. The more precise you are, the better your essay will be. Use active voice and present tense as much as possible.

ENRICHMENT

A. Research the Jamestown, VA, settlement. Contrast this settlement (1607) with the Pilgrim settlement (1620) and Puritan experiment (1630).

ANSWER: *The Jamestown settlement was a commercial enterprise; the Plymouth/Boston settlements were started for religious reasons. Even a cursory examination of letters from Jamestown and Plymouth show the contrast of these two views. This is the tension played out throughout American history: commercialism/privatism/individualism vs. religious/spiritual agendas. One of the worst investments in the early 17th century was an investment in the Virginia Company. The Virginia Company was a stock-option company set up to raise funds for new colonizing enterprises. Its first and only real undertaking was the Jamestown investment. The Jamestown settlement proved to be an extraordinarily bad investment because it lost vast amounts of money for its investors. This was principally due to the unwillingness of the early colonizers to do the necessary work of providing for themselves. At the same time, and in defense of the early settlers, the investors never really provided enough capital for supply of the venture. Nevertheless, how extraordinary that the United States—whose business is business President Calvin Coolidge once said—started as a bad business venture.*

Jamestown, Virginia, was the object of this investment venture and the site of the first permanent British settlement in North America. It was founded on May 14, 1607, and was located on a peninsula (later an island) in the James River in Virginia. It was named in honor of King James I.

From the beginning, the colony was unsure about its reason for existence. Ostensibly, it was founded for the sole purpose of making profit for its investors. One quick way to make money in the 17th century, of course, was to find gold. This method was especially appealing to the yeoman (middle class) farmer and second or third son of an aristocratic family (who had scant hope of inheriting any money in England), both of whom made up the majority element of early British settlers. Gold was and still is hard to come by in southeastern, tidewater Virginia. Finally, after starvation took over half the colony, the new colonists discovered that the cultivation of tobacco was about as good as gold. It was then grown everywhere—including the streets of Jamestown.

No one knows why the early profiteers chose such an unhealthy place as Jamestown for a settlement. No self-respecting Native American would be caught dead near the place. Situated in an unhealthful marshy area, the colony always had a small population because of a high death rate from disease. What disease did not kill, fire often did. In 1608 Jamestown was accidentally burned, and two years later it was about to be abandoned by its inhabitants when Thomas West, Lord De La Warr, arrived with new energy and new supplies. Other fires occurred in 1676 and 1698. Jamestown fell into decay when the seat of government of Virginia was moved in 1699 to the Middle Plantation (later Williamsburg). By this time quick profit had been abandoned for more long-term profit. However, from the beginning Jamestown was an experiment in profit making.

Meanwhile, in New England, Englishmen were starting a holy experiment. The historian Perry Miller argued that we cannot understand America unless we understand the Puritans. Indeed. But who were the Puritans? What is the difference between a Boston Puritan and a Plymouth Separatist? Were Puritans bigots? Saints? Puritanism, a movement arising within the Church of England in the latter part of the 16th century, sought to carry the reformation of that church beyond the point the early Anglican or Church of England had gone. The Church of England was attempting to establish a middle course between Roman Catholicism and the ideas of the Protestant reformers. This was unacceptable to a growing number of reformers, called Puritans, who wanted the Church of England to reject Anglicanism and embrace Calvinism. The term Puritanism was also used in a broader sense to refer to attitudes and values considered characteristic of these radical reformers. Thus, the Separatists (i.e., Pilgrims) in the 16th century, the Quakers in the 17th century, and Nonconformists after the Restoration were called Puritans, although they were no longer part of the established church. For our purposes, though, we shall refer to the Puritans in two ways: Puritans and Pilgrims.

The Pilgrims, Separatists, founders of Plymouth Colony in Massachusetts were, like their countrymen in Virginia, initially dependent upon private investments from profit-minded backers to finance their colony. In other ways, however, these intensely religious people were nothing like the Jamestown settlers. (James Stobaugh)

B. Describe how it might have felt to be a member of the Lenape Native American tribe. Your name is Mary White Feather. You are a mother of three children. Your husband is an average Native American brave. You are watching these strange people in their big ships land at Jamestown. Describe your fears and hopes.

ANSWER: *Answers will vary, but perhaps the Indians knew from the beginning that these new Europeans were poten-*

tially a disastrous threat to their civilization. Their feelings were ambivalent, however. They recognized that there were advantages in trading with the Europeans. They also recognized that some of the technological advantages (e.g., guns) offered them an advantage over their enemies. Study Squanto to learn more about this tension. The main Native American tribe in the Virginia area in the early 17ᵗʰ century was the Lenape Powhatan Tribe. By the time the English colonists had arrived the chief of the Powhatans, Chief Powhatan, ruled a formidable 30-tribe confederacy. He allegedly controlled 128 villages with about 9,000 inhabitants. Powhatan initially opposed the English settlement at Jamestown. According to legend, he changed his policy in 1607 when he released the captured Smith. In April 1614, Pocahontas, Powhatan's daughter, married the planter John Rolfe, and afterwards Powhatan negotiated a peace agreement with his son-in-law's people. Peace reigned until after Powhatan died in 1618. In 1622 a great war broke out between the English settlers and the Powhatan Confederacy. Initially the Powhatan Confederation very nearly destroyed the Jamestown settlement. In the long term, however, the war destroyed the Confederacy as a viable entity.

C. Describe how you would feel if you were an Englishman named Ebenezer Davis. It is 1619. You have survived a long harrowing sea voyage and are now a settler in Jamestown. You have left your family behind in Yorkshire, England. You have never seen anything like America, much less a Lenape Native American. What are your fears and expectations?

ANSWER: *Most Englishmen were lower middle class yeoman farmers. The excitement of owning one's own land was mitigated by the knowledge that they were in a dangerous, strange place. These fears were confirmed in the massacre of 1622.*

D. Pretend you are Joe Black (your English name) to your slave owners, but you know that your real name is Lomatata (your African name). You were captured and enslaved in West Africa two years ago. You have (had?) a wife and three children in Africa. You doubt that you will ever see them again. You have spent two years working in the West Indies. Now you are being sold to new owners in Jamestown, VA. It is 1619. What are your fears and hopes? What do you think about the Native Americans?

ANSWER: *From the beginning slaves were treated poorly. Historians disagree whether racism preceded slavery or vice versa, but within a decade after the first English settlers came to Jamestown, racism was a ubiquitous presence in American culture.*

E. Notwithstanding the somewhat fictionalized Disney version, Pocahontas was a real person. Research your history books and find out about this Native American princess.

ANSWER: *Pocahontas was indeed a real person who married an Englishman and died in England. It is interesting how Disney has made her into a New-Ager who worshipped nature. She was born around 1595 to one of Powhatan's many wives. They named her Matoaka, though she is better known as Pocahontas, which means "Little Wanton," a playful, frolicsome little girl. Pocahontas probably saw Europeans before they settled in Jamestown in May 1607.*

The first meeting of Pocahontas and John Smith is questionable if not entirely invented by Smith. He was leading an expedition in December 1607 when he was taken captive by some Indians. Days later, he was brought to Chief Powhatan where he was later saved by Pocahontas. There is some debate about whether or not this event really happened. Nevertheless, Pocahontas and Smith soon became friends. In October 1609, John Smith was badly injured by a gunpowder explosion and was forced to return to England. When Pocahontas next came to visit the fort, she was told that her friend Smith was dead. Pocahontas apparently married an Indian named Kocoum in 1610. She lived in Potomac country among Indians, but her relationship with the Englishmen was not over. When an energetic and resourceful member of the Jamestown settlement, Captain Samuel Argall, learned where she was, he devised a plan to kidnap her and hold her for ransom. With the help of Japazaws, lesser chief of the Patowomeck Indians, Argall lured Pocahontas onto his ship. Argall sent word that he would return Chief Powhatan's beloved daughter only when the chief had returned to him the English prisoners he held, the arms and tools that the Indians had stolen, and also some corn. After some time Powhatan sent part of the ransom and asked that they treat his daughter well. Argall returned to Jamestown in April 1613 with Pocahontas. She eventually moved to a new settlement, Henrico, where she began her education in the Christian Faith and met a successful tobacco planter named John Rolfe in July 1613. Pocahontas was allowed relative freedom within the settlement, and she began to enjoy her role in the relations between the colony and her people. She grew to love John Rolfe. John Rolfe, a committed Christian, agonized for many weeks over the decision to marry a "strange wife," a heathen Indian. He finally decided to marry Pocahontas after she had been converted to Christianity. Pocahontas was baptized, christened "Rebecca" and married John Rolfe on April 5, 1614. Rolfe returned to England, but in March 1617, he decided to return his family to Virginia. It was soon apparent, however, that Pocahontas would not survive the voyage home. She was ill from pneumonia or possibly tuberculosis. She was buried in a churchyard in Gravesend, England. She was 22 years old. (James Stobaugh)

During the 18th century, literature and the arts—in other words, popular culture—began to move away from the personalized, travelogue advertisements of their adventures written by John Smith and others. American culture began to develop into a style and worldview all its own. There was, as you have seen, a culture war—even then! The war was between the secularism of a John Smith and the piety of a William Bradford. Although there is no evidence that these two contemporaries met, they were nonetheless involved in a culture war. Ultimately, the worldview of John Smith won. Puritanism and its Christian Theism gave way in the 18th century to the subtle deism of Thomas Paine. In the Christian Theistic world of the Puritan, God was intimately involved in the affairs of man. In a Deistic world, God, the watchmaker, supposedly created a perfect world and then retreated allowing people to work out their own fate. Humanity was now in charge. Or so it thought . .

CRITICAL THINKING

What rhetorical devices does Patrick Henry employ to persuade his audience?

ANSWER: *Henry uses the strategy of rhetorical questions to persuade his listeners that they were actually irrational for not entering this war. Repetition is one of the stronger designs that Patrick uses to help stress the importance of taking on this battle now rather than waiting until it was too late. Henry had no doubt as to the outcome. Using resent events and facts as a technique to emphasize the need, Henry uses true and powerful statements.*

BIBLICAL APPLICATION

To a Christian, revolution is a very knotty issue. At what point, if ever, should a Christian rebellion against authority? Does Thomas Jefferson offer sufficient arguments to justify a revolution?

ANSWER: *Certainly in the context of that time period, rebellion seemed logical. Was the American Revolution entirely necessary? In light of other examples of British colonial rule—e.g., Canada and Australia—what would it have taken for the issue to have been resolved peacefully?*

ENRICHMENT

Men and women—like Phillis Wheatley, Patrick Henry, Thomas Jefferson, and Abigail Adams—were critical to this Revolutionary period. However, does history make people, or do people make history? In other words, were these famous Americans the product of their age, or did they actually create the events that unfolded in their age?

ANSWER: *Answers will vary.*

FINAL PROJECT

Students should correct and rewrite all essays and place them in their Final Portfolio.

LESSON 5 TEST

SHORT ANSWER QUESTIONS. (30 POINTS)

Answer in two or three sentences:

A. Did the Church support chattel slavery? Why?

B. Did slaves resist their masters? Why or why not? How did they resist?

C. Why did Phillis Wheatley so willingly accept her servitude?

CRITICAL THINKING (70 POINTS)

Carefully read the following poem by Phillis Wheatley and then summarize Wheatley's advice to Harvard College students.

To the University of Cambridge in New England (Harvard College)

While an intrinsic ardor prompts to write,
The muses promise to assist my pen;
'Twas not long since I left my native shore
The land of errors, and *Egyptian* gloom:
Father of mercy, 'twas thy gracious hand
Brought me in safety from those dark abodes.
Students, to you 'tis giv'n to scan the heights
Above, to traverse the ethereal space,
And mark the systems of revolving worlds.
Still more, ye sons of science ye receive
The blissful news by messengers from heav'n,
How *Jesus'* blood for your redemption flows.
See him with hands out-stretcht upon the cross;
Immense compassion in his bosom glows;
He hears revilers, nor resents their scorn:
What matchless mercy in the Son of God!
When the whole human race by sin had fall'n,
He deign'd to die that they might rise again,
And share with him in the sublimest skies
Life without death, and glory without end.
Improve your privileges while they stay,
Ye pupils, and each hour redeem, that bears
Or good or bad report of you to heav'n.
Let sin, that baneful evil to the soul,
By you be shun'd, nor once remit your guard;
Suppress the deadly serpent in its egg.
Ye blooming plants of human race divine,
An *Ethiop* tells you 'tis your greatest foe;
Its transient sweetness turns to endless pain,
And in immense perdition sinks the soul.
http://darkwig.uoregon.edu/~bear/wheatley.html

LESSON 5 TEST ANSWERS

SHORT ANSWERS (30 POINTS)

Answer in two or three sentences:

A. Did the Church support chattel slavery? Why?

ANSWER: *Yes. Only the Mennonites and Quakers systematically opposed slavery. Many felt it was defensible by Scripture.*

B. Did slaves resist their masters? Why or why not? How did they resist?

ANSWER: *Yes; they resisted in every way that they could: through work slow downs and by sabotaging the crops. Most of all, they resisted by forming their own culture.*

C. Why did Phillis Wheatley so willingly accept her servitude?

ANSWER:
She saw it as being God's will for her life.

CRITICAL THINKING (70 POINTS)

Summarize Wheatley's advice to Harvard College students.

ANSWER: *Wheatley advised college students to humble themselves before God and to learn knowledge to advance His kingdom. She deemed all other knowledge useless. Students, to you 'tis giv'n to scan the heights/Above, to traverse the ethereal space,/And mark the systems of revolving worlds./Still more, ye sons of science ye receive/The blissful news by messengers from heav'n,/How Jesus' blood for your redemption flows./See him with hands out-stretcht upon the cross;/Immense compassion in his bosom glows;/He hears revilers, nor resents their scorn:/What matchless mercy in the Son of God!*

LESSON 6
A GROWING NATION 1800-1840: NATIONAL PERIOD (Part 1)

Readings Due For This Lesson: Students should review "Thanatopsis," William Cullen Bryant and the short stories "The Devil and Tom Walker" and "The Legend of Sleepy Hollow," Washington Irving.

Reading Ahead: Students should review the poem "The Raven," and the short stories "Fall of the House of Usher" and "The Tell Tale Heart" both by Edgar Allan Poe. What makes Poe's short stories so perfect?

Goal: Students will analyze "Thanatopsis," William Cullen Bryant and the short stories "The Devil and Tom Walker" and "The Legend of Sleepy Hollow," Washington Irving.

Goals/Objectives: What is the purpose of this lesson?	Strategies to meet these goals: How will I obtain these goals/objectives?	Evaluation: How will I know when I have met these goals/ objectives?
Students will understand the following concept: Figurative language in "Thanatopsis." (cognitive goal)	Students will compose the following essay: Offer several examples of figurative language and discuss how Bryant uses them to advance the purposes of his poem. (Critical Thinking)	Students, with minimal errors, will clearly answer the assigned question in a 1-2 page essay.
Students will increase their vocabulary. (cognitive goal)	Students will collect at least five new vocabulary words from their reading and use these words in their essays. In "The Devil and Tom Walker" Irving uses an extensive vocabulary. Define each word and use it in a sentence: melancholy, parsimonious, propitiatory, ostentatious, and superfluous. (Critical Thinking A)	Students will use five vocabulary words in conversation during the week as well as use the words in their essays and in conversation.

Goals/Objectives: What is the purpose of this lesson?	Strategies to meet these goals: How will I obtain these goals/objectives?	Evaluation: How will I know when I have met these goals/objectives?
Students will manifest higher-level thinking as they discuss whether or not "Thanatopsis" has moved away from Theistic moorings. (cognitive goal)	Students will compose the following essay: Bryant hid "Thanatopsis" for many years because he was afraid that it would offend his Christian hearers. Was he justified in his fears? (Biblical Application)	Students, with minimal errors, will clearly answer the assigned question in a 1-2 page essay.
Students will understand humor in this novel. (cognitive goal)	The use of these difficult words makes his short story more humorous. How? (Critical Thinking B)	Students, with minimal errors, will clearly answer the assigned question in a 1-2 page essay.
Students will understand the concept of irony. (cognitive goal)	Students will write an essay on the following topic: Find the sentence in the conclusion of the short story where Tom makes an ironic statement. (Critical Thinking C)	Students, with minimal errors, will clearly answer the assigned question in a 1-2 page essay.
Students will review the concept of symbolism. (cognitive goal)	Students will write an essay on the following topic: What is the meaning of the Woodman's scoring of the trees in "The Devil and Tom Walker?" What do the trees symbolize? (Critical Thinking D)	Students, with minimal errors, will clearly answer the assigned question in a 1-2 page essay.
Students will understand the concept of Tom's conversion. (cognitive goal)	Students will write an essay on the following topic: As Tom ages, he becomes "a violent churchgoer." Is Tom's conversion genuine? Offer evidence to support your answer. (Critical Thinking E)	Students, with minimal errors, will clearly answer the assigned question in a two-page essay.
Students will understand the concept of hyperbole. (cognitive goal)	Students will write an essay on the following topic: Hyperbole is a figure of speech in which exaggeration of fact is used in order to produce humor. Give an example of hyperbole in "The Devil and Tom Walker." What purpose does hyperbole serve in this short story? (Critical Thinking F)	Students, with minimal errors, will clearly answer the assigned question in a 1-2 page essay.
Students will understand the concept of theme. (cognitive goal)	Students will compose the following essay: The theme of this book—selling one's soul to the devil—is a common theme in world literature. Offer at least one other example and compare that example to this short story. (Critical Thinking G)	Students, with minimal errors, will clearly answer the assigned question in a 2 page essay.

Goals/Objectives: What is the purpose of this lesson?	Strategies to meet these goals: How will I obtain these goals/objectives?	Evaluation: How will I know when I have met these goals/objectives?
Students will exhibit higher-level thinking as they write an expository essay describing two or three biblical characters who compromised their faith. (cognitive goal)	Students will answer the following question in an expository essay: Describe two or three biblical characters who compromised their faith for fame, fortune, or other reasons. (Biblical Application A)	Students, with minimal errors, will clearly answer the assigned question in a two-page essay.
Students will exhibit higher-level thinking as they write a creative, illustrative, essay. (cognitive essay)	Students will write an essay on the following topic: Create a modern version of "The Devil and Tom Walker." Your short story should be about five to ten pages. (Biblical Application B)	Students, with minimal errors, will clearly answer the assigned question in a ten-page essay.
Students will exhibit higher-level thinking as they write a comparison essay. (cognitive goal)	Students will write an essay on the following topic: Compare and contrast Irving's short story with Goethe's Faust. (Enrichment A)	Students, with minimal errors, will clearly answer the assigned question in a 1-2 page essay.
Students will write an evaluation essay. (cognitive goal)	Students will answer this question: Critic Harold Bloom in *The Western Canon* laments the propensity for other critics to discuss worldview in literary works. He argues that suggesting that literary works have a worldview cheapens their artistic value. Is it possible to read literature as if it does not have a worldview? Why do you agree or disagree with Bloom? (Enrichment B)	Students, with minimal errors, will clearly answer the assigned question in a 1-2 page essay.
Students will exhibit higher-level thinking as they write a comparison essay. (cognitive goal)	Students will compare "Sleepy Hollow" by Washington Irving with "The Devil and Tom Walker." (Enrichment C)	Students, with minimal errors, will clearly answer the assigned question in a 1-2 page essay.
Students will work in a group setting. (behavioral goal)	In a class, in a co-op experience, or during a family discussion, students will discuss Poe's description of a short story. (below)	Students will exhibit practical listening skills and will manifest understanding of opposing worldviews.
Students will be able to recall the information taught in the lesson. (cognitive goal)	Lesson 6 Test	Students will take the test at the end of this lesson and score at least 80%.

Goals/Objectives: What is the purpose of this lesson?	Strategies to meet these goals: How will I obtain these goals/objectives?	Evaluation: How will I know when I have met these goals/objectives?
Students will experience reflective writing. (affective/spiritual goal)	Using the Journal Guide Questions in the Appendices, students will record at least three entries this week. Suggested Scriptures: Isaiah 42	Students will show evidence that they have reflected on this issue, including informed discussions and written responses.

SUGGESTED
Weekly Implementation

DAY 1	DAY 2	DAY 3	DAY 4	DAY 5
Prayer journal. Students review the required reading(s) before the assigned lesson begins. Teacher may want to discuss assigned reading(s) with students. Teacher and students will decide on the number of required essays for this lesson, choosing two or three essays. The rest of the essays can be outlined, answered with shorter answers, or skipped. Students will review all readings for Lesson 6.	**Prayer journal.** Students should review reading(s) from next lesson. Students should outline essays due at the end of the week. Per teacher instructions, students may answer orally in a group setting some of the essays that are not assigned as formal essays.	**Prayer journal.** Students should write rough drafts of all assigned essays. The teacher and/or a peer evaluator may correct rough drafts.	**Prayer journal.** Student will re-write corrected copies of essays due tomorrow.	**Prayer journal.** Essays are due. Students should take the Lesson 6 test. Reading Ahead: Students should review the poem "The Raven," and the short stories "Fall of the House of Usher" and "The Tell Tale Heart" both by Edgar Allan Poe. Guide: What makes Poe's short stories so perfect?

Note: References to sources are in student edition

ENRICHMENT ACTIVITIES/PROJECTS

Students should choreograph the final scene where the Devil comes to get Walker.

The family should read this short story orally.

SUPPLEMENTAL RESOURCES

Aderman, Ralph, ed. *Critical Essays on Washington Irving.*

Bowden, Mary W. *Washington Irving.*

Myers, Andrew B., ed. *A Century of Commentary on the Works of Washington Irving, 1860-1974.*

Neider, Charles. ed. *The Complete Tales of Washington Irving.* Da Capo Press, 1998.

Notes:

William Cullen Bryant

CRITICAL THINKING

Offer several examples of figurative language and discuss how Bryant uses them to advance the purposes of his poem.

ANSWER: *This example of personification "She has a voice of gladness, and a smile" brings nature alive to the reader—an important goal for Bryant. The final simile "Like one who wraps the drapery of his couch/ About him, and lies down to pleasant dreams" invites the reader to embrace death as if it were a long, restful nap.*

BIBLICAL APPLICATION

Bryant hid "Thanatopsis" for many years because he was afraid that it would offend his Christian hearers. Was he justified in his fears?

ANSWER: *This poem obviously exhibits early Romanticism/Transcendentalism. The speaker goes forth to "commune" with nature, "to mix forever with the elements." Even in death "So live, that when thy summons comes to join/ The innumerable caravan, which moves/To that mysterious realm, where each shall take/ His chamber in the silent halls of death,/Thou go not, like the quarry-slave at night,/ Scourged to his dungeon, but, sustained and soothed/By an unfaltering trust, approach thy grave." Death is no more than a changing of consciousness with no mention of salvation by faith in Jesus Christ.*

Washington Irving

CRITICAL THINKING

A. In "The Devil and Tom Walker" Irving uses an extensive vocabulary. Define each word and use it in a sentence.

   melancholy   parsimonious   propitiatory
   ostentatious   superfluous

   ANSWER: *parsimonious (miserly)*
   propitiatory (fortunate)
   ostentatious (showy)
   superfluous (unnecessary)
   melancholy (sad)

B. The use of these difficult words makes his short story more humorous. How?

   ANSWER: *To the unsophisticated 19th century audience, pretentious language would have portrayed Tom Walker as the pompous, self-centered, shallow man that he was. The technique was popular among western literature. For example, Mrs. Misanthrope (as in "misanthropism") exhibited a similar flaw in Richard Sheridan's play* The Rival. *Irving's audience would have loved it.*

C. Find the sentence in the conclusion of the short story where Tom makes an ironic statement.

   ANSWER: *"The devil take me if I have made a farthing." That is of course exactly what happened.*

D. What is the meaning of the Woodman's scoring of the trees in "The Devil and Tom Walker?" What do the trees symbolize?

   ANSWER: *The scoring foreshadows the mark of the devil on Tom Walker. What do the trees symbolize? Just as the trees burn, so shall Walker someday burn.*

E. As Tom ages, he becomes "a violent churchgoer." Is Tom's conversion genuine? Offer evidence to support your answer.

   ANSWER: *Clearly, Tom was seeking "fire insurance." It was to no avail, however, as Irving makes abundantly clear by his ironic statements.*

F. Hyperbole is a figure of speech in which exaggeration of fact is used in order to produce humor. Give an example of hyperbole in "The Devil and Tom Walker." What purpose does it serve in this short story?

ANSWER: *"...female scold is generally considered a match for the devil."* http://classiclit.about.com/library/bl-etexts/wirving/bl-wirving-devil.htm

Again, Irving is using understatement to make a point. This invites the reader to laugh at a very serious subject.

G. The theme of this book—selling one's soul to the devil—is a common theme in world literature. Offer at least one other example and compare that example to this short story.

ANSWER: *The Tragedy of Faust, Goethe, but there are many other examples too. Christopher Marlowe wrote an English play Dr. Faustus about the same theme.*

H. Note unusual punctuation and sentence structure in Irving's writing.

ANSWER: *Irving uses excessive hyphenation, spellings with the British style of double consonants and ou rather than o, and comma and semi-colon punctuation that is inconsistent with what is acceptable today. Samples: clamour; neighbourhood; tranquility; broken-down; plow-horse. The following sentence contains unusual punctuation that would need serious revision in today's standards of written expression: "The tale was told of old Brouwer, a most heretical disbeliever in ghosts, how he met the Horseman returning from his foray into Sleepy Hollow, and was obliged to get up behind him; how they galloped over bush and brake, over hill and swamp, until they reached the bridge; when the Horseman suddenly turned into a skeleton, threw old Brouwer into the brook, and sprang away over the tree-tops with a clap of thunder."*

BIBLICAL APPLICATION

A. Write an expository essay describing two or three biblical characters who compromised their faith for fame, fortune, or other reasons.

ANSWER: *Possible choices include Samson, Saul, and Solomon.*

B. Create a modern version of "The Devil and Tom Walker." Your short story should be about five to ten pages.

ANSWER: *Answers will vary.*

ENRICHMENT

A. Compare and contrast Irving's short story with Goethe's *Faust*.

ANSWER: *Faust is a similar story, but much longer, and much more complicated than "The Devil and Tom Walker." There is no person quite like Goethe's Gretchen in Irving's "The Devil and Tom Walker." Also, the ending is much different from Goethe's Faust. Faust is allowed to escape eternal damnation; Walker does not escape anything. Nonetheless, both authors advance a romantic, subjective vision—although Goethe is a much better writer than Washington.*

B. Critic Harold Bloom in *The Western Canon* laments the propensity for other critics to discuss worldview in literary works. He argues that suggesting that literary works have a worldview cheapens their artistic value. Is it possible to read literature as if it does not have a worldview? Why do you agree or disagree with Bloom?

ANSWER: *At the beginning of the 21st century, in the midst of a culture war, to suggest that one should read books, watch movies, and pretend that they are only "art" appears absurd. One must discern worldviews. There is no "value free" culture anymore. Christians, especially, must be careful to guard their hearts.*

C. Compare "Sleepy Hollow" by Washington Irving with "The Devil and Tom Walker."

ANSWER:
The tone is very similar in both stories. Irving flirts with the supernatural in both short stories. The protagonists are somewhat bungling and awkward. At this point similarities end.

FINAL PROJECT

Students should correct and rewrite all essays and place them in their Final Portfolio.

LESSON 6 TEST

DISCUSSION QUESTIONS. (100 POINTS)

Read the following short story and complete the accompanying worksheet.

Great Stone Face

Nathaniel Hawthorne

One afternoon, when the sun was going down, a mother and her little boy sat at the door of their cottage, talking about the Great Stone Face. They had but to lift their eyes, and there it was plainly to be seen, though miles away, with the sunshine brightening all its features. And what was the Great Stone Face? Embosomed amongst a family of lofty mountains, there was a valley so spacious that it contained many thousand inhabitants. Some of these good people dwelt in log huts, with the black forest all around them, on the steep and difficult hillsides. Others had their homes in comfortable farm houses, and cultivated the rich soil on the gentle slopes or level surfaces of the valley. Others, again, were congregated into populous villages, where some wild, highland rivulet, tumbling down from its birthplace in the upper mountain region, had been caught and tamed by human cunning, and compelled to turn the machinery of cotton factories. The inhabitants of this valley, in short, were numerous, and of many modes of life. But all of them, grown people and children, had a kind of familiarity with the Great Stone Face, although some possessed the gift of distinguishing this grand natural phenomenon more perfectly than many of their neighbors.

The Great Stone Face, then, was a work of Nature in her mood of majestic playfulness, formed on the perpendicular side of a mountain by some immense rocks, which had been thrown together in such a position as, when viewed at a proper distance, precisely to resemble the features of the human countenance. It seemed as if an enormous giant, or a Titan, had sculptured his own likeness on the precipice. There was the broad arch of the forehead, a hundred feet in height; the nose, with its long bridge; and the vast lips, which, if they could have spoken, would have rolled their thunder accents from one end of the valley to the other. True it is, that if the spectator approached too near, he lost the outline of the gigantic visage, and could discern only a heap of ponderous and gigantic rocks, piled in chaotic ruin one upon another. Retracing his steps, however, the wondrous features would again be seen; and the farther he withdrew from them, the more like a human face, with all its original divinity intact, did they appear; until, as it grew dim in the distance, with the clouds and glorified vapor of the mountains clustering about it, the Great Stone Face seemed positively to be alive.

It was a happy lot for children to grow up to manhood or womanhood with the Great Stone Face before their eyes, for all the features were noble, and the expression was at once grand and sweet, as if it were the glow of a vast, warm heart, that embraced all mankind in its affections, and had room for more. It was an education only to look at it. According to the belief of many people, the valley owed much of its fertility to this benign aspect that was continually beaming over it, illuminating the clouds, and infusing its tenderness into the sunshine.

As we began with saying, a mother and her little boy sat at their cottage door, gazing at the Great Stone Face, and talking about it. The child's name was Ernest.

"Mother," said he, while the Titanic visage milled on him, "I wish that it could speak, for it looks so very kindly that its voice must needs be pleasant. If I were to See a man with such a face, I should love him dearly." "If an old prophecy should come to pass," answered his mother, "we may see a man, some time, for other, with exactly such a face as that." "What prophecy do you mean, dear mother?" eagerly inquired Ernest. "Pray tell me all about it!" So his mother told him a story that her own mother had told to her, when she herself was younger than little Ernest; a story, not of things that were past, but of what was yet to come; a story, nevertheless, so very old, that even the Indians, who formerly inhabited this valley, had heard it from their forefathers, to whom, as they affirmed, it had been murmured by the mountain streams, and whispered by the wind among the treetops. The purport was, that, at some future day, a child should be born hereabouts, who was destined to become the greatest and noblest personage of his time, and whose countenance, in manhood, should bear an exact resemblance to the Great Stone Face. Not a few old-fashioned people, and young ones likewise, in the ardor of their hopes, still cherished an enduring faith in this old prophecy. But others, who had seen more of the world, had watched and waited till they were weary, and had beheld no man with such a face, nor any man that proved to be much greater or nobler than his neighbors, concluded it to be nothing but an idle tale. At all events, the great man of the prophecy had not yet appeared."

O mother, dear mother!" cried Ernest, clapping his

hands above his head, "I do hope that I shall live to see him!"

His mother was an affectionate and thoughtful woman, and felt that it was wisest not to discourage the generous hopes of her little boy. So she only said to him, "Perhaps you may."

And Ernest never forgot the story that his mother told him. It was always in his mind, whenever he looked upon the Great Stone Face. He spent his childhood in the log cottage where he was born, and was dutiful to his mother, and helpful to her in many things, assisting her much with his little hands, and more with his loving heart. In this manner, from a happy yet often pensive child, he grew up to be a mild, quiet, unobtrusive boy, and sun-browned with labor in the fields, but with more intelligence brightening his aspect than is seen in many lads who have been taught at famous schools. Yet Ernest had had no teacher, save only that the Great Stone Face became one to him. When the toil of the day was over, he would gaze at it for hours, until he began to imagine that those vast features recognized him, and gave him a smile of kindness and encouragement, responsive to his own look of veneration. We must not take upon us to affirm that this was a mistake, although the Face may have looked no more kindly at Ernest than at all the world besides. But the secret was that the boy's tender and confiding simplicity discerned what other people could not see; and thus the love, which was meant for all, became his peculiar portion.

About this time there went a rumor throughout the valley, that the great man, foretold from ages long ago, who was to bear a resemblance to the Great Stone Face, had appeared at last. It seems that, many years before, a young man had migrated from the valley and settled at a distant seaport, where, after getting together a little money, he had set up as a shopkeeper. His name but I could never learn whether it was his real one, or a nickname that had grown out of his habits and success in life was Gathergold.

Being shrewd and active, and endowed by Providence with that inscrutable faculty which develops itself in what the world calls luck, he became an exceedingly rich merchant, and owner of a whole fleet of bulky bottomed ships. All the countries of the globe appeared to join hands for the mere purpose of adding heap after heap to the mountainous accumulation of this one man's wealth. The cold regions of the north, almost within the gloom and shadow of the Arctic Circle, sent him their tribute in the shape of furs; hot Africa sifted for him the golden sands of her rivers, and gathered up the ivory tusks of her great elephants out of the forests; the east came bringing him the rich shawls, and spices, and teas, and the effulgence of diamonds, and the gleaming purity of large pearls. The ocean, not to be behindhand with the earth, yielded up her mighty whales, that Mr. Gathergold might sell their oil, and make a profit on it. Be the original commodity what it might, it was gold within his grasp. It might be said of him, as of Midas, in the fable, that whatever he touched with his finger immediately glistened, and grew yellow, and was changed at once into sterling metal, or, which suited him still better, into piles of coin. And, when Mr. Gathergold had become so very rich that it would have taken him a hundred years only to count his wealth, he bethought himself of his native valley, and resolved to go back thither, and end his days where he was born. With this purpose in view, he sent a skillful architect to build him such a palace as should be fit for a man of his vast wealth to live in.

As I have said above, it had already been rumored in the valley that Mr. Gathergold had turned out to be the prophetic personage so long and vainly looked for, and that his visage was the perfect and undeniable similitude of the Great Stone Face. People were the more ready to believe that this must needs be the fact, when they beheld the splendid edifice that rose, as if by enchantment, on the site of his father's old weather-beaten farmhouse. The exterior was of marble, so dazzlingly white that it seemed as though the whole structure might melt away in the sunshine, like those humbler ones which Mr. Gathergold, in his young play-days, before his fingers were gifted with the touch of transmutation, had been accustomed to build of snow. It had a richly ornamented portico supported by tall pillars, beneath which was a lofty door, studded with silver knobs, and made of a kind of variegated wood that had been brought from beyond the sea. The windows, from the floor to the ceiling of each stately apartment, were composed, respectively of but one enormous pane of glass, so transparently pure that it was said to be a finer medium than even the vacant atmosphere. Hardly anybody had been permitted to see the interior of this palace; but it was reported, and with good semblance of truth, to be far more gorgeous than the outside, insomuch that whatever was iron or brass in other houses was silver or gold in this; and Mr. Gathergold's bed-chamber, especially, made such a glittering appearance that no ordinary man would have been able to close his eyes there. But, on the other hand, Mr. Gathergold was now so inured to wealth, that perhaps he could not have closed his eyes unless where the gleam of it was certain to find its way beneath his eyelids.

In due time, the mansion was finished; next came the upholsterers, with magnificent furniture; then, a whole troop of black and white servants, the haranguers of Mr. Gathergold, who, in his own majestic person, was expected to arrive at sunset. Our friend Ernest, meanwhile, had been deeply stirred by the idea that the great man, the noble man, the man of prophecy, after so many ages of delay, was at length to be made manifest to his native valley. He knew, boy as he was, that there were a thousand ways in which Mr. Gathergold, with his vast wealth, might transform himself into an angel of beneficence, and assume a control over human affairs as wide and benignant as the smile of the Great Stone Face. Full of faith and hope, Ernest doubted not that what the people said was true, and that now he was to behold the living likeness of those wondrous features on the mountainside. While the boy was still gazing up the valley, and fancying, as he always did, that the Great Stone Face returned his gaze and looked kindly at him, the rumbling of wheels was heard, approaching swiftly along the winding road.

"Here he comes!" cried a group of people who were assembled to witness the arrival. "Here comes the great Mr. Gathergold!"

A carriage, drawn by four horses, dashed round the turn of the road. Within it, thrust partly out of the window, appeared the physiognomy of the old man, with a skin as yellow as if his own Midas hand had transmuted it. He had a low forehead, small, sharp eyes, puckered about with innumerable wrinkles, and very thin lips, which he made still thinner by pressing them forcibly together.

"The very image or the Great Stone Face!" shouted the people. "Sure enough, the old prophecy is true; and here we have the great man come, at last!"

And, what greatly perplexed Ernest, they seemed actually to believe that here was the likeness which they spoke of. By the roadside there chanced to be an old beggar woman and two little beggar children, stragglers from some far-off region, who, as the carriage rolled onward, held out their hands and lifted up their doleful voices, most piteously beseeching charity. A yellow claw the very same that had dawed together so much wealth poked itself out of the coach window, and dropped some copper coins upon the ground; so that, though the great man's name seems to have been Gathergold, he might just as suitably have been nicknamed Scatter copper. Still, nevertheless, with an earnest shout, and evidently with as much good faith as ever, the people bellowed "He is the very image of the Great Stone Face!" But Ernest turned sadly from the wrinkled shrewdness of that sordid visage, and gazed up the valley, where, amid a gathering mist, gilded by the last sunbeams, he could still distinguish those glorious features which had impressed themselves into his soul. Their aspect cheered him. What did the benign lips seem to say?

"He will come! Fear not, Ernest; the man will come! "

The years went on, and Ernest ceased to be a boy. He had grown to be a young man now. He attracted little notice from the other inhabitants of the valley; for they saw nothing remarkable in his way of life, save that, when the labor of the day was over, he still loved to go apart and gaze and meditate upon the Great Stone Face. According to their idea of the matter, it was a folly, indeed, but pardonable, inasmuch as Ernest was industrious, kind, and neighborly, and neglected no duty for the sake of indulging this idle habit. They knew not that the Great Stone Face had become a teacher to him, and that the sentiment which was expressed in it would enlarge the young man's heart, and fill it with wider and deeper sympathies than other hearts. They knew not that thence would come a better wisdom than could be learned from books, and a better life than could be molded on the defaced example of other human lives. Neither did Ernest know that the thoughts and affections which came to him so naturally, in the fields and at the fireside, and wherever he communed with himself, were of a higher tone than those which all men shared with him. A simple soul simple as when his mother first taught him the old prophecy he beheld the marvelous features beaming down the valley, and still wondered that their human counterpart was so long in making his appearance.

By this time poor Mr. Gathergold was dead and buried; and the oddest part of the matter was, that his wealth, which was the body and spirit of his existence, had disappeared before his death, leaving nothing of him but a living skeleton, covered over with a wrinkled, yellow skin. Since the melting away of his gold, it had been very generally conceded that there was no such striking resemblance, after all, betwixt the ignoble features of the ruined merchant and that majestic face upon the mountainside. So the people ceased to honor him during his lifetime, and quietly consigned him to forgetfulness after his decease. Once in a while, it is true, his memory was brought up in connection with the magnificent palace which he had built, and which had long ago been turned into a hotel for the accommodation of strangers, multitudes of whom came, every summer, to visit that famous natural curiosity, the Great

Stone Face. Thus, Mr. Gathergold being discredited and thrown into the shade, the man of prophecy was yet to come.

It so happened that a native-born son of the valley, many years before, had enlisted as a soldier, and, after a great deal of hard fighting, had now become an illustrious commander. Whatever he may be called in history, he was known in camps and on the battlefield under the nickname of Old Blood and Thunder. This war worn veteran, being now infirm with age and wounds, and weary of the turmoil of a military life, and of the roll of the drum and the clangor of the trumpet, that had so long been ringing in his ears, had lately signified a purpose of returning to his native valley, hoping to find repose where he remembered to have left it. The inhabitants, his old neighbors and their grownup children, were resolved to welcome the renowned warrior with a salute of cannon and a public dinner; and all the more enthusiastically, it being affirmed that now, at last, the likeness of the Great Stone Face had actually appeared. An aide camp of Old Blood and Thunder, traveling through the valley, was said to have been struck with the resemblance. Moreover the schoolmates and early acquaintances of the general were ready to testify, on oath, that, to the best of their recollection, the aforesaid general had been exceedingly like the majestic image, even when a boy, only that the idea had never occurred to them at that period. Great, therefore, was the excitement throughout the valley; and many people, who had never once thought of glancing at the Great Stone Face for years before, now spent their time in gazing at it, for the sake of knowing exactly how General Blood and Thunder looked.

On the day of the great festival, Ernest, with all the other people of the valley, left their work, and proceeded to the spot where the sylvan banquet was prepared. As he approached, the loud voice of the Rev. Dr. Battleblast was heard, beseeching a blessing on the good things set before them, and on the distinguished friend of peace in whose honor they were assembled. The tables were arranged in a cleared space of the woods, shut in by the surrounding trees, except where a vista opened eastward, and afforded a distant view of the Great Stone Face. Over the general's chair, which was a relic from the home of Washington, there was an arch of verdant boughs, with the laurel profusely intermixed, and surmounted by his country's banner, beneath which he had won his victories. Our friend Ernest raised himself on his tiptoes, in hopes to get a glimpse of the celebrated guest; but there was a mighty crowd about the tables anxious to hear the toasts and speeches, and to catch any word that might fall from the general in reply; and a volunteer company, doing duty as a guard, pricked ruthlessly with their bayonets at any particularly quiet person among the throng. So Ernest, being of an unobtrusive character, was thrust quite into the background, where he could see no more of Old Blood and Thunder's physiognomy than if it had been still blazing on the battlefield. To console himself, he turned towards the Great Stone Face, which, like a faithful and long remembered friend, looked back and smiled upon him through the vista of the forest. Meantime, however, he could overhear the remarks of various individuals, who were comparing the features of the hero with the face on the distant mountainside.

"T' is the same face, to a hair!" cried one man, cutting a caper for joy.

"Wonderfully like, that's a fact!" responded another.

"Like! why, I call it Old Blood and Thunder himself, in a monstrous looking-glass!" cried a third.

"And why not? He's the greatest man of this or any other age, beyond a doubt."

And then all three of the speakers gave a great shout, which communicated electricity to the crowd, and called forth a roar from a thousand voices, that went reverberating for miles among the mountains, until you might have supposed that the Great Stone Face had poured its thunder breath into the cry. All these comments, and this vast enthusiasm, served the more to interest our friend; nor did he think of questioning that now, at length, the mountain visage had found its human counterpart. It is true, Ernest had imagined that this long looked for personage would appear in the character of a man of peace, uttering wisdom, and doing good, and making people happy. But, taking an habitual breadth of view, with all his simplicity, he contended that providence should choose its own method of blessing mankind, and could conceive that this great end might be effected even by a warrior and a bloody sword, should inscrutable wisdom see fit to order matters SO.

"The general! the general!" was now the cry. " Hush! silence! Old Blood and Thunder's going to make a speech."

Even so; for, the cloth being removed, the general's health had been drunk, amid shouts of applause, and he now stood upon his feet to thank the company. Ernest saw him. There he was, over the shoulders of the crowd, from the two glittering epaulets and embroidered collar upward, beneath the arch of green boughs with intertwined laurel, and the banner drooping as if to shade his brow! And there, too, visible in the same glance, through the vista of the forest, appeared the Great Stone Face! And was there, indeed, such a resemblance as the crowd had testified? Alas, Ernest could not recognize it! He beheld a war worn and weatherbeaten countenance, full of energy, and expressive of an iron will; but the gentle wisdom, the deep, broad, tender sympathies, were altogether wanting in Old Blood and Thunder's visage; and even if the Great Stone Face had assumed his look of stern command, the milder traits would still have tempered it.

"This is not the man of prophecy," sighed Ernest to himself, as he made his way out of the throng. "And must the world wait longer yet?"

The mists had congregated about the distant mountainside, and there were seen the grand and awful features of the Great Stone Face, awful but benignant, as if a mighty angel were sitting among the hills, and enrobing himself in a cloudvesture of gold and purple. As he looked, Ernest could hardly believe but that a smile beamed over the whole visage, with a radiance still brightening, although without motion of the lips. It was probably the effect of the western sunshine, melting through the thinly diffused vapors that had swept between him and the object that he gazed at. But as it always did the aspect of his marvelous friend made Ernest as hopeful as if he had never hoped in vain.

"Fear not, Ernest," said his heart, even as if the Great Face were whispering himself, "fear not, Ernest; he will come."

More years sped swiftly and tranquilly away. Ernest still dwelt in his native valley, and was now a man of middle age. By imperceptible degrees, he had become known among the people. Now, as heretofore, he labored for his bread, and was the same simple-hearted man that he had always been. But he had thought and felt so much, he had given so many of the best hours of his life to unworldly hopes for some great good to mankind, that it seemed as though he had been talking with the angels, and had imbibed a portion of their wisdom unawares. It was visible in the calm and well-considered beneficence of his daily life, the quiet stream of which had made a wide green margin all along its course. Not a day passed by, that the world was not the better because this man, humble as he was, had lived. He never stepped aside from his own path, yet would always reach a blessing to his neighbor. Almost involuntarily, too, he had become a preacher. The pure and high simplicity of his thought, which, as one of its manifestations, took shape in the good deeds that dropped silently from his hand, flowed also forth in

speech. He uttered truths that wrought upon and molded the lives of those who heard him. His auditors, it may be, never suspected that Ernest, their own neighbor and familiar friend, was more than an ordinary man; least of all did Ernest himself suspect it; but, inevitably as the murmur of a rivulet, came thoughts out of his mouth that no other human lips had spoken.

When the people's minds had had a little time to cool, they were ready enough to acknowledge their mistake in imagining a similarity between General Blood and Thunder's truculent physiognomy and the benign visage on the mountainside. But now, again, there were reports and many paragraphs in the newspapers, affirming that the likeness of the Great Stone Face had appeared upon the broad shoulders of a certain eminent statesman. He, like Mr. Gathergold and old Blood-and-Thunder, was a native of the valley, but had left it in his early days, and taken up the trades of law and politics. Instead of the rich man's wealth and the warrior's sword, he had but a tongue, and it was mightier than both together. So wonderfully eloquent was he, that whatever he might choose to say, his auditors had no choice but to believe him; wrong looked like right, and right like wrong; for when it pleased him, he could make a kind of illuminated fog with his mere breath, and obscure the natural daylight with it. His tongue, indeed, was a magic instrument: sometimes it rumbled like the thunder; sometimes it warbled like the sweetest music. It was the blast of war the song of peace; and it seemed to have a heart in it, when there was no such matter. In good truth, he was a wondrous man; and when his tongue had acquired him all other imaginable success when it had been heard in halls of state, and in the courts of princes and potentates after it had made him known all over the world, even as a voice crying from shore to shore it finally persuaded his countrymen to select him for the Presidency. Before this time indeed, as soon as he began to grow celebrated his admirers had found out the resemblance between him and the Great Stone Face; and so much were they struck by it, that throughout the country this distinguished gentleman was known by the name of Old Stony Phiz. The phrase was considered as giving a highly favorable aspect to his political prospects; for, as is likewise the case with the Popedom, nobody ever becomes President without taking a name other than his own.

While his friends were doing their best to make him President, Old Stony Phiz, as he was called, set out on a visit to the valley where he was born. Of course, he had no other object than to shake hands with his fellow citizens, and neither thought nor cared about any effect which his progress through the country might have upon the election. Magnificent preparations were made to receive the illustrious statesman; a cavalcade of horsemen set forth to meet him at the boundary line of the State, and all the people left their business and gathered along the wayside to see him pass. Among these was Ernest. Though more than once disappointed, as we have seen, he had such a hopeful and confiding nature that he was always ready to believe in whatever seemed beautiful and good.

He kept his heart continually open, and thus was sure to catch the blessing from on high when it should come. So now again, as buoyantly as ever, he went forth to behold the likeness of the Great Stone Face.

The cavalcade came prancing along the road, with a great clattering of hoofs and a mighty cloud of dust, which rose up so dense and high that the visage of the mountainside was completely hidden from Ernest's eyes. All the great men of the neighborhood were there on horseback; militia officers, in uniform; the member of Congress; the sheriff of the county; the editors of newspapers; and many a farmer, too, had mounted his patient steed, with his Sunday coat upon his back. It really was a very brilliant spectacle, especially as there were numerous banners flaunting over the cavalcade, on some of which were gorgeous portraits of the illustrious statesman and the Great Stone Face, smiling familiarly at one another, like two brothers. If the pictures were to be trusted, the mutual resemblance, it must be confessed, was marvelous. We must not forget to mention that there was a band of music, which made the echoes of the mountains ring and reverberate with the loud triumph of its strains; so that airy and soul-thrilling melodies broke out among all the heights and hollows, as if every nook of his native valley had found a voice, to welcome the distinguished guest. But the grandest effect was when the far-off mountain precipice flung back the music; for then the Great Stone Face itself seemed to be swelling the triumphant chorus, in acknowledgment, that, at length, the man of prophecy was come. All this while the people were throwing up their hats and shouting, with enthusiasm so contagious that the heart of Ernest kindled up, and he likewise threw up his hat, and shouted, as loudly as the loudest, "Huzza for the great man! Huzza for Old Stony Phiz!" But as yet he had not seen him.

"Here he is, now!" cried those who stood near Ernest. "There! There! Look at Old Stony Phiz and then at the Old Man of the Mountain, and see if they are not as like as two twin brothers!"

In the midst of all this gallant array came an open barouche, drawn by four white horses; and in the barouche, with his massive head uncovered, sat the illustrious statesman, Old Stony Phiz himself.

"Confess it," said one of Ernest's neighbors to him, "the Great Stone Face has met its match at last!"

Now, it must be owned that, at his first glimpse of the countenance which was bowing and smiling from the barouche, Ernest did fancy that there was a resemblance between it and the old familiar face upon the mountainside. The brow, with its massive depth and loftiness, and all the other features, indeed, were boldly and strongly hewn, as if in emulation of a more than heroic, of a Titanic model. But the sublimity and stateliness, the grand expression of a divine sympathy, that illuminated the mountain visage and etherealized its ponderous granite substance into spirit, might here be sought in vain. Something had been originally left out, or had departed. And therefore the marvelously gifted statesman had always a weary gloom in the deep caverns of his eyes, as of a child that has outgrown its playthings or a man of mighty faculties and little aims, whose life, with all its high performances, was vague and empty, because no high purpose had endowed it with reality.

Still, Ernest's neighbor was thrusting his elbow into his side, and pressing him for an answer.

"Confess! confess! Is not he the very picture of your Old Man of the Mountain?"

"No!" said Ernest, bluntly, "I see little or no likeness."

"Then so much the worse for the Great Stone Face!" answered his neighbor; and again he set up a shout for Old Stony Phiz.

But Ernest turned away, melancholy, and almost despondent: for this was the saddest of his disappointments, to behold a man who might have fulfilled the prophecy, and had not willed to do so. Meantime, the cavalcade, the banners, the music, and the barouches swept past him, with the vociferous crowd in the rear, leaving the dust to settle down, and the Great Stone Face to be revealed again, with the grandeur that it had worn for untold centuries.

"Lo, here I am, Ernest!" the benign lips seemed to say. "I have waited longer than thou, and am not yet weary. Fear not; the man will come."

The years hurried onward, treading in their haste on one another's heels. And now they began to bring white hairs, and scatter them over the head of Ernest; they made reverend wrinkles across his forehead, and furrows in his cheeks. He was an aged man. But not in vain had he grown old: more than the white hairs on his head were the sage thoughts in his mind; his wrinkles and furrows were inscriptions that Time had engraved, and in which he had written legends of wisdom that had been tested by the tenor of a life. And Ernest had ceased to be obscure. Unsought for, undesired, had come the fame which so many seek, and made him known in the great world, beyond the limits of the valley in which he had dwelt so quietly. College professors, and even the active men of cities, came from far to see and converse with Ernest; for the report had gone abroad that this simple husbandman had ideas unlike those of other men, not gained from books, but of a higher tone a tranquil and familiar majesty, as if he had been talking with the angels as his daily friends. Whether it were sage, statesman, or philanthropist, Ernest received these visitors with the gentle sincerity that had characterized him from boyhood, and spoke freely with them of whatever came uppermost, or lay deepest in his heart or their own. While they talked together, his face would kindle, unawares, and shine upon them, as with a mild evening light. Pensive with the fullness of such discourse, his guests took leave and went their way; and passing up the valley, paused to look at the Great Stone Face, imagining that they had seen its likeness in a human countenance, but could not remember where.

While Ernest had been growing up and growing old, a bountiful Providence had granted a new poet to this earth. He, likewise, was a native of the valley, but had spent the greater part of his life at a distance from that romantic region, pouring out his sweet music amid the bustle and din of cities. Often, however, did the mountains which had been familiar to him in his childhood lift their snowy peaks into the clear atmosphere of his poetry. Neither was the Great Stone Face forgotten, for the poet had celebrated it in an ode, which was grand enough to have been uttered by its own majestic lips. This man of genius, we may say, had come down from heaven with wonderful endowments. If he sang of a mountain, the eyes of all mankind beheld a mightier grandeur reposing on its breast, or soaring to its summit, than had before been seen there. If his theme were a lovely lake, a celestial smile had now been thrown over it, to gleam forever on its surface. If it were the vast old sea, even the deep immensity of its dread bosom seemed to swell the higher, as if moved by the emotions of the song. Thus the world assumed another and a better aspect from the hour that the poet blessed it with his happy eyes. The Creator had bestowed him, as the last best touch to his own handiwork. Creation

was not finished till the poet came to interpret, and so complete it.

The effect was no less high and beautiful, when his human brethren were the subject of his verse. The man or woman, sordid with the common dust of life, who crossed his daily path, and the little child who played in it, were glorified if they beheld him in his mood of poetic faith. He showed the golden links of the great chain that intertwined them with an angelic kindred; he brought out the hidden traits of a celestial birth that made them worthy of such kin. Some, indeed, there were, who thought to show the soundness of their judgment by affirming that all the beauty and dignity of the natural world existed only in the poet's fancy. Let such men speak for themselves, who undoubtedly appear to have been spawned forth by Nature with a contemptuous bitterness; she plastered them up out of her refuse stuff, after all the swine were made. As respects all things else, the poet's ideal was the truest truth. The songs of this poet found their way to Ernest. He read them after his customary toil, seated on the bench before his cottage door, where for such a length of time he had filled his repose with thought, by gazing at the Great Stone Face. And now as he read stanzas that caused the soul to thrill within him, he lifted his eyes to the vast countenance beaming on him so benignantly.

"O majestic friend," he murmured, addressing the Great Stone Face, "is not this man worthy to resemble thee?"

The face seemed to smile, but answered not a word.

Now it happened that the poet, though he dwelt so far away, had not only heard of Ernest, but had meditated much upon his character, until he deemed nothing so desirable as to meet this man, whose untaught wisdom walked hand in hand with the noble simplicity of his life.

One summer morning, therefore, he took passage by the railroad, and, in the decline of the afternoon, alighted from the cars at no great distance from Ernest's cottage. The great hotel, which had formerly been the palace of Mr. Gathergold, was close at hand, but the poet, with his carpetbag on his arm, inquired at once where Ernest dwelt, and was resolved to be accepted as his guest.

Approaching the door, he there found the good old man, holding a volume in his hand, which alternately he read, and then, with a finger between the leaves, looked lovingly at the Great Stone Face.

"Good evening," said the poet. "Can you give a traveler a night's lodging?"

"Willingly," answered Ernest; and then he added,

smiling, "Methinks I never saw the Great Stone Face look so hospitably at a stranger."

The poet sat down on the bench beside him, and he and Ernest talked together. Often had the poet held intercourse with the wittiest and the wisest, but never before with a man like Ernest, whose thoughts and feelings gushed up with such a natural feeling, and who made great truths so familiar by his simple utterance of them. Angels, as had been so often said, seemed to have wrought with him at his labor in the fields; angels seemed to have sat with him by the fireside; and, dwelling with angels as friend with friends, he had imbibed the sublimity of their ideas, and imbued it with the sweet and lowly charm of household words. So thought the poet. And Ernest, on the other hand, was moved and agitated by the living images which the poet flung out of his mind, and which peopled all the air about the cottage door with shapes of beauty, both gay and pensive. The sympathies of these two men instructed them with a profounder sense than either could have attained alone. Their minds accorded into one strain, and made delightful music which neither of them could have claimed as all his own, nor distinguished his own share from the other's. They led one another, as it were, into a high pavilion of their thoughts, so remote, and hitherto so dim, that they had never entered it before, and so beautiful that they desired to be there always.

As Ernest listened to the poet, he imagined that the Great Stone Face was bending forward to listen too. He gazed earnestly into the poet's glowing eyes.

"Who are you, my strangely gifted guest?" he said.

The poet laid his finger on the volume that Ernest had been reading.

"You have read these poems," said he. "You know me, then for I wrote them."

Again, and still more earnestly than before, Ernest examined the poet's features; then turned towards the Great Stone Face; then back, with an uncertain aspect, to his guest. But his countenance fell; he shook his head, and sighed.

"Wherefore are you sad?" inquired the poet. "Because," replied Ernest, "all through life I have awaited the fulfilment of a prophecy; and, when I read these poems, I hoped that it might be fulfilled in you."

"You hoped," answered the poet, faintly smiling, "to find in me the likeness of the Great Stone Face. And you are disappointed, as formerly with Mr. Gathergold, and old Blood-and-Thunder, and Old Stony Phiz. Yes, Ernest, it is my doom.

"You must add my name to the illustrious three, and record another failure of your hopes. For in shame and sadness do I speak it, Ernest I am not worthy to be typified by yonder benign and majestic image."

"And why?" asked Ernest. He pointed to the volume. "Are not those thoughts divine?"

"They have a strain of the Divinity," replied the poet. "You can hear in them the far-off echo of a heavenly song. But my life, dear Ernest, has not corresponded with my thought. I have had grand dreams, but they have been only dreams, because I have lived and that, too, by my own choice among poor and mean realities. Sometimes, even shall I dare to say it? I lack faith in the grandeur, the beauty, and the goodness, which my own works are said to have made more evident in nature and in human life. Why, then, pure seeker of the good and true, shouldst thou hope to find me, in yonder image of the divine?"

The poet spoke sadly, and his eyes were dim with tears. So, likewise, were those of Ernest.

At the hour of sunset, as had long been his frequent custom, Ernest was to discourse to an assemblage of the neighboring inhabitants in the open air. He and the poet, arm in arm, still talking together as they went along, proceeded to the spot. It was a small nook among the hills, with a gray precipice behind, the stern front of which was relieved by the pleasant foliage of many creeping plants that made a tapestry for the naked rock, by hanging their festoons from all its rugged angles. At a small elevation above the ground, set in a rich framework of verdure, there appeared a niche, spacious enough to admit a human figure, with freedom for such gestures as spontaneously accompany earnest thought and genuine emotion. Into this natural pulpit Ernest ascended, and threw a look of familiar kindness around upon his audience. They stood, or sat, or reclined upon the grass, as seemed good to each, with the departing sunshine falling obliquely over them, and mingling its subdued cheerfulness with the solemnity of a grove of ancient trees, beneath and amid the boughs of which the golden rays were constrained to pass. In another direction was seen the Great Stone Face, with the same cheer, combined with the same solemnity, in its benignant aspect.

"Ernest began to speak, giving to the people of what was in his heart and mind. His words had power, because they accorded with his thoughts; and his thoughts had reality and depth, because they harmonized with the life which he had always lived. It was not mere breath that this preacher uttered; they were the words of life, because a life of good deeds and holy love was melted into them. Pearls, pure and rich, had been dissolved into this precious draught. The poet, as he listened, felt that the being and character of Ernest were a nobler strain of poetry than he had ever written.

His eyes glistening with tears, he gazed reverentially at the venerable man, and said within himself that never was there an aspect so worthy of a prophet and a sage as that mild, sweet, thoughtful countenance, with the glory of white hair diffused about it. At a distance, but distinctly to be seen, high up in the golden light of the setting sun, appeared the Great Stone Face, with hoary mists around it, like the white hairs around .the brother of Ernest. Its look of grand beneficence seemed to embrace the world.

At that moment, in sympathy with a thought which he was about to utter, the face of Ernest assumed a grandeur of expression, so imbued with benevolence, that the poet, by an irresistible impulse, threw his arms aloft and shouted

"Behold! Behold! Ernest is himself the likeness of the Great Stone Face!"

Then all the people looked and saw that what the deep sighted poet said was true. The prophecy was fulfilled. But Ernest, having finished what he had to say, took the poet's arm, and walked slowly homeward, still hoping that some wiser and better man than himself would by and by appear, bearing a resemblance to the GREAT STONE FACE.

www.classicreader.com

SHORT STORY CHECKUP

NAME OF SHORT STORY: *Great Stone Face*
NAME OF AUTHOR: Nathaniel Hawthorne

I. BRIEFLY DESCRIBE: (20 Points)
PROTAGONIST–

ANTAGONIST-

OTHER CHARACTERS USED TO DEVELOP PROTAGONIST—

DO ANY OF THE CHARACTERS REMIND ME OF A BIBLE CHARACTER? WHO? WHY?

II. SETTING: (10 Points)

III. POINT OF VIEW: CIRCLE ONE: FIRST PERSON, THIRD PERSON, THIRD PERSON OMNISCIENT. (10 Points)

IV. BRIEF SUMMARY OF THE PLOT: (20 Points)

IDENTIFY THE CLIMAX OF THE SHORT STORY. (10 Points)

V. THEME. (THE QUINTESSENTIAL MEANING/PURPOSE OF THE STORY IN ONE OR TWO SENTENCES). (10 Points)

VI. AUTHOR'S WORLD VIEW:
HOW DO YOU KNOW THIS? WHAT BEHAVIORS DO(ES) THE CHARACTER(S) MANIFEST THAT LEAD YOU TO THIS CONCLUSION?
(10 Points)

VII. WHY DID YOU LIKE/DISLIKE THIS SHORT STORY? (10 Points)

Lesson 6 Test Answers

Discussion Questions. (100 Points)

ANSWER:
Short Story Checkup

NAME OF SHORT STORY: *Great Stone Face*
NAME OF AUTHOR: Nathaniel Hawthorne
I. BRIEFLY DESCRIBE:. (20 Points)
PROTAGONIST– *Ernest*
ANTAGONIST— *None*
OTHER CHARACTERS USED TO DEVELOP PROTAGONIST—*Mr. Gathergold, old Blood-and-Thunder, Old Stony Phiz, and the Poet.*
DO ANY OF THE CHARACTERS REMIND ME OF A BIBLE CHARACTER? WHO? WHY? *Ernest appears to be a Christlike figure; the Poet is perhaps John the Baptist.*
II. SETTING: (10 Points) *White Mountains in New Hampshire*

III. POINT OF VIEW: CIRCLE ONE: FIRST PERSON, THIRD PERSON, <u>THIRD PERSON OMNISCIENT</u>. (10 Points)

IV. BRIEF SUMMARY OF THE PLOT: (20 Points)
A young man grows up wondering who is the Great Stone Face. Eventually, he himself is the stone face by virtue of his imagination, disposition, reputation, character, hard work, and the embrace of his community.
IDENTIFY THE CLIMAX OF THE SHORT STORY. (10 Points) *When the poet visits at the end and commends Ernest to the community.*

V. THEME. (THE QUINTESSENTIAL MEANING/PURPOSE OF THE STORY IN ONE OR TWO SENTENCES). (10 Points) *A young man perseveres in his dreams and hopes and is rewarded by finding meaning in the stone face—himself.*

VI. AUTHOR'S WORLD VIEW:
HOW DO YOU KNOW THIS? WHAT BEHAVIORS DO(ES) THE CHARACTER(S) MANIFEST THAT LEAD YOU TO THIS CONCLUSION?
(10 Points) *There are elements of Romanticism but the embrace of community and ethical values indicates that Theism is the predominant worldview.*

VII. WHY DID YOU LIKE/DISLIKE THIS SHORT STORY? (10 Points)

LESSON 7

A GROWING NATION 1800-1840: NATIONAL PERIOD (Part 2)

Readings Due For This Lesson: Students should review the poem "The Raven" and the short stories "Fall of the House of Usher" and "The Tell Tale Heart," both by Edgar Allan Poe.

Reading Ahead: *The Scarlet Letter* and "The Birthmark," both by Nathaniel Hawthorne. What Romantic themes emerge in Hawthorne's novel *The Scarlet Letter* and the short story "The Birthmark?"

Goal: Students will analyze the poem "The Raven" and the short stories "Fall of the House of Usher" and "The Tell Tale Heart," both by Edgar Allan Poe.

Goals/Objectives: What is the purpose of this lesson?	Strategies to meet these goals: How will I obtain these goals/objectives?	Evaluation: How will I know when I have met these goals/ objectives?
Students will understand the concept of connotative language. (cognitive goal)	Students will compose an essay on the following question: Part of Poe's genius is his ability to create mood by the use of connotative language (language that suggests more than the words explicitly express). Write an essay describing how this literary technique is employed by Poe in "The Raven" and "The Fall of the House of Usher." (Critical Thinking A)	Students, with minimal errors, will clearly answer the assigned question in a 1-2 page essay.
Students will increase their vocabulary. (cognitive goal)	Students will collect at least five new vocabulary words from their reading and use these words in their essays.	Students will use five vocabulary words in conversation during the week as well as use the words in their essays and in conversation.
Students will understand the concept of characterization of Roberick Usher. (cognitive goal)	Students will write a characterization of Roderick Usher. (Critical Thinking B)	Students, with minimal errors, will clearly answer the assigned question in a 1-2 page essay.

Goals/Objectives: What is the purpose of this lesson?	Strategies to meet these goals: How will I obtain these goals/objectives?	Evaluation: How will I know when I have met these goals/objectives?
Students will understand the concept of symbolism. (cognitive goal)	Students will answer this essay question: In the third paragraph of the short story, Poe identifies the Usher family with what structure? Why? (Critical Thinking C)	Students, with minimal errors, will clearly answer the assigned question in a 1-2 page essay.
Students will understand the concept of reliable narration. (cognitive goal)	Students will answer this essay question: How does first-person narration enhance Poe's purposes to scare his readers? Who is the narrator? Is he reliable? Why or why not? (Critical Thinking D)	Students, with minimal errors, will clearly answer the assigned question in a 1-2 page essay.
Students will understand the concept of foreshadowing as a literary technique. (cognitive goal)	Students will answer this essay question: Find the narrator's description of Roderick's picture. How does this foreshadow future events? (Critical Thinking E)	Students, with minimal errors, will clearly answer the assigned question in a 1-2 page essay.
Students will exhibit higher level thinking as they compare two short stories. (cognitive goal)	Students will write a comparison essay. (cognitive goal) Students will read the "Tell Tale Heart" by Edgar Allan Poe and compare it to "The Fall of the House of Usher." (Enrichment)	Students, with minimal errors, will clearly answer the assigned question in a 1-2 page essay.
Students will exhibit higher level thinking as they discuss the problem of evil. (cognitive goal) Students will consider the generalization that evil is very much a part of the human condition. (cognitive/affective goal)	Students will answer this essay question: The problem of evil for Christians is a real one. Explore the biblical understanding of evil and create a theology. (Biblical Application A)	Students, with minimal errors, will clearly answer the assigned question in a 1-2 page essay.
Students will understand the concept of the Romantic worldview. (cognitive goal)	Students will answer this essay question: One problem with the Romantic worldview is the weak image of God. This presages the later naturalistic view that rejects an omnipotent God altogether. God, to the Romantic, is unable to overcome the power of nature and the human will. There is a moral vision but it is mitigated by sentimental notions about nature. Using the Bible as your main resource, critique this worldview. (Biblical Application B)	Students, with minimal errors, will clearly answer the assigned question in a 1-2 page essay.

Goals/Objectives: What is the purpose of this lesson?	Strategies to meet these goals: How will I obtain these goals/objectives?	Evaluation: How will I know when I have met these goals/ objectives?
Students will understand the concept of Eichmann as a very smart but immoral man. (cognitive goal) Students will consider the generalization that people can be very smart but also very immoral. (affective goal)	Students will answer this essay question: Christian teacher Thomas Merton, in an essay entitled "A Devout Meditation in Memory of Adolf Eichmann" (a Nazi leader who implemented the Holocaust) challenges modern man to rethink sanity. "One of the most disturbing facts," Merton begins, "that came out in the Eichmann trial was that a psychiatrist examined him and pronounced him perfectly sane." The fact is, given our world, we can no longer assume that because a person is "sane" or "adjusted" he/she is OK. Merton reminds us that such people can be well adjusted even in hell itself! Merton says, "The whole concept of sanity in a society where spiritual values have lost their meaning is itself meaningless." In light of biblical discussions of human depravity—especially as they appear in the book of Romans—write an essay reflecting on the accuracy of Merton's statement. (Biblical Application C)	Students, with minimal errors, will clearly answer the assigned question in a 1-2 page essay.
Students will work in a group setting. (behavioral goal)	In a class, in a co-op experience, or during a family discussion, students will answer this question: Some people argue that Poe's short stories are offensive to Christian readers. What do you think?	Students will exhibit practical listening skills and will manifest understanding of opposing worldviews.
Students will be able to recall the information taught in the lesson. (cognitive goal)	Lesson 7 Test	Students will take the test at the end of this lesson and score at least 80%.
Students will experience reflective writing. (affective/spiritual goal)	Using the Journal Guide Questions in the Appendices, students will record at least three entries this week. Suggested Scriptures: Exodus 3	Students will show evidence that they have reflected on this issue, including informed discussions and written responses.

SUGGESTED
Weekly *Implementation*

DAY 1	DAY 2	DAY 3	DAY 4	DAY 5
Prayer journal.	**Prayer journal.**	**Prayer journal.**	**Prayer journal.**	**Prayer journal.**
Students review the required reading (s) before the assigned lesson begins.	Student should review reading (s) from the next lesson.	Students should write rough drafts of all assigned essays.	Student will re-write corrected copies of essays due tomorrow.	Essays are due.
Teacher may want to discuss assigned reading (s) with students.	Students should outline essays due at the end of the week.	The teacher and/or a peer evaluator may correct rough drafts.		Students should take the Lesson 7 test.
Teacher and students will decide on the number of required essays for this lesson, choosing two or three essays. The rest of the essays can be outlined, answered with shorter answers, or skipped.	Per teacher instructions, students may answer orally in a group setting some of the essays that are not assigned as formal essays.			Reading ahead: Students should review *The Scarlet Letter* and "The Birthmark," by Nathaniel Hawthorne.
Students will review all readings for Lesson 7.				Guide: What Romantic themes emerge in Hawthorne's novel *The Scarlet Letter* and the short story "The Birthmark?"

Note: References to sources are in student edition.

ENRICHMENT ACTIVITIES/PROJECTS

Students should choreograph the "Tell Tale Heart."
    The family should read this short story orally.
    Students should rewrite "The Fall of the House of Usher" from the perspective of Frederick Usher.

SUPPLEMENTAL RESOURCES

Carlson, Eric W. Editor. *The Fall of the House of Usher.*
    A critical analysis of the best of Poe's short stories.

Quinn, Arthur Hobson. *Edgar Allan Poe: A Critical Biography*
One of the best biographies on the market.

Krutch, Joseph Wood. *Edgar Allan Poe: A Study in Genius.*
A very readable but well-crafted biography of Poe.

Price, Vincent, (Reader), Basil Rathbone. (Reader). *Edgar Allan Poe Audio Collection*
An excellent audio adaptation of Poe's short stories.

Notes:

CRITICAL THINKING

A. Part of Poe's genius is his ability to create mood by the use of connotative language (language that suggests more than what the words explicitly express). Write an essay describing how this literary technique is employed by Poe in "The Raven" and in "The Fall of the House of Usher."

ANSWER: *There are innumerable examples. One is "...dull, dark, and soundless day in the autumn of the year..."*

B. Write a characterization of Roderick Usher.

ANSWER: *Usher is a very bright but disturbed man. He is an injured, lifeless man. He is at the end of a declining, aristocratic family and has no heirs. Now his sister is apparently ill. Or so we think. In my opinion, Usher is representative of the old, dysfunctional life style/worldview that Poe finds objectionable. The visitor is the fresh, neutral observer who interprets the story.*

C. In the third paragraph of the short story, Poe identifies the Usher family with what structure? Why?

ANSWER: *A wealthy but flawed line of aristocrats, the Usher family is represented by the physical structure of the Usher mansion, which itself is in disrepair. This is a common Romantic theme (echoed in Mary Shelley's Frankenstein): the degeneration of the tired, old, ruling class.*

D. How does first-person narration enhance Poe's purposes to scare his readers? Who is the narrator? Is he reliable? Why or why not?

ANSWER: *The reader is drawn into the story through first-person narration. We sense that he is reliable since he is an observer, not a participant, in the story. This is a very common technique to enhance the credibility of the narration.*

E. Find the narrator's description of Roderick's picture. How does the description of the picture foreshadow future events?

ANSWER: *Throughout the short story the reader wonders if Usher is mad. The painting presented an Usher whose countenance had an expression of "low cunning and perplexity."*

ENRICHMENT

Read the "Tell Tale Heart" by Edgar Allan Poe and compare it to "The Fall of the House of Usher."

ANSWER: *Both short stories are written well with the narrator being critical to the story. However, the narrator in "Tell Tale Heart" is also the protagonist. He is not reliable. The narrator in "The Fall of the House of Usher" is reliable but he is not the protagonist. Both short stories exhibit the same melancholy tone. "Tell-Tale Heart" is much shorter with fewer characters. The plots are similar: the climax occurs at the end of the short story (with relatively no prose devoted to falling action). This arrangement is a typical mystery-tale approach.*

BIBLICAL APPLICATION

A. The problem of evil for Christians is a real one. Explore the biblical understanding of evil and create a theology.

ANSWER: *Evil enters the world in the second chapter of Genesis. It stays around. In fact by the time of Noah, God regrets creating the world altogether. (Genesis 6, 8) Evil separates a person from God. It takes life away from people. Evil was very much part of the New Testament. In fact Jesus tells His followers to pray, "Deliver us from evil." The problem is that Romanticism rejects the notion of evil, or at least original sin. Evil is something external to man, not a fissured nature or something endemic to the human condition. This is problematic, of course, to an orthodox Christian.*

B. One problem with the Romantic worldview is the weak image of God. This presages the later naturalistic view that rejects an omnipotent God altogether. God, to the Romantic, is unable to overcome the power of nature and the human will. There is a moral vision but it is mitigated by sentimental notions about nature. Using the Bible as your main resource, critique this worldview.

ANSWER: *The Bible is unequivocal in its view that God is omnipotent, omniscient, and omnipresent. He is not to be trifled with. He is a mighty, awesome God. The notion that human subjectivity has any place in the design of providence is laughable.*

C. Christian teacher Thomas Merton, in an essay entitled "A Devout Meditation in Memory of Adolf Eichmann" (a Nazi leader who implemented the Holocaust), challenges modern man to rethink sanity. "One of the most disturbing facts," Merton begins, "that came out in the Eichmann trial was that a psychiatrist examined him and pronounced him perfectly sane." The fact is, given our world, we can no longer assume that because a person is "sane" or "adjusted" he/she is OK. Merton reminds us that such people can be well adjusted even in hell itself! Merton says, "The whole concept of sanity in a society where spiritual values have lost their meaning is itself meaningless." In light of biblical discussions of human depravity—especially as they appear in the book of Romans—write an essay reflecting on the accuracy of Merton's statement.

ANSWER: *It is an accurate and unnerving statement. A big concern is that people can be very talented, and very smart, and very evil. That is the Achilles tendon of the Romantic Movement. It begins with a notion that man unshackled by authority and control is basically good. That leads to disastrous results. While it would be stretching it to call Eichmann a Romantic, his lack of fear of God—a Romantic tendency—led him to implement the murder of 8 million people.*

FINAL PROJECT

Students should correct and rewrite all essays and place them in their Final Portfolio.

Elements of Romanticism	Frontier is a vast expanse; It represents freedom, innocence, and opportunity.
Writing Techniques	1. Appeals to imagination; use of the "willing suspension of disbelief." 2. Stress on emotion and imagination rather than reason; optimism, geniality. 3. Subjectivity in form and meaning. 4. Prefers the remote setting in time and space. 5. Prefers the exotic and improbable plots. 6. Prefers aberrant characterization. 7. Form rises out of content, non-formal. 8. Prefers individualized, subjective writing.

LESSON 7 TEST
DISCUSSION QUESTIONS. (100 POINTS)

A. Poe believed in what he called "unity of effect." "Unity of effect" to Poe meant that the short story could be read at a single sitting. To Poe, tone was everything. He would deliberately subordinate everything in the story to tone. As a result, the short story became "poetic." Give examples of this effect in our two short stories "Fall of the House of Usher" and "The Tell Tale Heart." (20 Points)

B. Poe was accused of being a detective and horror story writer. However, he was a Romantic writer. Explain and give examples of Romanticism in these two short stories.

(20 Points)

C. Poe was fond of creating paradoxes in his short stories. Explain and give examples from these two short stories. (20 Points)

D. Describe Roderick. Why does he both repel and attract the reader? (20 Points)

E. Compare and contrast "Usher" to "Tell Tale Heart." (10 Points)

F. Which of the following passages is from Poe? How do you know? (10 Points)

#1 I was sick, sick unto death, with that long agony, and when they at length unbound me, and I was permitted to sit, I felt that my senses were leaving me. The sentence, the dread sentence of death, was the last of distinct accentuation which reached my ears. After that, the sound of the inquisitorial voices seemed merged in one dreamy indeterminate hum. It conveyed to my soul the idea of Revolution, perhaps from its association in fancy with the burr of a mill-wheel. This only for a brief period, for presently I heard no more. Yet, for a while, I saw, but with how terrible an exaggeration! I saw the lips of the black-robed judges. They appeared to me white—whiter than the sheet upon which I trace these words—and thin even to grotesqueness; thin with the intensity of their expression of firmness, of immovable resolution, of stern contempt of human torture. I saw that the decrees of what to me was fate were still issuing from those lips. I saw them writhe with a deadly locution. I saw them fashion the syllables of my name, and I shuddered, because no sound succeeded. I saw, too, for a few moments of delirious horror, the soft and nearly imperceptible waving of the sable draperies which enwrapped the walls of the apartment; and then my vision fell upon the seven tall candles upon the table. At first they wore the aspect of charity, and seemed white slender angels who would save me: but then all at once there came a most deadly nausea over my spirit, and I felt every fibre in my frame thrill, as if I had touched the wire of a galvanic battery, while the angel forms became meaningless specters, with heads of flame, and I saw that from them there would be no help. And then there stole into my fancy, like a rich musical note, the thought of what sweet rest there must be in the grave. The thought came gently and stealthily, and it seemed long before it attained full appreciation; but just as my spirit came at length properly to feel and entertain it, the figures of the judges vanished, as if magically, from before me; the tall candles sank into nothingness; their flames went out utterly; the blackness of darkness superceded; all sensations appeared swallowed up in a mad rushing descent as of the soul into Hades. Then silence, and stillness, and night were the universe.

#2 And I would have you believe, my sons, that the same Justice which punishes sin may also most graciously forgive it, and that no ban is so heavy but that by prayer and repentance it may be removed. Learn then from this story not to fear the fruits of the past, but rather to be circumspect in the future, that those foul passions whereby our family has suffered so grievously may not again be loosed to our undoing. "Know then that in the time of the Great Rebellion (the history of which by the learned Lord Clarendon I most earnestly commend to your attention) this... was held by Hugo of that name, nor can it be gainsaid that he was a most wild, profane, and godless man. This, in truth, his neighbour might have pardoned, seeing that saints have never flourished in those parts, but there was in him a certain wanton and cruel humor which made his name a byword through the West. It chanced that this Hugo came to love (if, indeed, so dark a passion may be known under so bright a name) the daughter of a yeoman who held lands near the Baskerville estate. But the young maiden, being discreet and of good repute, would ever avoid him, for she feared his evil name. So it came to pass that one Michaelmas this Hugo, with five or six of his idle and wicked companions, stole down upon the farm and carried off the maiden, her father and brothers being from home, as he well knew. When they had brought her to the Hall the maiden was placed in an upper chamber, while Hugo and his friends sat down to a long carouse, as was their nightly custom. Now, the poor lass upstairs was like to have her wits turned at the singing and shouting and terrible oaths which came up to her from below...

Lesson 7 Answers

Discussion Questions. (100 Points)

A. Poe believed in what he called "unity of effect." "Unity of effect" to Poe meant that the short story could be read at a single sitting. To Poe, tone was everything. He would deliberately subordinate everything in the story to tone. As a result, the short story became "poetic." Give examples of this effect in "Usher" and "Tell Tale." (20 Points)

ANSWER: *"Usher" has symmetry — the decaying owner lives in the decaying house. "During the whole of a dull, dark, and soundless day in the autumn of the year, when the clouds hung oppressively low in the heavens, had been passing alone, on horseback, through a singularly dreary tract of country; and at length found myself, as the shades of the evening drew on, within view of the melancholy House of Usher." "Tell Tale Heart" also has a unity of effect: "Presently, I heard a slight groan, and I knew it was the groan of mortal terror. It was not a groan of pain or of grief — oh no! It was the low stifled sound that arises from the bottom of the soul when overcharged with awe. I knew the sound well."*

B. Poe was accused of being a detective and a horror story writer. However, he was a Romantic writer. Explain and give examples of Romanticism in the two short stories "Fall of the House of Usher" and "The Tell Tale Heart." (20 Points)

ANSWER:
1. Appeals to imagination; use of the "willing suspension of disbelief."
2. Stress on emotion and imagination rather than reason; optimism, geniality.
3. Subjectivity in form and meaning.
4. Prefers the remote setting in time and space.
5. Prefers the exotic and improbable plots.
6. Prefers aberrant characterization.
7. Form rises out of content, non-formal.
8. Prefers individualized, subjective writing.

C. Poe was fond of creating paradoxes in his short stories. Explain and give examples from these two short stories. (20 Points)

ANSWER: *His life was basically insecure and highly emotional, but his writing is structured. Poe was a Romantic writer, but he emphasized rationality. He presented realistic details in Romantic/horror settings.*

D. Describe Roderick. Why does he both repel and attract the reader? (20 Points)

ANSWER: *Roderick is erudite, well-educated, but also very disturbed. His physical appearance, both fascinating and repulsive, declines as the story progresses.*

E. Compare and contrast "Usher" to "Tell Tale Heart." (10 Points)

ANSWER: *Both employ Romantic writing principles. Both build suspense. Both protagonists seem to be insane. "Tell Tale" however employs first person narration. "Usher" also is first person but functions as a neutral observer.*

F. Which of the following passages is from Poe? How do you know? (10 Points)

ANSWER: *The first is from "Pit and Pendulum." The second is Arthur Conan Doyle's "The Hounds of the Baskerville." The language and images in Poe are significantly more developed than in "Hounds." Poe, a vastly better writer than Doyle, uses well-developed characters to propel his plot forward and to influence the reader's mood. Doyle uses coincidence to propel the plot and setting to influence the reader's mood. Poe is a much more economical writer. Every word is important.*

LESSON 8
ROMANTICISM: NEW ENGLAND RENAISSANCE, *1840-1855*
(Part 1)

Readings Due For This Lesson: Students should review *The Scarlet Letter* and "The Birthmark," Nathaniel Hawthorne.

Reading Ahead: Students should review poems by Henry Wadsworth Longfellow, Oliver Wendell Holmes, James Russell Lowell, John Greenleaf Whittier, and Emily Dickinson. What moral vision do these poets present?

Goal: Students will analyze *The Scarlet Letter* and "The Birthmark," Nathaniel Hawthorne.

Goals/Objectives: What is the purpose of this lesson?	Strategies to meet these goals: How will I obtain these goals/objectives?	Evaluation: How will I know when I have met these goals/objectives?
Students will understand this concept: the way allegory is used in *Scarlet Letter*. (cognitive goal)	Students will write an essay on the following topic: An allegory is a narrative in which characters, action, and sometimes setting represent abstract concepts or moral qualities. What moral qualities are represented by Arthur? Hester? Roger? Write an illustrative essay describing the moral qualities each character represents. (Critical Thinking A)	Students, with minimal errors, will clearly answer the assigned question in a 1-2 page essay.
Students will increase their vocabulary. (cognitive goal)	Students will collect at least five new vocabulary words from their reading and use these words in their essays. They will also define the words provided in this lesson and use them in essays and in conversation.	Students will use five vocabulary words in conversation during the week as well as use the words in their essays and in conversation.
Students will apply the historical and worldview tensions of 1850 America to *Scarlet Letter*. (cognitive goal)	Students will write an essay on the following topic: *The Scarlet Letter* was one of the last books in American literature that had a Theistic moral vision. Although Hawthorne never hinted that	Students, with minimal errors, will clearly answer the assigned question in a 1-2 page essay.

Goals/Objectives: What is the purpose of this lesson?	Strategies to meet these goals: How will I obtain these goals/objectives?	Evaluation: How will I know when I have met these goals/objectives?
	Prynne's punishment was unjust, he seemed far more disturbed by Dimmesdale's deception and Chillingsworth's evil ways. In a two-page essay, using this book as a metaphor for the tensions existing in American society c. 1850, discuss these tensions and evidence them from the text. Who is the victim in this book? (Critical Thinking B)	
Students will exhibit higher-level thinking by writing a persuasive essay. (cognitive goal)	Students will value confession and repentance. (affective goal) Students will write an essay on the following topic: A recent television commercial argued, "Doesn't everyone deserve a second chance?" Do you agree or disagree with this statement? Why does this book offend or not offend your sense of justice? (Critical Thinking C)	Students, with minimal errors, will clearly answer the assigned question in a 1-2 page essay.
Students will exhibit higher-level thinking as they discuss contemporary reactions to Hester Prynne. (cognitive goal)	Students will write an essay on the following topic: Pretend that Hester Prynne lived in City Anywhere, USA. How would she be treated at a public school? At the grocery story? At your church? Defend your answer. (Critical Thinking D)	Students, with minimal errors, will clearly answer the assigned question in a 1-2 page essay.
Students will exhibit higher-level thinking as they evaluate the influence of Sophia Peabody on her husband. (cognitive goal) Students will consider the generalization that Christians should not marry unbelievers. (affective goal)	Students will write an essay on the following topic: Many scholars find evidence that Nathaniel Hawthorne was a believer. While there were evidences of Transcendentalism in his writings, Hawthorne admired and advanced the Puritan theistic vision. The ambivalence in his writing may have been from his Transcendalist/Universalist wife Sophia Peabody Hawthorne who no doubt influenced him. What evidence supports or fails to support this theory? Offer evidence in your essay from the *The Scarlet Letter* and other writings. (Critical Thinking E)	Students, with minimal errors, will clearly answer the assigned question in a 1-2 page essay.

Goals/Objectives: What is the purpose of this lesson?	Strategies to meet these goals: How will I obtain these goals/objectives?	Evaluation: How will I know when I have met these goals/objectives?
Students will understand the concept of characterization through Hester. (cognitive goal) In their assessment of this situation, students will consider the generalization that Hester's decision to stand and face the consequences of her sin was correct. (affective goal) Students will gain discussion skills. (behavioral goal)	Write an essay on the following topic: Give a characterization of Hester. What sort of woman is she? She could have run away with Arthur. Why doesn't she? (Critical Thinking F) Students should discuss this topic at length with their parents.	Students, with minimal errors, will clearly answer the assigned question in a 1-2 page essay.
Students will understand the concept of *foil*. (cognitive goal) Students will exhibit higher level thinking as they write comparison essays. (cognitive goal)	Students will write essays on the following topics: Pearl functions as a foil (a character whose primary purpose is to develop the main character.) Give evidence of this purpose. (Critical Thinking G) In another essay, compare the use of a foil in this book with another foil in another piece of literature. (Critical Thinking H) Compare Pearl to a foil in your favorite movie (e.g. the way Aubrey is used in the movie *Chariots of Fire*). (Critical Thinking I)	Students, with minimal errors, will clearly answer the assigned question in a 1-2 page essay.
Students will exhibit higher-level thinking as they contrast the adulterous woman story in John 8 and the Hester Prynne story in *Scarlet Letter*. (cognitive goal) Students will value honest admission of sin and forgiveness of sin. (affective goal) Students will write a contrast paper. (cognitive goal)	Students will write an essay: Contrast the way Hester's community handles her adultery and the way Jesus dealt with the adulterous woman who was brought to Him. (John 8) Also, contrast the way Hester handled her sin and the way the adulterous woman handled her sin. (Biblical Application A)	Students, with minimal errors, will clearly answer the assigned question in a 1-2 page essay.
Students will understand the concept of how to create a Biblical argument for their position. (cognitive goal)	Students will compose an essay on the following topic: While we may agree that Hester's community was somewhat rough on her, are we	Students, with minimal errors, will clearly answer the assigned question in a 1-2 page essay.

Goals/Objectives: What is the purpose of this lesson?	Strategies to meet these goals: How will I obtain these goals/objectives?	Evaluation: How will I know when I have met these goals/ objectives?
Students will grow in their walk with the Lord as they rethink their relationship with God. (affective goal) Students will understand these concepts: sin, repentance, and restoration.	willing to say that she and her companion in adultery should not have been punished? Do a Bible study on the whole topics of sin, repentance, and restoration. Start in Matthew 18. (Biblical Application B)	
Students will understand the concept of Salem witches. (cognitive essay)	Students will write an essay on the following topic: Do you really think there were witches in Salem? Defend your answer. (Enrichment A)	Students, with minimal errors, will clearly answer the assigned question in a 1-2 page essay.
Students will exhibit higher level thinking as they evaluate how our culture has been transformed by television and the entertainment industry. (cognitive goal)	Students will write an essay on the following topic: The message has become the medium. What do you think? Read Postman or use other materials and write an essay explaining how our culture has been transformed by television and the entertainment industry. (Enrichment B)	Students, with minimal errors, will clearly answer the assigned question in a 1-2 page essay.
Students will understand the concept of a comparison between Hester Prynne in *The Scarlet Letter* and Phoebe Pyncheon in *House of the Seven Gables*. (cognitive essay)	Students will write an essay on the following topic: Compare and contrast Hester Prynne in *The Scarlet Letter* and Phoebe Pyncheon in *House of the Seven Gables*. (Enrichment D)	Students, with minimal errors, will clearly answer the assigned question in a 1-2 page essay.
Students will exhibit higher level thinking as they analyze this short story looking for examples of Theism and Romanticism (cognitive goal).	Students will write an essay on the following topic: As stated previously, Hawthorne flirted with Transcendentalism/ Romanticism but never left his theistic Romanticism. Find examples of Theistic Romanticism in "The Birthmark." (Critical Thinking A)	Students, with minimal errors, will clearly answer the assigned question in a 1-2 page essay.
Students will understand the concept of Hawthorne's fear of science. (cognitive goal)	Students will write an essay on the following topic: Do you share Hawthorne's fear of the power of science? Why or why not? (Critical Thinking B)	Students, with minimal errors, will clearly answer the assigned question in a 1-2 page essay.

Goals/Objectives: What is the purpose of this lesson?	Strategies to meet these goals: How will I obtain these goals/objectives?	Evaluation: How will I know when I have met these goals/objectives?
Students will understand the concept of Aylmer's love for science and Georgiana. (cognitive goal)	Students will write an essay on the following topic: How can Aylmer love both science and Georgiana? Are these loves mutually contradictory? (Critical Thinking C)	Students, with minimal errors, will clearly answer the assigned question in a 1-2 page essay.
Students will understand the concept of comparison essay. (cognitive goal)	Students will write an essay on the following topic: What basic differences are there between Aylmer's world view and Transcendentalism? (Critical Thinking D)	Students, with minimal errors, will clearly answer the assigned question in a 1-2 page essay.
Students will exhibit higher level thinking as they answer this question: Aylmer's attempts to perfect Georgiana are doomed to failure. (cognitive goal)	Students will write an essay on the following topic: In the final analysis, Aylmer's attempts to perfect Georgiana are doomed to failure. Why? (Critical Thinking E)	Students, with minimal errors, will clearly answer the assigned question in a 1-2 page essay.
Students will understand this concept: allegory. (cognitive goal)	Students will write an essay on the following topic: This story is an allegory. What moral quality is represented by Aylmer? By Georgiana? Aminadab? In a two-page essay, describe how Hawthorne sets up this allegory. (Critical Thinking F)	Students, with minimal errors, will clearly answer the assigned question in a two-page essay.
Students will exhibit higher level thinking as they pretend to be Aylmer's pastor. (cognitive goal) Students will consider the generalization that we are all valuable because we are created in the image of God. (affective goal)	Students will write an essay on the following topic: Pretend you are Aylmer's pastor. He has come to you to seek advice about his wife's physical flaw. How do you respond? (Biblical Application)	Students, with minimal errors, will clearly answer the assigned question in a 1-2 page essay.
Students will understand the concept of a comparison essay of these two novels. (cognitive goal).	Students will write an essay on the following topic: Students will compare the theme(s) of this short story with the theme(s) of Mary Shelley's *Frankenstein*. (Enrichment A).	Students, with minimal errors, will clearly answer the assigned question in a 1-2 page essay.
Students will understand the concept of comparison and contrast of Aylmer and Chillingsworth. (cognitive essay)	Students will write an essay on the following topic: Students will compare and contrast Aylmer and Chillingsworth (*The Scarlet Letter*). (Enrichment B).	Students, with minimal errors, will clearly answer the assigned question in a 1-2 page essay.

Goals/Objectives: What is the purpose of this lesson?	Strategies to meet these goals: How will I obtain these goals/objectives?	Evaluation: How will I know when I have met these goals/objectives?
Students will understand the concept of tautology (cognitive essay)	Students will write an essay on the following topic: other tautologies in modern science? (Enrichment C)	Students, with minimal errors, will clearly answer the assigned question in a 1-2 page essay.
Students will work in a group setting. (behavioral goal)	In a class, in a co-op experience, or during a family discussion, students will answer the following question: Were there really witches in Salem during the Salem witch trials?	Students will exhibit practical listening skills and will manifest understanding of opposing world-views.
Students will be able to recall the information taught in the lesson. (cognitive goal)	Lesson 8 Test	Students will take the test at the end of this lesson and score at least 80%.
Students will experience reflective writing. (affective/spiritual goal)	Using the Journal Guide Questions in the Appendices, students will record at least three entries this week. Suggested Scriptures: 1 Samuel	Students will show evidence that they have reflected on this issue, including informed discussions and written responses.

SUGGESTED
Weekly *Implementation*

DAY 1	DAY 2	DAY 3	DAY 4	DAY 5
Prayer journal. Students review the required reading(s) before the assigned lesson begins. Teacher may want to discuss assigned reading(s) with students. Teacher and students will decide on the number of required essays for this lesson, choosing two or three essays. The rest of the essays can be outlined, answered with shorter answers, or skipped. Students review all readings for Lesson 8.	**Prayer journal.** Students review reading(s) from next lesson. Students outline essays due at the end of the week. Per teacher instructions, students may answer orally in a group setting some of the essays that are not assigned as formal essays.	**Prayer journal.** Students write rough drafts of all assigned essays. The teacher and/or a peer evaluator may correct rough drafts.	**Prayer journal.** Students re-write corrected copies of essays due tomorrow.	**Prayer journal.** Essays are due. Students take the Lesson 8 test. Reading ahead: Students review poems by Henry Wadsworth Longfellow, Oliver Wendell Holmes, James Russell Lowell, John Greenleaf Whittier, and Emily Dickinson. Guide: What moral vision do these poets present?

Note: References to sources are in student edition.

ENRICHMENT ACTIVITIES/PROJECTS

Students should visit Salem, Massachusetts if at all possible.

Students should read other Hawthorne novels.

Students should write a screen play of this book. Who will play each part?

Students should listen to an unabridged book tape/CD of this book.

Students should compare the similarities between artists of the 1960s. (Dylan, Hendrix, Warhol) and artists of the 1830s. (Emerson, Hawthorne, Thoreau, and Melville)

SUPPLEMENTAL RESOURCES

Bell, Millicent. (Editor), *Nathaniel Hawthorne—Collected Novels: Fanshawe, The Scarlet Letter, The House of the Seven Gables, The Blithedale Romance.*

An excellent collection, with editorial helps, of Hawthorne's five novels. A choice version for young readers.

Gaeddert, LouAnn. *A New England Love Story: Nathaniel Hawthorne and Sophia Peabody.*

For mature readers. Gaeddert gives great insights into the relationship of Sophia Peabody and Nathaniel Hawthorne.

Pearce, Roy Harvey. (Editor) *Nathaniel Hawthorne: Tales and Sketches.*

This book offers young readers an authoritative edition of Hawthorne's complete stories in a single comprehensive volume.

Sculley, Bradley, ed. *The Scarlet Letter: Backgrounds and Sources, Criticism.*

One of the best scholarly resources on Hawthorne and his works.

Turner, Arlin. *Nathaniel Hawthorne: A Biography.*

An unpretentious but readable biography of Hawthorne.

Notes:

SUGGESTED VOCABULARY WORDS

As you read the assigned prose, poetry, and novels, make vocabulary cards. On one side put the word you do not know. On the other side put the definition of the word and a sentence with the word used in it. Read 35-50 pages per night. (200 pages per week) At the same time, create 3/5 vocabulary cards. You should use five new words in each essay you write. The following are vocabulary works in *The Scarlet Letter*. Find more.

II   ignominy. (*disgrace*)
III   heterogeneous. (*mixed*)
      Iniquity. (*evil*)
VIII   imperious. (*contemptuous*)
XII   dauntless. (*fearless*)
      forlorn. (*dejected*)
      odious. (*detestable*)
      efficacious. (*useful*)
XIII   expiation. (*remorse; penance*)
      scurrilous. (*crude and offensive*)
XIX   misanthropy. (*hatred of people*)
XX   effluence. (*generously flowing out*)
      choleric. (*peevish*)
XXI   vicissitude. (*unpredictable change*)

BIBLICAL APPLICATION

A.   Contrast the way Hester's community handles her adultery and the way Jesus dealt with the adulterous woman who was brought to Him. (John 8)

ANSWER: *Hester's community was unable to forgive her. Nonetheless, Hester found forgiveness and wholeness through her contrite heart. Jesus announced the adulterous woman's forgiveness and invited others to forgive her too. Whether or not they did, the woman at the well, and Hester Prynne found forgiveness. Undeserved, unconditional love invited both heroines to be His disciple. Both individuals manifested a decidedly theistic response to bad choices. However, Hester openly accepted her sin in the midst of her community. The adulterous woman hid her sin from Christ until He identified it to her personally.*

B.   While we may agree that Hester's community was somewhat rough on her, are we willing to say that she, as well as her partner in adultery, should not have been punished? Do a Bible study on the whole topics of *sin, repentance,* and *restoration.* Start in Matthew 18.

ANSWER: *Answers will vary. One of the purposes of Christian discipline is to bring restoration. Therefore, holding someone responsible for his/her actions is necessary for restoration to even be an option. If there is no moral standard to be upheld, there can be no sin and therefore no restoration. This is the concern of the psychologist Karl Menninger when he wrote his influential work* Whatever Happened to Sin?

CRITICAL THINKING

A.   In *The Scarlet Letter,* as he did in most of his books, Hawthorne combined historical truth with imaginative detail to create an allegory. An allegory is a narrative in which characters, action, and sometimes setting represent abstract concepts or moral qualities. What moral qualities are represented by Arthur? Hester? Roger? Write an illustrative essay describing the moral qualities each character represents.

ANSWER: *Arthur Dimmesdale represents the flawed religious community. He is not hypocritical—he deeply feels his crime—but he is pusillanimous. Roger Chillingsworth is the villain of this novel. He is amoral. He is the cold, technical, bureaucrat who judges but refuses to get involved. He is only concerned about himself. He represents the Yankee commercialism that is* overtaking Hawthorne's community. He represents the cold, dispassionate scientist. (e.g., Dr. Frankenstein in Shelley's *Frankenstein*) Hester is a true heroine. Refusing to flee punishment, she realizes that repentance brings restoration. She is the strongest member of her community. True, strong, and faithful Hester inspires us all. She is a repentant, forgiven sinner who, ironically, is the only person who survives and becomes stronger through the journey.

B. *The Scarlet Letter* was one of the last books in American literature that had a Theistic moral vision. Although Hawthorne never hinted that Prynne's punishment was unjust, he seemed far more disturbed by Dimmesdale's deception and Chillingsworth's evil ways. Using this book as a metaphor for the tensions existing in American society c. 1850, discuss in a two-page essay these tensions and evidence them from the text. Who is the victim in this book?

ANSWER: *Surely the setting of The Scarlet Letter—the stern, joyless world of Puritan New England—appears to have very little potential for joy. Why did Hawthorne choose this dark world for his masterpiece? Why did Hawthorne reject the contemporary scene? Hawthorne reached back to Salem in the 1600s to find men and women who would speak directly to his creative imagination. The Puritan world of the mid-17th century apparently gave Hawthorne something he badly needed—people who lived their lives to the full. In the pages of The Scarlet Letter, the Puritans emerge from the shadows of an earlier time, direct of speech, and full of integrity. The Puritans had a moral vitality never again found on the American scene. For a writer like Hawthorne, intrigued with the subject of conscience, here were people with conscience to spare. The Puritans at least knew the difference between right and wrong. Hawthorne made no apologies for Hester's punishment. Likewise, Hawthorne clearly thought that Dimmesdale deserved punishment too. If there were ambivalence in Hawthorne's worldview—between Theism and Transcendentalism—it came forth honestly. Hawthorne, a Theist, was married to a beautiful Transcendentalist, Sophia Peabody. Their friends included Transcendentalists Melville, the Alcott sisters, Emerson, and Thoreau. Hawthorne, the Theist, was no doubt influenced by these individuals. In the life of Hawthorne the reader observes the movement of America's cultural worldview from Puritanism to Transcendentalism. By the time Melville wrote Billy Budd the protagonist was "saved" through good works and the Puritan theistic vision appeared to be dead. Hester Prynne was no Billy Budd. Hester Prynne committed adultery, repented, and was forgiven. In summary, what bothered Hawthorne was that Dr. Chillingsworth and Pastor Dimmesdale were unrepentant hypocrites. Chillingsworth, the realist (as Alymer in "The*

Birthmark"), and Dimmesdale, the coward/hypocrite, would not stand with Hester on the scaffold (until the end when Dimmesdale owned his sin). Hawthorne's characters knew no redemption until they understood and accepted the antidote to sin—the sacrifice of Jesus Christ at Calvary which is only accessible to a repentant heart. Really, Hawthorne would say we all are standing on the scaffold with Hester . . . All have sinned and fallen short . . . Ergo, in 1820-1850, when American society was changing so much, and there were so many alternative worldviews (viz., Realism, Transcendentalism, and Romanticism), Hawthorne, for the last time, promoted a Theistic/Puritan vision. Hawthorne, who wrote like a Romantic but believed like a Christian Theist, was making one last literary effort to make a stand for morality in the face of situation ethics (Realism); an unfeeling angry God (Naturalism); an impersonal God (Deism); a Nature-powered world (Romanticism); and a world that emphasizes human intuition (Transcendentalism). For the last time in American literature for two generations, a character stood up and took responsibility for her moral choices. Contrast this courage with a later novel A Farewell to Arms where the protagonist blamed fate for his problems. The world of which Hawthorne was a part invited him to step away from his Christian beliefs. He chose not to do so. That is the genius of his book. There were no victims—only men and women making decisions that have eternal consequences.

C. A recent television commercial argued, "Doesn't everyone deserve a second chance?" Why do you agree or disagree with this statement? Why does this book offend or not offend your sense of justice?

ANSWER: *Deserving a second chance is the wrong question to ask. The real question is, "Will a person admit his sin and find the only real antidote to that sin?" If a person confesses with his mouth and believes in his heart that Jesus Christ is Lord, he is both saved and forgiven. Christians should be anxious to forgive the* repentant *sinner and accept him into fellowship.*

D. Pretend that Hester Prynne lived in City Anywhere, USA. How would she be treated at a public school? At the grocery story? At your church? Defend your answer.

ANSWER: *Answers will have to be opinions.*

E. Many scholars find evidence that Nathaniel Hawthorne was a believer. While there were evidences of Transcendentalism in his writings, Hawthorne admired and advanced the Puritan Theistic vision. The ambivalence in his writing may have been from his Transcendalist/ Universalist wife Sophia Peabody Hawthorne and friends who no doubt influenced him. What evidence supports or fails to support this theory? In your essay offer evidence from the *The Scarlet Letter* and other writings.

ANSWER: *Hawthorne came dangerously close to embracing Transcendentalism. His use of the rose, for instance, and other symbolism resembled Emerson's writing. Also, Hawthorne seemed to borrow symbols of light and darkness which were powerful Transcendental symbols. On the other hand, he did not deify nature nor did he prosper immoral characters. Hawthorne wrote like a romantic but believed like a Christian.*

F. Give a characterization of Hester. What sort of woman is she? She could have run away with Arthur. Why doesn't she?

ANSWER: *Hester recognizes the value of punishment—a rare, and valuable character quality. She accepts suffering because she knows that it leads to redemption. She does not condemn others, though. In her attempt to be humble before God, referring to guilt and responsibilities of others, she speaks, "I know not. I know not."*

G. Pearl functions as a *foil* (a character whose primary purpose is to develop the main character). Give evidence of this purpose.

ANSWER: *Pearl is a wild, impish character who represents the fruit of Hester's and Arthur's sin. Even though she is an invitation to be wild and unholy, Hester never accepts that invitation.*

H. In another essay, compare the use of a foil in this book with another foil in another piece of literature.

ANSWER: *One of the best foils in American literature is Jim in Huckleberry Finn. In the movie <u>Chariots of Fire</u> Aubrey functions as a foil.*

I. Compare Pearl to a foil in your favorite movie. (e.g. the way Aubrey is used in the movie *Chariots of Fire*)

ANSWER: *An excellent foil in the movie <u>Iron Will</u> is the Native American Companion of Will Stoner.*

ENRICHMENT

A. Do you really think there were witches in Salem? Defend your answer.

ANSWER: *One of the most remarkable and bizarre—depending on the reader's perspective—events in early colonial history occurred during May through October 1692. Around Salem Village, Massachusetts, north of Boston, 19 convicted "witches" were hanged, and many other suspects were imprisoned in the town of Salem in the Massachusetts Bay Colony. Alarmed by tales told by a West Indian slave named Tituba, local officials, encouraged by Pastor Samuel Parris, set up a special court in Salem to try those accused of practicing witchcraft. The list of the accused increased (even Massachusetts governor William Phips's wife was implicated) until over a 100 people were put in jail. While there could well have been witches among the accused, this whole affair was reflective more of the growing concern that the hold of Puritanism was being replaced rapidly by a growing Yankee spirit of commercialism and secularism than it was about the punishment of witches.*

B. *The Scarlet Letter* was a critical success but not a best seller. In American society, so structured around entertainment, one wonders if Hawthorne would be able to find a publisher. In his book *Amusing Ourselves to Death* Neil Postman argues that television is transforming our culture into one vast arena for show business (p. 80). Television is the highest order of abstract thinking and consistently undermines critical thinking (p.41). The message has become the medium. What do you think? Read Postman or use other material and write an essay explaining how our culture has been transformed by television and the entertainment industry.

ANSWER: *Clearly Postman is correct. Our culture obtains its motifs, metaphors, and even its values from the media.*

C. Compare and contrast Hester Prynne in *The Scarlet Letter* and Phoebe Pyncheon in *House of the Seven Gables*.

ANSWER: *Both Phoebe and Prynne are strong, female, Theistic characters in a dark, Romantic world.*

CRITICAL THINKING

A. As stated previously, Hawthorne flirted with Transcendentalism/ Romanticism but never left his Theistic Romanticism. Find examples of Theistic Romanticism in "The Birthmark."

ANSWER: *Evidences of Romanticism are abundant. The use of the forest; the juxtaposition of nature and the personality of Aylmer; etc. Theism is also evident but in more subtle ways. Again, as <u>The Scarlet Letter</u>, Birthmark has a moral vision. There is only one God in Hawthorne's world, and He is not Chillingsworth or Aylmer, nor is it their rationalism.*

B. Aylmer was a character who represents a modern nineteenth century scientist. Hawthorne was one of the earliest writers to point out the limits of science. Others include Mary Shelley, *Frankenstein*, and Robert Louis Stevenson, *Dr. Jekyl and Mr. Hyde*. George Gaylord Simpson in his book *The Age of Evolution*, argues that science (especially evolution) can suggest that "man is the result of a purposeless and materialistic process that did not have him in mind . . . the universe. . . lacked any purpose or plan . . . (this) has the inevitable corollary that the workings of the universe cannot provide any automatic, universal, eternal or absolute criteria of right or wrong." Hawthorne believed, with all his heart that science could become a "god." What Hawthorne understood was how science related to knowledge (epistemology). Hawthorne understood the danger of Transcendentalism or any other worldview that replaced Christianity. With the disestablishment of Christianity, western society has wrestled with epistemology for the past several hundred years. If materialism were one's metaphysics, then scientism became one's dominant epistemology. Science became the way to know anything that was to be known. Do you share Hawthorne's fear of the power of science? Why or why not?

ANSWER: *Answers will vary. A healthy respect for science is paramount since our society enjoys the benefits of science. We can applaud progress that has been made over the years.*

C. How can Aylmer love both science and Georgiana? Are these loves mutually contradictory?

ANSWER: *To Hawthorne they are. Either man will worship the Creator or the creation. Science is the creation; God is the Creator. Aylmer most certainly cannot improve on God's handiwork—that is Georgiana.*

D. What basic differences are there between Aylmer's worldview and Transcendentalism?

ANSWER: *Aylmer is truly an interesting 19th century literary character. He is the rationalist; a Chillingsworth, a scientist. He is a type of modern man. He is the Faust of American literature. Transcendentalism, while celebrating "the human spirit" and "relativism," also tries to embrace science rationalism. However, the essence of Transcendentalism is the opposite of scientific rationalism: experience verses empiricism. It is a conflict as old as Aristotle and Plato. Plato argued that the metaphysical realm (that is, God) controls the natural world; Aristotle believed that the natural world defined God. All contemporary worldview discussions can be traced one way or another to Plato and Aristotle. Plato was the Pharisee of his day,*

the conservative, the one who believed that the gods were intimately involved with human beings. His "Republic" was a perfect society based on the notion that mankind was creating a city based on the word of the gods. Cosmology, or the presence of supernatural being(s), in other words, was very important to Plato. Likewise, to the Pharisee, who believed strongly in the Resurrection, the supernatural was very involved in human life. To Plato, the gods defined reality. Aristotle, on the other hand, in his important essay Poeticus *argued that the world was governed by impersonal laws. Aristotle argued that mankind defined who the gods were. While the gods are alive and well, they do not much concern themselves with the world. Therefore, mankind should be concerned about finding out about his world without worrying about the gods. This view was evident again in the Sadducees—who rejected the supernatural—and later philosophers like David Hume. Discussing Hellenistic philosophy, at this point, is for no other reason than to point out that the struggle in which our children will participate is over 3000 years old. It is the struggle that Elijah joined when he fought King Ahab. King Ahab was a good Jew; the problem was he did not live his life as if God were actually alive. Is God intentionally involved in the affairs of mankind or not? The answer to this question is more or less the battle that is raging on college campuses today. Paul, a student of Greek philosophy, was deeply affected by Plato. The Holy Spirit led Paul to write: "So we do not focus on what is seen, but on what is unseen; for what is seen is temporary, but what is unseen is eternal." (2 Cor. 4:18).*

E. In the final analysis, Aylmer's attempts to perfect Georgiana are doomed to failure. Why?

ANSWER: *Georgiana could not be changed by anyone but God. In the short story "The Birth Mark" by Nathaniel Hawthorne the main character is a scientist named Aylmer. Aylmer has a gentle, loving wife named Georgiana who has a birth mark on her cheek. Aylmer cannot stand this birth mark. Therefore, he convinces his wife to let him remove it. In the end, he removes the mark, but he kills her. Aylmer is the antithesis of a worldview/movement of the middle 19th century called Transcendentalism. What is Transcendentalism? It is a 19th-century movement of writers and philosophers in New England who were loosely bound together by adherence to an idealistic system of thought based on a belief in the essential unity of all creation, the innate goodness of man, and the supremacy of insight over logic and experience for the revelation of the deepest truths* (Encyclopedia Britannica). *In other words, Transcendentalism reveres subjectivity. Subjectivity celebrates individuality and creativity. It is a reality that grows from the heart of man; not from science. Aylmer can not understand, much less appreciate his beautiful Transcendental wife. Georgiana loves gardens, flowers, and anything else that draws out her innate feelings of goodness. The scientist Alymer does not have a clue.*

Georgiana's birthmark is certainly something that sets her apart from a genus or phallum. "Georgiana," said he, "has it ever occurred to you that the mark upon your cheek might be removed?" "No, indeed," she said, smiling; but perceiving the seriousness of his manner she blushed deeply. "To tell you the truth, it has been so often called a charm that I was simple enough to imagine it might be so." The Transcendentalist Georgiana values what is unique, different. It is a "charm." The scientist Aylmer who is always looking for the usual, the pattern, the repeated behavior cannot value or chooses not to value an aberration.

Aylmer also has a drive for everything to be perfect. Everything must be in perfect order. Every little thing filed away. But on his wife, whom he loves greatly, there is an imperfect spot. This spot drives him crazy. He will do anything to get rid of it.

In this short story, Nathaniel Hawthorne shows how this beautiful woman, with a birth mark that some would say was a "charm," was destroyed by this literalist, this empiricist monster, Aylmer. Beauty was destroyed for the passion of perfection. (Peter Stobaugh)

F. This story is an *allegory*. What moral quality is represented by Aylmer? By Georgiana? Aminadab? In a two-page essay, describe how Hawthorne sets up this allegory.

ANSWER: *Well intentioned but misplaced rationalism. He is the scientist, the empiricist.* By Georgiana? *Romanticism.* Aminadab? *Cautious rationalism.*

BIBLICAL APPLICATION

Pretend you are Aylmer's pastor. He has come to you to seek advice about his wife's physical flaw. How do you respond?

ENRICHMENT

A. Compare the theme(s) of this short story with the theme(s) of Mary Shelley's *Frankenstein*.

ANSWER: *Dr. Frankenstein sought to create perfect life, and he created a monster. Alymer could not accept limits on his science, and he killed the person he most loved. Both were betrayed by their modern tendencies to worship science/rationalism—a typical Romantic theme of both Shelley and Hawthorne.*

B. Compare and contrast Aylmer and Chillingsworth (*The Scarlet Letter*).

ANSWER: *Both Aylmer and Chillingsworth are anti-romantics, rationalists, scientists. They are men who accomplish their tasks by thought, science, and the objective. They reject something that cannot be analyzed, measured, or, most of all, duplicated. Aylmer cannot accept his "flawed" wife, and likewise, Chillingsworth cannot accept his "flawed" wife.*

C. One of the places that science has failed us is in the area of the origins of man. Phillip E. Johnson in his book *Darwin on Trial*, skillfully argues that Evolution—specifically natural selection—is a tautology. A tautology is a way of saying the same thing twice. Natural selection predicts that the fittest organisms will produce the most offspring, and it defines the fittest organisms as the ones that produce the most offspring! Can you find other tautologies in modern science?

ANSWER: *Either it will rain tomorrow or it will not rain tomorrow (American Heritage Dictionary).*

FINAL PROJECT

Students should correct and rewrite all essays and place them in their Final Portfolio.

LESSON 8 TEST

OBJECTIVE QUESTIONS. (25 POINTS)

_____ 1. In the first chapter, the image that suggests a moral symbol is the. (A) rusty church steeple. (B) angry dog barking at Pearl. (C) rose beside the door. (D) bearded man.

_____ 2. Hester continues to live in her community after she is shunned because she (A) wants to purge her sin by doing public penance. (B) wishes to bring revenge on Dimmesdale. (C) hopes that her husband will forgive her. (D) cannot afford to leave.

_____ 3. Chillingsworth's suspicion of the cause of Dimmesdale's illness is verified by (A) a conversation with another congregant. (B) pulling back the sleeping minister's bed clothes. (C) a conversation he hears between Hester and the minister. (D) finding the minister's secret diary.

_____ 4. Hester's feeling toward Mistress Hibbins is that of (A) anger. (B) indifference. (C) deep love. (D) mild pity.

_____ 5. Symbolically, the appearance of the meteor during the night Arthur Dimmesdale is on the scaffold (A) lights his soul as well as the night sky. (B) confirms Dimmesdale's hypocrisy and guilt. (C) vindicates Chillingsworth's position. (D) enables Prynne to forgive herself.

IDENTIFICATION (10 POINTS)

Which themes appeared in what writings?

Theme	The Scarlet Letter	Birthmark
Alienation		
Science vs. Romanticism		
Allegory		
Unforgiveness		
Individual vs. Society		
Problem of Guilt		
Fate vs. Free Will		
Pride		
Hypocrisy		

DISCUSSION QUESTIONS (40 POINTS)

A. What is the purpose of the introductory chapter "The Custom House" in Hawthorne's _The Scarlet Letter_?

B. Discuss Pearl's role in _The Scarlet Letter_.

C. _The Scarlet Letter_ is a battleground between two worldviews: Christian Theism (Puritanism) and Romanticism. Give examples of both worldviews in this novel.

D. What is the significance of the following passages:

This rose-bush, by a strange chance, has been kept alive in history; but whether it had merely survived out of the stern old wilderness, so long after the fall of the gigantic pines and oaks that originally overshadowed it, or whether, as there is far authority for believing, it had sprung up under the footsteps of the sainted Ann Hutchinson as she entered the prison-door, we shall not take upon us to determine. Finding it so directly on the threshold of our narrative, which is now about to issue from that inauspicious portal, we could hardly do otherwise than pluck one of its flowers, and present it to the reader. It may serve, let us hope, to symbolize some sweet moral blossom that may be found along the track, or relieve the darkening close of a tale of human frailty and sorrow . . . Ch. 1.

We have as yet hardly spoken of the infant, that little creature, whose innocent life had sprung, by the inscrutable decree of Providence, a lovely and immortal flower, out of the rank luxuriance of a guilty passion. How strange it seemed to the sad woman, as she watched the growth, and the beauty that became every day more brilliant, and the intelligence that threw its quivering sunshine over the tiny features of this child! Her Pearl—for so had Hester called her; not as a name expressive of her aspect, which had nothing of the calm, white, unimpassioned lustre that would be indicated by the comparison. But she named the infant "Pearl," as being of great price—purchased with all she had—her mother's only treasure! How strange, indeed! Man had marked this woman's sin by a scarlet letter, which had such potent and disastrous efficacy that no human sympathy could reach her, save it were sinful like herself. God, as a direct consequence of the sin which man thus punished, had given her a lovely child, whose place was on that same dishonoured bosom, to connect her parent for ever with the race and descent of mortals, and to be finally a blessed soul in heaven! Yet these thoughts affected Hester Prynne less with hope than apprehension. She knew that her deed had been evil; she could have no faith, therefore, that its result would be good. Day after day she looked fearfully into the child's expanding nature, ever dreading to detect some dark and wild peculiarity that should correspond with the guiltiness to which she owed her being. (Ch. 6)

E. In this passage, Dimmesdale visits the platform where Hester stood at the beginning of the novel. "Why, then, had he come hither?"

It was an obscure night in early May. An unwearied pall of cloud muffled the whole expanse of sky from zenith to horizon. If the same multitude which had stood as eye-witnesses while Hester Prynne sustained her punishment could now have been summoned forth, they would have discerned no face above the platform nor hardly the outline of a human shape, in the dark grey of the midnight. But the town was all asleep. There was no peril of discovery. The minister might stand there, if it so pleased him, until morning should redden in the east, without other risk than that the dank and chill night air would creep into his frame, and stiffen his joints with rheumatism, and clog his throat with catarrh and cough; thereby defrauding the expectant audience of to-morrow's prayer and sermon. No eye could see him, save that ever-wakeful one which had seen him in his closet, wielding the bloody scourge. Why, then, had he come hither? (Ch. 12)

ESSAY QUESTIONS (15 POINTS)

The following are quotes from critics about *The Scarlet Letter*. Paraphrase each criticism and agree or disagree with each one.

A. The personages in it with whom the reader will interest himself are four—the husband, the minister who has been the sinful lover, the woman, and the child. The reader is expected to sympathize only with the woman—and will sympathize only with her. The husband, an old man who has knowingly married a young woman who did not love him, is a personification of that feeling of injury which is supposed to fall upon a man when his honor has been stained by the falseness of a wife. He has left her and has wandered away, not even telling her of his whereabouts. He comes back to her without a sign. The author tells us that he had looked to find his happiness in her solicitude and care for him.

The reader, however, gives him credit for no love. But the woman was his wife, and he comes back and finds that she had gone astray. Her he despises, and is content to leave her to the ascetic cruelty of the town magistrates; but to find the man out and bring the man to his grave by slow torture is enough of employment for what is left to him of life and energy. (1879)

B. Above all it is Hester Prynne whose passion and beauty dominate every other person, and color each event. Hawthorne has conceived her as he has conceived his scene, in the full strength of his feeling for ancient New England. He is the Homer of that New England, and Hester is its most heroic creature. Tall, with dark and abundant hair and deep black eyes, a rich complexion that makes modern women (says Hawthorne) pale and thin by comparison, and a dignity that throws into low relief the "delicate, evanescent, and indescribable grace" by which gentility in girls has since come to be known, from the very first—and we believe it—she is said to cast a spell over those who behold her. (Martin Van Doren, 1949)

C. "The Custom House" throws light on a theme in *The Scarlet Letter* which is easily overlooked amid the ethical concerns of the book. Every character, in effect, re-enacts "The Custom House" scene in which Hawthorne himself contemplated the letter, so that the entire "romance" becomes a kind of exposition on the nature of symbolic perception. Hawthorne's subject is not only the meaning of adultery but also meaning in general; not only what the focal symbol means but also how it gains significance. (Charles Feidelson, Jr., 1953)

D. Hawthorne was morally, in an appreciative degree, a chip off the old block. His forefathers crossed the Atlantic for conscience sake, and it was the idea of the urgent conscience that haunted the imagination of their so-called degenerate successor. The Puritan strain in his blood ran clear—there are passages in his diaries, kept during his residence in Europe, which might almost have been written by the grimmest of the old Salem worthies. (Henry James, 1879)

E. In *The Scarlet Letter*, passion justifies nothing, while its denial justifies all. The fallen Eden of this world remains fallen; but the sinful priest purges himself

by public confession, becomes worthy of his sole
remaining way to salvation, death. Even Hester,
though sin and suffering have made her an almost
magical figure, a polluted but still terrible goddess,
must finally accept loneliness and self-restraint
instead of the love and freedom she dreamed. . .
(Leslie A. Fiedler, 1968)

LESSON 8 TEST ANSWERS

OBJECTIVE QUESTIONS (25 POINTS)

1. __C__
2. __A__
3. __B__
4. __D__
5. __A__

IDENTIFICATION (10 POINTS)

Which themes appeared in what writings?

Theme	*The Scarlet Letter*	*Birthmark*
Alienation	Yes	No
Science vs. Romanticism	Yes	Yes
Allegory	Yes	Yes
Unforgiveness	Yes	No
Individual vs. Society	Yes	No
Problem of Guilt	Yes	No
Fate vs. Free Will	Yes	Yes
Pride	Yes	Yes
Hypocrisy	Yes	Yes

DISCUSSION QUESTIONS (50 POINTS)

A. What is the purpose of the introductory chapter "The Custom House" in Hawthorne's *The Scarlet Letter*?

ANSWER: *There is some debate about that. Some critics argue that it is supercilious. Others insist that it is a vital door through with the reader must walk. On the surface, it is the place where the author discovers the story that is related in* The Scarlet Letter.

B. Discuss Pearl's role in *The Scarlet Letter*.

ANSWER: *Pearl's role is also much debated. Is she Hester's alter-ego? Is she the "wild side" of Hester kept under control by Puritan laws? In any event, Pearl is the quintessential foil.*

C. *The Scarlet Letter* is a battleground between two worldviews: Christian Theism (Puritanism) and Romanticism. Give examples of both worldviews in this novel.

ANSWER: *The community is a place of laws, order, and safety (Puritanism). Nature, while it is appealing and beautiful, is dangerous because it is outside the laws of man (Romanticism). Stylistically it is a Romantic novel—Hawthorne describes an aberration vs. ordinary events (Realism). The worldview, however, is clearly Christian theism.*

D. What is the significance of the following passages:

This rose-bush, by a strange chance, has been kept alive in history; but whether it had merely survived out of the stern old wilderness, so long after the fall of the gigantic pines and oaks that originally overshadowed it, or whether, as there is far authority for believing, it had sprung up under the footsteps of the sainted Ann Hutchinson as she entered the prison-door, we shall not take upon us to determine. Finding it so directly on the threshold of our narrative, which is now about to issue from that inauspicious portal, we could hardly do otherwise than pluck one of its flowers, and present it to the reader. It may serve, let us hope, to symbolize some sweet moral blossom that may be found along the track, or relieve the darkening close of a tale of human frailty and sorrow . . . Ch. 1.

ANSWER: *This of course is the famous scene in which the present events are tied symbolically to the Puritan past. Hester stands with the scarlet A that ties her to the rose planted by the Puritans. Both symbols imply life and hope.*

We have as yet hardly spoken of the infant, that little creature, whose innocent life had sprung, by the inscrutable decree of Providence, a lovely and immortal flower, out of the rank luxuriance of a guilty passion. How strange it seemed to the sad woman, as she watched the growth, and the beauty that became every day more brilliant, and the intelligence that threw its quivering sunshine over the tiny features of this child! Her Pearl—for so had Hester called her; not as a name expressive of her aspect, which had nothing of the calm, white, unimpassioned lustre that would be indicated by the comparison. But she named the infant "Pearl," as being of great price—purchased with all she had—her mother's only treasure! How strange, indeed! Man had marked this woman's sin by a scarlet letter, which had such potent and disastrous efficacy that no human sympathy could reach her, save it were sinful like herself. God, as a direct consequence of the sin which man thus punished, had given her a lovely child, whose place was on that same dishonoured bosom, to connect her parent for ever with the race and descent of mortals, and to be finally a blessed soul in heaven! Yet these thoughts affected Hester Prynne less with hope than apprehension. She knew that her deed had been evil; she could have no faith, therefore, that its result would be good. Day after day she looked fearfully into the child's expanding nature, ever dreading to detect some dark and wild peculiarity that should correspond with the guiltiness to which she owed her being. (Ch. 6)

ANSWER: *This is the scene in which Pearl is introduced. She is an enigma. On one hand, she is wildly beautiful, but she lies outside the bounds of Puritan society. See comments above.*

E. In this passage, Dimmesdale visits the platform where Hester stood at the beginning of the novel. "Why, then, had he come hither?"

It was an obscure night in early May. An unwearied pall of cloud muffled the whole expanse of sky from zenith to horizon. If the same multitude which had stood as eye-witnesses while Hester Prynne sustained her punishment could now have been summoned forth, they would have discerned no face above the platform nor hardly the outline of a human shape, in the dark grey of the midnight. But the town was all asleep. There was no peril of discovery. The minister might stand there, if it so pleased him, until morning should redden in the east, without other risk than that the dank and chill night air would creep into his frame, and stiffen his joints with rheumatism, and clog his throat with catarrh and cough; thereby defrauding the expectant audience of to-morrow's prayer and sermon. No eye could see him, save that ever-wakeful one which had seen him in his closet, wielding the bloody scourge. Why, then, had he come hither? (Ch. 12)

ANSWER: *He futilely tried to atone for his sins privately.*

ESSAY QUESTIONS (15 POINTS)

The following are quotes from critics about *The Scarlet Letter.* Paraphrase each criticism and agree or disagree with each one.

A. ANSWER: *First, Hawthorne does not "pity" Hester. He respects and honors her. She is the person of integrity and honor—not desirous of pity. She deserves none—she is redeemed by her walk with God. Secondly, Chillingsworth, full of unforgiveness is neither a victim nor a hero. He is despicable. He could have forgiven his wife and had her as his wife again—but chose to participate in evil machinations and rejected her.*

B. ANSWER: *This is accurate.*

C. ANSWER: *Intriguing idea, but perhaps this critic is making too much of the custom house since Hawthorne only mentions it in the beginning of the novel and never again.*

D. ANSWER: *A bit harsh, this critic nonetheless is correct in saying that Hawthorne advanced Puritan/Christian Theist values.*

E. ANSWER: *He is right on target with Dimmesdale but misses Hester all together. In fact, she is happy, and more than that. She experiences the pleasure of living a Christian Theistic life.*

LESSON 9

ROMANTICISM: NEW ENGLAND RENAISSANCE, *1840-1855* (Part 2)

Readings Due For This Lesson: Students should review poems by Henry Wadsworth Longfellow, Oliver Wendell Holmes, James Russell Lowell, John Greenleaf Whittier, and Emily Dickinson. What moral vision do these poets present?

Reading Ahead: Reading ahead: Students should review poems by Ralph Waldo Emerson. In what ways are Emerson's poems religious?

Goal: Students will analyze poems by Henry Wadsworth Longfellow, Oliver Wendell Holmes, James Russell Lowell, John Greenleaf Whittier, and Emily Dickinson. What moral vision do these poets present?

Goals/Objectives: What is the purpose of this lesson?	Strategies to meet these goals: How will I obtain these goals/objectives?	Evaluation: How will I know when I have met these goals/objectives?
Students will understand the concept of Romanticism. (cognitive goal)	Students will write an essay on this topic: Find examples of Romanticism in each poem. (Critical Thinking A)	Students, with minimal errors, will clearly answer the assigned question in a 1-2 page essay.
Students will increase their vocabulary. (cognitive goal)	Students will collect at least five new vocabulary words from their reading and use these words in their essays. They will also define the words provided in this lesson and use them in essays and in conversation.	Students will use five vocabulary words in conversation during the week as well as use the words in their essays and in conversation.
Students will understand the concept of satire (cognitive goal)	Students will write an essay on this topic: Give an example of satire in "The Biglow Papers" and discuss its purpose. (Critical Thinking B)	Students, with minimal errors, will clearly answer the assigned question in a 1-2 page essay.
Students will exhibit higher-level thinking by discussing Holmes' view of heaven. (cognitive goal)	Students will write an essay on this topic: What is Holmes' view of heaven? (Critical Thinking C)	Students, with minimal errors, will clearly answer the assigned question in a 1-2 page essay.

Goals/Objectives: What is the purpose of this lesson?	Strategies to meet these goals: How will I obtain these goals/objectives?	Evaluation: How will I know when I have met these goals/ objectives?
Students will exhibit higher-level thinking as they discuss their opinions of Longfellow's poetry (cognitive goal)	Students will write an essay on this topic: Longfellow was popular among ordinary people but mostly criticized by scholars. People loved the very thing that critics disliked: the predictable narrative enclosed in tiresome rimes. Agree or disagree with the critics. (Critical Thinking D)	Students, with minimal errors, will clearly answer the assigned question in a 1-2 page essay.
Students will exhibit higher-level thinking as they discuss why Dickinson's poetry is modern. (cognitive goal)	Students will write an essay on this topic: What is so modern about Dickinson's poetry? (Critical Thinking E)	Students, with minimal errors, will clearly answer the assigned question in a 1-2 page essay.
Students will work in a group setting. (behavioral goal)	In a class, in a co-op experience, or during a family discussion, students will answer this question: Which of the assigned poets is my favorite? Why?	Students will exhibit practical listening skills and will manifest understanding of opposing worldviews.
Students will be able to recall the information taught in the lesson. (cognitive goal)	Lesson 9 Test	Students will take the test at the end of this lesson and score at least 80%.
Students will experience reflective writing. (affective/spiritual goal)	Using the Journal Guide Questions in the Appendices, students will record at least three entries this week. Suggested Scriptures: 1 Samuel	Students will show evidence that they have reflected on this issue, including informed discussions and written responses.

SUGGESTED
Weekly *Implementation*

DAY 1	DAY 2	DAY 3	DAY 4	DAY 5
Prayer journal. Students review the required reading(s) before the assigned lesson begins. Teacher may want to discuss assigned reading(s) with students. Teacher and students will decide on the number of essays required for this lesson, choosing two or three essays. The rest of the essays can be outlined, answered with shorter answers, or skipped. Students will review all readings for Lesson 9.	**Prayer journal.** Student should review reading(s) from next lesson. Student should outline essays due at the end of the week. Per teacher instructions, students may answer orally in a group setting some of the essays that are not assigned as formal essays.	**Prayer journal.** Students should write rough drafts of all assigned essays. The teacher or a peer evaluator may correct rough drafts.	**Prayer journal.** Student will re-write corrected copies of essays due tomorrow.	**Prayer journal.** Essays are due. Students should take the Lesson 9 test. Reading ahead: Students should review: Poems by Ralph Waldo Emerson. Guide: In what ways are Emerson's poems religious?

Note: References to sources are in student edition.

ENRICHMENT ACTIVITIES/PROJECTS
Students should memorize a poem by each poet.

SUPPLEMENTAL RESOURCES
Buell, Lawrence. (Editor), *Ralph Waldo Emerson: A Collection of Critical Essays.*

A great overview of scholarship surrounding Emerson's works.

Buranelli, Vincent. *Edgar A. Poe.*
   A readable and scholarly study of Poe's life and works.

Gorman, Herbert S. *A Victorian American.*
   An intriguing study on Henry W. Longfellow.

Habegger, Alfred. *My Wars Are Laid Away in Books: The Life of Emily Dickinson.*

Even though Habegger makes too much of Emily Dickinson's feminism (she was not a feminist at all) his biography of Dickinson is one of the best on the market.

Howe, Susan. *My Emily Dickinson.*
A poet's bird's-eye view of the very elusive Emily Dickinson.

Hutchison, William R. *The Transcendentalist Ministers; Church Reform in the New England Renaissance.*
A Harvard professor highly knowledgeable about the Transcendentalists.

Meltzer, Milton. *Walt Whitman: A Biography.*

Tharp, Louise Hall. *The Peabody Sisters of Salem.*
The Peabody sisters had a profound impact on America through their influence on the Alcott sisters and N. Hawthorne.

Notes:

CRITICAL THINKING

A. Find examples of Romanticism in each poem.

ANSWER: *All the poems, in one way or another, celebrate nature. Every one of them has metaphors and images that celebrate nature. An exception would be the poem by Lowell which is more political satire than anything else.*

B. Give an example of satire in "The Biglow Papers" and discuss its purpose.

ANSWER: *"it's a marcy we've gut folks to tell us/the rights an' the wrongs o' these matters" is a satirical comment (and also a Romantic comment which celebrates subjectivity and personal choice). www.bartleby.com*

C. What is Holmes' view of heaven?

ANSWER: *A higher consciousness—"Leave thy low-vaulted past!/Let each new temple, nobler than the last,/Shut thee from heaven with a dome more vast,/Till thou at length art free,/Leaving thine outgrown shell by life's unresting sea!" www.bartleby.com*

D. Longfellow was popular among ordinary people but negatively criticized by scholars. People loved the very thing that critics disliked: the predictable narrative enclosed in tiresome rimes. Agree or disagree with the critics.

ANSWER: *Answers will vary but this reader agrees with the critics.*

E. What is so modern about Dickinson's poetry?

ANSWER: *In form it is free verse. It explores the interior life—like most Romantic poetry—but she also treats her subjects as individuals and she is always concerned about the present—not the future. These are decidedly modern approaches.*

FINAL PROJECT
Students should correct and rewrite all essays and place them in their Final Portfolio.

LESSON 9 TEST

DISCUSSION QUESTION (100 POINTS)

Paraphrase "A Psalm of Life" and explain why you agree or disagree with its worldview. What are Longfellow's favorite words and metaphors?

The Psalm of Life
Henry Wadsworth Longfellow

Tell me not, in mournful numbers,
Life is but an empty dream!
For the soul is dead that slumbers,
And things are not what they seem.

Life is real! Life is earnest!
And the grave is not its goal;
Dust thou art, to dust returnest,
Was not spoken of the soul.

Not enjoyment, and not sorrow,
Is our destined end or way;
But to act, that each tomorrow
Find us farther than today.

Art is long, and Time is fleeting,
And our hearts, though stout and brave,
Still, like muffled drums, are beating
Funeral marches to the grave.

In the world's broad field of battle,
In the bivouac of Life,
Be not dumb, driven cattle!
Be a hero in the strife!

Trust no Future, howe'er pleasant!
Let the dead Past bury its dead!
Act,—act in the living Present!
Heart within, and God o'erhead!

Lives of great men all remind us
We can make our lives sublime,
And, departing, leave behind us
Footprints on the sands of time;

Footprints, that perhaps another,
Sailing o'er life's solemn main,
A forlorn and shipwrecked brother,
Seeing, shall take heart again.

Let us, then, be up and doing,
With a heart for any fate;
Still achieving, still pursuing,
Learn to labor and to wait.
www.bartleby.com

LESSON 9 TEST ANSWERS

DISCUSSION QUESTIONS (100 POINTS)

Paraphrase "A Psalm of Life" and explain why you agree or disagree with its worldview.

What are Longfellow's favorite words and metaphors?

ANSWER: *This poem is a typical Romantic response to life. It invites the reader to make the most of time—carpe diem—addressing neither the consequences nor the after life. Certainly the poem has merit, but ultimately it falls short in its quest for eternal meaning to life. Longfellow's favorite metaphor is sand on a beach washed by the ocean of time.*

LESSON 10

ROMANTICISM: NEW ENGLAND RENAISSANCE, *1840-1855* (*Part 3*)

Readings Due For This Lesson: Students should review poems by Ralph Waldo Emerson.

Reading Ahead: Students should review *Walden*, Henry David Thoreau. Is this novel a charming reflection on nature or a vitriolic diatribe against the Protestant ethic?

Goal: Students will analyze poems by Ralph Waldo Emerson.

Goals/Objectives: What is the purpose of this lesson?	Strategies to meet these goals: How will I obtain these goals/objectives?	Evaluation: How will I know when I have met these goals/objectives?
Students will understand the concept of Transcendentalism and the effect it had on American thought. (cognitive goal) Students will review how to write a report. (cognitive goal)	Students will write a report on Transcendentalism and the effect it had on American thought. (Critical Thinking A)	Students, with minimal errors, will clearly answer the assigned question in a 1-2 page report.
Students will increase their vocabulary. (cognitive goal)	Students will collect at least five new vocabulary words from their reading and use these words in their essays.	Students will use five vocabulary words in conversation during the week as well as use the words in their essays.
Students will exhibit higher level thinking as they explain why Romanticism/ Transcendentalism flourished in America during the 1960s, as it did in the 1830s. (cognitive goal) Students will review how to write a comparison essay. (cognitive goal)	Students will explain why Romanticism/ Transcendentalism flourished in America during the 1960s, as it did in the 1830s. (Literary Criticism B)	Students, with minimal errors, will clearly answer the assigned question in a 1-2 page essay.
Students will exhibit higher level thinking as they analyze a poem by R. Waldo Emerson. (cognitive goal)	Students will write an essay on this topic: The last six lines of "The Snowstorm" contain a description of the events of the next morning.	Students, with minimal errors, will clearly answer the assigned question in a 1-2 page essay.

Goals/Objectives: What is the purpose of this lesson?	Strategies to meet these goals: How will I obtain these goals/objectives?	Evaluation: How will I know when I have met these goals/objectives?
	What is Emerson saying? What is his worldview? Which does the author consider the true artist? Support your conclusions with references from the poem. (Enrichment A)	
Students will write an essay on this topic: In Emerson's poem "Day," why is the day scornful? (cognitive goal) Students will exhibit higher thinking—specifically analytical skills—as they write an essay explaining the scorn at whom the poem "Day" is directed. (cognitive goal)	Students will write an essay on this topic: In Emerson's poem "Day," why is the day scornful? Write an essay explaining at whom the scorn is directed. (Enrichment B)	Students, with minimal errors, will clearly answer the assigned question in a 1-2 page essay.
Students will exhibit higher level thinking as they answer this question: Based on "The Rhodora," what is Emerson's idea of a god. (cognitive goal) Students will consider the generalization that someone can be religious without being a Christian theist. (affective goal) Students will be able to discern spirituality that is not Christ-centered. (affective goal)	Students will write an essay on this topic: Based on "The Rhodora," what is Emerson's idea of a god? (Enrichment C)	Students, with minimal errors, will clearly answer the assigned question in a 1-2 page essay.
Students will find evidences of Transcendentalism in the enclosed poems. (cognitive goal) Students will exhibit higher thinking—specifically analysis skills. (cognitive goal)	Students will write an essay on this topic: Give several evidences of Transcendentalism from these poems. Defend your answer in a 2 page essay. (Enrichment D)	Students, with minimal errors, will clearly answer the assigned question in a 2 page essay.
Students will exhibit higher level thinking as they compare the poetry of Ralph Waldo Emerson with that of another New England poet, Anne Bradstreet. (cognitive goal)	Students will write an essay on this topic: Compare the poetry of Ralph Waldo Emerson with that of another New England poet, Anne Bradstreet. (Enrichment E)	Students, with minimal errors, will clearly answer the assigned question in a 1-2 page essay.

Goals/Objectives: What is the purpose of this lesson?	Strategies to meet these goals: How will I obtain these goals/objectives?	Evaluation: How will I know when I have met these goals/objectives?
Students will exhibit higher level thinking skills as they read four or five essays that Emerson wrote and compare and contrast the themes of these essays with his poetry. (cognitive goal)	Students will exhibit higher thinking—specifically comparison/contrast evaluation skills. (cognitive goal) Students will write an essay on this topic: Read four or five essays that Emerson wrote and compare and contrast the themes of these essays with his poetry. (Enrichment F)	Students, with minimal errors, will clearly answer the assigned question in a 1-2 page essay.
Students will consider the generalization that Puritanism had a permanent, ameliorating effect on American culture. (affective goal) Students will write a higher critical thinking paper evaluating the demise of this culture's impact on American culture. (cognitive goal)	Students will answer this question: Puritans saw the world in terms of individual sin and of principalities and powers. They saw themselves as being part of a larger, more important cosmological story. They knew, without a doubt, that every knee would bow, every tongue confess. With the rise of Lockian. (i.e., John Locke) rationalism and its emphasis on individual rights, supported so vigorously by such men as Thomas Jefferson, Americans privatized their faith and morality. Morality was defined according to each individual preference and Americans avoided static moral biblical structures. For the first time in American thought, man's agendas were more important than the Word of God. Theism was still everywhere present in America, but for the first time morality was loosed from its biblical moorings—with disastrous results. Agree or disagree with this assessment. (Biblical Application A)	Students, with minimal errors, will clearly answer the assigned question in a 1-2 page essay.
Students will exhibit higher level thinking skills as they write an essay on this topic: At the same time that Emerson was writing, the well-attended revivals led by Charles Finney were being held in upstate New York. In fact, this revival had a greater impact than Emerson's essays and poetry on American society. (cognitive goal)	Students will answer this question: At the same time that Emerson was writing, the well-attended revivals led by Charles Finney were being held in upstate New York. In fact, this revival had a greater impact than Emerson's essays and poetry on American society. Write a 1 page *report* on this revival. (Biblical Application B)	Students, with minimal errors, will clearly answer the assigned question in a 1 page *report*.

127

Goals/Objectives: What is the purpose of this lesson?	Strategies to meet these goals: How will I obtain these goals/objectives?	Evaluation: How will I know when I have met these goals/objectives?
Students will exhibit higher level thinking as they write an essay discussing the demise of Puritanism and the effect of this demise on American culture. (cognitive essay)	Students will write an essay on this topic: Transcendentalism is a sad commentary on the failure of American Puritanism. By the end of the 17th Century Puritanism was declining because of a lack of conversions and disrespect for authority. As a result of this demise, American society lost a strong sense of community. Agree or disagree with this statement in an essay and offer evidence to support your answer. (Biblical Application C)	Students, with minimal errors, will clearly answer the assigned question in a 1-2 page essay.
Students will exhibit higher level thinking as they analyze Emersonian thought in light of Christian Theism. (cognitive goal)	In what way is the following statement about Jesus by the Transcendentalist/ Romantic Emerson inconsistent with a Christian theistic world view? "An immense progress in natural and religious knowledge has been made since his death. Even his genius cannot quicken all that stark nonsense about the blessed and the damned. Yet in the 'Life of Christ' I have thought him a Christian Plato; so rich and great was his philosophy. Is it possible the intellect should be so inconsistent with itself? It is singular also that the bishop's morality should sometimes trip, as in his explanation of false witness." (Biblical Application D)	Students, with minimal errors, will clearly answer the assigned question in a 1-2 page essay.
Students will exhibit higher level thinking as they refute Emerson's worldview by advancing the truth as they find it in the Bible. (cognitive/affective goal) Students will articulate their own faith statement based on the Word of God (affective goal)	Students will refute Emerson's worldview by advancing the truth as they find it in the Bible. (Biblical Application E)	Students, with minimal errors, will clearly answer the assigned question in a 1-2 page essay.
Students will exhibit higher-level thinking as they find instances in the Bible where Nature is controlled by God (cognitive goal)	Students will write an essay on this topic: Find instances in the Bible where Nature is controlled by God. (Biblical Application F)	Students, with minimal errors, will clearly answer the assigned question in a 1-2 page essay.

Goals/Objectives: What is the purpose of this lesson?	Strategies to meet these goals: How will I obtain these goals/objectives?	Evaluation: How will I know when I have met these goals/objectives?
Students will work in a group setting. (behavioral goal)	In a class, in a co-op experience, or during a family discussion, students will answer this question: What remains of Puritanism in American culture today?	Students will exhibit practical listening skills and will manifest understanding of opposing worldviews.
Students will be able to recall the information taught in the lesson. (cognitive goal)	Lesson 10 Test	Students will take the test at the end of this lesson and score at least 80%.
Students will experience reflective writing. (affective/spiritual goal)	Using the Journal Guide Questions in the Appendices, students will record at least three entries this week. Suggested Scriptures: Gals 2-3	Students will show evidence that they have reflected on this issue, including informed discussions and written responses.

SUGGESTED
Weekly *Implementation*

DAY 1	DAY 2	DAY 3	DAY 4	DAY 5
Prayer journal.	**Prayer journal.**	**Prayer journal.**	**Prayer journal.**	**Prayer journal.**
Students review the required reading(s) before the assigned lesson begins.	Student should review reading(s) from next lesson.	Students should write rough drafts of all assigned essays.	Student will re-write corrected copies of essays due tomorrow.	Essays are due.
Teacher may want to discuss assigned reading(s) with students.	Student should outline essays due at the end of the week.	The teacher and/or a peer evaluator may correct rough drafts.		Students should take the Lesson 10 test.
Teacher and students will decide on the required essays for this lesson, choosing two or three essays. The rest of the essays can be outlined, answered with shorter answers, or skipped.	Per teacher instructions, students may answer orally in a group setting some of the essays that are not assigned as formal essays.			Reading ahead: Students should review *Walden*, Henry David Thoreau.
Students will review all readings for Lesson 10.				Guide: Is this novel a charming reflection on nature or a vitriolic diatribe against the Protestant ethic?

Note: References to sources are in student edition.

ENRICHMENT ACTIVITIES/PROJECTS

For a whole week, the family should pretend that they are a Puritan family. What will they do for entertainment?

Write a report on Puritanism from the perspective of Roger Williams and Anne Hutchinson.

SUPPLEMENTAL RESOURCES

Buell, Lawrence (Editor). *Ralph Waldo Emerson: A Collection of Critical Essays.*
A great overview of scholarship surrounding Emerson's works.

Hutchison, William R. *The Transcendentalist Ministers; Church Reform in the New England Renaissance.*
Written by a Harvard professor very knowledgeable about Transcendentalists.

Notes:

CRITICAL THINKING

A. Research Transcendentalism and the effect it had on American thought.

   ANSWER: *Themes of Transcendentalism that should be*

identified include: absence of an omnipotent God; omniscient nature. The concept of a ubiquitous fate is absent; contrast this with the Greek concept of fate. Nature is venerated, if not worshiped. Subjectivity is celebrated—empiricism is suspect. Transcendentalism was a major crack in the Theistic vision that was, until Emerson, endemic to the American ethos. For the first time there was a worldview that invited men and women to follow their "feelings" and "intuition." In other words, to use Old Testament language, they felt justified in doing what was right in their own eyes.

B. Explain why Romanticism/Transcendentalism flourished in America during the 1960s, as it did in the 1830s.

ANSWER: *In both eras subjectivity and individualism were celebrated, almost worshipped. The notion that the world could be perfect, if mankind were left to its own devices, was supreme. So, people in both eras flocked to utopian communities, and they celebrated nature as some sort of ubiquitous entity.*

C. The last six lines of "The Snowstorm" contain a description of the events of the next morning. What is Emerson saying? What is his worldview? Which does the author consider the true artist? Support your conclusions with references from the poem.

ANSWER: *The last six lines are: "And when his hours are numbered, and the world/Is all his own, retiring, as he were not,/Leaves, when the sun appears, astonished Art/To mimic in slow structures, stone by stone,/Built in an age, the mad wind's night-work,/The frolic architecture of the snow." The snowstorm is over. All creation is at rest. This scene evokes the same sobriety of the creation scene in Genesis 1. As God rested in Genesis 1, nature rests at the end of "The Snowstorm." Likewise, it was good—"The frolic architecture of the snow." Emerson is saying that the world is good, that God is good, and that man is good—so long as he behaves himself and does not intrude on nature's handiwork. The true artist is a mindless, benevolent deity called nature. Gone are the central tenants of Theism: an omnipotent, loving God, who created man in His own image. In Theism, mankind is not an anemic version of creation, to be placed next to, or behind, the perfection of nature. Man is the ruler of, and is separate from, nature. Nature to the Romantic is beautiful and inviting. To the Theist, God's order, His Word, and His Son Jesus Christ are beautiful and inviting. To Emerson, nature is the true artist. To the Theist, God of the Old and New Testament is the artist.*

D. In Emerson's poem "Days," why is the day scornful? Write an essay explaining at whom the scorn is directed.

ANSWER: *To the Transcendentalist time is the problem. Romanticism is able to address such issues as the human soul, human life, and even human morality. However, Romanticism is quite weak in its discussion about death. Romanticism has no convincing answer to the question, "What happens to human beings when they die?" That is where the Christian Theistic worldview is vastly superior.*

E. Based on "The Rhodora," what is Emerson's idea of a god? Emerson could not accept the idea of a God separate from man and nature; in other words, Emerson was not a Christian believer. Yet, in his own way, he was a deeply religious person. How is this revealed in the last four lines of the poem? Using the poems "The Snow Storm" and "Days" and other Emerson writings, show how Emerson was "religious."

ANSWER: *Emerson was religious in that he fervently believed in transcendent truth, but he was unwilling to put a specific name or classification on that truth. That meant very little to the American society that Emerson knew. In fact, at the time Emerson was writing, the great Charles Finney revival was spreading across upstate New York. America still basically embraced Judeo-Christian values. Transcendentalism was an aberration in the middle of the 19th century; it became the order of the day in the 20th century. Finney spoke to more folks and brought more social change in one city than Emerson did through his whole career.*

ENRICHMENT

A. Give several evidences of Transcendentalism from these poems. Defend your answer in a two page essay.

ANSWER: *The image of nature having a powerful presence and the celebration of the human spirit exemplifies Transcendentalism. The celebration of human subjectivity is advanced in every poem. Truth is uncovered by observing a snowstorm—not by reading the Word of God. Finally, man is equal—not superior—to nature: "Why thou wert there, O rival of the rose!/I never thought to ask, I never knew./But, in my simple ignorance, suppose/The self-same Power that brought me there brought you."*

B. Compare the poetry of Ralph Waldo Emerson with that of another New England poet, Anne Bradstreet.

ANSWER: *Ralph Waldo Emerson, while he is obviously a gifted poet, represents a Transcendentalist position. This view is in direct contradiction to Anne Bradstreet's viewpoint, a*

Christian view of life. In Emerson's poem "The Snowstorm" the reader sees a powerful but impersonal nature. Nature seems to be alive. In verses 10-15 nature is compared to a mason. "Come see the north wind's masonry…" (vs. 10). Humankind is clearly not in control; nature is in control. There is no God in Emerson's poem or, if there is a God, he would be nature. In the poem "Days," nature is called fate. Fate is an impersonal force that seems to have no more interest in people than it would have in a rainstorm. "Daughters of Time, the hypocritic Days,/Muffled and dumb like barefoot dervishes." (vs.1-2). Nature unites people with all creatures. There seems to be no difference, for instance, between a flower—the Rhodora—and a man. "The self-same Power that brought me there brought you" (vs. 16) in "The Rhodora." There is a power outside humankind that exists to Bradstreet, but it is not impersonal. It is intimately involved with everything that happens to people. "It" is a loving God. "Shall I then praise the earth, the trees, the earth?" (section 20, vs 2). Of course Bradstreet would say no, she does not praise nature. She praises God. With the line "to My Dear and Loving Husband" she recognizes that human relationships require perseverance (vs 11). But, while pain and misery are part of life, they are not inflicted by an impersonal force like fate. They are allowed to happen by a loving God. Bradstreet feels pain, disappointment, and disaster, but she finds hope in God not in her earthly belongings or circumstances. There is no fate to Bradstreet. She believes in providence, not fate. For instance, she is not worried about her house burning down, growing old, leaving her beloved husband. She does not sentimentalize flowers or snowy days. Why? Because beautify to her is to be found in relationship with her God. Besides, temporal things have relatively no interest to her when they are compared to the future. While she may suffer now, and will experience physical death, she is nonetheless acutely aware that she will live forever with God in heaven. She is forever separated from "flowers" and "snowstorms" because she is created in the image of God. They are not. She does not need to paint pretty pictures of bad things in her life because she knows that God loves her and has great plans for her life.

In Emerson's poetry and in Bradstreet's poetry we see two entirely different worldviews. One celebrates a loving, personal God. The other reaches for meaning in nature. One is fearful of fate. The other rests in an all powerful God. In his book <u>Toward a Recovery of Christian Belief</u> (1990), Carl H. Henry tells a story that illustrates what happens when Romanticism replaces Theism as the main cultural worldview of a nation. When flying with a friend the pilot announces that their spotter had just died. "What does that mean?" Henry asked. "It means no one knows where we are," the pilot answered. "With the rise of Romanticism America lost her morals and epistemic (i.e., knowledge) moral compass bearings," Henry concludes.

BIBLICAL APPLICATION

A. Puritans saw the world in terms of individual sin and of principalities and powers. They always saw themselves as being part of a larger, more important cosmological story. They knew, without a doubt, that every knee would bow, every tongue confess. With the rise of Lockian (i.e., John Locke) rationalism and its emphasis on individual rights, supported so vigorously by such men as Thomas Jefferson, Americans privatized their faith and morality. Morality was defined according to each individual preference, and Americans avoided static moral biblical structures. For the first time in American thought, man's agendas were more important than the Word of God. Theism was still everywhere present in America, but for the first time morality was loosed from its biblical moorings—with disastrous results. *Agree or disagree with this assessment.*

ANSWER: *Answers may vary, however, this reader agrees. The Puritan era was an unprecedented era in the life of a community and has had permanent results on American history. To a large degree, the providential blessing that America enjoys is partly if not mostly due to the faith of these early setters.*

B. At the same time that Emerson was writing, the well-attended revivals led by Charles Finney were being held in upstate New York. In fact, this revival had a greater impact than Emerson's essays and poetry on American society. Write a one page *report* on this revival.

ANSWER: *Finney's upstate New York revivals were epic in proportion to Emerson's influence on America. Thousands of people committed their lives to Christ. In fact, the entire sociological structure of upstate New York was indelibly changed by Finney's revivals. His revivals became part of what was called the Second Great Awakening.*

C. Transcendentalism is a sad commentary on the failure of American Puritanism. By the end of the 17th Century, Puritanism was declining because of a lack of conversions and disrespect for authority. As a result of this demise, American society lost a strong sense of community. Some thinkers, such as sociologist Peter Berger, argue that one feature of modern America has been the loss of mediating institutions so that America is now full of increasingly atomistic individuals. This variety is maintained by a powerful state, with no buffers between government and people. Berger also argues that we Americans have lost all sense of community. Puritans rarely talked about themselves—they just lived their lives in the community of the Lord. Contemporary Americans talk about community so much because they experience it so little in their lives. The 17th and 18th Century Church ceased to be a mediating institution as it was in Puritan New England. As a result, Christianity lost credibility as a viable institution and Transcendentalism arose. *Agree or disagree with this statement in an essay and offer evidence to support your answer.*

ANSWER: *A core of moral truth is at the center of all viable civilizations. Joshua knew that when he prepared the nation of Israel to enter the Promised Land in the last chapters of Deuteronomy. He urged his nation to choose this day whom they would serve. In our nation, as we have rejected our Judeo-Christian biblical roots, that moral core has been severely eroded. The Puritan vision, which was a decidedly Christian Theistic vision, lost its pervasive influence by the 19th century in all but the most covert ways.*

D. In what way is the following statement about Jesus by the Transcendentalist/ Romantic Emerson inconsistent with a Christian Theistic worldview? "An immense progress in natural and religious knowledge has been made since his death. Even his genius cannot quicken all that stark nonsense about the blessed and the damned. Yet in the 'Life of Christ' I have thought him a Christian Plato; so rich and great was his philosophy. Is it possible the intellect should be so inconsistent with itself? It is singular also that the bishop's morality should sometimes trip, as in his explanation of false witness."

ANSWER: *Jesus Christ is not a "rationalistic, perfect man;" he is the Son of the living, most high God. The idea of a "Christian Plato" ironically, is a high compliment from the Transcendentalist Emerson. He is comparing him to the "high priest" of Transcendentalism. Plato developed the idea of the "form" or perfect idea that naturally would appeal to Emerson. However, while this reader finds Emerson's thought to be consistent, it is nonetheless wrong.*

E. Born in 1803, Emerson began his working life as a Unitarian preacher. Early widowhood plunged him into a crisis of faith (already weakened by Unitarian Universalism), and he resigned his ministry in 1832. He abandoned any semblance of Theism. In Nature alone he found comfort and direction, but Emerson had an ambivalent viewpoint towards nature. He

loved and respected Nature and considered Nature all-powerful and reverent. Emerson's faith ultimately strayed into pantheistic nature-worship. PanTheism argues that god is alive everywhere—in animate and inanimate objects alike. There is nothing new under the sun! Emerson's panTheism was very common in the Bible. In the Old Testament BAAL worship (attacked by Elijah) was very similar to Emerson's Transcendentalism. Compare and contrast the BAAL worship that such men as Joshua and Elijah fought so vigorously with the Nature worship that Transcendentalism advanced. Use the following passages as a guide for your discussion. Refute Emerson's worldview by advancing the truth as you find it in the Bible.

The texts below are from *Nature* (1836)

ANSWER:
The Lie: Direct revelation comes to man through nature.

The foregoing generations beheld God face to face; we, through their eyes. Why should not we also enjoy an original relation to the universe? Why should not we have... a religion by revelation to us, and not the history of theirs? Embosomed for a season in nature, whose floods of life stream around and through us, and invite us by the powers they supply, to action...?

The Truth: *Revelation comes to man through God; He has chosen to speak most definitively to us through the Word of God.*

The Lie: "God" exists everywhere—but especially in Nature.

One might think the atmosphere was made transparent with this design, to give man, in the heavenly bodies, the perpetual presence of the sublime... If the stars should appear one night in a thousand years, how would men believe and adore; and preserve for many generations the remembrance of the City of God which had been shown! But all natural objects make a kindred impression, when the mind is open to their influence...Nature says, he is my creature...

The Truth: *God is omniscient, but He is also omnipotent. He is not to be sentimentalized. He is to be worshiped. He is no man's creature!*

The Lie: Nature unifies us all.

A leaf, a drop, a crystal, a moment of time is related to the whole, and partakes of the perfection of the whole. Each particle is a microcosm, and faithfully renders the likeness of the world.... So intimate is this Unity, that, it is easily seen, it lies under the undermost garment of nature, and betrays its source in the Universal Spirit....

The Truth: *Man is hopelessly lost without the Lord Jesus Christ. All have sinned; all are separated from God and one another without the miraculous intervention of God. Furthermore, man is separate from animals. He has a soul and was commanded by God in the Bible to rule over the other animals. Only man is created in the image of God.*

F. Find instances in the Bible where Nature is controlled by God.

ANSWER: *Clearly God is not controlled by His creation as evidenced in the following stories: Creation, the Red Sea, Elijah on Mt. Carmel—among others. God is very much in control of all elements of His creation.*

FINAL PROJECT

Students should correct and rewrite all essays and place them in their Final Portfolio.

LESSON 10 TEST

DISCUSSION QUESTIONS. (100 POINTS)

A. Discuss the way Americans view themselves in Transcendentalism and contrast it to Puritanism. Cite several poems to argue your case.

B. Transcendentalism became, by and large, a northeastern phenomenon centered in the Boston area. It was very much an elitist movement. There were many critics of this movement. "I was given to understand that whatever was unintelligible would be certainly Transcendental," Charles Dickens wrote. Define Transcendentalism and then evaluate its credibility as a worldview.

C. In the 17th century the best histories were written by Puritan ministers who saw history as the working out of God's will. Based on the concept of the chosen people of God, America was presented as a Promised Land for God's faithful people. Later historians ridiculed this view of history. However, in a real sense, at least in Puritan New England, this was a fairly accurate appraisal of the motivations of an entire generation of early settlers. Why was it so difficult for later historians to believe that people can be motivated strictly by their faith?

D. By their own admission, New England Puritans saw themselves as being intolerant. They felt no obligation to accept in their midst worldviews that they perceived as heretical. Was this a correct way to establish an English colony?

E. Have we Evangelicals lost the fire and passion of our Puritan ancestors?

LESSON 10 TEST ANSWERS

DISCUSSION QUESTIONS. (100 POINTS)

A. Discuss the way Americans view themselves in Transcendentalism and contrast it to Puritanism. Cite several poems to argue your case.

ANSWERS: *Transcendentalists are humanists—man centered. They worship intuition and subjectivity. They are in stark contrast to the Puritans who worship and glorify God. One could choose any poem by Emerson to compare with Bradstreet.*

B. Transcendentalism became, by and large, a northeastern phenomenon centered in the Boston area. It was very much an elitist movement. There were many critics of this movement. "I was given to understand that whatever was unintelligible would be certainly Transcendental," Charles Dickens wrote. Define Transcendentalism and then evaluate its credibility as a worldview.

ANSWER: *Transcendentalists are very subjective and then somewhat vague in their pursuit of truth. This reader agrees with Dickens. The reader feels that it was an esoteric, illogical, movement with no substance in fact.*

C. In the 17th century the best histories were written by Puritan ministers who saw history as the working out of God's will. Based on the concept of the chosen people of God, America was presented as a Promised Land for God's faithful people. Later historians ridiculed this view of history. However, in a real sense, at least in Puritan New England, this was a fairly accurate appraisal of the motivations of an entire generation of early settlers. Why was it so difficult for later historians to believe that people can be motivated strictly by their faith?

ANSWER: *In the modern era, it is virtually impossible for secular historians to believe that people would go anywhere, or do anything, because of something as abstract as faith. They looked for motivation in other more measurable directions: economic, political, and other reasons.*

D. By their own admission, New England Puritans saw themselves as being intolerant. They felt no obligation to accept in their midst worldviews that they perceived as heretical. Was this a correct way to establish an English colony?

ANSWER: *Answers will vary but students should be careful not to put a 21st century worldview on 17th century society. The whole notion of toleration has changed significantly since the Puritans settled New England.*

E. Have we Evangelicals lost the fire and passion of our Puritan ancestors?

ANSWER: *Answers will be opinions. Students should carefully defend their arguments.*

LESSON 11

ROMANTICISM: NEW ENGLAND RENAISSANCE, *1840-1855*
(Part 4)

> **Readings Due For This Lesson:** Students should review *Walden*, Henry David Thoreau.
>
> **Reading Ahead:** Students should review *Billy Budd*, Herman Melville. In what way is Billy Budd a Christ-like figure? In what way does this book mark the end of Christian orthodoxy in American literature?
>
> **Goal:** Students will analyze *Walden*, Henry David Thoreau.

Goals/Objectives: What is the purpose of this lesson?	Strategies to meet these goals: How will I obtain these goals/objectives?	Evaluation: How will I know when I have met these goals/objectives?
Students will exhibit higher-level thinking as they discuss whether or not they agree with Ezra Pound's comments. (cognitive goal)	Students will write an essay on this topic: The poet Ezra Pound said that Thoreau wrote *Walden* as the "First intellectual reaction to the mere approach of industrialization: Thoreau tried to see how little he need bother about other humanity." Agree or disagree with this statement. (Critical Thinking)	Students, with minimal errors, will clearly answer the assigned question in a 1-2 page essay.
Students will increase their vocabulary. (cognitive goal)	Students will collect at least five new vocabulary words from their reading and use these words in their essays.	Students will use five vocabulary words in conversation during the week as well as use the words in their essays.
Students will understand this concept: Thoreau's views on death and whether or not they line up with biblical teachings. (cognitive goal)	Students will write an essay on this topic: In his concluding chapter Thoreau reflects on death. What does he conclude and does it parallel biblical teachings? (Biblical Application)	Students, with minimal errors, will clearly answer the assigned question in a 1-2 page essay.
Students will exhibit higher-level thinking as they analyze Thoreau's attitude toward work. (cognitive goal)	Students will write an essay on this topic: Thoreau extols hard work while doing very little of it. Is he a sensitive observer of nature, a lazy over-educated snob hanging out doing nothing for a year, or—? (Enrichment A)	Students, with minimal errors, will clearly answer the assigned question in a 1-2 page essay.

Goals/Objectives: What is the purpose of this lesson?	Strategies to meet these goals: How will I obtain these goals/objectives?	Evaluation: How will I know when I have met these goals/objectives?
Students will exhibit higher thinking as they consider why this book was so popular in the 1960s. (cognitive goal)	Students will write an essay on this topic: Why was this book so popular in the 1960s? (Enrichment B)	Students, with minimal errors, will clearly answer the assigned question in a 1-2 page essay.
Students will work in a group setting. (behavioral goal)	In a class, in a co-op experience, or during a family discussion, students will answer this question: Is *Walden* a harmless, "feel-good" book?	Students will exhibit practical listening skills and will manifest understanding of opposing worldviews.
Students will be able to recall the information taught in the lesson. (cognitive goal)	Lesson 11 Test	Students will take the test at the end of this lesson and score at least 80%.
Students will experience reflective writing. (affective/spiritual goal)	Using the Journal Guide Questions in the Appendices, students will record at least three entries this week. Suggested Scriptures: Mark	Students will show evidence that they have reflected on this issue, including informed discussions and written responses.

SUGGESTED
Weekly *Implementation*

DAY 1	DAY 2	DAY 3	DAY 4	DAY 5
Prayer journal.	**Prayer journal.**	**Prayer journal.**	**Prayer journal.**	**Prayer journal.**
Students review the required reading(s) before the assigned lesson begins. Teacher may want to discuss assigned reading(s) with students. Teacher and students will decide on the number of required essays for this lesson, choosing two or three essays. The rest of the essays can be outlined, answered with shorter answers, or skipped. Students will review all readings for Lesson 11.	Student should review reading(s) from next lesson. Student should outline essays due at the end of the week. Per teacher instructions, students may answer orally in a group setting some of the essays that are not assigned as formal essays.	Students should write rough drafts of all assigned essays. The teacher or a peer evaluator may correct rough drafts.	Student will re-write corrected copies of essays due tomorrow.	Essays are due. Students should take the Lesson 11 test. Reading ahead: Students should review *Billy Budd*, Herman Melville. Guide: In what way is Billy Budd a Christ-like figure? In what way does this book mark the end of Christian orthodoxy in American literature?

Note: References to sources are in student edition.

ENRICHMENT ACTIVITIES/PROJECTS

Students should read *Walden Two*, B. F. Skinner, and compare it to Thoreau's book.

If possible, students should visit Walden Pond, near Concord, Massachusetts.

SUPPLEMENTAL RESOURCES

Bridges, William E. *Spokesmen for the Self: Emerson, Thoreau, Whitman.*

Shanley, James L. *The Making of Walden, with the Text of the First Version.*

Stern, Philip Van Doren, ed. *The Annotated Walden.*

Stern manages to overcome his fawning attitude toward Thoreau to provide some helpful insights.

Notes:

CRITICAL THINKING

The poet Ezra Pound said that Thoreau wrote *Walden* as the "First intellectual reaction to the mere approach of industrialization: Thoreau tried to see how little he need bother about other humanity." Agree or disagree with this statement.

ANSWER: *There may be nothing particularly political in this book. I would disagree with Mr. Pound. It's simply a journal with reflections of a man's stay on the edge of a New England lake.*

BIBLICAL APPLICATION

In his concluding chapter Thoreau reflects on death. What does he conclude and does it parallel biblical teachings?

ANSWER: *There is a sort of ending to his sojourn on Walden Pond that reflects the end of life. With the coming of spring there is both life and death. Wild geese fly overhead, reminding Thoreau that change is in the air. Thoreau feels that old arguments should be forgotten and old sins forgiven because of spring time. Finally, Thoreau believes that death in such an atmosphere would not be so bad. Redemption, unfortunately, cannot be bought by the advent of a season. Death, too, with all its mystery, will not be escaped or blunted by a Romantic experience next to a pond. However, in Thoreau's defense, it is fair to say that he had no intention of making a theological statement.*

ENRICHMENT

A. Thoreau extols hard work while doing very little of it. Is he a sensitive observer of nature, a lazy over-educated snob hanging out doing nothing for a year, or — ?

   ANSWER: *Answers will have to be opinions.*

B. Why was this book so popular in the 1960s?

   ANSWER: *Forced to simplify his life, Thoreau concludes that it is best "as long as possible" to "live free and uncommitted." Thoreau sought to live free of obligations and full of leisure. He happily lived far from the post office and all the constraining social relationships the mail system represented. He lived away from people and enjoyed the solitude. "I am monarch of all I survey," he stated. This spirit was a central theme in the highly individualistic 1960s.*

FINAL PROJECT

Students should correct and rewrite all essays and place them in their Final Portfolio.

LESSON 11 TEST

OBJECTIVE QUESTIONS (50 POINTS)

1. _____ Originally, Thoreau wanted (A) to buy a nearby farm (B) to live in Italy (C) to attend graduate school at Yale (D) to move to Alaska.

2. _____ Thoreau finished his cabin (A) in the fall of 1845 (B) in the spring of 1845 (C) in the spring of 1846 (D) in the winter of 1844.

3. _____ The property on which he built his cabin belonged to (A) Herman Melville (B) Abraham Lincoln (C) George Eliot (D) Ralph Waldo Emerson.

4. _____ Thoreau cannot completely escape technology because (A) he hears a steamboat on the Merrimac River (B) he hears airplanes overhead (C) he hears a nearby railroad (D) his cousin visits him with a mini-cotton gin.

5. _____ Thoreau received visits from (A) Melville and Emerson (B) Blair and Smith (C) Channing and Alcott (D) Davis and Hawthorne.

DISCUSSION QUESTION (50 POINTS)

"Economy" to Thoreau is not only an economic term. What does it mean to him?

LESSON 11 TEST ANSWERS

OBJECTIVE QUESTIONS (50 POINTS)

1. __A__
2. __B__
3. __D__
4. __C__
5. __C__

DISCUSSION QUESTION (50 POINTS)

"Economy" to Thoreau is not only an economic term. What does it mean to him?

ANSWER: *Thoreau follows Emerson in exploring the higher dimensions of individualism. In Transcendentalist thought the self is the absolute center of reality. Therefore, subjectivity is more important than reason. Everything external, including the entire universe, is an expression of the self that gets its reality from our inner selves. "Economizing," then, to Thoreau, is removing the external things that hinder the development of one's inner self or "soul."*

LESSON 12

ROMANTICISM: NEW ENGLAND RENAISSANCE 1840-1855 (Part 5)

Readings Due For This Lesson: Students should review *Billy Budd*, Herman Melville.

Reading Ahead: Students should review "Oh Captain! My Captain!" Walt Whitman; Negro Spirituals; "The Gettysburg Address," Abraham Lincoln; and "Surrender Speech," Chief Joseph. Is Whitman a Romantic? What were the purposes of the Negro Spirituals?

Goal: Students will evaluate the romantic/naturalistic novel *Billy Budd*, by Herman Melville.

Goals/Objectives: What is the purpose of this lesson?	Strategies to meet these goals: How will I obtain these goals/objectives?	Evaluation: How will I know when I have met these goals/objectives?
Students will understand the concept of tragedy. (cognitive goal)	Students will write an essay on the following topic: In what way is *Billy Budd* a modern tragedy? What does this show about the way American society is changing? (Critical Thinking A)	Students, with minimal errors, will clearly answer the assigned question in a 1-2 page essay.
Students will increase their vocabulary. (cognitive goal)	Students will collect at least five new vocabulary words from their reading and use these words in their essays.	Students will use five vocabulary words in conversation during the week as well as use the words in their essays and in conversation.
Students will exhibit higher-level thinking skills as they write an evaluation essay to determine the flaws in David Hume's philosophy. (cognitive goal)	Students will write an essay on the following topic: How does David Hume's philosophy conflict with a theistic/biblical worldview. (Critical Thinking B)?	Students, with minimal errors, will clearly answer the assigned question in a 1-2 page essay.
Students will understand the concept of symbolism. (cognitive goal)	Students will give at least two examples of symbolism in this book. (Critical Thinking C)	Students, with minimal errors, will clearly answer the assigned question in a 1-2 page essay.

Goals/Objectives: What is the purpose of this lesson?	Strategies to meet these goals: How will I obtain these goals/objectives?	Evaluation: How will I know when I have met these goals/objectives?
Students will understand the following concept: biblical understanding of sin vs. classical understanding of sin. (cognitive goal) Students will consider the generalization that all have sinned and fall short of the Kingdom of God. (affective goal)	Students will write an essay on the following topic: Melville intentionally rejects Judeo-Christian notions of sin and depravity. Thus, Claggart is described as being depraved in a Platonic way. Plato defined depravity as "a depravity according to nature." What does the Bible say about sin? Why would Melville reject a biblical understanding of sin and go to a classical definition? (Critical Thinking D)	Students, with minimal errors, will clearly answer the assigned question in a 1-2 page essay.
Students will analyze the use of setting to reveal character. (cognitive goal)	Students will write an essay on the following topic: In *Billy Budd* the setting helps to reveal character and to shape events. Give evidence for this statement. (Critical Thinking E)	Students, with minimal errors, will clearly answer the assigned question in a 1-2 page essay.
Students will discuss how Melville creates his characters. (cognitive goal)	Students will write an essay on the following topic: How does Melville create his characters? (Critical Thinking F)	Students, with minimal errors, will clearly answer the assigned question in a 1-2 page essay.
Students will write an evaluation essay. (cognitive goal)	Students will discuss in what way *Billy Budd* is autobiographical. (Critical Thinking G)	Students, with minimal errors, will clearly answer the assigned question in a 1-2 page essay.
Students will understand the concept of Ahab and his worldview. (cognitive goal)	Students will write an essay on the following topic: Research another Theist named Ahab. (1 Kings) who also struggled to be both a Theist and a pagan at the same time. (Biblical Application A)	Students, with minimal errors, will clearly answer the assigned question in a 1-2 page essay.
Students will understand the concept of Billy Budd as a Christ-like figure. (cognitive/affective goal)	Students will write an essay on the following topic: Billy Budd is obviously a Christ-like figure. From the book find evidence to support this idea. Compare and contrast Melville's view with the New Testament account of Christ's crucifixion. (Biblical Application B)	Students, with minimal errors, will clearly answer the assigned question in a two-page essay.

Goals/Objectives: What is the purpose of this lesson?	Strategies to meet these goals: How will I obtain these goals/objectives?	Evaluation: How will I know when I have met these goals/ objectives?
Students will write an evaluation essay. (cognitive goal) Students will accept the generalization that all have sinned and fall short of the Kingdom of God. (affective goal) Students will witness to an unsaved person. (behavior)	Students will write an essay on the following topic: This is the first time in American literature that reverse salvation happens, and it does not bode well for future literature. Find evidence to support this view and find Scripture to show a way to discuss salvation with an unbeliever. (Biblical Application C)	Students, with minimal errors, will clearly answer the assigned question in a 1-2 page essay.
Students will exhibit higher-level thinking as they write an evaluation essay comparing worldviews. (cognitive goal)	Students will write an essay on the following topic: Agree or disagree with Wells' statement and find examples both in this book and in contemporary life that support or refute this statement. (Enrichment A)	Students, with minimal errors, will clearly answer the assigned question in a 1-2 page essay.
Students will understand this concept: plurality of truth. (cognitive goal)	Students will write an essay on this topic: Using Billy Budd as evidence, discuss how Melville is advocating a plurality of truth. (Enrichment B)	Students, with minimal errors, will clearly answer the assigned question in a 1-2 page essay.
Students will write a *report*. (cognitive goal)	Students will write a report on early nineteenth century whaling and other commercial enterprises related to the sea. (Enrichment C)	Students, with minimal errors, will clearly answer the assigned question in a 1-2 page essay.
Students will evaluate this essay and compare it to other Melville writings. (cognitive/affective goal)	Students will write an essay on the following topic how Melville is poking fun at his friend Ralph Waldo Emerson and other romantics in his essay "I and my Chimney." (Enrichment D)	Students, with minimal errors, will clearly answer the assigned question in a two-page essay.
Students will work in a group setting. (behavioral goal)	In a class, in a co-op experience, or during a family discussion, Students will answer the following question: Is God in control of our lives, or is he like an absent landlord who owns the place and set everything in motion, but is now absent?	Students will exhibit practical listening skills and will manifest understanding of opposing worldviews.

Goals/Objectives: What is the purpose of this lesson?	Strategies to meet these goals: How will I obtain these goals/objectives?	Evaluation: How will I know when I have met these goals/objectives?
Students will be able to recall the information taught in the lesson. (cognitive goal)	Lesson 12 Test	Students will take the test at the end of this lesson and score at least 80%.
Students will experience reflective writing. (affective/spiritual goal)	Using the Journal Guide Questions in the Appendices, students will record at least three entries this week. Suggested Scriptures: 1 Kings	Students will show evidence that they have reflected on this issue, including discussions and written responses.

SUGGESTED
Weekly *Implementation*

DAY 1	DAY 2	DAY 3	DAY 4	DAY 5
Prayer journal.	Prayer journal.	Prayer journal.	Prayer journal.	Prayer journal.
Students review the required reading(s) before the assigned lesson begins. Teacher may want to discuss assigned reading(s) with students. Teacher and students will decide on the number of required essays for this lesson, choosing at least two or three essays. The rest of the essays can be outlined, answered with shorter answers, or skipped. Students will review all readings for Lesson 12.	Student should review reading(s) from next lesson. Students should outline essays due at the end of the week. Per teacher instructions, students may answer orally in a group setting some of the essays that are not assigned as formal essays.	Students should write rough drafts of all assigned essays. The teacher and/or a peer evaluator may correct rough drafts.	Student will re-write corrected copies of essays due tomorrow.	Essays are due. Students should take Lesson 12 test. Reading ahead: Students should review "Oh Captain! My Captain!" Walt Whitman; Negro Spirituals; "The Gettysburg Address," Abraham Lincoln; and "Surrender Speech," Chief Joseph. Guide: Is Whitman a Romantic? What were the purposes of the Negro Spirituals?

Note: References to sources are in student edition.

ENRICHMENT ACTIVITIES/PROJECTS

Over the next few weeks students should take on the character of a person who is born in 1820 and dies in 1920. Follow the instructions provided:

Keep a personal diary. Reflect on historical events as they unfold in your pretend life.

Obviously, each historical event will have different degrees of relevance to your situation; however, about every event state your opinion reflecting a correct historical understanding of the event and its significance to American history. Some historical research will be required to accomplish this task.

REBECCA HAWTHORNE. You are a white, Boston born resident. Your father is a whaler. While delivering your little brother, your mother will die from tuberculosis when you are ten.

PRISCILLA DINWIDDIE. You are a black slave living in Virginia. You have assumed the name of your master, Dinwiddie. Your master is a wealthy plantation owner who owns hundreds of slaves. When you are twelve your mother and father will be sold to a plantation in South Carolina. Your grandmother will raise you.

ROBERT STRONG. You are a white person living in Tennessee. Your father owns three slaves. You have fourteen brothers and sisters.

DAVID ARMSTRONG. You are born into a white Pennsylvania farm family. When you are six, your father is killed in a farming accident.

WHITEWATER RAPIDS. You are a Sioux warrior. You were born in Illinois, but before long the white men come and drive you off your land.... Before you are twenty years old, four family members die from Smallpox.

You should begin each entry with "Dear diary..." and you should write about one-page for each entry. Each entry should be in essay form.

—It is 1828. President Jackson has just been elected president. How did your parents react?

—It is 1832. The Cherokees have been relocated to Oklahoma in the "trail of tears." What is this?

—Two things happen this year: Your relatives are part of the Underground Railroad. What is it? How does it affect you? And, you hear about the Alamo. What year is this? You are married to an immigrant from Germany who does not know how to speak English (or your language).

—Your parents obtain a copy of William Lloyd Garrison's newspaper *The Liberator*. What is their reaction? Why?

—It is 1845. The Mexican War has started. Your older brother joins up. Several members of your hometown think it is a bad war. In fact, your closet friend was arrested for civil disobedience. How do your parents react?

—Nat Turner is a name that terrorizes your household. Why?

—The Fugitive Slave Act is passed. What is it? Does it bother your wife?

—You fight in the Civil War and are wounded at Cold Harbor. Create a diary with entries about the way the whole war affected you. Have at least ten entries.

—You join the Klu Klux Klan; your husband joins the Klan; or you have been hurt by the Klan.

SUPPLEMENTAL RESOURCES

Auden, W. H. "The Christian Tragic Hero." In *New York Times Book Review*, December 16, 1945

Auden is an incredible poet and respectable critic. This article is seminal in studies on Romanticism.

Consider the Sea. (VHS Tape)

This fine video is informational for studying Melville, et al.

Famous Authors: Herman Melville. (VHS Tape)

This exhaustive video presents Melville's life.

Field Trip Possibility: The New Bedford Whaling Museum. (New Bedford, MA)

This museum is located across from the famous chapel in *Moby Dick*.

Field Trip Dream: Youghal, Ireland: the filming site of the film version of *Moby Dick*.

A delightful, friendly small Irish town with local music and landscape.

Fiedler, Leslie. *Love and Death in the American Novel.*

This book is only tangentially connected to Melville, but Fiedler's criticisms of literary works are impressive.

Levin, Harry. *The Power of Blackness: Hawthorne, Poe, Melville.*

The use of darkness in Romantic writers. Interesting.

Miller, Perry. "Melville and Transcendentalism." In *Virginia Quarterly Review*, 29. (Autumn 1953)

Perhaps no one is better able to speak to the tension

in Melville's transition from Romanticism to Realism.

Van Doren, Carl. *The American Novel.*

A great, general overview of the rise of the American novel (of which *Billy Budd* held prominence).

Wright, Nathalia. *Melville's Use of the Bible.*

Hard to find resource that discusses Melville's biblical motifs.

Notes:

SUGGESTED VOCABULARY WORDS

motley (*many colored*)
retinue (*escort*)
genial (*cordial*)
decorum (*propriety*)
deference (*submission*)
appellation (*name*)
felonious (*criminal*)
comely (*handsome*)
clandestine (*secret*)
immured (*confined*)

CRITICAL THINKING

A. *Billy Budd* is a tragedy. There are two concepts of tragedy—the classic and the modern. Aristotle defines the classic tragedy as: "imitation of an action that is serious." The tragic hero must have a tragic flaw, and he must recognize the reason for his downfall. The modern concept of tragedy can be found in the ideas of Arthur Miller who wrote *The Crucible* and *The Death of a Salesman.* The audience witnesses a tragedy when the characters are unable to achieve happiness, when the characters are misunderstood. In what way is *Billy Budd* a modern tragedy, and what does this show about the way American society is changing?

ANSWER: *Billy is a tragic figure in that he is unable to achieve happiness and is misunderstood. Certainly, he is a tragic figure, but to another generation of readers his tragedy would be determined along more cosmological terms. Namely, Billy Budd is unsaved on the day he dies. He was approached by a weak chaplain who discusses existential philosophy with him instead of sharing the Gospel with him. Billy is being executed for a crime he did not commit, and that is tragic. What is more*

tragic is that his life ends without any discussion of his eternal destiny. Melville, of course, would not see it that way and did not write it that way.

B. How does David Hume's philosophy conflict with a theistic/biblical worldview?

ANSWER: *Except Nietzsche, probably no philosopher is more disturbing to the Christian reader than David Hume. For the first time in western history, Hume seriously suggested that there was no necessary connection between cause and effect. If there is no necessary effect from any necessary cause, how can there be a God, much less an omnipotent God? Hume argued that people were captured by their senses. For better or worse all they had were their senses. Nothing else was real. There were no permanently necessary connections between different objects. Effects associated with particular causes were merely coincidental patterns of experience. Thus, with no predictable effect from a cause, there was no reason to fear any consequences resulting from any behavior—because there was no judgment. Morality was a wholly human construct governed by human needs and demands rather than by a higher authority (e.g., God). Hume opened the door to modern worldviews of naturalism and realism.*

C. Give at least two examples of symbolism in this book.

ANSWER: *There are several. Begin by looking at the names of the ships.*

D. Melville intentionally rejects Judeo-Christian notions of sin and depravity. Thus, Claggart is described as being depraved in a Platonic way. Plato defined depravity as "a depravity according to nature." What does the Bible say about sin? Why would Melville reject a biblical understanding of sin and go to a classical definition?

ANSWER: *Like Emerson, Melville felt more comfortable with a Platonic concept of "form" rather than the Christian concept of "sanctification." He needed some form of perfection but found Christian/Puritan/theistic views to be dogmatic. Therefore, He embraced Greek philosophy—a very popular romantic tendency. Plato stressed the intellectual basis of virtue, identifying virtue with wisdom. Plato believed that the world was made of forms, such as a rock, and ideas, such as virtue. The ability of human beings to appreciate forms made a person virtuous. Knowledge came from the gods; opinion was from man. Virtuous activity, then, was dependent upon knowledge of the forms. This was made-to-order for the romantic-in-transition-to-naturalism Melville.*

E. In *Billy Budd* the setting helps to reveal character and to shape events. Give evidence for this statement.

ANSWER: *In microcosm the inhospitable sea is the world into which Melville wants his romantics to wander. It is cruel and dangerous but beautiful. In fact, though, human society on this ocean is far more malevolent.*

F. How does Melville create his characters?

ANSWER: *Inevitably Melville introduces his characters through the medium of an introductory description and narrative.*

G. In what way is *Billy Budd* autobiographical?

ANSWER: *In the early part of Melville's life he was a sailor. There is no evidence that he knew about a situation exactly like Billy Budd's situation.*

BIBLICAL APPLICATION

A. Melville (who was a transitional romantic) and contemporary romantic writers tried to embrace the best of both cosmological worlds. They believed in God, although they diluted His person and substance with natural science, but they also believe in human ingenuity and subjectivity. It was very hard to keep both of these worldviews parallel. Research another theist named Ahab (1 Kings) who also struggled to be both a theist and a pagan at the same time.

ANSWER: *It is difficult to maintain one's sanity if one is trying to be religious and secular simultaneously. Ahab sought to hedge his bets, so to speak. He wanted to remain a good Jew, but he also wanted to satisfy his pagan/Baal-worshiper contingent. What irritated Ahab about Elijah was not that he was a faithful follower of God—Ahab saw himself in that role too. What bothered Ahab was that Elijah claimed there was one and only one God. The post-modern world in which we live is bothered by someone who takes a stand for Christ; it is absolutely livid with someone who claims that Christ is the one and only Savior of the world.*

B. Billy Budd is obviously a Christlike figure. From the book find evidence to support this idea. Compare and contrast Melville's view with the New Testament account of Christ's crucifixion.

ANSWER: *Innocent Billy dies for another's sin. He struggles a night before he dies. An unnatural event occurs at his burial. Billy cries "God bless Captain Vere" at his death. This is similar to Christ's cry on the cross. (Luke 23:34)*

C. Billy is "saved" the night before he dies—but not through Christ. In fact, the chaplain, who presumably represents the Christian view of salvation, lis-

tens to Billy and finds his strength through this event—much like the disciples listened to Christ at the Last Supper. This time, however, Billy saves the pastor! The romantic saves the theist! This reverse salvation is the first for American literature, and it does not bode well for future literature. Find evidence to support this view and find Scripture to show a way to discuss salvation with an unbeliever.

ANSWER: *The pastor presages an ominous development in American literature. Instead of the hardy, principled Dimmesdale (Scarlet Letter), for a generation the American reader will feast on a hardy diet of weak, unprincipled pastors and parsons. In literature gone are the Cotton Mathers and other lights who guide society in the way of Truth. True salvation comes as a person accepts his sin, believes in his heart that Jesus Christ is Lord, and confesses this belief with his mouth.*

ENRICHMENT

A. Perhaps the best characterization of Melville is found in the writings of his good friend Nathaniel Hawthorne. Hawthorne describes Melville:

We took a pretty long walk together, and sat down in a hollow among the sand hills. . . Melville, as he always does, began to reason of Providence and futurity, and of everything that lies beyond human ken, and informed me that he had 'pretty much made up his mind to be annihilated'; but still he does not seem to rest in that anticipation; and, I think, will never rest until he gets hold of a definite belief . . . He can neither believe, nor be comfortable in his unbelief; and he is too honest and courageous not to try to do one or the other. . .

http://www.melville.org/hawthorne.htm

He can neither believe, nor be comfortable in his unbelief. What a marvelous description of modern man. In his book *God in the Wasteland: The Reality of Truth in a World of Fading Dreams*, David F. Wells is convinced that since the middle of the last century human society has embraced "an ironic recapitulation of the first dislocation in which God's creatures replaced their Creator and exiled Him from His own world." Find examples of this development in *Billy Budd*. Agree or disagree with Wells' statement and find examples both in this book and contemporary life that support or refute this statement.

ANSWER: *The free and flawed biblical analogies, the divorce of morality from its Judeo-Christian roots, and the pri-*

macy of human experience over biblical truth foreshadow much trouble for the American soul. In that sense Melville is a metaphor both for Ahab (Moby Dick) and Billy. (Billy Budd)

B. Two quintessential questions our culture raises by its nature and development are *what is truth* and *what can we believe?* Our culture doesn't know the answer. It never has. The Puritans knew that. They looked beyond themselves. They looked to God, but from this point forward in American literature we enter a wasteland . . . . After humorist Mark Twain wrote his satire and early realism, American writers lost confidence in a single truth and came to the conclusion that truth is unattainable. Today we hold to a plurality of truths, and the *tolerance* of them is now a *virtue*. To our secular world, truth is discovered in this struggle. Using *Billy Budd* as evidence, discuss how Melville is advocating a plurality of truth.

ANSWER: *There is no one absolutely wrong in this book. There are protagonists and antagonists, but they are not connected with any moral vision. In other words, Billy is not better than others because he is moral. He is merely innocent—or not guilty of what he is charged. Gone is proactive good. This is no Hester Prynne standing up for her sin and basking in redemption. This is a young man who gains salvation through insightful reflection of truth. He is nearer the naturalist character Henry Fleming in Red Badge of Courage who finds his "salvation" in a cynical rejection of subjectivity. Billy Budd is a new perspective—the person who has no control over his fate but*

can only react to circumstances. Truth, then, is couched in these plural, subjective terms. The truth on which Billy Budd bases his life is completely his own to hold. He is not concerned about convincing others. He quietly goes to the gallows. Alone. The beauty of Billy's life is his silent struggle against the "gods" with no notion of life's outcome. This character is replicated in American literature for the next 150 years.

C. Write a *report* on early nineteenth century whaling and other commercial enterprises related to the sea.

ANSWER: *Whaling was quite dangerous and profitable. Investors could make a fortune on only one sailing venture. Whaling was finally terminated when cheaper petroleum replaced whale oil in lamps.*

D. In a two-page essay, discuss how Melville is poking fun at his friend Ralph Waldo Emerson and other romantics in his essay "I and my Chimney."

ANSWER: *Melville is comparing the chimney to nature. He shows how absurd Romantics can be. While the chimney is necessary to a house, it is not necessarily beautiful—likewise a snowstorm. He also pokes fun at the Romantics who intersect human relationship (i.e., the protagonist and his wife) with the chimney. Like nature, the chimney is an inanimate object.*

FINAL PROJECT

Students should correct and rewrite all essays and place them in their Final Portfolio.

LESSON 12 TEST

OBJECTIVE QUESTIONS. (50 POINTS)

_____ 1. The only person to warn Billy of Claggart's ill-will was (A) the chaplain. (B) the Dansker. (C) the cook.

_____ 2. Billy's reaction to Claggart's allegation was impeded by his (A) anger. (B) speech problems. (C) retardation.

_____ 3. The main feeling of the court in response to Billy's testimony before them was one of (A) repulsion. (B) commiseration. (C) incredulity.

_____ 4. The final court verdict upon Billy was prompted by strict adherence to (A) biblical witness. (B) Billy's confession. (C) the civil law.

_____ 5. Billy's burial was marked by the appearance of (A) birds. (B) stormy seas. (C) an earthquake.

DISCUSSION QUESTIONS. (50 POINTS)

A. Like so much of Romantic literature, _Billy Budd_ examines in great detail the problem of good and evil. Explain.

B. Hawthorne undertook a similar quest in his books. Compare and contrast the views of Hawthorne and Melville on this important problem.

C. Several of the characters have biblical parallels. Compare at least three characters to biblical characters.

D. Likewise, the plot itself, parallels several biblical references/stories. Identify at least three.

E. The protagonist Billy Budd is a quintessential Romantic man. Explain.

LESSON 12 TEST ANSWERS

OBJECTIVE QUESTIONS. (50 POINTS)

1. __B__
2. __B__
3. __B__
4. __C__
5. __A__

DISCUSSION QUESTIONS. (50 POINTS)

A. Like so much of Romantic literature, *Billy Budd* examines in great detail the problem of Good and Evil. Explain.

ANSWER: *A young man is unjustly accused of a crime he did not commit (Evil). He is executed because of a greater Good—the need for wartime discipline. Ultimately, though, the implication is that Good overcomes Evil in the person of Billy Budd.*

B. Hawthorne undertook a similar quest in his books. Compare and contrast the views of Hawthorne and Melville on this important problem of Good and Evil.

ANSWER: *Hawthorne's Billy Budd figure would be Hester Prynne—but Hawthorne, who is essentially a theist, accepts that Hester is really guilty. There can be no redemption without a willing admission of guilt, Hawthorne argues. Melville, on the other hand, is a truer romantic: Good is the absence of intrusive human moral structure.*

C. Several of the characters have biblical parallels. Compare at least three characters to biblical characters.

ANSWER: *Billy Budd = Jesus Christ; Captain Vere = Pilate; and Captain Vere = Abraham sacrificing his favorite son Isaac (Billy Budd).*

D. Likewise, the plot itself, parallels several biblical references/stories. Identify at least three.

ANSWER: *Billy would be Adam before the fall; Saul (Claggart) and David (Billy Budd) in the story about jealousy; the story of Ananias (conspiracy).*

E. The protagonist Billy Budd is a quintessential romantic man. Explain.

ANSWER: *Billy is the natural, naive, man, unpolluted by human machination and intrigue. He is much to be admired. He is much like the Native Americans, free and unpolluted by civilization, in the popular, romantic Last of the Mohicans, James Fenimore Cooper.*

LESSON 13
DIVISION, WAR, AND RECONCILIATION *1855-1865 (Part 1)*

Readings Due For This Lesson: Students should review "Oh Captain! My Captain!" Walt Whitman; Negro Spirituals; "The Gettysburg Address," Abraham Lincoln; and "Surrender Speech," Chief Joseph.

Reading Ahead: *Narrative of the Life of Frederick Douglass,* Frederick Douglass. How was Douglass' life typical or atypical of most African-American slave lives?

Goal: Students will analyze "Oh Captain! My Captain!" Walt Whitman; Negro Spirituals; "The Gettysburg Address," Abraham Lincoln; and "Surrender Speech," Chief Joseph.

Goals/Objectives: What is the purpose of this lesson?	Strategies to meet these goals: How will I obtain these goals/objectives?	Evaluation: How will I know when I have met these goals/objectives?
Students will exhibit higher-level thinking as they discuss what metaphor Whitman uses to communicate his grief at the death of Abraham Lincoln. (cognitive goal)	Students will write an essay on this topic: In "Oh Captain! My Captain!" what metaphor does Whitman use to communicate his grief at the death of Abraham Lincoln? (Critical Thinking A)	Students, with minimal errors, will clearly answer the assigned question in a 1-2 page essay.
Students will increase their vocabulary. (cognitive goal)	Students will collect at least five new vocabulary words from their reading and use these words in their essays.	Students will use five vocabulary words in conversation during the week as well as use the words in their essays and in conversation.
Students will exhibit higher-level thinking skills as they discuss in what sense Whitman's poetry is modern. (cognitive goal)	Students will write an essay on this topic: In what sense is this poetry modern? In what sense is this poetry Romantic? (Critical Thinking B)	Students, with minimal errors, will clearly answer the assigned question in a 1-2 page essay.
Students will understand this concept: slave resistance. (cognitive goal)	Students will write an essay on this topic: In what ways were Negro spirituals a form of resistance to chattel slavery? (Biblical Application)	Students, with minimal errors, will clearly answer the assigned question in a 1-2 page essay.

Goals/Objectives: What is the purpose of this lesson?	Strategies to meet these goals: How will I obtain these goals/objectives?	Evaluation: How will I know when I have met these goals/objectives?
Students will understand this concept: Native American and Anglo-European conflict. (cognitive goal)	Students will write an essay on this topic: What does Geronimo say is the primary reason whites and Native Americans did not get along? (Enrichment)	Students, with minimal errors, will clearly answer the assigned question in a 1-2 page essay.
Students will work in a group setting. (behavioral goal)	In a class, in a co-op experience, or during a family discussion, students will answer this question: Was Abraham Lincoln a born again Christian?	Students will exhibit practical listening skills and will manifest understanding of opposing worldviews.
Students will be able to recall the information taught in the lesson. (cognitive goal)	Lesson 13 Test	Students will take the test at the end of this lesson and score at least 80%.
Students will experience reflective writing. (affective/spiritual goal)	Using the Journal Guide Questions in the Appendices, students will record at least three entries this week. Suggested Scriptures: Romans 6	Students will show evidence that they have reflected on this issue, including informed discussions and written responses.

SUGGESTED
Weekly *Implementation*

DAY 1	DAY 2	DAY 3	DAY 4	DAY 5
Prayer journal.	**Prayer journal.**	**Prayer journal.**	**Prayer journal.**	**Prayer journal.**
Students review the required reading(s) before the assigned lesson begins.	Student should review reading(s) from next lesson.	Students should write rough drafts of all assigned essays.	Student will re-write corrected copies of essays due tomorrow.	Essays are due.
Teacher may want to discuss assigned reading(s) with students.	Student should outline essays due at the end of the week.	The teacher and/or a peer evaluator may correct rough drafts.		Students should take the Lesson 13 test.
Teacher and students will decide on required essay for this lesson, choosing two or three essays.	Per teacher instructions, students may answer orally in a group setting some of the essays that are not assigned as formal essays.			Reading ahead: Students should review Reading Ahead: *Narrative of the Life of Frederick Douglass*, Frederick Douglass. Guide Question: How was Douglass' life typical or atypical of most African-American slave lives?
The rest of the essays can be outlined, answered with shorter answers, or skipped.				
Students will review all readings for Lesson 13.				

Note: References to sources are in student edition.

ENRICHMENT ACTIVITIES/PROJECTS

A. In the last few years Christians have been practicing what some are calling "mapping." Mapping is a technique where Christian leaders ascertain sins committed in a particular area by one people group toward another people group. A case in point is the violation of Native American rights by white Americans. These Christian leaders call white Americans to repent for the sins of their forefathers. Students should reflect on this practice and argue the pros and cons of its implementation.

B. Students should memorize the "Gettysburg Address."

SUPPLEMENTAL RESOURCES

Foote, Shelby. *The Civil War: A Narrative History.*
    By far, the finest series on the Civil War in print.

Craven, A. O. *The Coming of the Civil War.*

Notes:

CRITICAL THINKING

A. In "Oh Captain! My Captain!" what metaphor does Whitman use to communicate his grief at the death of Abraham Lincoln?

ANSWER: *Lincoln is a captain of a ship trying to get the ship into port. The ship makes it; the captain does not.*

B. In what sense is this poetry modern? In what sense is this poetry Romantic?

ANSWER: *The poem is modern in form, Romantic in theme. Whitman avoids traditional structures because he wants to show that his is truly American—not indebted to previous poets from other countries. The notion of transcendent beauty, of the immutability of the soul, is a Romantic theme. While Whitman consciously chose ordinary subjects in most of his poetry, there is something in Lincoln's life that goes beyond present circumstances. As Secretary of Defense Stanton proclaimed, "He belongs to the Ages."*

BIBLICAL APPLICATION

In what ways were Negro spirituals a form of resistance to chattel slavery?

ANSWER: *African-American slaves were originally converted by the witnessing of their white captors. They now take the Old Testament stories and employ them as a subtle way to proclaim their freedom.*

ENRICHMENT

Other than Chief Joseph, the most famous Native war chief was Geronimo. Geronimo (1829-1909) was chief of an Apache tribe in present-day Arizona. In 1876 the United States government attempted to move the Apaches from their ancestral home to New Mexico. Geronimo then began a ten year war against white settlements. Ultimately, Geronomo was captured and converted to Christianity before he died. The following is from Geronimo's autobiography:

> About ten years later some more white men came. These were all warriors. They made their camp on the Gila River south of Hot Springs. At first they were friendly and we did not dislike them, but they were not as good as those who came first.

> After about a year some trouble arose between them and the Indians, and I took the war path

as a warrior, not as a chief. I had not been wronged, but some of my people bad been, and I fought with my tribe; for the soldiers and not the Indians were at fault.

Not long after this some of the officers of the United States troops invited our leaders to hold a conference at Apache Pass (Fort Bowie). Just before noon the Indians were shown into a tent and told that they would be given something to eat. When in the tent they were attacked by soldiers. Our chief and several other warriors, by cutting through the tent, escaped; but most of the warriors were killed or captured. Among the Bedonkohe Apaches killed at this time were Sanza, Kladetahe, Niyokahe, and Gopi. After this treachery the Indians went back to the mountains and left the fort entirely alone. I do not think that the agent had anything to do with planning this, for he had always treated us well. I believe it was entirely planned by the soldiers.

From the very first the soldiers sent out to our western country, and the officers in charge of them, did not hesitate to wrong the Indians. They never explained to the Government when an Indian was wronged but always reported the misdeeds of the Indians. Much that was done by mean white men was reported at Washington as the deeds of my people.

The Indians always tried to live peaceably with the white soldiers and settlers. One day during the time that the soldiers were stationed at Apache Pass I made a treaty with the post. This was done by shaking hands and promising to be brothers. Cochise and Mangus-Colorado did likewise. I do not know the name of the officer in command, but this was the first regiment that ever came to Apache Pass. This treaty was made about a year before we were attacked in a tent, as above related. In a few days after the attack at Apache Pass we organized in the mountains and returned to fight the soldiers. There were two tribes-the Bedonkohe and the Chokonen Apaches, both commanded by Cochise. After a few days' skirmishing we attacked a freight train that was coming in with supplies for the Fort. We killed some of the men and captured the others. These prisoners our chief offered to trade for the Indians whom the soldiers had captured at the massacre in the tent. This the officers refused, so we killed our prisoners, disbanded, and went into hiding in the mountains. Of those who took part in this affair I am the only one now living.

In a few days troops were sent out to search for us, but as we were disbanded, it was, of course, impossible for them to locate any hostile camp. During the time they were searching for us many of our warriors (who were thought by the soldiers to be peaceable Indians) talked to the officers and men, advising them where they might find the camp they sought, and while they searched we watched them from our hiding places and laughed at their failures.

After this trouble all of the Indians agreed not to be friendly with the white men any more. There was no general engagement, but a long struggle followed. Sometimes we attacked the white men, sometimes they attacked us. First a few Indians would be killed and then a few soldiers. I think the killing was about equal on each side. The number killed in these troubles did not amount to much, but this treachery on the part of the soldiers had angered the Indians and revived memories of other wrongs, so that we never again trusted the United States troops.

What does Geronimo say is the primary reason whites and Native Americans did not get along?

ANSWER: *The Native Americans tried to live peacefully with the Anglo-European settlers, but they were constantly betrayed.*

FINAL PROJECT

Students should correct and rewrite all essays and place them in their Final Portfolio.

LESSON 13 TEST

DISCUSSION QUESTION (100 POINTS)

Compare "Pioneers! O Pioneers!" written early in Whitman's life, and "When lilacs last in the Dooryard Bloom'd," written later in his life.

Pioneers! O Pioneers

Come my tan-faced children,
Follow well in order, get your weapons ready,
Have you your pistols? have you your sharp-edged
    axes?
Pioneers! O pioneers!
For we cannot tarry here,
We must march my darlings, we must bear the brunt
    of danger,
We the youthful sinewy races,
all the rest on us depend,
Pioneers! O pioneers!
O you youths,
Western youths,
So impatient, full of action, full of manly pride and
    friendship

When lilacs last in the Dooryard Bloom'd

WHEN lilacs last in the dooryard bloom'd,
And the great star early droop'd in the western sky in
    the night,
I mourn'd, and yet shall mourn with ever-returning
    spring. Ever-returning spring, trinity sure to me
    you bring, Lilac blooming perennial and drooping
    star in the west,
And thought of him I love.
powerful western fallen star!
shades of night—
moody, tearful night! great star disappear'd—
the black murk that hides the star! cruel hands that
    hold me powerless—
helpless soul of me!
harsh surrounding cloud that will not free my soul.
In the dooryard fronting an old farm-house near the
    white-wash'd palings,
Stands the lilac-bush tall-growing with heart-shaped
    leaves of rich green,
With many a pointed blossom rising delicate, with the
    perfume strong I love,
With every leaf a miracle—and from this bush in the
    dooryard,
With delicate-color'd blossoms and heart-shaped
    leaves of rich green,
A sprig with its flower I break.
In the swamp in secluded recesses,
A shy and hidden bird is warbling a song.
Solitary the thrush,
The hermit withdrawn to himself, avoiding the settle-
    ments,
Sings by himself a song. Song of the bleeding throat,
Death's outlet song of life (for well dear brother I
    know,
If thou wast not granted to sing thou would'st surely
    die).

LESSON 13 TEST ANSWERS

DISCUSSION QUESTION (100 POINTS)

Compare "Pioneers! O Pioneers!" written early in Whitman's life, and "When lilacs last in the Dooryard Bloom'd," written later in his life.

ANSWER: *The Civil War diminished Whitman's faith in democratic America and in human nature in general. The casualty during the Civil War was greater than anyone expected. Whitman was a volunteer nurse in the Union Army and saw the carnage first hand. Reconstruction, which began to fail almost immediately after it was begun, further disappointed Whitman. Thus, when the images in the poem "When lilacs last in the Dooryard Bloom'd" was written, Whitman had given up on humanity altogether.*

LESSON 14
DIVISION, WAR, AND RECONCILIATION *1855-1865 (Part 2)*

> **Readings Due For This Lesson:** Students should review *Narrative of the Life of Frederick Douglass*, Frederick Douglass.
>
> **Reading Ahead:** Students should review *The Adventures of Huckleberry Finn*, by Mark Twain.
>
> **Guide:** Is Twain writing a humorous farce or is he writing a very serious, even cynical, novel?
>
> **Goal:** Students will analyze *Narrative of the Life of Frederick Douglass*, Frederick Douglass.

Goals/Objectives: What is the purpose of this lesson?	Strategies to meet these goals: How will I obtain these goals/objectives?	Evaluation: How will I know when I have met these goals/objectives?
Students will exhibit higher-level thinking as they discuss the eloquent style of Frederick Douglas. (cognitive goal)	Students will write an essay on Douglas' writing style. (Critical Thinking A)	Students, with minimal errors, will clearly answer the assigned question in a 1-2 page essay.
Students will increase their vocabulary. (cognitive goal)	Students will collect at least five new vocabulary words from their reading and use these words in their essays.	Students will use five vocabulary words in conversation during the week as well as use the words in their essays and in conversation.
Students will exhibit higher-level thinking as they discuss Douglas' use of form.	Students will write an essay on Douglas' literary form.	Students will answer the assigned question in a 1-2 page essay.
Students will understand this concept: slave resistance. (cognitive goal)	Students will write an essay on this topic: Douglas' faith journey. (Biblical Application)	Students, with minimal errors, will clearly answer the assigned question in a 1-2 page essay.

Goals/Objectives: What is the purpose of this lesson?	Strategies to meet these goals: How will I obtain these goals/objectives?	Evaluation: How will I know when I have met these goals/objectives?
Students will be able to recall the information taught in the lesson. (cognitive goal)	Lesson 13 Test	Students will take the test at the end of this lesson and score at least 80%.
Students will experience reflective writing. (affective/spiritual goal)	Using the Journal Guide Questions in the Appendices, students will record at least three entries this week. Suggested Scriptures: Romans 6	Students will show evidence that they have reflected on this issue, including informed discussions and written responses.

SUGGESTED
Weekly *Implementation*

DAY 1	DAY 2	DAY 3	DAY 4	DAY 5
Prayer journal.	**Prayer journal.**	**Prayer journal.**	**Prayer journal.**	**Prayer journal.**
Students review the required reading(s) before the assigned lesson begins.	Student should review reading(s) from next lesson.	Students should write rough drafts of all assigned essays.	Student will re-write corrected copies of essays due tomorrow.	Essays are due.
Teacher may want to discuss assigned reading(s) with students.	Student should outline essays due at the end of the week.	The teacher and/or a peer evaluator may correct rough drafts.		Students should take the Lesson 14 test.
Teacher and students will decide on required essays for this lesson, choosing two or three essays.	Per teacher instructions, students may answer orally in a group setting some of the essays that are not assigned as formal essays.			Reading ahead: Students should review: *The Adventures of Huckleberry Finn*, by Mark Twain.
The rest of the essays can be outlined, answered with shorter answers, or skipped.				Guide: Is Twain writing a humorous farce or is he writing a very serious, even cynical, novel?
Students will review all readings for Lesson 14.				

Note: References to sources are in student edition.   Notes:

ENRICHMENT ACTIVITIES/PROJECTS

If possible, students should visit the Carter Plantation, Williamsburg, VA.

SUPPLEMENTAL RESOURCES

Gates, Jr. Henry Louis. *Figures in Black.*

Usry, Glenn and Craig S. Keener. *Black Man's Religion.*

Woodward, C. Vann. *The Strange Career of Jim Crow.*

CRITICAL THINKING

A. Douglass writes in a very eloquent style, which contributes to the effectiveness of his work. Many people who thought African-Americans were inferior in intelligence were shown to be mistaken with the writings of Frederick Douglass.

Discuss the form that Douglass employs in his masterpiece.

ANSWER: *Douglas gives both his own life stories and a strong statement against slavery.*

B. What does Douglass learn that is the key to freedom?

ANSWER: *It was from Hugh Auld that Douglass learned the notion that knowledge must be the way to freedom, because Auld forbade his wife to teach Douglass how to read and write. Auld knew that literary education would ultimately bring freedom. Auld unwittingly revealed the strategy by which slave holders kept blacks as slaves and by which blacks might free themselves. Douglass saw his own education as the primary means by which he would be able to free himself and as his greatest tool to work for the freedom of all slaves.*

BIBLICAL APPLICATION

Discuss Douglass's faith journey.

ANSWER: *"Previous to my contemplation of the anti-slavery movement, and its probable results, my mind had been seriously awakened to the subject of religion. I was not more than thirteen years old, when I felt the need of God, as a father and protector. My religious nature was awakened by the preaching of a white Methodist minister, named Hanson. He thought that all men, great and small, bond and free, were sinners in the sight of God; that they were, by nature, rebels against His government; and that they must repent of their sins, and be reconciled to God, through Christ. I cannot say that I had a very distinct notion of what was required of me; but one thing I knew very well—I was wretched, and had no means of making myself otherwise. Moreover, I knew that I could pray for light. I consulted a good colored man, named Charles Johnson; and, in tones of holy affection, he told me to pray, and what to pray for. I was, for weeks, a poor, brokenhearted mourner, traveling through the darkness and misery of doubts and fears. I finally found that change of heart which comes by 'casting all one's cares' upon God, and by having faith in Jesus Christ, as the Redeemer, Friend, and Savior of those who diligently seek Him.*

After this, I saw the world in a new light. I seemed to live in a new world, surrounded by new objects, and to be animated by new hopes and desires. I loved all mankind—slaveholders not excepted; though I abhorred slavery more than ever. My great concern was, now, to have the world converted. The desire for knowledge increased, and especially did I want a thorough acquaintance with the contents of the Bible. I have gathered scattered pages from this holy book, from the filthy street gutters of Baltimore, and washed and dried them, that in the moments of my leisure, I might get a word or two of wisdom from them. While thus religiously seeking knowledge, I became acquainted with a good old colored man, named Lawson. A more devout man than he, I never saw. He drove a dray for Mr. James Ramsey, the owner of a rope-walk on Fell's Point, Baltimore. This man not only prayed three time a day, but he prayed as he walked through the streets, at his work—on his dray everywhere. His life was a life of prayer, and his words (when he spoke to his friends,) were about a better world. Uncle Lawson lived near Master Hugh's house; and, becoming deeply attached to the old man, I went often with him to prayer-meeting, and spent much of my leisure time with him on Sunday. The old man could read a little, and I was a great help to him, in making out the hard words, for I was a better reader than he. I could teach him 'the letter,' but he could teach me 'the spirit'; and high, refreshing times we had together, in singing, praying and glorifying God." (Ch. 12 My Bondage and My Freedom)

ENRICHMENT

Compare Phillis Wheatley and Frederick Douglass.

ANSWER:

Douglass was far more aggressive in his pursuit of the abolition of slavery than Wheatley, but of course he lived 50 years after she did. Wheatley wrote more religious-related works than Douglass. Nonetheless, they were both brilliant writers of their age.

FINAL PROJECT

Students should correct and rewrite all essays and place them in their Final Portfolio.

LESSON 14 TEST

ESSAY (100 POINTS)

Answer the following question in a 1 page essay: Is *Narrative of the Life of Frederick Douglass* strictly an autobiography?

LESSON 14 TEST ANSWER

ESSAY (100 POINTS)

Answer the following question in a 1 page essay: Is *Narrative of the Life of Frederick Douglass* strictly an autobiography?

ANSWER: *An autobiography is the history of a person written by that person. Douglass's* Narrative *is strictly an autobiography at certain points, but it exhibits conventions of other narrative genres as well. For example, at times Douglass intends his life story to stand as representative of a typical slave life. He also takes every opportunity to argue for abolitionism.*

LESSON 15

REALISM, NATURALISM, AND THE FRONTIER, *1865-1915* (*Part 1*)

Readings Due For This Lesson: Students should review *The Adventures of Huckleberry Finn* by Mark Twain.

Reading Ahead: Students will review *Red Badge of Courage*, Stephen Crane. Who is the "god" the reader encounters in this seminal, naturalistic novel (Lesson 17)?

Goal: Students will evaluate this first, and greatest, realistic novel in American literary history.

Goals/Objectives: What is the purpose of this lesson?	Strategies to meet these goals: How will I obtain these goals/objectives?	Evaluation: How will I know when I have met these goals/objectives?
Students will exhibit higher-level thinking as they compare two different persons with significant different worldviews. (cognitive goal) Students will consider Samuel's worldview to be superior over Huck's. (affective goal)	Students will write an essay on this topic: Compare Huckleberry Finn to the young Samuel of the Old Testament (1 Sam.1-3). (Biblical Application)	Students, with minimal errors, will clearly answer the assigned question in a 1-2 page essay.
Students will increase their vocabulary. (cognitive goal)	In addition to the words presented in this lesson, students will collect at least five new vocabulary words from their reading and use these words in their essays.	Students will use five vocabulary words in conversation during the week as well as use the words in their essays and in conversation.
Students will understand this concept: characterization. (cognitive goal)	Students will write an essay on this topic: As Huck Finn progresses we learn to love Jim, loyal to a fault, trusting, and hardworking. The reader is drawn to this pillar of fecundity. Describe in detail the way Twain develops this character. (Critical Thinking A) Students will write an essay on this topic: Huck is not a static character.	Students, with minimal errors, will clearly answer the assigned question in a 1-2 page essay.

Goals/Objectives: What is the purpose of this lesson?	Strategies to meet these goals: How will I obtain these goals/objectives?	Evaluation: How will I know when I have met these goals/objectives?
	As the novel progresses, he matures. What additional knowledge about the problems of life has Huck acquired by the time he gets to the Phelps' farm? In an essay, explain how Huck has changed by this point. (Critical Thinking B)	
Students will understand this concept: situational irony. (cognitive goal)	Students will write an essay on this topic: Ironically, Jim and Huck are trying to escape from slavery by floating down the Mississippi River. Why is this escape ironic? (Critical Thinking C)	Students, with minimal errors, will clearly answer the assigned question in a 1-2 page essay.
Students will understand these literary concepts: 1. satire 2. symbolism 3. allegory 4. foreshadowing (cognitive goal)	Students will write an essay on this topic: Mark Twain used several literary devices. Look up the meaning of each of the following literary terms and find at least one example from the book. 1. satire 2. symbolism 3. allegory 4. foreshadowing (Critical Thinking D)	Students, with minimal errors, will clearly answer the assigned question in a 1-2 page essay.
Students will understand this concept: literary point of view. (cognitive goal)	Students will write an essay on this topic: Twain uses first person point of view to tell his story. What advantages and disadvantages does this present Twain. (Critical Thinking E)?	Students, with minimal errors, will clearly answer the assigned question in a two-page essay.
Students will exhibit higher-level thinking as they contrast the Realist Huck Finn with the Romantic Henry David Thoreau. (cognitive goal)	Students will write an essay on this topic: Can you imagine Huck joining the transcendentalist Henry David Thoreau for a year on the edge of Walden Pond? Why or why not? (Enrichment A)?	Students, with minimal errors, will clearly answer the assigned question in a 1-2 page essay.
Students will exhibit higher-level thinking as they define Realism. (cognitive goal)	Students will write an essay on this topic: Define Realism. Give examples of Realism in Huckleberry Finn. (Enrichment B)	Students, with minimal errors, will clearly answer the assigned question in a 1-2 page essay.

Goals/Objectives: What is the purpose of this lesson?	Strategies to meet these goals: How will I obtain these goals/objectives?	Evaluation: How will I know when I have met these goals/objectives?
Students will exhibit higher-level thinking as he analyzes contemporary culture and extrapolate upon what response Christians should have. (affective/cognitive goals)	Students will write an essay on this topic: Find contemporary examples where Christian theism is clashing with Realism. (Enrichment C)	Students, with minimal errors, will clearly answer the assigned question in a 1-2 page essay.
Students will work with their parents. (behavioral goal)	Students will learn how to participate in spiritual warfare. (affective goal) Students will discuss with their parents what spiritual warfare is. They will practice this warfare with their parents. NOTE: This author considers spiritual warfare to be speaking spiritual truth in places of deception: if someone feels unimportant, he could quote Psalm 119 as a response.	Students will speak openly about spiritual warfare with their parents and peers.
Students will work in a group setting. (behavioral goal)	In a class, in a co-op experience, or during a family discussion, students will answer this question: Did you like this novel? Why?	Students will exhibit practical listening skills and will manifest understanding of opposing worldviews.
Students will be able to recall the information taught in the lesson. (cognitive goal)	Lesson 15 Test	Students will take the test at the end of this lesson and score at least 80%.
Students will experience reflective writing. (affective/spiritual goal)	Using the Journal Guide Questions in the Appendices, students will record at least three entries this week. Suggested Scriptures: Daniel 1-3	Students will show evidence that they have reflected on this issue, including informed discussions and written responses.

SUGGESTED
Weekly *Implementation*

DAY 1	DAY 2	DAY 3	DAY 4	DAY 5
Prayer journal. Students should review the required reading(s) before the assigned lesson begins. Teacher may want to discuss assigned reading(s) with students. Teacher and students will decide on required essays for this lesson, choosing two or three essays. The rest of the essays can be outlined, answered with shorter answers, or skipped. Students will review all readings for Lesson 15	**Prayer journal.** Student should review reading(s) from next lesson. Student should outline essays due at the end of the week. Per teacher instructions, students may answer orally in a group setting some of the essays that are not assigned as formal essays.	**Prayer journal.** Students should write rough drafts of all assigned essays. The teacher and/or a peer evaluator may correct rough drafts.	**Prayer journal.** Student will re-write corrected copies of essays due tomorrow.	**Prayer journal.** Essays are due. Students should take the Lesson 15 test. Reading ahead: Students should review *Red Badge of Courage*, Stephen Crane (Lesson 17). Guide: Who is the "god" the reader encounters in this seminal, naturalistic novel?

Note: References to sources are in student edition.

ENRICHMENT ACTIVITIES/PROJECTS

A. Students should write a creative essay describing a vacation in an episodic style like *The Adventures of Huckleberry Finn*.

B. Students should choose a series of adventures between Huck and Jim and make a pictorial album.

SUPPLEMENTAL RESOURCES

Burns, Ken. *Mark Twain.* (PBS Program)
    A wonderful documentary on the life of Mark Twain.

Burns, Ken, Dayton Duncan, and Geoffrey C. Ward. *Mark Twain, An Illustrated Biography.*
    The book version of the PBS documentary.

Holbrook, Hal. *Mark Twain Tonight.* (DVD)
    Hal Holbrook is the perfect Mark Twain in this 1967 television special.

Robinson, Forrest G., ed. *The Cambridge Companion to Mark Twain.*

Single best secondary resource on Mark Twain.

Notes:

SUGGESTED VOCABULARY WORDS

Students should use these words in essays they write this week.

temperance. (*abstinence*)
reticule. (*handbag*)
wince. (*draw back*)
pensive. (*thoughtful*)
degraded. (*debased*)
histrionic. (*theatrical*)
obsequies. (*funeral rites*)
ingenious. (*inventive*)

BIBLICAL APPLICATION

Compare Huckleberry Finn to the young Samuel of the Old Testament. (1 Sam.1-3)

ANSWER: *Huck Finn was a moralistic young man. Samuel was a man who followed God's laws. There is a significant difference. Huck did what seemed right to him. He does good works, but he is amoral, but not immoral. Everything is relative to Huck. He is good natured and kind. Inevitably, though, the end justifies the means. On the other hand, Samuel obeyed God's Word. He was moral and just. Huck's vision was a realistic vision; Samuel's vision was theistic. Huck basically responded to each situation and made his choices; Samuel obeyed God at all costs. There is a sort of nostalgia about Huck—who is the quintessential, good-natured, modern character—that does not exist in Samuel.*

CRITICAL THINKING

A. As *Huck Finn* progresses we learn to love Jim, loyal to a fault, trusting, and hardworking. The reader is drawn to this pillar of fecundity. Describe in detail the way that Twain develops this character.

ANSWER: *In American literature Jim is one of the few 19th century African-American characters who has a well-developed personality. While Jim (whose last name remains*

unknown) still exhibits residual "Sambo" qualities, Twain nonetheless uses Jim as an excellent foil. He is used to develop Huck and several other characters in this novel (e.g., Tom Sawyer and the Duke). Primarily, Twain uses Jim's conversations with Huck to show how Huck develops. Jim is not a static character, however. He matures as a man/character. For example, by the end of the novel, he exhibits hurt when Huck lets him down.

B. Huck is not a static character. As the novel progresses, he matures. What additional knowledge about the problems of life has Huck acquired by the time he gets to the Phelps' farm? In an essay, explain how Huck has changed by this point.

ANSWER: *Huck develops from a self-centered, selfish boy to an insightful—not yet pensive—thinking young man. Huck is now concerned about the outcome of his actions, and the actions of others. He is suspicious of unnecessary violence. This change occurs as he floats down the Mississippi River. At the end of the novel Huck abdicates leadership to Tom. However, Huck's more mature grasp of the realities of this situation is still quite evident.*

C. Jim and Huck are ironically trying to escape from slavery by floating down the Mississippi River. Why is this escape ironic?

ANSWER: *They are escaping on a floating raft without any artificial power. Thus, they are moving down river toward New Orleans where Jim will stay a slave—not North where Jim could be free.*

D. Mark Twain used several literary devices. Look up the meaning of each of the following literary terms and find at least one example from the book.

1. satire
2. symbolism
3. allegory
4. foreshadowing

ANSWER:

1. satire. (the description of the people at the camp meeting)

2. symbolism. (the way the two confidence men "pay" for their escape)

3. allegory. (the journey downriver, the story of the Duke and the Dauphin)

4. foreshadowing. (Huck's early thoughts about helping a runaway slave)

E. Twain uses first person point of view to tell his story. What advantages and disadvantages does this present Twain?

ANSWER: *The reader has more intimate, first-hand details as they unfold and in that sense the narrator is reliable. On the other hand, the reader sees everything from Huck's viewpoint—hardly a reliable witness. Everything is colored by the eyes of a young, ambivalent, moralistic, somewhat sentimental white southern boy. This viewpoint is especially evident in Huck's ambivalence about escaping with Jim. First-person narration also allows Twain to use dialogue to present humor.*

ENRICHMENT

A. Can you imagine Huck joining the transcendentalist Henry David Thoreau for a year on the edge of Walden Pond? Why or why not?

ANSWER: *They would drive each other crazy! Thoreau is the subjective, pensive thinker/romantic. Huck is the forthright, moral pragmatist/realist. They are opposites.*

B. Define Realism. Give examples of Realism in *Huckleberry Finn.*

ANSWER: *Realism, like most worldviews, has an artistic component and a worldview component. There is an insistence upon the experienced commonplace. Character is more important than plot. Morality is fluid not static. Situation ethics is the rule of the day. The purpose of writing is to instruct and to entertain. Realists were pragmatic, relativistic, democratic, and experimental. The morality of Realism is intrinsic and relativistic. Emphasis is placed upon scenic presentation, de-emphasizing authorial comment and evaluation. Realistic novels rarely use the omniscient point of view. The novel itself—with the journey motif—is realistic. The novel deals with ordinary events in 19th century America. There is no forgiven*

adulterer standing on a scaffold (A Scarlet Letter) or a crazy sea captain chasing a white whale (Moby Dick). Huck Finn is the perfectly modern character: he never considers his eternal destiny. There is no interest in the mind of Huck Finn in the cosmos. He lives in, and relates to, the present. He is a young man without a past and without a future.

C. Realism, which is an ideological cousin to Naturalism, attacks the two most important tenants of Christianity. The basic ontological (i.e., science of beginnings) axiom is the living God. It is theoretically as legitimate for a Christian theist to view God as the cause of the universe as for a realist to view nature as a chaos that happened to arise. Next, the basic epistemological (i.e., science of knowledge) axiom is divine revelation. To the realist, there is no divine revelation. The realist's base of operation lies in rationalism and experience. The Christian theist's base of operation lies in God's divine revelation. Find contemporary examples where Christian theism is clashing with Realism.

ANSWER: *The whole debate about legalizing homosexual marriages smacks of Realism. The pro-homosexual marriage lobby argues that homosexuality is normal and commonplace, thus it should be legal. There is no attempt to defend this social stand by referring to any moral code, Christian or otherwise.*

FINAL PROJECT

Students should correct and rewrite all essays and place them in their Final Portfolio.

LESSON 15 TEST

OBJECTIVE QUESTIONS. (50 POINTS)

_____ 1. Tom proved his honesty early by (A) leaving five cents for the "borrowed" candles. (B) telling Aunt Polly about Jim. (C) refusing to aid Jim. (D) returning what Huck had stolen.

_____ 2. When Huck's father's body was found (A) Huck felt guilty (B) Tom took Huck home to spare Huck's feelings. (C) Jim covered the body to spare Huck's feelings. (D) Huck suspected that he had been murdered by Indian Joe.

_____ 3. The attempted lynching of Col. Sherburn was precipitated by (A) Jim's disappearance. (B) the death of Boggs. (C) the disappearance of the silver coins. (D) Tom's false accusation.

_____ 4. Tom rejected Huck's escape plan for Jim because (A) it would not work. (B) it was too simple. (C) it put Jim into too much danger. (D) it was discovered by Mr. Phelps.

_____ 5. Jim was finally freed by (A) the Emancipation Proclamation. (B) Huck's pleading. (C) a will. (D) a shooting.

DISCUSSION QUESTIONS. (50 POINTS)

A. Most critics agree that _The Adventures of Huckleberry Finn_ is one of the best, if not the best, American novels ever written. Yet, at the same time, it is a deceptively easy book to read. In fact, the same critics argue that it is one of the most difficult books really to understand and to analyze effectively. Why?

B. One must be skeptical about most of what Huck says in order to hear what Twain is saying. Why?

C. Is Twain speaking through Huck or Jim?

D. "All right, then, I'll go to Hell," Huck says when he decides not to return Jim to slavery. Huck is convinced that his reward for defying the moral norms of his society will be eternal damnation. What is the right thing for Huck to do?

E. _The Adventures of Huckleberry Finn_ really is a different kind of book from what we have read so far this year. Explain.

F. Most readers assume that Huck is the hero and center of the story and consider Jim to be a foil. Is it possible they are wrong with Jim being the main character and Huck the foil?

G. One of the major criticisms of _Huck Finn_ has been that Jim is a racist stereotype and that the implication is that African-Americans are stupid, superstitious, and passive. To what extent is Jim a stereotype? Does he break out of this role?

H. What do you think is the climax of the novel? Why?

I. Why do you think the author chose a carefree, uneducated character as the voice through which to tell this story?

J. Do you think it was necessary for Twain to use the word "nigger?" Why or why not?

LESSON 15 TEST ANSWERS

OBJECTIVE QUESTIONS. (50 POINTS)

1. __A__
2. __C__
3. __B__
4. __B__
5. __C__

DISCUSSION QUESTIONS. (50 POINTS)

A. Most critics agree that *The Adventures of Huck Finn* is one of the best, if not the best, American novels ever written. Yet, at the same time, it is a deceptively easy book to read. In fact, the same critics argue that it is one of the most difficult books to really understand and to analyze effectively. Why?

ANSWER: *There are so many layers of meaning in this novel. On one hand, it appears to be a children's story—the continuation of the Tom Sawyer saga, which is a children's story. On the other hand, it is the first major Realistic (worldview) novel written in America. While Melville is a transition writer, there is no doubt that Twain is breaking new ground with this novel.*

B. One must be skeptical about most of what Huck says in order to hear what Twain is saying. Why?

ANSWER: *Twain teases his reader by understatement, hyperbole, and irony. These literary elements all conspire to warn the reader to read between the lines to really hear what Twain is saying.*

C. Is Twain speaking through Huck or Jim?

ANSWER: *Primarily, Twain is speaking through Huck because Huck is the main character and we see the story unfold through Huck's mind.*

D. "All right, then, I'll go to Hell," Huck says when he decides not to return Jim to slavery. Huck is convinced that his reward for defying the moral norms of his society will be eternal damnation. What is the right thing for Huck to do?

ANSWER: *When man's laws (e.g., abortion) violate God's laws, man should obey God's laws and be prepared to accept the consequences of breaking civil laws.*

E. *The Adventures of Huck Finn* really is a different kind of book from what we have read so far this year. Explain.

ANSWER: *Romanticism—both as a worldview and as a literary technique—is dead in this novel. In the scene where Huck is in Arkansas, we especially see the consequences of Romanticism—a crazy feud murders a generation. The characterizations are real; the setting is real too—not an aberration.*

F. Most readers assume that Huck is the hero and center of the story and consider Jim to be a foil. Is it possible they are wrong, with Jim being the main character and Huck the foil?

ANSWER: *I believe Huck is the protagonist. Frankly I do not think Twain was an anti-slavery person, nor do I see evidence that he was any different from other 19th century Americans—he also exhibited some racism. Jim was merely there to develop Huck.*

G. One of the major criticisms of *Huck Finn* has been that the Jim is a racist stereotype and that the implication is that African-Americans are stupid, superstitious, and passive. To what extent is Jim a stereotype? Does he break out of this role?

ANSWER: *He breaks out of his role at the end while he is in prison. Twain is no different from his contemporaries in his views of African-Americans.*

H. What do you think is the climax of the novel? Why?

ANSWER: *The whole novel is about a journey, an escape, and the climax occurs when Jim is released at the end.*

I. Why do you think the author chose a carefree, uneducated character as the voice through which to tell this story?

ANSWER: *This is a brilliant way to poke fun at Romanticism and to take the focus off Huck and onto the matter at hand. His lack of sophistication is disarming and charming!*

J. Do you think it was necessary for Twain to use the word "nigger?" Why or why not?

ANSWER: *This novel is a realistic novel; therefore, it requires the use of this pejorative expression.*

LESSON 16
REALISM, NATURALISM, AND THE FRONTIER *1865-1915* (*Part 2*)

Readings Due For This Lesson: Students should review *The Adventures of Huckleberry Finn* by Mark Twain.

Reading Ahead: Students should review *Red Badge of Courage*, Stephen Crane. Guide Question: Who is the "god" the reader encounters in this seminal, naturalistic novel?

Goal: Students will evaluate this first, and greatest, realistic novel in American literary history.

Goals/Objectives: What is the purpose of this lesson?	Strategies to meet these goals: How will I obtain these goals/objectives?	Evaluation: How will I know when I have met these goals/objectives?
Students will exhibit higher-level thinking as they analyze the ending of this novel. (cognitive goal)	Students will write an essay on this topic: Some critics find the end of the novel to be very disappointing. They feel that after Huck arrives at the Phelps' house, the plot deteriorates rapidly. On the other hand, many critics find the end of the book to be entirely consistent with the tone of the book. What do you think? Defend your answer with specific details from the book. (Critical Thinking A)	Students, with minimal errors, will clearly answer the assigned question in a 1-2 page essay.
Students will increase their vocabulary. (cognitive goal)	Students will collect at least five new vocabulary words from their reading and use these words in their essays.	Students will use five vocabulary words in conversation during the week as well as use the words in their essays and in conversation.
Students will understand this concept: Twain's attitudes toward Christianity. (cognitive goal)	Students will write an essay on this topic: Twain's handling of Christianity wavers between outright scorn and mockery (Chapter I) to veiled superstition. Describe Twain's attitudes toward Christianity in *Huckleberry Finn*. Defend your answer with specific passages from the book. (Critical Thinking B)	Students, with minimal errors, will clearly answer the assigned question in a 1-2 page essay.

Goals/Objectives: What is the purpose of this lesson?	Strategies to meet these goals: How will I obtain these goals/objectives?	Evaluation: How will I know when I have met these goals/objectives?
Students will understand this concept: Twain's cynicism. (cognitive goal)	Students will write an essay on this topic: Give at least one example of Twain's cynicism. (Critical Thinking C)	Students, with minimal errors, will clearly answer the assigned question in a 1-2 page essay.
Students will exhibit higher-level thinking as they discuss Huck's journey. (cognitive goal)	Students will write an essay on this topic: Every journey must have a goal. What is the goal of Huck's journey? (Critical Thinking D)	Students, with minimal errors, will clearly answer the assigned question in a 1-2 page essay.
Students will understand this concept: chattel slavery report. (cognitive goal)	Students will write an essay on this topic: Write a five-page research paper on chattel slavery in the United States as it evolved from 1619 to the American Civil War (1861). (Enrichment A)	Students, with minimal errors, will clearly answer the assigned question in a 5 page research paper.
Students will understand this concept: civil disobedience. (cognitive/affective goal)	Students will write an essay on this topic: Huck's decision to run away with Jim—a slave—is an unlawful act. Huck, though, decides to commit a civil disobedient act. When, if ever, is civil disobedience appropriate? In your answer, reference writings from Thoreau. (Enrichment B)	Students, with minimal errors, will clearly answer the assigned question in a two-page essay.
Students will understand this concept: tone in Twain's short story and *Huck Finn*. (cognitive goal)	Students will write an essay on this topic: Compare the tone of the following short story with the tone in *Huck Finn*. (Enrichment C)	Students, with minimal errors, will clearly answer the assigned question in a 1-2 page essay.
Students will exhibit higher-level thinking as they agree or disagree with this statement: as Huckleberry regularly relativized his situation on the banks of the Mississippi, many modern Americans conduct their lives in the same way. (cognitive goal)	Students will write an essay on this topic: *Huckleberry Finn* is one of the earliest novels in which the issue of motivation and self are paramount. In his book *The Saturated Self: Dilemmas of Identity in Contemporary Life*, Kenneth J. Gergen argues that self- motivation appeared by	Students, with minimal errors, will clearly answer the assigned question in a 1-2 page essay.

Goals/Objectives: What is the purpose of this lesson?	Strategies to meet these goals: How will I obtain these goals/objectives?	Evaluation: How will I know when I have met these goals/ objectives?
	the end of the 20th century as a sort of selfishness that was very destructive to Christianity. As Huckleberry regularly relativized his situation on the banks of the Mississippi, many modern Americans conducted their lives in the same way. Agree or disagree with this statement and offer evidence to support your answer. (Enrichment D)	
Students will work in a group setting. (behavioral goal)	In a class, in a co-op experience, or during a family discussion, students will answer this question: When is Civil Disobedience appropriate?	Students will exhibit practical listening skills and will manifest understanding of opposing worldviews.
Students will be able to recall the information taught in the lesson. (cognitive goal)	Lesson 16 Test	Students will take the test at the end of this lesson and score at least 80%.
Students will experience reflective writing. (affective/spiritual goal)	Using the Journal Guide Questions in the Appendices, students will record at least three entries this week. Suggested Scriptures: Philemon	Student will show evidence that they have reflected on this issue, including informed discussions and written responses.

SUGGESTED
Weekly *Implementation*

DAY 1	DAY 2	DAY 3	DAY 4	DAY 5
Prayer journal.	**Prayer journal.**	**Prayer journal.**	**Prayer journal.**	**Prayer journal.**
Students review the required reading(s) before the assigned lesson begins.	Student should review reading(s) from next lesson.	Students should write rough drafts of all assigned essays.	Student will re-write corrected copies of essays due tomorrow.	Essays are due.
Teacher may want to discuss assigned reading(s) with students.	Students should outline essays due at the end of the week.	The teacher and/or a peer evaluator may correct rough drafts.		Students should take the Lesson 16 test.
Teacher and students will decide on required essays for this lesson, choosing two or three essays.	Per teacher instructions, students may answer orally in a group setting some of the essays that are not assigned as formal essays.			Reading ahead: Students should review *Red Badge of Courage*, Stephen Crane.
The rest of the essays can be outlined, answered with shorter answers, or skipped.				Guide: Who is the "god" the reader encounters in this seminal, naturalistic novel?
Students will review all readings for Lesson 16				

Note: References to sources are in student edition.

ENRICHMENT ACTIVITIES/PROJECTS

A. Students should write an imaginary fictional story where they undertake a similar trip on the Mississippi River to save a friend.

B. Students should choose a series of river experiences from the novel and draw pictures to present in a pictorial portfolio.

SUPPLEMENTAL RESOURCES

Burns, Ken. *Mark Twain.* (PBS Program)
    A wonderful documentary on the life of Mark Twain.

Burns, Ken, Dayton Duncan, and Geoffrey C. Ward. *Mark Twain, An Illustrated Biography.*
    The book version of the PBS documentary.

Holbrook, Hal. *Mark Twain Tonight.* (DVD)
    Hal Holbrook is the perfect Mark Twain in this 1967 television special.

Robinson, Forrest G. ed. *The Cambridge Companion to Mark Twain.*

Single best secondary resource on Mark Twain.

Notes:

CRITICAL THINKING

A. Some critics find the end of the novel to be very disappointing. They feel that after Huck arrives at the Phelps' house, the plot deteriorates rapidly. On the other hand, many critics find the end of the book to be entirely consistent with the tone of the book. What do you think? Defend your answer with specific details from the book.

ANSWER: *Those critics who do not like the ending argue that the Huck Finn/Tom Sawyer incidence is reminiscent of the inferior novel,* Tom Sawyer. *They argue that this serious, brilliant, realistic novel degenerates into a juvenile, humorous moral tale. Each reader must decide for himself, however.*

B. Twain's handling of Christianity wavers between outright scorn and mockery (Chapter I) to veiled superstition. Describe Twain's attitudes toward Christianity in *Huckleberry Finn.* Defend your answer with specific passages from the book.

ANSWER: *Obviously Huck did not have a vital, living faith. "After supper she (Widow Douglas) learned me about Moses . . . but when I discovered he had been dead a considerable long time . . . I don't take no stock in dead people." (p. 2) The whole novel, in effect, is the story of a boy in conflict. Perhaps the one significant change in Huck Finn during the course of the book is his duty to Jim, a morality loosely based on New Testament ethic.*

C. Give at least one example of Twain's cynicism.

ANSWER: *When he had Colonel Sherburn taunt the mob. When he described the Duke putting up the notice, "Ladies and Children not Admitted." "There, if that line don't fetch them, I don't know Arkansaw." These are only two contempts for humanity that Twain exhibits.*

D. Every journey must have a goal. What is the goal of Huck's journey?

ANSWER: *Throughout the book there is an ever-increasing engagement between the world of the raft and the world on shore. As the book progresses there is less and less notice taken of the raft and more and more of the river bank world. The world on shore—the real world—is singularly unsatisfactory, disingenuous, and immoral. The world on the raft—exhibited by the friendship of Huck and Jim is genuine and wholesome.*

ENRICHMENT: THE HISTORICAL SETTING

A. Write a <u>five-page report</u> on chattel slavery in the United States as it evolved from 1619 to the American Civil War. (1861)

ANSWER: *There is much debate about what came first to the American shore: racism or slavery. Where the first slaves indentured servants or chattel slavery? In any event, by the time Eli Whitney invented the cotton gin, slavery was a significant part of southern, as well as northern, society.*

B. Huck's decision to run away with Jim—a slave—is an unlawful act. Huck, though, decides to commit a civil disobedient act. When, if ever, is civil disobedience appropriate? In your answer, reference writings from Thoreau.

ANSWER: *When man's laws violate God's laws Christians are obligated to follow God's laws no matter what the consequences. Thus, since chattel slavery, I believe, is against God's laws, Huck has every right to violate that law; however, once an act of civil disobedience is committed, the perpetrator of the act is obligated to accept the punishment for the crime. Civil disobedience <u>never</u> justifies an act of violence.*

C. Compare the tone of the following short story with the tone in *Huck Finn.*

ANSWER: *Both short stories use colloquial language and misanthropisms to generate interest in their readers. The similarities end here. There is no serious, vitriolic message in the "Celebrated Jumping Frog."*

D. *Huckleberry Finn* is one of the earliest novels in which the issue of motivation and self are paramount. In his book *The Saturated Self: Dilemmas of Identity in Contemporary Life,* Kenneth J. Gergen argues that self motivation appeared by the end of the 20th century as a sort of selfishness that was very destructive to Christianity. As Huckleberry regularly relativized his situation on the banks of the Mississippi, many modern Americans conducted their lives in the same way. Agree or disagree with this statement and offer evidence to support your answer.

ANSWER: *Many readers agree. Since Sigmund Freud*

invited people to reject conviction (he called it "guilt"), the whole concept of personal responsibility has lost all meaning. Combine this obsession with human motivation with romantic notions of human subjectivity, and the results are inevitable. Most people freely relativize their situations and make decisions out of perceived need and self-interest rather than according to a code of ethics.

FINAL PROJECT

Students should correct and rewrite all essays and place them in their Final Portfolio.

LESSON 16 TEST

DISCUSSION QUESTIONS. (50 POINTS)

State what worldview–Romanticism or Realism–is exhibited in each passage below. Defend your answer.

A. It was Sunday, and, according to his custom on that day, McTeague took his dinner at two in the afternoon at the car conductors' coffee-joint on Polk Street. He had a thick gray soup; heavy, underdone meat, very hot, on a cold plate; two kinds of vegetables; and a sort of suet pudding, full of strong butter and sugar. On his way back to his office, one block above, he stopped at Joe Frenna's saloon and bought a pitcher of steam beer. It was his habit to leave the pitcher there on his way to dinner. *McTeague*, Frank Norris.

B. I am by birth a Genevese; and my family is one of the most distinguished of that republic. My ancestors had been for many years counselors and syndics; and my father had filled several public situations with honor and reputation. He was respected by all who knew him for his integrity and indefatigable attention to public business. He passed his younger days perpetually occupied by the affairs of his country; a variety of circumstances had prevented his marrying early, nor was it until the decline of life that he became a husband and the father of a family. *Frankenstein*, Mary Shelley.

C. The village lay under two feet of snow, with drifts at the windy corners. In a sky of iron the points of the Dipper hung like icicles and Orion flashed his cold fires. The moon had set, but the night was so transparent that the white house-fronts between the elms looked gray against the snow, clumps of bushes made black stains on it, and the basement windows of the church sent shafts of yellow light far across the endless undulations. Young Ethan Frome walked at a quick pace along the deserted street, past the bank and Michael Eady's new brick store and Lawyer Varnum's house with the two black Norway spruces at the gate. Opposite the Varnum gate, where the road fell away toward the Corbury valley, the church reared its slim white steeple and narrow peristyle. As the young man walked toward it the upper windows drew a black arcade along the side wall of the building, but from the lower openings, on the side where the ground sloped steeply down to the Corbury road, the light shot its long bars, illuminating many fresh furrows in the track leading to the basement door, and showing, under an adjoining shed, a line of sleighs with heavily blanketed horses. *Ethan Frome*, Edith Wharton.

D. The little farmers watched debt creep up on them like the tide. They sprayed the trees and sold no crop, they pruned and grafted and could not pick the crop. And the men of knowledge have worked, have considered, and the fruit is rotting on the ground, and the decaying mash in the wine vats is poisoning the air. And taste the wine—no grape flavor at all, just sulphor and tannic acid and alcohol. This little orchard will be part of a great holding next year, for the debt will have choked the owner. This vineyard will belong to the bank. Only the great owners can survive, for they own the canneries too. And four pears peeled and cut in half, cooked and canned, still cost fifteen cents. And the canned pears do not spoil. They will last for years. The decay spreads over the State, and the sweet smell is a great sorrow on the land. Men who can graft the trees and make the seed fertile and big can find no way to let the hungry people eat their produce. Men who have created new fruits in the world cannot create a system whereby their fruits may be eaten and the failure hangs over the State like a great sorrow. The works of the roots of the vines, of the trees, must be destroyed to keep up the price, and this is the saddest, bitterest thing of all. Carloads of oranges dumped on the ground. The people come from miles to take the fruit, but this could not be. How would they buy oranges at twenty cents a dozen if they could drive out and pick them up? And men with hoses squirt kerosine on the oranges, and they are angry at the crime, angry at the people who have come to take the fruit. A million people hungry, needing the fruit—and kerosine sprayed over the golden mountains. And the smell of rot fills the country. Burn coffee for fuel in the ships. Burn corn to keep warm, it makes a hot fire. Dump potatoes in the rivers and place guards along the banks to keep the hungry people from fishing them out. Slaughter the pigs and bury them, and let the putrescence drip down into the earth. *Grapes of Wrath*, John Steinbeck.

E. On the human imagination, events produce the effects of time. Thus, he who has traveled far and seen much, is apt to fancy that he has lived long;

and the history that most abounds in important incidents, soonest assumes the aspect of antiquity. In no other way can we account for the venerable air that is already gathering around American annals. When the mind reverts to the earliest days of colonial history, the period seems remote and obscure, the thousand changes that thicken along the links of recollections, throwing back the origin of the nation to a day so distant as seemingly to reach the mists of time; and yet four lives of ordinary duration would suffice to transmit, from mouth to mouth, in the form of tradition, all that civilized man has achieved within the limits of the republic. Although New York, alone, possesses a population materially exceeding that of either of the four smallest kingdoms of Europe, or materially exceeding that of the entire Swiss Confederation, it is little more than two centuries since the Dutch commenced their settlement, rescuing region from the savage state. Thus, what seems venerable by an accumulation of changes, is reduced to familiarity when we come seriously to consider it solely in connection with time. *Deerslayer*, James Fenimore Cooper.

F. Found among the papers of the late Diedrech Knickerbocker. A pleasing land of drowsy head it was, Of dreams that wave before the half-shut eye; And of gay castles in the clouds that pass, Forever flushing round a summer sky. Castle of Indolence. In the bosom of one of those spacious coves which indent the eastern shore of the Hudson, at that broad expansion of the river denominated by the ancient Dutch navigators the Tappan Zee, and where they always prudently shortened sail and implored the protection of St. Nicholas when they crossed, there lies a small market town or rural port, which by some is called Greensburgh, but which is more generally and properly known by the name of Tarry Town. This name was given, we are told, in former days, by the good housewives of the adjacent country, from the inveterate propensity of their husbands to linger about the village tavern on market days. Be that as it may, I do not vouch for the fact, but merely advert to it, for the sake of being precise and authentic. Not far from this village, perhaps about two miles, there is a little valley or rather lap of land among high hills, which is one of the quietest places in the whole world. A small brook glides through it, with just murmur enough to lull one to repose; and the occasional whistle of a quail or tapping of a woodpecker is almost the only sound that ever breaks in upon the uniform tranquillity. *The Legend of Sleep Hollow*, Washington Irving.

G. I'm not! And if turning up my hair makes me one, I'll wear it in two tails till I'm twenty, cried Jo, pulling off her net, and shaking down a chestnut mane. I hate to think I've got to grow up, and be Miss March, and wear long gowns, and look as prim as a China Aster! It's bad enough to be a girl, anyway, when I like boy's games and work and manners! I can't get over my disappointment in not being a boy. And it's worse than ever now, for I'm dying to go and fight with Papa. And I can only stay home and knit, like a poky old woman! *Little Women*, Lousia Alcott

H. Shaking off the sleet from my ice-glazed hat and jacket, I seated myself near the door, and turning sideways was surprised to see Queequeg near me. Affected by the solemnity of the scene, there was a wondering gaze of incredulous curiosity in his countenance. This savage was the only person present who seemed to notice my entrance; because he was the only one who could not read, and, therefore, was not reading those frigid inscriptions on the wall. Whether any of the relatives of the seamen whose names appeared there were now among the congregation, I knew not; but so many are the unrecorded accidents in the fishery, and so plainly did several women present wear the countenance if not the trappings of some unceasing grief, that I feel sure that here before me were assembled those, in whose unhealing hearts the sight of those bleak tablets sympathetically caused the old wounds to bleed afresh. *Moby Dick*, Herman Melville

I. The Time Traveler (for so it will be convenient to speak of him) was expounding a recondite matter to us. His grey eyes shone and twinkled, and his usually pale face was flushed and animated. The fire burned brightly, and the soft radiance of the incandescent lights in the lilies of silver caught the bubbles that flashed and passed in our glasses. Our chairs, being his patents, embraced and caressed us rather than submitted to be sat upon, and there was that luxurious after-dinner atmosphere when thought roams gracefully free of the trammels of precision. And he put it to us in this way—marking the points with a lean forefinger—as we sat and lazily admired his earnestness over this new paradox (as we thought it:) and his fecundity. *The Time Machine*, H. G. Wells

J. On an exceptionally hot evening early in July a young man came out of the garret in which he lodged in S. Place and walked slowly, as though in hesitation, towards K. bridge. He had successfully avoided meeting his landlady on the staircase. His garret was under the roof of a high, five-storied house, and was more like a cupboard than a room. The landlady, who provided him with garret, dinners, and attendance, lived on the floor below, and every time he went out he was obliged to pass her kitchen, the door of which invariably stood open. And each time he passed, the young man had a sick, frightened feeling, which made him scowl and feel ashamed. He was hopelessly in debt to his landlady, and was afraid of meeting her. *Crime and Punishment*, Fydor Doestoevsky

DISCUSSION QUESTIONS. (50 POINTS)

A. State why you agree or disagree with these critics. (30 Points)

All modern American literature comes from one book called *Huckleberry Finn* by Mark Twain. If you read it, you must stop where the Nigger Jim is stolen from the boys. That is the real end. The rest is just cheating, but it's the best book we've had. All American writing comes from that. There was nothing before. There has been nothing as good since. –Ernest Hemingway. (1959)

Huck Finn is alone: there is no more solitary character in fiction. The fact that he has a father only emphasizes his loneliness; and he views his father with a terrifying detachment. So we come to see Huck himself in the end as one of the permanent symbolic figures of fiction; not unworthy to take a place with Ulysses, Faust, Don Quixote, Don Juan, Hamlet and other great discoveries that man has made about himself. –T. S. Eliot. (1959)

In one sense, Huckleberry Finn seems a circular book, ending as it began with a refused adoption and a projected flight; and certainly it has the effect of refusing the reader's imagination passage into the future. But there is a break-through in the last pages, especially in the terrible sentence which begins,"But I reckon I got to light out for the territory ahead of the rest...." In these words, the end of childhood is clearly signaled; and we are forced to ask the question, which, duplicitously, the book refuses to answer: what will become of Huck if he persists in his refusal to return to the place where he has been before? —Leslie A. Fiedler. (1982)

B. The following was quoted in an 1885 newspaper, "The Concord Public Library committee has decided to exclude Mark Twain's latest book from the library. One member of the committee says that, while he does not wish to call it immoral, he thinks it contains but little humor, and that of a very coarse type. He regards it as the veriest trash. The librarian and the other members of the committee entertain similar views, characterizing it as rough, coarse and inelegant, dealing with a series of experiences not elevating, the whole book being more suited to the slums that to intelligent, respectable people." Agree or disagree with the Concord Public Library. (10 Points)

C. One newspaper editor observed in an obituary that "in ages to come, if historians and archaeologists would know the thoughts, the temper, the characteristic psychology of the American of the latter half of the nineteenth century, he will need only to read *Innocents Abroad*, *Tom Sawyer*, and *Huckleberry Finn*." What is the "characteristic psychology" to which he is referring? (10 Points)

LESSON 16 TEST ANSWERS

DISCUSSION QUESTIONS. (50 POINTS)

State what world view–Romanticism or Realism–that is exhibited in each passage below. Defend your answer.

A. **ANSWER:** *Realism (and Naturalism). Notice the every day details, the unadorned writing, and the ordinary setting.*

B. **ANSWER:** *Romanticism. Shelley chooses the extraordinary setting to develop her protagonist. In fact, Dr. Frankenstein is a sort of Alymer (in Birthmark).*

C. **ANSWER:** *Realism. The realistic, cold, unappetizing setting is a metaphor for the empty lives we shall soon observe unfold in this novel.*

D. **ANSWER:** *Realism. Steinbeck is one of the most famous American Realism writers. Notice the earthy details.*

E. **ANSWER:** *Romanticism. To Cooper, nature is ubiquitous. In fact, Native Americans are "noble" and nature in its pure form (i.e., untouched by human civilization) is pristine.*

F. **ANSWER:** *Romanticism. Nature has a powerful effect on the setting.*

G. **ANSWER:** *Romanticism. The characters and setting conspire to celebrate the extraordinary—the family is extraordinary, the setting is extraordinary.*

H. **ANSWER:** *This is a tough call. Melville is a Romantic writer but this book is a transition from Romanticism to Naturalism.*

I. **ANSWER:** *While Wells wrote science fiction, the images are ordinary, and the main characters are ordinary.*

J. **ANSWER:** *While this is a theistic novel, Doestoevsky writes in a Realistic style.*

DISCUSSION QUESTIONS. (50 POINTS)

A. Agree or disagree with these critics. (30 Points)

All modern American literature comes from one book by Mark Twain called Huckleberry Finn. If you read it you must stop where the Nigger Jim is stolen from the boys. That is the real end. The rest is just cheating. But it's the best book we've had. All American writing comes from that. There was nothing before. There has been nothing as good since. –Ernest Hemingway. (1959)

ANSWER: *Realism, Social Darwinism (i.e., the feud in Arkansas), and racism were all a part of the cultural scene of post-Civil War America. This reader categorically disagrees. At this point the climax has not occurred—Jim's struggle from freedom in the prison is a great opportunity for Twain to develop Jim and Huck.*

Huck Finn is alone: there is no more solitary character in fiction. The fact that he has a father only emphasizes his loneliness; and he views his father with a terrifying detachment. So we come to see Huck himself in the end as one of the permanent symbolic figures of fiction; not unworthy to take a place with Ulysses, Faust, Don Quixote, Don Juan, Hamlet and other great discoveries that man has made about himself. –T. S. Eliot. (1959)

ANSWER: *I agree. Huck, in spite of his proximity to other characters, is actually very alone. Twain creates Huck this way so that his journey, so to speak, belongs to the reader and Huck and to no one else.*

In one sense, Huckleberry Finn seems a circular book, ending as it began with a refused adoption and a projected flight; and certainly it has the effect of refusing the reader's imagination passage into the future. But there is a break-through in the last pages, especially in the terrible sentence which begins, "But I reckon I got to light out for the territory ahead of the rest...." In these words, the end of childhood is clearly signaled; and we are forced to ask the question, which, duplicitously, the book refuses to answer: what will become of Huck if he persists in his refusal to return to the place where he has been before? _Leslie A. Fiedler. (1982)

ANSWER: *This is a critical question whose answer is pure speculation. The sense is that Huck is a changed young man and cannot return to the racism and duplicity that was the ante-bellum South.*

B. The following was quoted in an 1885 newspaper, "The Concord Public Library committee has decided to exclude Mark Twain's latest book from the library. One member of the committee says that, while he does not wish to call it immoral, he thinks it contains but little humor, and that of a very coarse type. He regards it as the veriest trash. The librarian and the other members of the committee entertain similar views, characterizing it as rough, coarse and inelegant, dealing with a series of experiences not elevating, the whole book being more suited to the slums that to intelligent, respectable people." Agree or disagree with the Concord Public Library. (10 Points)

ANSWER: *We must be careful not to place present moral standards on 1885 America. At that time, according to their standards, it probably was obscene. However, I found the novel mild compared to a Hemingway, Steinbeck, or Salinger.*

C. One newspaper editor observed in an obituary that "in ages to come, if historians and archaeologists would know the thoughts, the temper, the characteristic psychology of the American of the latter half of the nineteenth century, he will need only to read *Innocents Abroad*, *Tom Sawyer*, and *Huckleberry Finn*." What is the "characteristic psychology" to which he is referring? (10 Points)

ANSWER: *Realism, Social Darwinism (i.e., the feud in Arkansas), and racism were all a part of the cultural scene of post-Civil War America.*

LESSON 17
REALISM, NATURALISM, AND THE FRONTIER,
1865-1915 (Part 3)

Readings Due For This Lesson: Students should review *The Red Badge of Courage*, Stephen Crane.

Reading Ahead: Students should review *The Red Badge of Courage*, Stephen Crane. Is Henry Fleming a patriotic war hero or a fatalist waving a flag on the hill of futility? Who is the "god" the reader encounters in this seminal, naturalistic novel?

Reading Ahead: Students should review "Outcasts of Poker Flat," Bret Harte; "The Story of an Hour," Kate Chopin; "Luke Havergal" and "Credo," Edwin Arlington Robinson; "Lucinda Matlock," Edgar Lee Masters. (Lesson 19) What new styles and themes emerge in these late 19th century works?

Goal: Students will analyze *Red Badge of Courage*, Stephen Crane.

Goals/Objectives: What is the purpose of this lesson?	Strategies to meet these goals: How will I obtain these goals/objectives?	Evaluation: How will I know when I have met these goals/objectives?
Students will understand this concept: a comparison of Stephen Crane's view of death with Jack London's view of death. (cognitive goal)	Students will write an essay on this topic: Compare and contrast Stephen Crane's view of death with Jack London's view of death in this short story. They are both naturalist writers. (Critical Thinking A)	Students, with minimal errors, will clearly answer the assigned question in a 1-2 page essay.
Students will increase their vocabulary. (cognitive goal)	Besides defining the recommended words, students will collect at least five new vocabulary words from their reading and use these words in their essays.	Students will use five vocabulary words in conversation during the week as well as use the words in their essays and in conversation.
Students will exhibit higher-level thinking as they discuss if Crane appeared to have been in a real battle. (cognitive goal)	Students will write an essay on this topic: When he wrote this book, Crane had never shot a gun in anger or seen a battle. Can you tell? (Critical Thinking B)	Students, with minimal errors, will clearly answer the assigned question in a 1-2 page essay.

Goals/Objectives: What is the purpose of this lesson?	Strategies to meet these goals: How will I obtain these goals/objectives?	Evaluation: How will I know when I have met these goals/ objectives?
Students will understand this concept: whether or not the protagonist matured in the novel. (cognitive goal)	Students will write an essay on this topic: Define maturity. How was Henry more mature at the end of the novel than he was at the beginning? (Critical Thinking C)	Students, with minimal errors, will clearly answer the assigned question in a 1-2 page essay.
Students will consider the generalization that Christian theism is a vastly superior, wholesome worldview. (affective goal)	Students will find examples of this hopelessness in modern movies, television programs, and music. Why, as Christian believers, should we reject this pessimism? (Biblical Application)	Students, with minimal errors, will clearly answer the assigned question in a 1-2 page essay.
Students will exhibit higher-level thinking as they agree or disagree with the main thesis of B. F. Skinner's *Beyond Freedom and Dignity*. (cognitive goal)	Students will write an essay on this topic: A contemporary and very popular proponent of *Naturalism* is B. F. Skinner. In his book *Beyond Freedom and Dignity*, Skinner argues that the problems we face today are caused by outside forces (e.g., Nature) and can be solved by also changing these outside forces. Changing hearts is irrelevant. Agree or disagree. (Enrichment)	Students, with minimal errors, will clearly answer the assigned question in a 1-2 page essay.
Students will work in a group setting. (behavioral goal)	In a class, in a co-op experience, or during a family discussion, Students will discuss what it was like to be in a Civil War battle.	Students will exhibit practical listening skills and will manifest understanding of opposing worldviews.
Students will be able to recall the information taught in the lesson. (cognitive goal)	Lesson 17 Test	Students will take the test at the end of this lesson and score at least 80%.
Students will experience reflective writing. (affective/spiritual goal)	Using the Journal Guide Questions in the Appendices, students will record at least three entries this week. Suggested Scriptures: Exodus 20	Students will show evidence that they have reflected on this issue, including informed discussions and written responses.

SUGGESTED
Weekly Implementation

DAY 1	DAY 2	DAY 3	DAY 4	DAY 5
Prayer journal.	**Prayer journal.**	**Prayer journal.**	**Prayer journal.**	**Prayer journal.**
Students review the required reading (s) before the assigned lesson begins.	Students should review reading (s) from next lesson.	Students should write rough drafts of all assigned essays.	Student will re-write corrected copies of essays due tomorrow.	Essays are due.
Teacher may want to discuss assigned reading(s) with students.	Student should outline essays due at the end of the week.	The teacher and/or a peer evaluator may correct rough drafts.		Students should take the Lesson 17 test.
Teacher and students will decide on required essays for this lesson, choosing two or three essays.	Per teacher instructions, students may answer orally in a group setting some of the essays that are not assigned as formal essays.			Reading Ahead: Students should review "Outcasts of Poker Flat," Bret Harte; "The Story of an Hour," Kate Chopin; "Luke Havergal" and "Credo," Edwin Arlington Robinson; "Lucinda Matlock," Edgar Lee Masters. (Lesson 19)
The rest of the essays can be outlined, answered with shorter answers, or skipped.				Guide: What new styles and themes emerge in these late 19th century works?
Students will review all readings for Lesson 17				

Note: References to sources are in student edition.

ENRICHMENT ACTIVITIES/PROJECTS

A particularly popular writer of the Gilded Age social history was Sinclair Lewis. Lewis brought late 19th century Americans into the small towns and bedrooms of American homes all over the land. Students should read one of his books.

Students should watch the popular Disney film *Newsies*. It is a fairly accurate picture of early labor problems in the Gilded Age.

SUPPLEMENTAL RESOURCES

Ahnebrink, Lars. *The Beginnings of Naturalism in American Fiction.*
Appears to be an excellent resource.

Bassan, Maurice. *Stephen Crane: A Collection of Critical Essays.*
Somewhat pedantic, but insightful essays on Crane's *major works.*

Crane, Stephen. *Great Short Works of Stephen Crane: Red Badge of Courage, Monster, Maggie, Open Boat, Blue Hotel, Bride Comes to Yellow Sky and Other Works.*
An excellent, unedited version of Crane's works.

Katz. Joseph, (Editor). *The Complete Poems of Stephen Crane.*

While Crane is a less accomplished poet than many others, his works are worth examining.

The Red Badge of Courage. (1951) Movie.

This epic version of Crane's novel, starring Audie Murphy, is a fairly accurate version of the book.

Notes:

Suggested Vocabulary Words

I	hilarious	(comical)
III	impregnable	(invincible)
III	impetus	(force)
	perambulating	(strolling)
VI	imprecations	(curses)
	querulous	(irritable)
IX	trepidation	(fear)
X	perfunctory	(cursory)
XIX	petulantly	(angry)
	deprecating	(condemning)
XXI	temerity	(shyness)
XXIV	imperious	(overbearing)
	expletive	(exclamation)
	stentorian	(very loud)

Critical Thinking

A. When he wrote this book, Crane had never shot a gun in anger or seen a battle. Can you tell?

ANSWER: *The charge scenes are more like American soldiers storming San Juan Hill in the Spanish American War than a hill in Northern Virginia during the American Civil War. The characters in the novel are far more modern than American Civil War soldiers, who, to a man, were theists. The struggles which Fleming experienced were mostly foreign to Civil War Americans. Not for a moment can I imagine an American in 1861 wondering if there was a God.*

B. Define maturity. How was Henry more mature at the end of the novel than he was at the beginning?

ANSWER: *This reader defines maturity partly as "delaying pleasure." I find Henry to be more mature, or is he just a modern, unfeeling American? I am not sure. I find Hester Prynne to be a far more mature character. Nonetheless, at the beginning of the novel Fleming is an incorrigible romantic. By*

the end of the novel he is a naturalist. He no longer cares what happens to him—he is a fatalist. He figures that he has no control over his fate—so why worry or be brave? At the end of the novel he has not matured to a brave man; he has been transformed into a cynical naturalist.

C. Compare and contrast Stephen Crane's view of death with Jack London's view of death in this short story. They are both naturalist writers.

ANSWER: *Actually their views are very similar. Death is a biological fact—not a cosmological event. Like all creatures, mankind dies and disappears into an abyss. The naturalist is not willing to argue there is no God at all, but if there is one, he certainly is malevolent or impersonal. Thus, death is not connected to any higher power or to any eternal destiny. Later, naturalists turned existentialists, like Jean Paul Sartre (in his play* No Exit*), take this viewpoint to the next logical step: there is a reality and it is the here-and-now. It is a sort of hell.*

Biblical Application

A man said to the universe: "Sir, I exist!" "However," replied the universe, "The fact has not created in me a sense of obligation." (In Humanity, http://quotes.prolix,mi/Authors/).

He never created a Hester Prynne who gave her life to absolute truth or a Huck Finn who had affectionate tolerance toward differing opinions. Crane's world was cynical and very dangerous. His world was full of opportunistic "demons" who sought to do him in. He was "A man adrift on a slim spar/A horizon smaller than the rim of a bottle/Tented waves rearing lashy dark points/The near whine of froth in circles./God is cold." (http://www.americanpoems.com/F from the poem "Adrift on a Spar") In a short story entitled "The Open Boat" Crane hauntingly described the frustration of being in an open boat near enough to see the shore but unable to reach the shore and safety (http://www.gonzaga.edu/faculty/campbell/crane/):

> If I am going to be drowned—if I am going to be drowned—if I am going to be drowned, why, in the name of the seven mad gods who rule the sea, was I allowed to come thus far and contemplate sand and trees? Was I brought here merely to have my nose dragged away as I was about to nibble the sacred cheese of life?

The morbidity expressed by Crane becomes a recurring theme in American literature. Gone is the God of the Puritans and even the God whom Hester Prynne so faithfully served. The great-great-grandchildren of Anne Bradstreet doubted God really loved them at all. "Fate" was the true power that determined their future.

Question: Find examples of this hopelessness in modern movies, television programs, and music. Why, as Christian believers, should we reject this pessimism?

ANSWER: *Even a cursory examination of modern movies (through advertisements, not necessarily through watching them) exhibits the following characteristics: the protagonists are inevitably divorced, single, or involved in some sort of dysfunctional relationship. There is excessive violence (Naturalism) and sexuality (Realism) in most movies. There is a sort of maudlin, moralizing in some moves, but by and large this is only a digression from the hopeless plot. Inevitably an unhappy occurrence or doomed relationship ultimately prevails. Why, as Christian believers, should we reject this pessimism? Because it is patently untrue. In all these things we are more than victorious through Him who loved us. (Romans 8) Because we have been remarkably and wonderfully made. (Psalm 139) We have a wonderful destiny ahead of us. (1 Corinthians 15) O, death where is thy sting? Christians have nothing to fear in the world because of what our God has done in and outside this world.*

ENRICHMENT

A contemporary and very popular proponent of *Naturalism* is B. F. Skinner. In his book *Beyond Freedom and Dignity*, Skinner argues that the problems we face today are caused by outside forces (e.g., Nature) and can be solved by changing these outside forces. Changing hearts is irrelevant. Agree or disagree.

ANSWER: *B. F. Skinner, like most deterministic, naturalistic, behaviorists, believes that people are merely one more species responding to stimuli around them. They have no control over their fate and make no decision based on metaphysics. People function out of self-interest and reward. They are no more than sensory automatons. If it feels good people do it; if not, they don't. This is wrong. People are created in the image of God, and, once converted, are able to do unselfish acts in the name of Christ. This is the whole foundation of modern, western society (Max Weber).*

FINAL PROJECT

Students should correct and rewrite all essays and place them in their Final Portfolio.

LESSON 17 TEST

DISCUSSION QUESTIONS (100 POINTS)

Find 5 examples of *Naturalism* in the following short story, state the paragraph number, and defend your answer.

The Open Boat

Stephen Crane

1 None of them knew the color of the sky. Their eyes glanced level, and were fastened upon the waves that swept toward them. These waves were of the hue of slate, save for the tops, which were of foaming white, and all of the men knew the colors of the sea. The horizon narrowed and widened, and dipped and rose, and at all times its edge was jagged with waves that seemed thrust up in points like rocks.

2 Many a man ought to have a bath-tub larger than the boat which here rode upon the sea. These waves were most wrongfully and barbarously abrupt and tall, and each froth-top was a problem in small boat navigation.

3 The cook squatted in the bottom and looked with both eyes at the six inches of gunwale which separated him from the ocean. His sleeves were rolled over his fat forearms, and the two flaps of his unbuttoned vest dangled as he bent to bail out the boat. Often he said: "Gawd! That was a narrow clip." As he remarked it he invariably gazed eastward over the broken sea.

4 The oiler, steering with one of the two oars in the boat, sometimes raised himself suddenly to keep clear of water that swirled in over the stern. It was a thin little oar and it seemed often ready to snap.

5 The correspondent, pulling at the other oar, watched the waves and wondered why he was there.

6 The injured captain, lying in the bow, was at this time buried in that profound dejection and indifference which comes, temporarily at least, to even the bravest and most enduring when, willy nilly, the firm fails, the army loses, the ship goes down. The mind of the master of a vessel is rooted deep in the timbers of her, though he command for a day or a decade, and this captain had on him the stern impression of a scene in the grays of dawn of seven turned faces, and later a stump of a top-mast with a white ball on it that slashed to and fro at the waves, went low and lower, and down. Thereafter there was something strange in his voice. Although steady, it was deep with mourning, and of a quality beyond oration or tears.

7 "Keep'er a little more south, Billie," said he.

8 "'A little more south,' sir," said the oiler in the stern.

9 A seat in this boat was not unlike a seat upon a bucking broncho, and, by the same token, a broncho is not much smaller. The craft pranced and reared, and plunged like an animal. As each wave came, and she rose for it, she seemed like a horse making at a fence outrageously high. The manner of her scramble over these walls of water is a mystic thing, and, moreover, at the top of them were ordinarily these problems in white water, the foam racing down from the summit of each wave, requiring a new leap, and a leap from the air. Then, after scornfully bumping a crest, she would slide, and race, and splash down a long incline and arrive bobbing and nodding in front of the next menace.

10 A singular disadvantage of the sea lies in the fact that after successfully surmounting one wave you discover that there is another behind it just as important and just as nervously anxious to do something effective in the way of swamping boats. In a ten-foot dingey one can get an idea of the resources of the sea in the line of waves that is not probable to the average experience, which is never at sea in a dingey. As each slaty wall of water approached, it shut all else from the view of the men in the boat, and it was not difficult to imagine that this particular wave was the final outburst of the ocean, the last effort of the grim water. There was a terrible grace in the move of the waves, and they came in silence, save for the snarling of the crests.

11 In the wan light, the faces of the men must have been gray. Their eyes must have glinted in strange ways as they gazed steadily astern. Viewed from a balcony, the whole thing would doubtlessly have been weirdly picturesque. But the men in the boat had no time to see it, and if they had had leisure there were other things to occupy their minds. The sun swung steadily up the sky, and they knew it was broad day because the color of the sea changed from slate to emerald-green, streaked with amber lights, and the foam was like tumbling snow. The process of the breaking day was unknown to them. They were aware only of this effect upon the color of the waves that rolled toward them.

12 In disjointed sentences the cook and the correspondent argued as to the difference between a life-saving station and a house of refuge. The cook had said: "There's a house of refuge just north of the Mosquito Inlet Light, and as soon as they see us, they'll come off in their boat and pick us up."

13 "As soon as who see us?" said the correspondent.

14 "The crew," said the cook.

15 "Houses of refuge don't have crews," said the correspondent. "As I understand them, they are only places where clothes and grub are stored for the benefit of shipwrecked people. They don't carry crews."

16 "Oh, yes, they do," said the cook.

17 "No, they don't," said the correspondent.

18 "Well, we're not there yet, anyhow," said the oiler, in the stern.

19 "Well," said the cook, "perhaps it's not a house of refuge that I'm thinking of as being near Mosquito Inlet Light. Perhaps it's a life-saving station."

20 "We're not there yet," said the oiler, in the stern.

II.

21 As the boat bounced from the top of each wave, the wind tore through the hair of the hatless men, and as the craft plopped her stern down again the spray slashed past them. The crest of each of these waves was a hill, from the top of which the men surveyed, for a moment, a broad tumultuous expanse; shining and wind-riven. It was probably splendid. It was probably glorious, this play of the free sea, wild with lights of emerald and white and amber.

22 "Bully good thing it's an on-shore wind," said the cook. "If not, where would we be? Wouldn't have a show."

23 "That's right," said the correspondent.

24 The busy oiler nodded his assent.

25 Then the captain, in the bow, chuckled in a way that expressed humor, contempt, tragedy, all in one. "Do you think we've got much of a show, now, boys?" said he.

26 Whereupon the three were silent, save for a trifle of hemming and hawing. To express any particular optimism at this time they felt to be childish and stupid, but they all doubtless possessed this sense of the situation in their mind. A young man thinks doggedly at such times. On the other hand, the ethics of their condition was decidedly against any open suggestion of hopelessness. So they were silent.

27 "Oh, well," said the captain, soothing his children, "we'll get ashore all right."

28 But there was that in his tone which made them think, so the oiler quoth: "Yes! If this wind holds!"

29 The cook was bailing: "Yes! If we don't catch hell in the surf."

30 Canton flannel gulls flew near and far. Sometimes they sat down on the sea, near patches of brown sea-weed that rolled over the waves with a movement like carpets on line in a gale. The birds sat comfortably in groups, and they were envied by some in the dingey, for the wrath of the sea was no more to them than it was to a covey of prairie chickens a thousand miles inland. Often they came very close and stared at the men with black bead-like eyes. At these times they were uncanny and sinister in their unblinking scrutiny, and the men hooted angrily at them, telling them to be gone. One came, and evidently decided to alight on the top of the captain's head. The bird flew parallel to the boat and did not circle, but made short sidelong jumps in the air in chicken-fashion. His black eyes were wistfully fixed upon the captain's head. "Ugly brute," said the oiler to the bird. "You look as if you were made with a jack-knife." The cook and the correspondent swore darkly at the creature. The captain naturally wished to knock it away with the end of the heavy painter, but he did not dare do it, because anything resembling an emphatic gesture would have capsized this freighted boat, and so with his open hand, the captain gently and carefully waved the gull away. After it had been discouraged from the pursuit the captain breathed easier on account of his hair, and others breathed easier because the bird struck their minds at this time as being somehow gruesome and ominous.

31 In the meantime the oiler and the correspondent rowed. And also they rowed.

32 They sat together in the same seat, and each rowed an oar. Then the oiler took both oars; then the correspondent took both oars; then the oiler; then the correspondent. They rowed and they rowed. The very ticklish part of the business was when the time came for the reclining one in the stern to take his turn at the oars. By the very last star of truth, it is easier to steal eggs from under a hen than it was to change seats in the dingey. First the man in the stern slid his hand along the thwart and moved with care, as if he were of Sevres. Then the man in the rowing seat slid his hand along the other thwart. It was all done with the most extraordinary care. As the two sidled past each other, the whole party kept watchful eyes on the coming wave, and the captain cried: "Look out now! Steady there!"

33 The brown mats of sea-weed that appeared from time to time were like islands, bits of earth. They were traveling, apparently, neither one way nor the other. They were, to all intents stationary. They informed the men in the boat that it was making progress slowly toward the land.

34 The captain, rearing cautiously in the bow, after the dingey soared on a great swell, said that he had seen the lighthouse at Mosquito Inlet. Presently the cook remarked that he had seen it. The correspondent was at

the oars, then, and for some reason he too wished to look at the lighthouse, but his back was toward the far shore and the waves were important, and for some time he could not seize an opportunity to turn his head. But at last there came a wave more gentle than the others, and when at the crest of it he swiftly scoured the western horizon.

35 "See it?" said the captain.

36 "No," said the correspondent, slowly, "I didn't see anything."

37 "Look again," said the captain. He pointed. "It's exactly in that direction."

38 At the top of another wave, the correspondent did as he was bid, and this time his eyes chanced on a small still thing on the edge of the swaying horizon. It was precisely like the point of a pin. It took an anxious eye to find a lighthouse so tiny.

39 "Think we'll make it, captain?"

40 "If this wind holds and the boat don't swamp, we can't do much else," said the captain.

41 The little boat, lifted by each towering sea, and splashed viciously by the crests, made progress that in the absence of sea-weed was not apparent to those in her. She seemed just a wee thing wallowing, miraculously, top-up, at the mercy of five oceans. Occasionally, a great spread of water, like white flames, swarmed into her.

42 "Bail her, cook," said the captain, serenely.

43 "All right, captain," said the cheerful cook.

III

44 IT would be difficult to describe the subtle brotherhood of men that was here established on the seas. No one said that it was so. No one mentioned it. But it dwelt in the boat, and each man felt it warm him. They were a captain, an oiler, a cook, and a correspondent, and they were friends, friends in a more curiously iron-bound degree than may be common. The hurt captain, lying against the water-jar in the bow, spoke always in a low voice and calmly, but he could never command a more ready and swiftly obedient crew than the motley three of the dingey. It was more than a mere recognition of what was best for the common safety. There was surely in it a quality that was personal and heartfelt. And after this devotion to the commander of the boat there was this comradeship that the correspondent, for instance, who had been taught to be cynical of men, knew even at the time was the best experience of his life. But no one said that it was so. No one mentioned it.

45 "I wish we had a sail," remarked the captain.

"We might try my overcoat on the end of an oar and give you two boys a chance to rest." So the cook and the correspondent held the mast and spread wide the overcoat. The oiler steered, and the little boat made good way with her new rig. Sometimes the oiler had to scull sharply to keep a sea from breaking into the boat, but otherwise sailing was a success.

46 Meanwhile the light-house had been growing slowly larger. It had now almost assumed color, and appeared like a little gray shadow on the sky. The man at the oars could not be prevented from turning his head rather often to try for a glimpse of this little gray shadow.

47 At last, from the top of each wave the men in the tossing boat could see land. Even as the light-house was an upright shadow on the sky, this land seemed but a long black shadow on the sea. It certainly was thinner than paper. "We must be about opposite New Smyrna," said the cook, who had coasted this shore often in schooners. "Captain, by the way, I believe they abandoned that life-saving station there about a year ago."

48 "Did they?" said the captain.

49 The wind slowly died away. The cook and the correspondent were not now obliged to slave in order to hold high the oar. But the waves continued their old impetuous swooping at the dingey, and the little craft, no longer under way, struggled woundily over them. The oiler or the correspondent took the oars again.

50 Shipwrecks are apropos of nothing. If men could only train for them and have them occur when the men had reached pink condition, there would be less drowning at sea. Of the four in the dingey none had slept any time worth mentioning for two days and two nights previous to embarking in the dingey, and in the excitement of clambering about the deck of a foundering ship they had also forgotten to eat heartily.

51 For these reasons, and for others, neither the oiler nor the correspondent was fond of rowing at this time. The correspondent wondered ingenuously how in the name of all that was sane could there be people who thought it amusing to row a boat. It was not an amusement; it was a diabolical punishment, and even a genius of mental aberrations could never conclude that it was anything but a horror to the muscles and a crime against the back. He mentioned to the boat in general how the amusement of rowing struck him, and the weary-faced oiler smiled in full sympathy. Previously to the foundering, by the way, the oiler had worked double-watch in the engine-room of the ship.

52 "Take her easy, now, boys," said the captain. "Don't spend yourselves. If we have to run a surf you'll

need all your strength, because we'll sure have to swim for it. Take your time."

53 Slowly the land arose from the sea. From a black line it became a line of black and a line of white, trees, and sand. Finally, the captain said that he could make out a house on the shore. "That's the house of refuge, sure," said the cook. "They'll see us before long, and come out after us."

54 The distant light-house reared high. "The keeper ought to be able to make us out now, if he's looking through a glass," said the captain. "He'll notify the life-saving people."

55 "None of those other boats could have got ashore to give word of the wreck," said the oiler, in a low voice. "Else the life-boat would be out hunting us."

56 Slowly and beautifully the land loomed out of the sea. The wind came again. It had veered from the northeast to the southeast. Finally, a new sound struck the ears of the men in the boat. It was the low thunder of the surf on the shore. "We'll never be able to make the light-house now," said the captain. "Swing her head a little more north, Billie," said the captain.

57 "'A little more north,' sir," said the oiler.

58 Whereupon the little boat turned her nose once more down the wind, and all but the oarsman watched the shore grow. Under the influence of this expansion doubt and direful apprehension was leaving the minds of the men. The management of the boat was still most absorbing, but it could not prevent a quiet cheerfulness. In an hour, perhaps, they would be ashore.

59 Their back-bones had become thoroughly used to balancing in the boat and they now rode this wild colt of a dingey like circus men. The correspondent thought that he had been drenched to the skin, but happening to feel in the top pocket of his coat, he found therein eight cigars. Four of them were soaked with sea-water; four were perfectly scatheless. After a search, somebody produced three dry matches, and thereupon the four waifs rode in their little boat, and with an assurance of an impending rescue shining in their eyes, puffed at the big cigars and judged well and ill of all men. Everybody took a drink of water.

IV

60 "COOK," remarked the captain, "there don't seem to be any signs of life about your house of refuge."

61 "No," replied the cook. "Funny they don't see us!"

62 A broad stretch of lowly coast lay before the eyes of the men. It was of low dunes topped with dark vegetation. The roar of the surf was plain, and some-times they could see the white lip of a wave as it spun up the beach. A tiny house was blocked out black upon the sky. Southward, the slim light-house lifted its little gray length.

63 Tide, wind, and waves were swinging the dingey northward. "Funny they don't see us," said the men.

64 The surf's roar was here dulled, but its tone was, nevertheless, thunderous and mighty. As the boat swam over the great rollers, the men sat listening to this roar. "We'll swamp sure," said everybody.

65 It is fair to say here that there was not a life-saving station within twenty miles in either direction, but the men did not know this fact and in consequence they made dark and opprobrious remarks concerning the eyesight of the nation's life-savers. Four scowling men sat in the dingey and surpassed records in the invention of epithets.

66 "Funny they don't see us."

67 The light-heartedness of a former time had completely faded. To their sharpened minds it was easy to conjure pictures of all kinds of incompetency and blindness and indeed, cowardice. There was the shore of the populous land, and it was bitter and bitter to them that from it came no sign.

68 "Well," said the captain, ultimately, "I suppose we'll have to make a try for ourselves. If we stay out here too long, we'll none of us have strength left to swim after the boat swamps."

69 And so the oiler, who was at the oars, turned the boat straight for the shore. There was a sudden tightening of muscles. There was some thinking.

70 "If we don't all get ashore—" said the captain. "If we don't all get ashore, I suppose you fellows know where to send news of my finish?"

71 They then briefly exchanged some addresses and admonitions. As for the reflections of the men, there was a great deal of rage in them. Perchance they might be formulated thus: "If I am going to be drowned — if I am going to be drowned — if I am going to be drowned, why, in the name of the seven mad gods who rule the sea, was I allowed to come thus far and contemplate sand and trees? Was I brought here merely to have my nose dragged away as I was about to nibble the sacred cheese of life? It is preposterous. If this old ninny-woman, Fate, cannot do better than this, she should be deprived of the management of men's fortunes. She is an old hen who knows not her intention. If she has decided to drown me, why did she not do it in the beginning and save me all this trouble. The whole affair is absurd. . . . But, no, she cannot mean to drown me. She dare not drown me. She cannot drown me. Not after all this work." Afterward the man might have had

an impulse to shake his fist at the clouds: "Just you drown me, now, and then hear what I call you!"

72 The billows that came at this time were more formidable. They seemed always just about to break and roll over the little boat in a turmoil of foam. There was a preparatory and long growl in the speech of them. No mind unused to the sea would have concluded that the dingey could ascend these sheer heights in time. The shore was still afar. The oiler was a wily surfman. "Boys," he said, swiftly, "she won't live three minutes more and we're too far out to swim. Shall I take her to sea again, captain?"

73 "Yes! Go ahead!" said the captain.

74 This oiler, by a series of quick miracles, and fast and steady oarsmanship, turned the boat in the middle of the surf and took her safely to sea again.

75 There was a considerable silence as the boat bumped over the furrowed sea to deeper water. Then somebody in gloom spoke. "Well, anyhow, they must have seen us from the shore by now."

76 The gulls went in slanting flight up the wind toward the gray desolate east. A squall, marked by dingy clouds, and clouds brick-red, like smoke from a burning building, appeared from the southeast.

77 "What do you think of those life-saving people? Ain't they peaches?"

78 "Funny they haven't seen us."

79 "Maybe they think we're out here for sport! Maybe they think we're fishin'. Maybe they think we're damned fools."

80 It was a long afternoon. A changed tide tried to force them southward, but wind and wave said northward. Far ahead, where coast-line, sea, and sky formed their mighty angle, there were little dots which seemed to indicate a city on the shore.

81 "St. Augustine?"

82 The captain shook his head. "Too near Mosquito Inlet."

82 And the oiler rowed, and then the correspondent rowed. Then the oiler rowed. It was a weary business. The human back can become the seat of more aches and pains than are registered in books for the composite anatomy of a regiment. It is a limited area, but it can become the theater of innumerable muscular conflicts, tangles, wrenches, knots, and other comforts.

84 "Did you ever like to row, Billie?" asked the correspondent.

85 "No," said the oiler. "Hang it."

86 When one exchanged the rowing-seat for a place in the bottom of the boat, he suffered a bodily depression that caused him to be careless of everything save

an obligation to wiggle one finger. There was cold seawater swashing to and fro in the boat, and he lay in it. His head, pillowed on a thwart, was within an inch of the swirl of a wave crest, and sometimes a particularly obstreperous sea came in-board and drenched him once more. But these matters did not annoy him. It is almost certain that if the boat had capsized he would have tumbled comfortably out upon the ocean as if he felt sure it was a great soft mattress.

87 "Look! There's a man on the shore!"

88 "Where?"

89 "There! See 'im? See 'im?"

90 "Yes, sure! He's walking along."

91 "Now he's stopped. Look! He's facing us!"

92 "He's waving at us!"

93 "So he is! By thunder!"

94 "Ah, now, we're all right! Now we're all right! There'll be a boat out here for us in half an hour."

95 "He's going on. He's running. He's going up to that house there."

96 The remote beach seemed lower than the sea, and it required a searching glance to discern the little black figure. The captain saw a floating stick and they rowed to it. A bath-towel was by some weird chance in the boat, and, tying this on the stick, the captain waved it. The oarsman did not dare turn his head, so he was obliged to ask questions.

97 "What's he doing now?"

98 "He's standing still again. He's looking, I think. . . . There he goes again. Toward the house. . . . Now he's stopped again."

99 "Is he waving at us?"

100 "No, not now! he was, though."

101 "Look! There comes another man!"

102 "He's running."

103 "Look at him go, would you."

104 "Why, he's on a bicycle. Now he's met the other man. They're both waving at us. Look!"

105 "There comes something up the beach."

106 "What the devil is that thing?"

107 "Why, it looks like a boat."

108 "Why, certainly it's a boat."

109 "No, it's on wheels."

110 "Yes, so it is. Well, that must be the life-boat. They drag them along shore on a wagon."

111 "That's the life-boat, sure."

112 "No, by — — , it's—it's an omnibus."

113 "I tell you it's a life-boat."

114 "It is not! It's an omnibus. I can see it plain. See? One of these big hotel omnibuses."

115 "By thunder, you're right. It's an omnibus, sure

as fate. What do you suppose they are doing with an omnibus? Maybe they are going around collecting the life-crew, hey?"

116 "That's it, likely. Look! There's a fellow waving a little black flag. He's standing on the steps of the omnibus. There come those other two fellows. Now they're all talking together. Look at the fellow with the flag. Maybe he ain't waving it."

117 "That ain't a flag, is it? That's his coat. Why, certainly, that's his coat."

118 "So it is. It's his coat. He's taken it off and is waving it around his head. But would you look at him swing it."

119 "Oh, say, there isn't any life-saving station there. That's just a winter resort hotel omnibus that has brought over some of the boarders to see us drown."

120 "What's that idiot with the coat mean? What's he signaling, anyhow?"

121 "It looks as if he were trying to tell us to go north. There must be a life-saving station up there."

122 "No! He thinks we're fishing. Just giving us a merry hand. See? Ah, there, Willie."

123 "Well, I wish I could make something out of those signals. What do you suppose he means?"

124 "He don't mean anything. He's just playing."

125 "Well, if he'd just signal us to try the surf again, or to go to sea and wait, or go north, or go south, or go to hell—there would be some reason in it. But look at him. He just stands there and keeps his coat revolving like a wheel. The ass!"

126 "There come more people."

127 "Now there's quite a mob. Look! Isn't that a boat?"

128 "Where? Oh, I see where you mean. No, that's no boat."

129 "That fellow is still waving his coat."

130 "He must think we like to see him do that. Why don't he quit it. It don't mean anything."

131 "I don't know. I think he is trying to make us go north. It must be that there's a life-saving station there somewhere."

132 "Say, he ain't tired yet. Look at 'im wave."

133 "Wonder how long he can keep that up. He's been revolving his coat ever since he caught sight of us. He's an idiot. Why aren't they getting men to bring a boat out. A fishing boat — one of those big yawls — could come out here all right. Why don't he do something?"

134 "Oh, it's all right, now."

135 "They'll have a boat out here for us in less than no time, now that they've seen us."

136 A faint yellow tone came into the sky over the low land. The shadows on the sea slowly deepened. The wind bore coldness with it, and the men began to shiver.

137 "Holy smoke!" said one, allowing his voice to express his impious mood, "if we keep on monkeying out here! If we've got to flounder out here all night!"

138 "Oh, we'll never have to stay here all night! Don't you worry. They've seen us now, and it won't be long before they'll come chasing out after us."

139 The shore grew dusky. The man waving a coat blended gradually into this gloom, and it swallowed in the same manner the omnibus and the group of people. The spray, when it dashed uproariously over the side, made the voyagers shrink and swear like men who were being branded.

140 "I'd like to catch the chump who waved the coat. I feel like soaking him one, just for luck."

141 "Why? What did he do?"

142 "Oh, nothing, but then he seemed so damned cheerful."

143 In the meantime the oiler rowed, and then the correspondent rowed, and then the oiler rowed. Gray-faced and bowed forward, they mechanically, turn by turn, plied the leaden oars. The form of the light-house had vanished from the southern horizon, but finally a pale star appeared, just lifting from the sea. The streaked saffron in the west passed before the all-merging darkness, and the sea to the east was black. The land had vanished, and was expressed only by the low and drear thunder of the surf.

144 "If I am going to be drowned—if I am going to be drowned—if I am going to be drowned, why, in the name of the seven mad gods, who rule the sea, was I allowed to come thus far and contemplate sand and trees? Was I brought here merely to have my nose dragged away as I was about to nibble the sacred cheese of life?"

145 The patient captain, drooped over the water-jar, was sometimes obliged to speak to the oarsman.

146 "Keep her head up! Keep her head up!"

147 "'Keep her head up,' sir." The voices were weary and low.

148 This was surely a quiet evening. All save the oarsman lay heavily and listlessly in the boat's bottom. As for him, his eyes were just capable of noting the tall black waves that swept forward in a most sinister silence, save for an occasional subdued growl of a crest.

149 The cook's head was on a thwart, and he looked without interest at the water under his nose. He was deep in other scenes. Finally he spoke. "Billie," he mur-

mured, dreamfully, "what kind of pie do you like best?"

V

150 "PIE," said the oiler and the correspondent, agitatedly. "Don't talk about those things, blast you!"

151 "Well," said the cook, "I was just thinking about ham sandwiches, and—"

152 A night on the sea in an open boat is a long night. As darkness settled finally, the shine of the light, lifting from the sea in the south, changed to full gold. On the northern horizon a new light appeared, a small bluish gleam on the edge of the waters. These two lights were the furniture of the world. Otherwise there was nothing but waves.

153 Two men huddled in the stern, and distances were so magnificent in the dingey that the rower was enabled to keep his feet partly warmed by thrusting them under his companions. Their legs indeed extended far under the rowing-seat until they touched the feet of the captain forward. Sometimes, despite the efforts of the tired oarsman, a wave came piling into the boat, an icy wave of the night, and the chilling water soaked them anew. They would twist their bodies for a moment and groan, and sleep the dead sleep once more, while the water in the boat gurgled about them as the craft rocked.

154 The plan of the oiler and the correspondent was for one to row until he lost the ability, and then arouse the other from his sea-water couch in the bottom of the boat.

155 The oiler plied the oars until his head drooped forward, and the overpowering sleep blinded him. And he rowed yet afterward. Then he touched a man in the bottom of the boat, and called his name. "Will you spell me for a little while?" he said, meekly.

156 "Sure, Billie," said the correspondent, awakening and dragging himself to a sitting position. They exchanged places carefully, and the oiler, cuddling down to the sea-water at the cook's side, seemed to go to sleep instantly.

157 The particular violence of the sea had ceased. The waves came without snarling. The obligation of the man at the oars was to keep the boat headed so that the tilt of the rollers would not capsize her, and to preserve her from filling when the crests rushed past. The black waves were silent and hard to be seen in the darkness. Often one was almost upon the boat before the oarsman was aware.

158 In a low voice the correspondent addressed the captain. He was not sure that the captain was awake, although this iron man seemed to be always awake.

"Captain, shall I keep her making for that light north, sir?"

159 The same steady voice answered him. "Yes. Keep it about two points off the port bow."

160 The cook had tied a life-belt around himself in order to get even the warmth which this clumsy cork contrivance could donate, and he seemed almost stove-like when a rower, whose teeth invariably chattered wildly as soon as he ceased his labor, dropped down to sleep.

161 The correspondent, as he rowed, looked down at the two men sleeping under foot. The cook's arm was around the oiler's shoulders, and, with their fragmentary clothing and haggard faces, they were the babes of the sea, a grotesque rendering of the old babes in the wood.

162 Later he must have grown stupid at his work, for suddenly there was a growling of water, and a crest came with a roar and a swash into the boat, and it was a wonder that it did not set the cook afloat in his life-belt. The cook continued to sleep, but the oiler sat up, blinking his eyes and shaking with the new cold.

163 "Oh, I'm awful sorry, Billie," said the correspondent, contritely.

164 "That's all right, old boy," said the oiler, and lay down again and was asleep.

165 Presently it seemed that even the captain dozed, and the correspondent thought that he was the one man afloat on all the oceans. The wind had a voice as it came over the waves, and it was sadder than the end.

166 There was a long, loud swishing astern of the boat, and a gleaming trail of phosphorescence, like blue flame, was furrowed on the black waters. It might have been made by a monstrous knife.

167 Then there came a stillness, while the correspondent breathed with the open mouth and looked at the sea.

168 Suddenly there was another swish and another long flash of bluish light, and this time it was alongside the boat, and might almost have been reached with an oar. The correspondent saw an enormous fin speed like a shadow through the water, hurling the crystalline spray and leaving the long glowing trail.

169 The correspondent looked over his shoulder at the captain. His face was hidden, and he seemed to be asleep. He looked at the babes of the sea. They certainly were asleep. So, being bereft of sympathy, he leaned a little way to one side and swore softly into the sea.

170 But the thing did not then leave the vicinity of the boat. Ahead or astern, on one side or the other, at

intervals long or short, fled the long sparkling streak, and there was to be heard the whiroo of the dark fin. The speed and power of the thing was greatly to be admired. It cut the water like a gigantic and keen projectile.

171 The presence of this biding thing did not affect the man with the same horror that it would if he had been a picnicker. He simply looked at the sea dully and swore in an undertone.

172 Nevertheless, it is true that he did not wish to be alone with the thing. He wished one of his companions to awaken by chance and keep him company with it. But the captain hung motionless over the water-jar and the oiler and the cook in the bottom of the boat were plunged in slumber.

VI

173 "IF I am going to be drowned—if I am going to be drowned—if I am going to be drowned, why, in the name of the seven mad gods, who rule the sea, was I allowed to come thus far and contemplate sand and trees?"

174 During this dismal night, it may be remarked that a man would conclude that it was really the intention of the seven mad gods to drown him, despite the abominable injustice of it. For it was certainly an abominable injustice to drown a man who had worked so hard, so hard. The man felt it would be a crime most unnatural. Other people had drowned at sea since galleys swarmed with painted sails, but still—

175 When it occurs to a man that nature does not regard him as important, and that she feels she would not maim the universe by disposing of him, he at first wishes to throw bricks at the temple, and he hates deeply the fact that there are no bricks and no temples. Any visible expression of nature would surely be pelleted with his jeers.

176 Then, if there be no tangible thing to hoot he feels, perhaps, the desire to confront a personification and indulge in pleas, bowed to one knee, and with hands supplicant, saying: "Yes, but I love myself."

177 A high cold star on a winter's night is the word he feels that she says to him. Thereafter he knows the pathos of his situation.

178 The men in the dingey had not discussed these matters, but each had, no doubt, reflected upon them in silence and according to his mind. There was seldom any expression upon their faces save the general one of complete weariness. Speech was devoted to the business of the boat.

179 To chime the notes of his emotion, a verse mysteriously entered the correspondent's head. He had even forgotten that he had forgotten this verse, but it suddenly was in his mind.

180 A soldier of the Legion lay dying in Algiers,

181 There was lack of woman's nursing, there was dearth of woman's tears;

182 But a comrade stood beside him, and he took that comrade's hand

183 And he said: "I shall never see my own, my native land."

184 In his childhood, the correspondent had been made acquainted with the fact that a soldier of the Legion lay dying in Algiers, but he had never regarded the fact as important. Myriads of his school-fellows had informed him of the soldier's plight, but the dinning had naturally ended by making him perfectly indifferent. He had never considered it his affair that a soldier of the Legion lay dying in Algiers, nor had it appeared to him as a matter for sorrow. It was less to him than breaking of a pencil's point.

185 Now, however, it quaintly came to him as a human, living thing. It was no longer merely a picture of a few throes in the breast of a poet, meanwhile drinking tea and warming his feet at the grate; it was an actuality—stern, mournful, and fine.

186 The correspondent plainly saw the soldier. He lay on the sand with his feet out straight and still. While his pale left hand was upon his chest in an attempt to thwart the going of his life, the blood came between his fingers. In the far Algerian distance, a city of low square forms was set against a sky that was faint with the last sunset hues. The correspondent, plying the oars and dreaming of the slow and slower movements of the lips of the soldier, was moved by a profound and perfectly impersonal comprehension. He was sorry for the soldier of the Legion who lay dying in Algiers.

187 The thing which had followed the boat and waited had evidently grown bored at the delay. There was no longer to be heard the slash of the cut-water, and there was no longer the flame of the long trail. The light in the north still glimmered, but it was apparently no nearer to the boat. Sometimes the boom of the surf rang in the correspondent's ears, and he turned the craft seaward then and rowed harder. Southward, someone had evidently built a watch-fire on the beach. It was too low and too far to be seen, but it made a shimmering, roseate reflection upon the bluff back of it, and this could be discerned from the boat. The wind came stronger, and sometimes a wave suddenly raged out like a mountain-cat and there was to be seen the sheen and sparkle of a broken crest.

188 The captain, in the bow, moved on his water-jar and sat erect. "Pretty long night," he observed to the correspondent. He looked at the shore. "Those life-saving people take their time."

189 "Did you see that shark playing around?"

190 "Yes, I saw him. He was a big fellow, all right."

191 "Wish I had known you were awake."

192 Later the correspondent spoke into the bottom of the boat.

193 "Billie!" There was a slow and gradual disentanglement. "Billie, will you spell me?"

194 "Sure," said the oiler.

195 As soon as the correspondent touched the cold comfortable sea-water in the bottom of the boat, and had huddled close to the cook's life-belt he was deep in sleep, despite the fact that his teeth played all the popular airs. This sleep was so good to him that it was but a moment before he heard a voice call his name in a tone that demonstrated the last stages of exhaustion. "Will you spell me?"

196 "Sure, Billie."

197 The light in the north had mysteriously vanished, but the correspondent took his course from the wide-awake captain.

198 Later in the night they took the boat farther out to sea, and the captain directed the cook to take one oar at the stern and keep the boat facing the seas. He was to call out if he should hear the thunder of the surf. This plan enabled the oiler and the correspondent to get respite together. "We'll give those boys a chance to get into shape again," said the captain. They curled down and, after a few preliminary chatterings and trembles, slept once more the dead sleep. Neither knew they had bequeathed to the cook the company of another shark, or perhaps the same shark.

199 As the boat caroused on the waves, spray occasionally bumped over the side and gave them a fresh soaking, but this had no power to break their repose. The ominous slash of the wind and the water affected them as it would have affected mummies.

200 "Boys," said the cook, with the notes of every reluctance in his voice, "she's drifted in pretty close. I guess one of you had better take her to sea again." The correspondent, aroused, heard the crash of the toppled crests.

201 As he was rowing, the captain gave him some whiskey and water, and this steadied the chills out of him. "If I ever get ashore and anybody shows me even a photograph of an oar — "

202 At last there was a short conversation.

203 "Billie. . . . Billie, will you spell me?"

204 "Sure," said the oiler.

VII

205 WHEN the correspondent again opened his eyes, the sea and the sky were each of the gray hue of the dawning. Later, carmine and gold was painted upon the waters. The morning appeared finally, in its splendor with a sky of pure blue, and the sunlight flamed on the tips of the waves.

206 On the distant dunes were set many little black cottages, and a tall white wind-mill reared above them. No man, nor dog, nor bicycle appeared on the beach. The cottages might have formed a deserted village.

207 The voyagers scanned the shore. A conference was held in the boat. "Well," said the captain, "if no help is coming, we might better try a run through the surf right away. If we stay out here much longer we will be too weak to do anything for ourselves at all." The others silently acquiesced in this reasoning. The boat was headed for the beach. The correspondent wondered if none ever ascended the tall wind-tower, and if then they never looked seaward. This tower was a giant, standing with its back to the plight of the ants. It represented in a degree, to the correspondent, the serenity of nature amid the struggles of the individual — nature in the wind, and nature in the vision of men. She did not seem cruel to him, nor beneficent, nor treacherous, nor wise. But she was indifferent, flatly indifferent. It is, perhaps, plausible that a man in this situation, impressed with the unconcern of the universe, should see the innumerable flaws of his life and have them taste wickedly in his mind and wish for another chance. A distinction between right and wrong seems absurdly clear to him, then, in this new ignorance of the grave-edge, and he understands that if he were given another opportunity he would mend his conduct and his words, and be better and brighter during an introduction, or at a tea.

208 "Now, boys," said the captain, "she is going to swamp sure. All we can do is to work her in as far as possible, and then when she swamps, pile out and scramble for the beach. Keep cool now and don't jump until she swamps sure."

209 The oiler took the oars. Over his shoulders he scanned the surf. "Captain," he said, "I think I'd better bring her about, and keep her head-on to the seas and back her in."

210 "All right, Billie," said the captain. "Back her in." The oiler swung the boat then and, seated in the stern, the cook and the correspondent were obliged to look over their shoulders to contemplate the lonely and indifferent shore.

211 The monstrous inshore rollers heaved the boat high until the men were again enabled to see the white sheets of water scudding up the slanted beach. "We won't get in very close," said the captain. Each time a man could wrest his attention from the rollers, he turned his glance toward the shore, and in the expression of the eyes during this contemplation there was a singular quality. The correspondent, observing the others, knew that they were not afraid, but the full meaning of their glances was shrouded.

212 As for himself, he was too tired to grapple fundamentally with the fact. He tried to coerce his mind into thinking of it, but the mind was dominated at this time by the muscles, and the muscles said they did not care. It merely occurred to him that if he should drown it would be a shame.

213 There were no hurried words, no pallor, no plain agitation. The men simply looked at the shore. "Now, remember to get well clear of the boat when you jump," said the captain.

214 Seaward the crest of a roller suddenly fell with a thunderous crash, and the long white comber came roaring down upon the boat.

215 "Steady now," said the captain. The men were silent. They turned their eyes from the shore to the comber and waited. The boat slid up the incline, leaped at the furious top, bounced over it, and swung down the long back of the waves. Some water had been shipped and the cook bailed it out.

216 But the next crest crashed also. The tumbling boiling flood of white water caught the boat and whirled it almost perpendicular. Water swarmed in from all sides. The correspondent had his hands on the gunwale at this time, and when the water entered at that place he swiftly withdrew his fingers, as if he objected to wetting them.

217 The little boat, drunken with this weight of water, reeled and snuggled deeper into the sea.

218 "Bail her out, cook! Bail her out," said the captain.

219 "All right, captain," said the cook.

220 "Now, boys, the next one will do for us, sure," said the oiler. "Mind to jump clear of the boat."

221 The third wave moved forward, huge, furious, implacable. It fairly swallowed the dingey, and almost simultaneously the men tumbled into the sea. A piece of life-belt had lain in the bottom of the boat, and as the correspondent went overboard he held this to his chest with his left hand.

222 The January water was icy, and he reflected immediately that it was colder than he had expected to find it off the coast of Florida. This appeared to his dazed mind as a fact important enough to be noted at the time. The coldness of the water was sad; it was tragic. This fact was somehow mixed and confused with his opinion of his own situation that it seemed almost a proper reason for tears. The water was cold.

223 When he came to the surface he was conscious of little but the noisy water. Afterward he saw his companions in the sea. The oiler was ahead in the race. He was swimming strongly and rapidly. Off to the correspondent's left, the cook's great white and corked back bulged out of the water, and in the rear the captain was hanging with his one good hand to the keel of the overturned dingey.

224 There is a certain immovable quality to a shore, and the correspondent wondered at it amid the confusion of the sea.

225 It seemed also very attractive, but the correspondent knew that it was a long journey, and he paddled leisurely. The piece of life-preserver lay under him, and sometimes he whirled down the incline of a wave as if he were on a hand-sled.

226 But finally he arrived at a place in the sea where travel was beset with difficulty. He did not pause swimming to inquire what manner of current had caught him, but there his progress ceased. The shore was set before him like a bit of scenery on a stage, and he looked at it and understood with his eyes each detail of it.

227 As the cook passed, much farther to the left, the captain was calling to him, "Turn over on your back, cook! Turn over on your back and use the oar."

228 "All right, sir!" The cook turned on his back, and, paddling with an oar, went ahead as if he were a canoe.

229 Presently the boat also passed to the left of the correspondent with the captain clinging with one hand to the keel. He would have appeared like a man raising himself to look over a board fence, if it were not for the extraordinary gymnastics of the boat. The correspondent marveled that the captain could still hold to it.

230 They passed on, nearer to shore — the oiler, the cook, the captain — and following them went the water-jar, bouncing gayly over the seas.

231 The correspondent remained in the grip of this strange new enemy — a current. The shore, with its white slope of sand and its green bluff, topped with little silent cottages, was spread like a picture before him. It was very near to him then, but he was impressed as one who in a gallery looks at a scene from Brittany or Algiers.

232 He thought: "I am going to drown? Can it be possible? Can it be possible? Can it be possible?" Perhaps an individual must consider his own death to be the final phenomenon of nature.

233 But later a wave perhaps whirled him out of this small deadly current, for he found suddenly that he could again make progress toward the shore. Later still, he was aware that the captain, clinging with one hand to the keel of the dingey, had his face turned away from the shore and toward him, and was calling his name. "Come to the boat! Come to the boat!"

234 In his struggle to reach the captain and the boat, he reflected that when one gets properly wearied, drowning must really be a comfortable arrangement, a cessation of hostilities accompanied by a large degree of relief, and he was glad of it, for the main thing in his mind for some moments had been horror of the temporary agony. He did not wish to be hurt.

235 Presently he saw a man running along the shore. He was undressing with most remarkable speed. Coat, trousers, shirt, everything flew magically off him.

236 "Come to the boat," called the captain.

237 "All right, captain." As the correspondent paddled, he saw the captain let himself down to bottom and leave the boat. Then the correspondent performed his one little marvel of the voyage. A large wave caught him and flung him with ease and supreme speed completely over the boat and far beyond it. It struck him even then as an event in gymnastics, and a true miracle of the sea. An overturned boat in the surf is not a plaything to a swimming man.

238 The correspondent arrived in water that reached only to his waist, but his condition did not enable him to stand for more than a moment. Each wave knocked him into a heap, and the under-tow pulled at him.

239 Then he saw the man who had been running and undressing, and undressing and running, come bounding into the water. He dragged ashore the cook, and then waded toward the captain, but the captain waved him away, and sent him to the correspondent. He was naked, naked as a tree in winter, but a halo was about his head, and he shone like a saint. He gave a strong pull, and a long drag, and a bully heave at the correspondent's hand. The correspondent, schooled in the minor formulae, said: "Thanks, old man." But suddenly the man cried: "What's that?" He pointed a swift finger. The correspondent said: "Go."

240 In the shallows, face downward, lay the oiler. His forehead touched sand that was periodically, between each wave, clear of the sea.

241 The correspondent did not know all that transpired afterward. When he achieved safe ground he fell, striking the sand with each particular part of his body. It was as if he had dropped from a roof, but the thud was grateful to him.

242 It seems that instantly the beach was populated with men with blankets, clothes, and flasks, and women with coffee-pots and all the remedies sacred to their minds. The welcome of the land to the men from the sea was warm and generous, but a still and dripping shape was carried slowly up the beach, and the land's welcome for it could only be the different and sinister hospitality of the grave.

243 When it came night, the white waves paced to and fro in the moonlight, and the wind brought the sound of the great sea's voice to the men on shore, and they felt that they could then be interpreters.

LESSON 17 TEST ANSWERS

DISCUSSION QUESTIONS (100 POINTS)

Find 5 examples of *Naturalism* in the following short story, state the paragraph number, and defend your answer.

ANSWER: *The following are only representative of many examples of Naturalism:*

1. The men are introduced without names. They are nameless, animals facing the unknown and fate. They are together, but separate—both at the same time (lines 1ff)

2. Men are confused and disoriented by the exigencies of life (lines 6ff)

3. Nature is unfriendly and indifferent (line 11)

4. Naturalism is full of irony. There is a life saving station but no crew to man it (lines 13-15)!

5. If there is brotherhood there is a sense that they are all doomed together. Or they are in the same game together with the same advantages and disadvantages (lines 44ff)

LESSON 18

REALISM, NATURALISM, AND THE FRONTIER, *1865-1915* (*Part 4*)

Readings Due For This Lesson: Students should review *The Red Badge of Courage*, Stephen Crane.

Reading Ahead: Students should review "Outcasts of Poker Flat," Bret Harte; "The Story of an Hour," Kate Chopin; "Luke Havergal" and "Credo," Edwin Arlington Robinson; "Lucinda Matlock," Edgar Lee Masters. Guide Question: What new styles and themes emerge in these late 19th century works?

Goal: Students will analyze *Red Badge of Courage*, Stephen Crane.

Goals/Objectives: What is the purpose of this lesson?	Strategies to meet these goals: How will I obtain these goals/objectives?	Evaluation: How will I know when I have met these goals/objectives?
Students will understand this concept: the plot of this novel. (cognitive goal)	Students will write an essay on this topic: The plot of *Red Badge of Courage*, to some critics, has major flaws. For instance, after running farther and faster than anyone else, Henry Fleming proves to be one of the bravest soldiers in the regiment. Some critics feel that this is unbelievable. Do you agree? If you feel that the transformation is believable, explain why you do with reasons from the book. (Critical Thinking A)	Students, with minimal errors, will clearly answer the assigned question in a 1-2 page essay.
Students will increase their vocabulary. (cognitive goal)	Students will collect at least five new vocabulary words from their reading and use these words in their essays.	Students will use five vocabulary words in conversation during the week as well as use the words in their essays and in conversation.
Students will understand this concept: tone and writing style of this novel (cognitive goal)	Students will write an essay on this topic: Analyze Crane's tone and writing style. (Critical Thinking B)	Students, with minimal errors, will clearly answer the assigned question in a 1-2 page essay.

Goals/Objectives: What is the purpose of this lesson?	Strategies to meet these goals: How will I obtain these goals/objectives?	Evaluation: How will I know when I have met these goals/ objectives?
Students will exhibit higher-level thinking skills as they speculate upon whether or not Henry should be court marshaled for desertion. (cognitive goal)	Students will write an essay on this topic: Pretend that Henry was court marshaled for desertion. Should he be convicted? Why or why not? (Critical Thinking C)	Students, with minimal errors, will clearly answer the assigned question in a 1-2 page essay.
Students will exhibit higher-level thinking as they compare Crane's view of nature with earlier Romantic writers' views of nature. (cognitive goal)	Students will write an essay on this topic: To Crane, nature has lost all contact with humanity. "It was surprising that Nature had gone tranquilly on with her golden process in the midst of so much devilment." Contrast this view with some of the earlier Romantic writers (e.g., Hawthorne). (Critical Thinking D)	Students, with minimal errors, will clearly answer the assigned question in a 1-2 page essay.
Students will understand this concept: determinism. (cognitive goal)	Students will write an essay on this topic: Naturalism stresses the discoverable, deterministic laws of nature. Write an essay that argues your perspective. (Biblical Application)	Students, with minimal errors, will clearly answer the assigned question in a 1-2 page essay.
Students will understand this concept: Social Darwinism. (cognitive goal) Students will consider the generalization that Social Darwinism contradicts the truth of Scripture. (affective goal)	Students will write an essay on this topic: How was Crane affected by Social Darwinism? (Enrichment A) Students will answer this question: Why do social scientists indulge themselves in such contrived chicanery and what are its ramifications? (Enrichment B)?	Students, with minimal errors, will clearly answer the assigned question in a 1-2 page essay.
Students will understand the concept: naturalistic themes in "Blue Hotel." (cognitive goal)	Students will read the short story by Crane entitled "Blue Hotel" (1898) and write an essay highlighting naturalistic themes. (Enrichment C)	Students, with minimal errors, will clearly answer the assigned question in a 1-2 page essay.
Students will exhibit higher-level thinking as they discuss evidence of Naturalism in American culture. (cognitive goal)	What evidence of Naturalism do you find in American culture today? (Enrichment D)?	Students, with minimal errors, will clearly answer the assigned question in a 1-2 page essay.

Goals/Objectives: What is the purpose of this lesson?	Strategies to meet these goals: How will I obtain these goals/objectives?	Evaluation: How will I know when I have met these goals/ objectives?
Students will work in a group setting. (behavioral goal)	In a class, in a co-op experience, or during a family discussion, students will answer this question: Discuss evidences of naturalism in contemporary society.	Students will exhibit practical listening skills and will manifest understanding of opposing worldviews.
Students will be able to recall the information taught in the lesson. (cognitive goal)	Lesson 18 Test	Students will take the test at the end of this lesson and score at least 80%.
Students will experience reflective writing. (affective/spiritual goal)	Using the Journal Guide Questions in the Appendices, students will record at least three entries this week. Suggested Scriptures: Exodus 20	Students will show evidence that they have reflected on this issue, including informed discussions and written responses.

SUGGESTED
Weekly *Implementation*

DAY 1	DAY 2	DAY 3	DAY 4	DAY 5
Prayer journal.	**Prayer journal.**	**Prayer journal.**	**Prayer journal.**	**Prayer journal.**
Students review the required reading (s) before the assigned lesson begins.	Student should review reading (s) from next lesson.	Students should write rough drafts of all assigned essays.	Student will re-write corrected copies of essays due tomorrow.	Essays are due.
Teacher may want to discuss assigned reading (s) with students.	Student should outline essays due at the end of the week.	The teacher and/or a peer evaluator may correct rough drafts.		Students should take the Lesson 18 test.
Teacher and students will decide on required essays for this lesson, choosing two or three essays. The rest of the essays can be outlined, answered with shorter answers, or skipped.	Per teacher instructions, students may answer orally in a group setting some of the essays that are not assigned as formal essays.			"Outcasts of Poker Flat," Bret Harte; "The Story of an Hour,"Kate Chopin; "Luke Havergal" and "Credo," Edwin Arlington Robinson; "Lucinda Matlock," Edgar Lee Masters.
Students will review all readings for Lesson 18				Guide: What new styles and themes emerge in these late 19th century works?

Note: References to sources are in student edition.

ENRICHMENT ACTIVITIES/PROJECTS
Students should do a *report* on the Spanish American War.
    Students should watch a Civil War re-enactment.
    Students should watch the movie *Rough Riders.* (1997)

SUPPLEMENTAL RESOURCES
Ahnebrink, Lars. *The Beginnings of Naturalism in American Fiction.*
    Appears to be an excellent resource.

Bassan, Maurice. *Stephen Crane: A Collection of Critical Essays.*
    Somewhat pedantic, but insightful essays on Crane's major works.

Crane, Stephen. *Great Short Works of Stephen Crane: Red Badge of Courage, Monster, Maggie, Open Boat, Blue Hotel, Bride Comes to Yellow Sky and Other Works.*
    An excellent, unedited version of Crane's works.

Katz, Joseph (Editor). *The Complete Poems of Stephen Crane.*
    While Crane is a less accomplished poet than many others, his works are worth examining.

The Red Badge of Courage. (1951) Movie.

This epic version of Crane's novel, starring Audie Murphy, is a fairly accurate version of the book.

Notes:

CRITICAL THINKING

A. The plot of *Red Badge of Courage*, to some critics, has major flaws. For instance, after running farther and faster than anyone else, Henry Fleming proves to be one of the bravest soldiers in the regiment. Some critics feel that this is unbelievable. Do you agree? If you feel that the transformation is believable, explain why you do with reasons from the book

ANSWER: *There is a certain episodic feature in Crane's organization. At the same time, we watch Henry discard his idealism for realism. So there are two levels in the plot: the metaphysical realm and the actual plot. Most readers confusingly see this novel as a Civil War novel. In fact, when one examines the worldview war that is occurring, one sees that this is a novel about naturalism vs. romanticism—in other words, a worldview conflict. Still, it is difficult to imagine most 18th century Americans rejecting metaphysics the way Henry Fleming does.*

B. Analyze Crane's tone and writing style.

ANSWER: *Crane writes in a terse, powerful style. His images are vivid and striking. While his metaphors are rich, they are cogent and precise. His dialogue is succinct. There is no hyperbole in Crane! He wastes no words. He is no James Fenimore Cooper! This style is later imitated by other naturalistic writers (e.g., Ernest Hemingway).*

C. Pretend that Henry was court marshaled for desertion. Should he be convicted? Why or why not?

ANSWER: *The question implies guilt and in fact he was guilty. He deserted his friends and regiment in the face of hostile fire, which was punishable by death. Crane would say no. To the naturalist, though, fleeing from danger was understandable, permissible, even desirable. It made no more sense to stand and fight than it did to flee. The fatalistic Fleming saw it that way. That was his "red badge of courage." The title itself is a mockery of romanticism. To Crane, it is an oxymoron. He only followed his instincts—one could expect nothing else. To Crane, who has no absolute moral paradigm with which to run his life, Fleming is free to act in his best interests.*

D. To Crane, nature has lost all contact with humanity.

"It was surprising that Nature had gone tranquilly on with her golden process in the midst of so much devilment." Contrast this view with some of the earlier Romantic writers. (e.g., Hawthorne)

ANSWER: *Hawthorne's Nature is merely a reflection of God. It is not a separate entity. To Crane, a Naturalist, nature is neither omniscient nor omnipotent, but it is malevolent. To Hawthorne, Emerson, and Cooper nature is omniscient and it is benevolent. To the Puritans, God is benevolent, personal, and omnipotent. Nature is under God's control and merely another one of His creations.*

BIBLICAL APPLICATION

Naturalism stresses the discoverable, deterministic laws of nature. If God exists in the naturalistic word, He is, like nature, cold and indifferent. As the fleeing Henry trips over his dead friend, he notices that a squirrel is playing innocently around his dead friend's body. The birds sing beautiful songs impervious to the death occurring all around them. The contrast of the carnage of human warfare and the malevolent beauty of nature is at the heart of Naturalism. Naturalism posits that nature is both ubiquitous and impersonal. What Scripture verses can you find that contradict this view? Write an essay that argues your perspective.

ANSWER: *Psalm 139:1-15, "Lord, You have searched me and known me. You know when I sit down and when I stand up; You understand my thoughts from far away. You observe my travels and my rest; You are aware of all my ways. Before a word is on my tongue, You know all about it, Lord. You have encircled me; You have placed Your hand on me. [This] extraordinary knowledge is beyond me. It is lofty; I am unable to [reach] it. Where can I go to escape Your Spirit? Where can I flee from Your presence? If I go up to heaven, You are there; if I make my bed in Sheol, You are there. If I live at the eastern horizon or settle at the western limits, even there Your hand will lead me; Your right hand will hold on to me. If I say, "Surely the darkness will hide me, and the light around me will become night"— even the darkness is not dark to You. The night shines like the day; darkness and light are alike to You. For it was You who created my inward parts; You knit me together in my mother's womb. John 3:16: "For God loved the world in this way: He gave His One and Only Son, so that everyone who believes in Him will not perish but have eternal life." Our God is literally very interested in all of us!*

ENRICHMENT

A. Social Darwinism was a social theory popular at the end of the nineteenth century. It argued that a social structure and a human organism both survive according to natural laws; i.e., survival of the fittest. How was Crane affected by Social Darwinism?

ANSWER: *The strongest survive. The weak do not. Charles Darwin published in 1859 <u>On The Origin of Species by Means of Natural Selection, or the Preservation of Favoured Races in the Struggle for Life</u>. Darwin in 1858 had co-authored (with Alfred Russell Wallace) the theory of natural selection, which says that superior biological variations tend to be preserved. In the struggle for existence, the fit are not those who survive but those who reproduce. Natural selection also leads to diversification as different organisms adapt to particular ecological circumstances. Darwin said all biological similarities and differences are caused by descent with modification. He concluded that all organisms are descended from only one ancestor. Evolution is the name for this biological process that goes back to one common ancestor 3-1/2 billion years ago. Charles Darwin, then, was the father of the theory of evolution.*

"We have reason to believe, as stated in the first chapter, that a change in the conditions of life, by specially acting on the reproductive system, causes or increases variability; and in the foregoing case the conditions of life are supposed to have undergone a change, and this would manifestly be favourable to natural selection, by giving a better chance of profitable variations occurring; and unless profitable variations do occur, natural selection can do nothing. Not that, as I believe, any extreme amount of variability is necessary; as man can certainly produce great results by adding up in any given direction mere individual differences, so could Nature, but far more easily, from having incomparably longer time at her disposal. Nor do I believe that any great physical change, as of climate, or any unusual degree of isolation to check immigration, is actually necessary to produce new and unoccupied places for natural selection to fill up by modifying and improving some of the varying inhabitants. For as all the inhabitants of each country are struggling together with nicely balanced forces, extremely slight modifications in the structure or habits of one inhabitant would often give it an advantage over others; and still further modifications of the same kind would often still further increase the advantage." <u>The Origin of Species</u>

B. In *Principles of Psychology* (1855) Herbert Spencer, a British philosopher, took Darwin's theory into the social realm. He influenced a generation of sociologists and authors like Stephen Crane. He wrote that all organic matter originated in a unified state and that individual characteristics gradually developed through evolution. The evolutionary progression from simple to more complex and diverse states was an important theme in most of Spencer's later works. In summary, Spencer argued that the strongest individuals and social systems survived. The weakest did not. This was an example of a scientific theory being transposed on human society and experience. The same thing happened with Einstein's theory of relativity. "Who would imagine that this simple law (constancy of the velocity of light) has plunged the conscientiously thoughtful physicist into the greatest intellectual difficulties?" Einstein wrote. He was horrified that social scientists took his theory about the quantum nature of light, a description of molecular motion, and the special theory of relativity and created a social theory called Relativism. Relativism argued that persons should make decisions based upon the "relative worth" of that decision based on circumstances. In other words, people were free to do what was relatively beneficial to their situation regardless of the consequences to others. Why d social scientists indulge themselves in such contrived chicanery and what are its ramifications?

ANSWER: *There is an aura of respectability that surrounds science that all the social sciences seek to be "scientific." It adds to their credibility. In the course of seeking credibility, some social sciences go too far. Both scientific theory and social science theory is cheapened. The above are two examples.*

C. Read the short story by Crane entitled "Blue Hotel" (1898) and write an essay highlighting Naturalistic themes.

ANSWER: *Notice the way Crane uses the setting. In naturalistic writings the setting is almost always dreary and incidental. Also, naturalistic and realistic characters are ordinary—like the person who lives next door. Crane uses irony—an important naturalist technique. Indeed, irony is everywhere. It is ironical that a naïve, easterner, is merciless killed by a westerner. There is no deep meaning here—it is just ironical that two people fight over something insignificant. In fact one even dies.*

D. Naturalism is essentially a literary expression of determinism. Associated with bleak, realistic depictions of lower-class life, determinism denies Christianity as a motivating force in the world and instead perceives the universe as a machine. It is hard to imagine that a born again Christian could be a naturalist. Eighteenth century Enlightenment thinkers also imagined the world as a machine, but as a perfect one, invented by God and tending toward progress and human betterment. Naturalists imagined society, instead, as a blind machine, godless and out of control.

The 19th century American historian and social thinker Henry Adams constructed an elaborate theory of history involving the idea of the dynamo, or machine force, and entropy, or decay of force. Instead of progress, Adams saw inevitable decline in human society. This pessimism was reinforced by the rise of Social Darwinism (the survival of the fittest). God is dead in American literature. God in American literature died when Nathaniel Hawthorne set aside his pen after writing *The Scarlet Letter*.

Like romanticism, naturalism first appeared in Europe. Naturalism flourished as Americans became urbanized and aware of the importance of large, impersonal economic and social forces.

FINAL PROJECT

Students should correct and rewrite all essays and place them in their Final Portfolio.

LESSON 18 TEST

ESSAY (100 POINTS)

While participating in an American literature college course discussion, you courageously mentioned that *The Red Badge of Courage* is not about the Civil War. The instructor and his students are shocked. To reward you for your insightful comments, the instructors ask you to write a 150 word essay defending your argument. In the space below, and on the back of this paper, argue that *The Red Badge of Courage* is really not about the Civil War.

LESSON 19 TEST ANSWERS

ESSAY (100 POINTS)

While participating in an American literature college course discussion, you courageously mentioned that *The Red Badge of Courage* is not about the Civil War. The instructor and his students are shocked. To reward you for your insightful comments, the instructor asks you to write a 150 word essay defending your argument. In the space below, and on the back of this paper, argue that *The Red Badge of Courage* is really not about the Civil War.

ANSWER: *First Crane was not old enough to participate in the American Civil War; however, he was a correspondent in Cuba during the Spanish American War. Secondly, Henry Fleming is too "modern" to be a real Civil War hero. His speculation about the cosmos, about God and His sovereignty, imply a worldview far beyond 1865. Red Badge exhibits a worldview — naturalism — that belongs in the late 19th century.*

LESSON 19

REALISM, NATURALISM, AND THE FRONTIER *1865-1915*
(Part 5)

Readings Due For This Lesson: Students should review "Outcasts of Poker Flat," Bret Harte; "The Story of an Hour," Kate Chopin; "Luke Havergal" and "Credo," Edwin Arlington Robinson; "Lucinda Matlock," Edgar Lee Masters. Guide Question: What new styles and themes emerge in these late 19th century works?

Reading Ahead: Students should review *Ethan Frome*, Edith Wharton. In what way is *Ethan Frome* a Naturalistic novel?

Goal: Students will analyze "Outcasts of Poker Flat," Bret Harte; "The Story of an Hour," Kate Chopin; "Luke Havergal" and "Credo," Edwin Arlington Robinson; "Lucinda Matlock," Edgar Lee Masters. Guide Question: What new styles and themes emerge in these late 19th century works?

Goals/Objectives: What is the purpose of this lesson?	Strategies to meet these goals: How will I obtain these goals/objectives?	Evaluation: How will I know when I have met these goals/objectives?
Students will understand this concept: creation of humor. (cognitive goal)	Students will write an essay on this topic: How does Bret Harte create humor in his short story "Outcasts of Poker Flat?" (Critical Thinking A)	Students, with minimal errors, will clearly answer the assigned question in a 1-2 page essay.
Students will increase their vocabulary. (cognitive goal)	Students will collect at least five new vocabulary words from their reading and use these words in their essays.	Students will use five vocabulary words in conversation during the week as well as use the words in their essays and in conversation.
Students will understand this concept: the joy that killed Mrs. Mallard. (cognitive goal)	Students will write an essay on this topic: the joy that killed Mrs. Mallard. (Critical Thinking B)	Students, with minimal errors, will clearly answer the assigned question in a 1-2 page essay.

Goals/Objectives: What is the purpose of this lesson?	Strategies to meet these goals: How will I obtain these goals/objectives?	Evaluation: How will I know when I have met these goals/objectives?
Students will exhibit higher-level thinking skills as they speculate upon what Robinson means by these lines "God slays Himself with every leaf that flies,/ And hell is more than half of paradise." (cognitive goal)	Students will write an essay on this topic: What does Robinson mean by these lines "God slays Himself with every leaf that flies,/ And hell is more than half of paradise"? (Critical Thinking C)	Students, with minimal errors, will clearly answer the assigned question in a 1-2 page essay.
Students will exhibit higher-level thinking as they discuss what Lucinda Matlock means when she says, "It takes life to love Life." (cognitive goal)	Students will write an essay on this topic: What does Lucinda Matlock mean when she says, "It takes life to love Life"? (Critical Thinking D)	Students, with minimal errors, will clearly answer the assigned question in a 1-2 page essay.
Students will understand this concept: comparison of Mrs. Mallard to Lucinda Matlock. (cognitive goal)	Students will write an essay on this topic: Compare Mrs. Mallard to Lucinda Matlock. (Enrichment)	Students, with minimal errors, will clearly answer the assigned question in a 1-2 page essay.
Students will work in a group setting. (behavioral goal)	In a class, in a co-op experience, or during a family discussion, students will answer this question: Why Kate Chopin's works should or should not be reprinted.	Students will exhibit practical listening skills and will manifest understanding of opposing world-views.
Students will be able to recall the information taught in the lesson. (cognitive goal)	Lesson 19 Test	Students will take the test at the end of this lesson and score at least 80%.
Students will experience reflective writing. (affective/spiritual goal)	Using the Journal Guide Questions in the Appendices, students will record at least three entries this week. Suggested Scriptures: Esther	Students will show evidence that they have reflected on this issue, including informed discussions and written responses.

SUGGESTED
Weekly *Implementation*

DAY 1	DAY 2	DAY 3	DAY 4	DAY 5
Prayer journal. Students review the required reading(s) before the assigned lesson begins. Teacher may want to discuss assigned reading(s) with students. Teacher and students will decide on required essays for this lesson, choosing two or three essays. The rest of the essays can be outlined, answered with shorter answers, or skipped. Students will review all readings for Lesson 19	**Prayer journal.** Student should review reading(s) from next lesson. Student should outline essays due at the end of the week. Per teacher instructions, students may answer orally in a group setting some of the essays that are not assigned as formal essays.	**Prayer journal.** Students should write rough drafts of all assigned essays. The teacher or a peer evaluator may correct rough drafts.	**Prayer journal.** Student will re-write corrected copies of essays due tomorrow.	**Prayer journal.** Essays are due. Students should take the Lesson 19 test. Reading Ahead: Students should review *Ethan Frome*, Edith Wharton. Guide: In what way is *Ethan Frome* a Naturalistic novel?

Note: References to sources are in student edition.

ENRICHMENT ACTIVITIES/PROJECTS
Students should compare and contrast "Cassandra", "Richard Cory," and "Mr. Flood's Party," all by Edwin Arlington Robinson.

SUPPLEMENTARY RESOURCES
Arp, Thomas R. (Editor), *Perrine's Literature: Structure, Sound and Sense.*
    An excellent resource on poetry.

Friedman, Norman. *E. E. Cummings: The Art of His Poetry.*

Perrine, Laurence. *Perrine's Sound and Sense: An Introduction to Poetry.*
    Perrine set the standard for poetry interpretation.

Schwartz, Sanford. *The Matrix of Modernism: Pound, Eliot, and Early Twentieth-Century Thought.*

Notes:

CRITICAL THINKING
A. How does Bret Harte create humor in his short story "Outcasts of Poker Flat?"

ANSWER: *Harte uses dramatic irony: "Some months before he had chanced upon a stray copy of Mr. Pope's ingenious translation of the Iliad. He now proposed to narrate the principal incidents of that poem—having thoroughly mastered the argument and fairly forgotten the words—in the current vernacular of Sandy Bar." He also gives great insights into the characters. His insights are so candid that the reader is disarmed and then pleasured by the spontaneity and freshness of his prose.*

B. What was the joy that killed Mrs. Mallard?

ANSWER: *In this short story Chopin is revealing women's private, submerged lives. In her novel* The Awakening *the protagonist "was beginning to realize her position in the universe as a human being and to recognize her relations as an individual to the world within and about her." The great sadness of losing her husband was shocking, but she was also free to explore new vistas in her life. This was the discovery that Mrs. Mallard made.*

C. What does Robinson mean by these lines "God slays Himself with every leaf that flies,/And hell is more than half of paradise"?

ANSWER: *This is an extremely powerful Naturalistic statement. Robinson is presenting an extremely anemic God who proves conclusively that He is indeed the impersonal, ineffectual Naturalistic God that Robinson knew.*

D. What does Lucinda Matlock mean when she says, "It takes life to love Life?"

ANSWER: *Her life was hard but it was life. And a person cannot love life without having a life to love. This celebration of life, for its own sake, is unusual for late 19th century Naturalistic America. Never having done anything that was famous, Lucinda Matlock's life was ordinary and ended at the age of 96. Nevertheless, she threw a scornful challenge to younger generations, accusing them of not loving life enough, for what has any famous person done that Lucinda did not match? She loved her husband and was loved by him. She gave birth to 12 children and outlived at least eight of them. She shouted to the forested hills and sang to the green valleys. Best of all, she died as she had lived, willingly, without a sense of loss or of the unreachable dream just across the next hill, round the next corner, beyond the horizon. She found life in her life: it takes life to love life!*

ENRICHMENT

Compare Mrs. Mallard to Lucinda Matlock.

ANSWER: *Both women felt deeply about the changes that occurred in their lives. It appears that Lucinda Matlock was more satisfied with her life than Mrs. Mallard.*

FINAL PROJECT

Students should correct and rewrite all essays and place them in their Final Portfolio.

LESSON 19 TEST

CREATIVE WRITING (25 POINTS)

Following the pattern established by Harte, Chopin, Robinson, or Masters, write a short story or poem imitating that writer's style.

DISCUSSION QUESTIONS (75 POINTS)

A. In a 75-150 word essay analyze the following poem. In your essay discuss the theme, setting, rhyme scheme, literary techniques (e.g., alliteration, metaphor), and other literary elements (e.g., symbolism).

The Pity of the Leaves
Edwin Arlington Robinson

Vengeful across the cold November moors,
Loud with ancestral shame there came the bleak
Sad wind that shrieked, and answered with a shriek,
Reverberant through lonely corridors.
The old man heard it; and he heard, perforce,
Words out of lips that were no more to speak—
Words of the past that shook the old man's cheek
Like dead, remembered footsteps on old floors.
And then there were the leaves that plagued him so!
The brown, thin leaves that on the stones outside
Skipped with a freezing whisper. Now and then
They stopped, and stayed there—just to let him know
How dead they were; but if the old man cried,
They fluttered off like withered souls of men.

B. Compare Robinson's "Leaves" with Ralph Waldo Emerson's "The Snow Storm."

The Snow Storm
R. W. Emerson

Announced by all the trumpets of the sky,
Arrives the snow, and, driving o'er the fields,
Seems nowhere to alight: the whited air
Hides hills and woods, the river, and the heaven,
And veils the farm-house at the garden's end.
The sled and traveller stopped, the courier's feet
Delayed, all friends shut out, the housemates sit
Around the radiant fireplace, enclosed
In a tumultuous privacy of storm.

Come see the north wind's masonry.
Out of an unseen quarry evermore
Furnished with tile, the fierce artificer
Curves his white bastions with projected roof
Round every windware stake, or tree, or door.
Speeding, the myriad-handed, his wild work
So fanciful, so savage, nought cares he
For number or proportion. Mockingly,
On coop or kennel he hangs Parian wreaths;

A swan-like form invests the hidden thorn;
Fills up the farmer's lane from wall to wall,
Maugre the farmer's sighs; and at the gate
A tapering turret overtops the work.
And when his hours are numbered, and the world
Is all his own, retiring, as he were not,
Leaves, when the sun appears, astonished Art
To mimic in slow structures, stone by stone,
Built in an age, the mad wind's night-work,
The frolic architecture of the snow.

LESSON 19 TEST ANSWERS

CREATIVE WRITING (25 POINTS)

Following the pattern established by Harte, Chopin, Robinson, or Masters, write a short story or poem imitating that writer's style.

ANSWERS: *Answers will vary.*

DISCUSSION QUESTION (75 POINTS)

A. In a 75-150 word essay analyze the following poem. In your essay discuss the theme, setting, rhyme scheme, literary techniques (e.g., alliteration, metaphor), and other literary elements (e.g., symbolism).

The Pity of the Leaves
Edwin Arlington Robinson

Vengeful across the cold November moors, *a*
Loud with ancestral shame there came the bleak *b*
Sad wind that shrieked, and answered with a shriek, *a*
Reverberant through lonely corridors. *a*
The old man heard it; and he heard, perforce, *c*
Words out of lips that were no more to speak *∂*
Words of the past that shook the old man's cheek *∂*
Like dead, remembered footsteps on old floors. *a*
And then there were the leaves that plagued him so! *e*
The brown, thin leaves that on the stones outside *f*
Skipped with a freezing whisper. Now and then *g*
They stopped, and stayed there—just to let him know *b*
How dead they were; but if the old man cried, *i*
They fluttered off like withered souls of men. *g*

ANSWER: *On the surface this poem offers the reader an image of leaves falling and blowing in the wind. It is both beautiful and sad. The image reminds the old man that his life is ending too. There is also an agnostic conclusion—the speaker does not know what is in store for him after death.*

B. Compare Robinson's "Leaves" with Ralph Waldo Emerson's "The Snow Storm."

The Snow Storm
R. W. Emerson

Announced by all the trumpets of the sky,
Arrives the snow, and, driving o'er the fields,
Seems nowhere to alight: the whited air
Hides hills and woods, the river, and the heaven,
And veils the farm-house at the garden's end.
The sled and traveller stopped, the courier's feet
Delayed, all friends shut out, the housemates sit
Around the radiant fireplace, enclosed
In a tumultuous privacy of storm.

Come see the north wind's masonry.
Out of an unseen quarry evermore
Furnished with tile, the fierce artificer
Curves his white bastions with projected roof
Round every windware stake, or tree, or door.
Speeding, the myriad-handed, his wild work
So fanciful, so savage, nought cares he
For number or proportion. Mockingly,
On coop or kennel he hangs Parian wreaths;

A swan-like form invests the hidden thorn;
Fills up the farmer's lane from wall to wall,
Maugre the farmer's sighs; and at the gate
A tapering turret overtops the work.
And when his hours are numbered, and the world
Is all his own, retiring, as he were not,
Leaves, when the sun appears, astonished Art
To mimic in slow structures, stone by stone,
Built in an age, the mad wind's night-work,
The frolic architecture of the snow.

ANSWER: *The Romantic Emerson expresses nothing but positive things about nature. The Naturalist Robinson is less generous with nature. In fact, nature is malevolent.*

LESSON 20
THE MODERN AGE, 1915-1946: LATE ROMANTICISM/ NATURALISM *(Part 1)*

Readings Due For This Lesson: Students should review *Ethan Frome*, Edith Wharton.

Reading Ahead: Students should review selections from 20th century poetry. What worldviews in this old genre surface in this new century?

Goal: Students will analyze *Ethan Frome*, Edith Wharton.

Goals/Objectives: What is the purpose of this lesson?	Strategies to meet these goals: How will I obtain these goals/objectives?	Evaluation: How will I know when I have met these goals/ objectives?
Students will understand this concept: narration in *Ethan Frome*. (cognitive goal)	Students will write an essay on this topic: The man telling the story is never real. Why? (Critical Thinking A)	Students, with minimal errors, will clearly answer the assigned question in a 1-2 page essay.
Students will increase their vocabulary. (cognitive goal)	Students will collect at least five new vocabulary words from their reading and use these words in their essays.	Students will use five vocabulary words in conversation during the week as well as use the words in their essays and in conversation.
Students will understand this concept: stream of consciousness. (cognitive goal)	Students will write an essay on this topic: Time and time again the reader is invited to interpret the story through Ethan's eyes. We watch Mattie dance, for instance, through Ethan's eyes before we meet her. This technique is called *stream of consciousness*. What effect does this technique have on the story? (Critical Thinking B)	Students, with minimal errors, will clearly answer the assigned question in a 1-2 page essay.

Goals/Objectives: What is the purpose of this lesson?	Strategies to meet these goals: How will I obtain these goals/objectives?	Evaluation: How will I know when I have met these goals/objectives?
Students will understand this concept: theme in *Ethan Frome*. (cognitive goal)	Students will write an essay on this topic: The life span of a story—or the number of years that it will be read—is determined to a large degree by its deeper meaning, or *theme*. Apart from the characters, apart from the plot a book must have a powerful theme or it will die. *The Odyssey*, by Homer, for instance, is such a story. The theme of journey is eternal and always interesting. The theme of someone returning to someone he loves is equally interesting. What is the theme of *Ethan Frome*? (Critical Thinking C)	Students, with minimal errors, will clearly answer the assigned question in a 1-2 page essay.
Students will understand this concept: irony. (cognitive goal)	Students will write an essay on this topic: This tragic book is marked by *irony*. *Irony* is defined as a contradiction between what is said and what is expected. Mattie ironically becomes the opposite of what she was as a youth. How do Zeena and Ethan change by the end of the novel? What other instances of irony do you find in Mrs. Hale's conversation? (Critical Thinking D)	Students, with minimal errors, will clearly answer the assigned question in a 1-2 page essay.
Students will understand this concept: imagery. (cognitive goal)	Students will write an essay on this topic: Find examples of *imagery* in this book. (Critical Thinking E)	Students, with minimal errors, will clearly answer the assigned question in a 1-2 page essay.
Students will exhibit higher-level thinking as they analyze the plot and discuss how the narrator draws the reader into the story. (cognitive goal)	Students will write an essay on this topic: How does the narrator draw the reader into this story. (Critical Thinking F)?	Students, with minimal errors, will clearly answer the assigned question in a 1-2 page essay.
Students will understand this concept: how interest is increased by the conversation between Mattie and Denis Eady. (cognitive goal)	Students will write an essay on this topic: How is interest increased by the conversation between Mattie and Denis Eady. (Critical Thinking G)?	Students, with minimal errors, will clearly answer the assigned question in a 1-2 page essay.

Goals/Objectives: What is the purpose of this lesson?	Strategies to meet these goals: How will I obtain these goals/objectives?	Evaluation: How will I know when I have met these goals/objectives?
Students will understand and consider the biblical view of divorce. (affective/behavioral)	Students will write an essay on this topic: Why do you think that Ethan did or did not have a right to leave Zeena? What does the Bible say? (Biblical Application A)	Students, with minimal errors, will clearly answer the assigned question in a 1-2 page essay.
Students will exhibit higher-level thinking as they reflect on how the personal lives of authors affect their writing style. (cognitive goal)	Students will write an essay on this topic: Wharton herself was struggling in a difficult marriage. Do you think this helped her make this novel more credible? How much do the personal lives of authors affect their writing style? (Biblical Application B)	Students, with minimal errors, will clearly answer the assigned question in a 1-2 page essay.
Students will accept the generalization that unforgiveness is wrong. (affective goal)	Students will exhibit higher-level thinking as they compare this theme in *Ethan Frome*, Edith Wharton, and *No Exit*, Jean Paul Sartre. (cognitive goal) Students will write an essay on this topic: At the end of the novel we observe three people captured by unforgiveness. They are, in effect, in a "living hell." What does the Bible say about unforgiveness? How can you forgive someone who has grievously wronged you? In fact, *Ethan Frome* has a similar theme to the existential play *No Exit*, by the French writer Jean Paul Sartre. Read this short play and compare it to *Ethan Frome* in an essay.	Students, with minimal errors, will clearly answer the assigned question in a 1-2 page essay.
Students will exhibit higher-level thinking as they answer these questions: In what ways is this novel a pessimistic view of life? In what ways does Wharton retain some moral vision? (cognitive goal)	Students will answer this question: Research the problems of the American city at the end of the nineteenth century. Contrast the views of Wharton with Dwight L. Moody an urban evangelist who transformed Chicago. This book presages the pessimism that grew after the First World War. In what ways is this novel a pessimistic view of life? In what ways does Wharton retain some moral vision? (Enrichment A)	Students, with minimal errors, will clearly answer the assigned question in a 1-2 page essay.

Goals/Objectives: What is the purpose of this lesson?	Strategies to meet these goals: How will I obtain these goals/objectives?	Evaluation: How will I know when I have met these goals/objectives?
Students will understand this concept: natural selection (cognitive goal) Students will consider the generalization that natural selection is wrong as a theory of science and as a theory of sociology. (cognitive goal)	Students will define natural selection and explain why this scientific theory is anti-Christian. (Enrichment B)	Students, with minimal errors, will clearly answer the assigned question in a 1-2 page essay.
Students will understand this concept: suspense in *Ethan Frome*. (cognitive goal)	Students will write an essay on this topic: Producing interest in the plot is called creating *suspense*. How does Wharton create suspense? (Enrichment A)	Students, with minimal errors, will clearly answer the assigned question in a 1-2 page essay.
Students will exhibit higher-level thinking as they reflect on what they would say to Frome after he tried to commit suicide. (cognitive goal)	Students will write an essay on this topic: What would be your advice to them? What would you say to Frome after he tried to commit suicide? (Enrichment B)	Students, with minimal errors, will clearly answer the assigned question in a 1-2 page essay.
Students will work in a group setting. (behavioral goal)	In a class, in a co-op experience, or during a family discussion, students will answer this question: When is divorce Scripturally acceptable?	Students will exhibit practical listening skills and will manifest understanding of opposing worldviews.
Students will be able to recall the information taught in the lesson. (cognitive goal)	Lesson 20 Test	Students will take the test at the end of this lesson and score at least 80%.
Students will experience reflective writing. (affective/spiritual goal)	Using the Journal Guide Questions in the Appendices, students will record at least three entries this week. Suggested Scriptures: Matthew 5-6	Students will show evidence that they have reflected on this issue, including informed discussions and written responses.

SUGGESTED
Weekly *Implementation*

DAY 1	DAY 2	DAY 3	DAY 4	DAY 5
Prayer journal. Students review the required reading (s) before the assigned lesson begins. Teacher may want to discuss assigned reading (s) with students. Teacher and students will decide on required essays for this lesson, choosing two or three essays. The rest of the essays can be outlined, answered with shorter answers, or skipped. Students will review all readings for Lesson 20	**Prayer journal.** Student should review reading (s) from next lesson. Student should outline essays due at the end of the week. Per teacher instructions, students may answer orally in a group setting some of the essays that are not assigned as formal essays.	**Prayer journal.** Students should write rough drafts of all assigned essays. The teacher and/or a peer evaluator may correct rough drafts.	**Prayer journal.** Student will re-write corrected copies of essays due tomorrow.	**Prayer journal.** Essays are due. Students should take the Lesson 20 test. Reading ahead: 20th century poetry. Guide: What world-views in this old genre surface in this new century?

Note: References to sources are in student edition.

ENRICHMENT ACTIVITIES/PROJECTS
Students could see the movie *Ethan Frome*. (1993)

SUPPLEMENTARY RESOURCES
Bell, Millicent ed. *The Cambridge Companion to Edith Wharton.*
   Bell offers a wonderful, insightful companion to the Wharton corpus.

Bloom, Harold, ed. *Edith Wharton: New Essays in Criticism.*
   Bloom is one of the best literary critics of the 20th century.

Ethan Frome. (VHS)
   A very fine, true-to-the-book video. However, parents should give permission before   students rent it.

Hofstadter, Richard. *Social Darwinism in American Thought.*
   Hofstadter is a brilliant Revisionist historian who presents an accurate picture of social   Darwinism (a worldview popular among Naturalists).

Johnson, Paul. *Modern Times.*

This is a very helpful history of the period in which Wharton lived. A sample on page 48 reads, "Among the advanced races, the decline and ultimately the collapse of the religious impulse would leave a huge vacuum. The history of modern times is in great part the history of how that vacuum is filled. Nietzsche (whom Davis calls post-modern) rightly perceived that the most likely candidate would be what he called the 'Will to Power,' which offered a far more comprehensive and in the end more plausible explanation of human behavior than either Marx or Freud. In place of religious belief, there would be secular ideology. Those who once filled the ranks of the totalitarian clergy would become totalitarian politicians. And, above all, the Will to Power would produce a new kind of messiah, uninhibited by any religious sanctions whatever, and with an unappeasable appetite for controlling mankind. The end of the old order, with an unguided world adrift in a relativistic universe, was a summons to such gangster-statesmen to emerge. They were not slow to make their appearance."

Moberg, David O. *The Great Reversal: Evangelism and Social Concern.*

Moberg offers a foil to Naturalist criticisms of Evangelical Christianity (see Stephen Crane, *Maggie*). He says "The question of how to deal with poverty and the numerous other interrelated problems of our day has divided Christians into two camps. One of them builds a strong case for evangelism as the basic solution, while the other emphasizes direct social involvement. Each accuses the other of being untrue to the essential nature of Christianity." (p. 13)

Price, Alan. *The End of the Age of Innocence: Edith Wharton and the First World War.*

Price places Wharton and her writings in her time period.

Simpson, George Gaylord. *The Meaning of Evolution.*

Simpson elucidates the dangers of evolution (a bedrock tenant of Naturalism). He states "Man is the result of a purposeless and materialistic process that did not have him in mind. He was not planned... discovery that the universe... lacked any purpose or plan has the inevitable corollary that the workings of the universe cannot provide any automatic, universal, eternal, or absolute criteria of Right and wrong."

Notes:

Ethan Frome
Edith Wharton (1911)

VOCABULARY WORDS

Prologue	taciturnity *(reserved)*
	Exanimate *(lifeless)*
Chapter I	sardonically *(mockingly)*
	oblique *(indirect)*
Chapter III	scintillating *(sparkling)*
	querulous *(fretful)*
Chapter V	languidly *(listlessly)*
Chapter VI	ominous *(threatening)*

CRITICAL THINKING

A. The man telling the story is never real. Why?

ANSWER: *Wharton does not want us to be distracted. The story is not about an outsider/visitor. The naturalist Wharton needs a neutral narrator, unimpressed by metaphysics, the uninterested spectator, to tell the story dispassionately.*

B. Time and time again the reader is invited to interpret the story through Ethan's eyes. We watch Mattie dance, for instance, through Ethan's eyes before we meet her. This technique is called *stream of consciousness.* What effect does this technique have on the story?

ANSWER: *Readers begin to see events and people from Ethan's perspective, building empathy between the reader and Ethan. Most readers willingly identify with Ethan. He is trapped. Ethan is a likeable person and the reader is tempted to see him as a victim. However, to do so would buy into a morality structure that presumes that adultery is acceptable under certain conditions. Of course, Ethan never committed adultery in actuality and the reader is sorry that Ethan and Mattie were injured, but at the same time Christians must be careful not to condone his actions.*

C. The life span of a story—or the number of years that it will be read—is determined to a large degree by its deeper meaning, or *theme.* Apart from the characters, apart from the plot, a book must have a powerful theme or it will die. *The Odyssey*, by Homer, for instance, is such a story. The theme of journey is eternal and always interesting. The theme of someone returning to someone he loves is equally interesting. What is the theme of *Ethan Frome*?

ANSWER: *Love, human effort, even hard work ultimately fail in the face of destiny.*

D. This tragic book is marked by *irony*. *Irony* is defined as a contradiction between what is said and what is expected. Mattie ironically becomes the opposite of what she was as a youth. How do Zeena and Ethan change by the end of the novel? What other instances of irony do you find in Mrs. Hale's conversation?

ANSWER: *Ethan, who was so afraid of silence, is now in silence all the time. Zeena, once the weakest, is ironically called to be the strongest member of the family. What other instances of irony do you find in Mrs. Hale's conversation? The fading New England woman is an unlikely interpreter of the Ethan Frome narrative to her visitor.*

E. Find examples of *imagery* in this book.

ANSWER: *There are many examples. "The village lay under two feet of snow, with drifts at the windy corners. In a sky of iron the points of the Dipper hung like icicles and Orion flashed his cold fires. The moon had set, but the night was so transparent that the white house-fronts between the elms looked gray against the snow, clumps of bushes made black stains on it, and the basement windows of the church sent shafts of yellow light far across the endless undulations." (Ch. 1)*

F. How does the narrator draw the reader into this story?

ANSWER: *Readers are given information in small increments as they are drawn into the tragedy, maintaining suspense and interest. It is not the nature, however, of naturalistic writers to "surprise" their readers. Normally they give ample warning through foreshadowing. However, in this case at least, the reader will most likely not see the ending coming. Only the dialogue at the end of this short novel gave warning.*

G. How is interest increased by the conversation between Mattie and Denis Eady?

ANSWER: *Jealous Ethan is obviously in love with Mattie. This gives the reader a hint of what may happen next. Few readers, however, guess what actually happens! Ethan is jealous—an uncharacteristic personality trait. The reader observes that Ethan is more complicated than he first appeared.*

BIBLICAL APPLICATION

A. Why do you think that Ethan did have or did not have a right to leave Zeena? What does the Bible say?

ANSWER: *Answers will vary. A typically accepted Christian interpretation is that divorce is Scripturally, and therefore, morally acceptable under specific conditions. These conditions were not met in this case.*

B. Wharton herself was struggling in a difficult marriage. Do you think this helped her make this novel more credible? How much do the personal lives of authors affect their writing style?

ANSWER: *The answer to this question must be an opinion. Typically accepted belief among some literary scholars is that the personal lives of the authors do indeed affect their narration. No doubt Wharton identified with Ethan since she was married to an abusive alcoholic.*

C. At the end of the novel we observe three people captured by unforgiveness. They are, in effect, in a "living hell." What does the Bible say about unforgiveness? How can you forgive someone who has grievously wronged you? In fact, *Ethan Frome* has a similar theme to the existential play *No Exit*, by the French writer Jean Paul Sartre. Read this short play and compare it to *Ethan Frome* in an essay.

ANSWER: *Forgiveness is a major tenet of Christian theology. However, it is important to understand the basis of how forgiveness is sought and offered; God requires repentance.*

A. Research the problems of the American city at the end of the nineteenth century. Contrast the views of Wharton with Dwight L. Moody, an urban evangelist who transformed Chicago. This book presages the pessimism that grew after the First World War. In what way is this novel a pessimistic view of life? In what ways does Wharton retain some moral vision?

ANSWER: *The notion that nameless, cold fate is in control of everything (if there is any control at all) is depressing. The negative image of marriage fidelity that Wharton presents is somewhat depressing. Nonetheless, Wharton honors Ethan for his moral stand—after all he deliberately chose not to commit active adultery.*

B. One individual who had a profound effect on America when Edith Wharton was alive was Charles Darwin (1809-1882). In 1859 Charles Darwin published *On The Origin of Species by Means of Natural Selection*, or the *Preservation of Favoured Races in the Struggle for Life*. In 1858 Darwin had co-authored (with Alfred Russel Wallace) the theory of natural selection, which says that superior biological variations tend to be preserved. In the struggle for existence, the fit are not those who survive but those who reproduce. Natural selection also leads to diversification as different organisms adapt to particular ecological circumstances. Darwin said all biological similarities and differences are caused by descent with modification. He concluded that all organisms are descended from only one ancestor. Evolution is the name for this biological process that goes back to one common ancestor 3-1/2 billion years ago. Charles Darwin, then, was the father of the theory of evolution:

We have reason to believe, as stated in the first chapter, that a change in the conditions of life, by specially acting on the reproductive system, causes or increases variability; and in the foregoing case the conditions of life are supposed to have undergone a change, and this would manifestly be favourable to natural selection, by giving a better chance of profitable variations occurring; and unless profitable variations do occur, natural selection can do nothing. Not that, as I believe, any extreme amount of variability is necessary; as man can certainly produce great results by adding up in any given direction mere individual differences, so could Nature, but far more easily, from having incomparably longer time at her disposal. Nor do I believe that any great physical change, as of climate, or any unusual degree of isolation to check immigration, is actually necessary to produce new and unoccupied places for natural selection to fill up by modifying and improving some of the varying inhabitants. For as all the inhabitants of each country are struggling together with nicely balanced forces, extremely slight modifications in the structure or habits of one inhabitant would often give it an advantage over others; and still further modifications of the same kind would often still further increase the advantage.—*The Origin of Species*

Define natural selection and explain why this scientific theory is anti-Christian?

ANSWER: *Natural selection assumes that species are evolving from a lower complexity and utilitarian structure to a more complicated complexity and advantageous structure. This theory argues that scientific forces—not God—are at work in the world. In fact, God is dead altogether. If this is the case, then man is not created in the image of God and onerous, evil practices like abortion and euthanasia make a lot of sense.*

C. Producing interest in the plot is called creating *suspense*. How does Wharton create suspense?

ANSWER: *She controls the information that is given. After subtle hints (e.g., the scene at the dance), the reader wonders what will happen next. We know that Ethan and Mattie are debilitated. It is a skilled writer who tells his/her readers the ending the first chapter in the book.*

D. Wharton knew much too well the frustration of a failed marriage—such as Ethan and Zeena's. Teddy Wharton was thirteen years older than his wife and a totally unsuitable mate for her. She bored him, and he scoffed at her literary and intellectual pursuits. When Teddy's health began to fail, the marriage became still more strained. He crabbed and complained much of the time. In fits of temper he verbally abused his wife. Twice he suffered nervous breakdowns. Edith Wharton told the story of her marriage in various writings, including her literary autobiography, *A Backward Glance* (1934). If Edith's version is accurate, though, she wins our sympathy as the wronged partner in the marriage, just as most readers sympathize with Ethan Frome for being stuck with Zeena, his sickly, ill-tempered wife. But Ethan's is also a one-sided story. We can only guess what Zeena thinks about him by reading between the lines. It seems certain, however, that Ethan Frome is a product of Edith Wharton's long and serious contemplation of the mutual obligations of marriage partners. Ethan chose to die rather than stay with his spouse. That wasn't a satisfactory solution for Wharton, though. In 1913, two years after Ethan Frome was published, she filed for divorce. Pretend that you are Ethan Frome's and/or Edith Wharton's pastor. What would be your advice to them? What would you say to Frome after he tried to commit suicide?

ANSWER: *There are three serious issues here: suicide, divorce, and forgiveness. All three issues will need to be addressed. Answers will be opinions and interpretations of biblical concepts.*

FINAL PROJECT

Students should correct and rewrite all essays and place them in their Final Portfolio.

LESSON 20 TEST

OBJECTIVE QUESTIONS (50 POINTS)

_____ 1. Telling the story is (A) a family friend, (B) Ethan, (C) Zeena, (D) a neutral observer.

_____ 2. Life is very hard for Ethan because (A) his wife Zeena has an outside job (B) his barn recently burned (C) his wife Zeena was an unhappy hypochondriac (D) he cannot read.

_____ 3. Life improved considerably for everyone when (A) Zeena's cousin Mattie came to help (B) the Fromes won the lottery (C) Zeena died (D) Ethan stopped worrying about Zeena.

_____ 4. Mattie and Ethan took things into their own hands and (A) ran away (B) tried to commit suicide (C) secretly married (D) decided not to continue their relationship.

_____ 5. At the end of the novel (A) Zeena dies and Mattie and Ethan live happily ever after (B) Zeena, wounded Mattie, and Ethan live in unhappiness (C) Mattie dies suddenly (D) everyone goes his own way.

DISCUSSION QUESTIONS (50 POINTS)

A. The nameless narrator only appears in the prologue and in the epilogue of the novel. Some critics argue that he is a young engineer with time to kill in Starkfield. With the instinct of a scientist, he investigates Ethan, and with the skill of an experienced writer he tells Ethan's story. Why does Wharton choose this particular narrator and why doesn't she have him be a part of the story?

B. It is interesting that the scientist or engineer is scorned by Hawthorne (e.g., Chillingsworth and Alymer) but extolled by Wharton. Why?

C. What are two possible themes of *Ethan Frome*?

D. How does Wharton use the setting to advance her themes?

E. Why, in Wharton's world, are Ethan and Maggie doomed?

F. What role does Mrs. Andrew Hale play in this novel?

G. The use of darkness and light is an important motif for Romantic writers. Likewise, Wharton uses darkness and light to make a point. The contrast between the brilliant light inside the church and the darkness outside is drawn vividly. She does it several other times too. Why? What is her point?

H. Several of the novels we have read this year have characters who are isolated. Hester Prynne is isolated from her community; Huck Finn is isolated and living alone; Henry Fleming is isolated and alone when he flees from the battlefield; now Ethan is isolated from all others by his shyness and social inadequacies. Yet, there is a considerable difference between Hester's isolation and all the rest. Why?

I. Mattie has virtually no personality at all. She is critical to the plot but remains completely undeveloped. Why?

J. Because Edith Wharton came from high society, some scholars doubted that Wharton had the insight to write about ordinary country people. One scholar wrote that *Ethan Frome* "was not a New England story and certainly not the granite 'folk tale' of New England its admirers have claimed it to be. (Mrs. Wharton) knew little of the New England common world and perhaps cared even less. She never knew how the poor lived in Paris or London; she knew even less of how they lived in the New England villages where she spent an occasional summer." Agree or disagree with this critic and defend your answer.

LESSON 20 TEST ANSWERS

OBJECTIVE QUESTIONS (50 POINTS)

1. __D__
2. __C__
3. __A__
4. __B__
5. __B__

DISCUSSION QUESTIONS (50 POINTS)

A. The nameless narrator only appears in the prologue and in the epilogue of the novel. Some critics argue that he is a young engineer with time to kill in Starkfield. With the instinct of a scientist, he investigates Ethan, and with the skill of an experienced writer he tells Ethan's story. Why does Wharton choose this particular narrator and why doesn't she have him be a part of the story?

ANSWER: *The Naturalistic Wharton values a neutral, uninterested, uninvolved narrator. Contrast this with the narrator in Poe's short story "The Fall of the House of Usher." He likewise is a reliable narrator but he is not an engineer.*

B. It is interesting that the scientist or engineer is scorned by Hawthorne (e.g., Chillingsworth and Alymer) but extolled by Wharton. Why?

ANSWER: *Continuing the previous discussion, Chillingsworth and Alymer would be useful to the empiricist/Naturalist Wharton. Romanticist Hawthorne prefers the poet (see "Old Stone Face") to the scientist.*

C. What are two possible themes of *Ethan Frome*?

ANSWER: *Alienation and loneliness or moribundity (i.e., death).*

D. How does Wharton use the setting to advance her themes?

ANSWER: *When Ethan is gloomy the weather is gloomy; when he is happy there is sunshine. The harsh New England winters suit Wharton just fine.*

E. Why, in Wharton's world, are Ethan and Maggie doomed?

ANSWER: *They harbor romantic hopes in a naturalistic world. They actually think that they can be happy. Just as Henry Fleming must lose his romantic worldview in* Red Badge *or be killed, likewise Ethan and Maggie need to discard morality and do the "naturalistic thing"—which presumably is to do what is right in their own eyes.*

F. What role does Mrs. Andrew Hale play in this novel?

ANSWER: *She is Ethan's conscience—he can't possibly pressure or cheat Mr. Hale when Mrs. Hale is obviously so fine a woman. This forces Ethan to stay the course with his moral position.*

G. The use of darkness and light is an important motif for Romantic writers. Likewise, Wharton uses darkness and light to make a point. The contrast between the brilliant light inside the church and the darkness outside is drawn vividly. She does it several other times too. Why? What is her point?

ANSWER: *To Hawthorne, darkness is evil and light is openness and goodness. To Wharton darkness is ignorance and secrecy—both anathemas to the empiricist/Naturalist. Likewise, to Wharton, light implies beauty and to her, false hope. Maggie, for instance, lights up Ethan's face.*

H. Several of the novels we have read this year have characters who are isolated. Hester Prynne is isolated from her community; Huck Finn is isolated and living alone; Henry Fleming is isolated and alone when he flees from the battlefield; now Ethan is isolated from all others by his shyness and social inadequacies. Yet, there is a considerable difference between Hester's isolation and all the rest. Why?

ANSWER: *Within her isolated repentance Hester finds new life and hope. Ethan's isolation ultimately leads to disaster.*

I. Mattie has virtually no personality at all. She is critical to the plot but remains completely undeveloped. Why?

ANSWER: *Her only purpose is to develop Ethan and to help Wharton make a Naturalistic statement about the cosmos.*

J. Because Edith Wharton came from high society, some scholars doubted that Wharton had the insight to write about ordinary country people. On scholar wrote that *Ethan Frome* "was not a New England story and certainly not the granite 'folk tale' of New England its admirers have claimed it to be. (Mrs. Wharton) knew little of the New England common world and perhaps cared even less. She never knew how the poor lived in Paris or London; she knew even less of how they lived in the New England villages where she spent an occasional summer." Agree or disagree with this critic and defend your answer.

ANSWER: *Wharton's novel is far more than a social statement about New England—it is a statement about the cosmos—it advances the naturalist worldview. Thus her first-hand knowledge about the New England rural lower middle class is irrelevant.*

THE MODERN AGE, 1915-1946: LATE ROMANTICISM/
NATURALISM *(Part 2)*

Readings Due For This Lesson: Students should review selections from 20th century poetry.

Reading Ahead: Students should read *A Farewell to Arms*, Ernest Hemingway. What is Hemingway's vision? How is the protagonist Frederick Henry in *A Farewell to Arms* similar to Henry Fleming in *A Red Badge of Courage*? Stylistically, how is *A Farewell to Arms* similar to *The Adventures of Huckleberry Finn*?

Goal: Students will analyze 20th century poetry.

Goals/Objectives: What is the purpose of this lesson?	Strategies to meet these goals: How will I obtain these goals/objectives?	Evaluation: How will I know when I have met these goals/objectives?
Students will understand this concept: Ezra Pound's racism. (cognitive goal)	Students will write an essay on this topic: Ezra Pound was a notorious racist and supporter of the Nazi party in Germany. Do you see evidence of his racism in his poems? Should we avoid reading his poetry because he is a racist? Why? (Critical Thinking A)	Students, with minimal errors, will clearly answer the assigned question in a 1-2 page essay.
Students will increase their vocabulary. (cognitive goal)	Students will collect at least five new vocabulary words from their reading and use these words in their essays.	Students will use five vocabulary words in conversation during the week as well as use the words in their essays and in conversation.
Students will exhibit higher-level thinking as they agree or disagree with these critics. (cognitive goal)	Students will write an essay on this topic: Agree or disagree with each critic. (Critical Thinking B)	Students, with minimal errors, will clearly answer the assigned question in a 1-2 page essay.
Students will exhibit higher-level thinking as they compare themes in works by Frost and Wharton. (cognitive goal)	Students will write an essay on this topic: Read "Home Burial" and "Death of a Hired Hand" by Robert Frost and compare the themes of these poems with *Ethan Frome*, Edith Wharton. Identify elements of Naturalism and Realism	Students, with minimal errors, will clearly answer the assigned question in a 1-2 page essay.

Goals/Objectives: What is the purpose of this lesson?	Strategies to meet these goals: How will I obtain these goals/objectives?	Evaluation: How will I know when I have met these goals/objectives?
	in these literary works. How does nature function in these two writer's prose/poetry? How does each author use irony? Why is irony a particularly effective literary device for naturalistic writers to use? (Critical Thinking C)?	
Students will understand this concept: Langston Hughes' poetry and the theme of anger. (cognitive goal)	Read as many of Langston Hughes' poems as you can. Do you find examples of anger in his poetry? Explain. (Critical Thinking D)	Students, with minimal errors, will clearly answer the assigned question in a 1-2 page essay.
Students will exhibit higher-level thinking as they evaluate how good a poet Millay is. (cognitive goal)	Students will write this essay: Some scholars argue that Edna St. Vincent Millay is a second-rate poet. Support what you think. (Critical Thinking E)	Students, with minimal errors, will clearly answer the assigned question in a 1-2 page essay.
Students will understand this concept: tone and how it relates to the content of Frost's poems. (cognitive goal)	Students will write this essay: In Robert Frost's poem *Fire and Ice*, what is the speaker's tone of voice in the first two lines? Is it surprising? How does his tone suit or contrast with the content of what he is saying? What gives the poem its power? (Critical Thinking F)	Students, with minimal errors, will clearly answer the assigned question in a 1-2 page essay.
Students will exhibit higher-level thinking as they argue for their favorite poet (cognitive goal).	Students will answer this question in essay form: You are retained by a major publisher to put together an anthology of the best American poetry of the 20th century. What 5 American poets and poems would you include and why? (Enrichment)	Students, with minimal errors, will clearly answer the assigned question in a 1-2 page essay.
Students will work in a group setting. (behavioral goal)	In a class, in a co-op experience, or during a family discussion, students will answer this question: Examine contemporary song lyrics. Which ones are appropriate and which ones are not? What are your criteria for defining "appropriate"?	Students will exhibit practical listening skills and will manifest understanding of opposing worldviews.
Students will be able to recall the information taught in the lesson. (cognitive goal)	Lesson 21 Test	Students will take the test at the end of this lesson and score at least 80%.

Goals/Objectives: What is the purpose of this lesson?	Strategies to meet these goals: How will I obtain these goals/objectives?	Evaluation: How will I know when I have met these goals/objectives?
Students will experience reflective writing. (affective/spiritual goal)	Using the Journal Guide Questions in the Appendices, students will record at least three entries this week. Suggested Scriptures: Matthew 5-6	Students will show evidence that they have reflected on this issue, including informed discussions and written responses.

SUGGESTED

Weekly *Implementation*

DAY 1	DAY 2	DAY 3	DAY 4	DAY 5
Prayer journal.	Prayer journal.	Prayer journal.	Prayer journal.	Prayer journal.
Students review the required reading(s) before the assigned lesson begins.	Student should review reading(s) from next lesson.	Students should write rough drafts of all assigned essays.	Student will re-write corrected copies of essays due tomorrow.	Essays are due.
Teacher may want to discuss assigned reading(s) with students.	Student should outline essays due at the end of the week.	The teacher and/or a peer evaluator may correct rough drafts.		Students should take the Lesson 21 test.
Teacher and students will decide on required essays for this lesson, choosing two or three essays.	Per teacher instructions, students may answer orally in a group setting some of the essays that are not assigned as formal essays.			Reading ahead: review *A Farewell to Arms*, Ernest Hemingway.
The rest of the essays can be outlined, answered with shorter answers, or skipped.				Guide: How is the protagonist Frederick Henry in *A Farewell to Arms* similar to Henry Fleming in *A Red Badge of Courage?* Stylistically, how is *A Farewell to Arms* similar to *The Adventures of Huckleberry Finn?*
Students will review all readings for Lesson 21				

Note: References to sources are in student edition.

ENRICHMENT ACTIVITIES/PROJECTS

Students should memorize 150 lines from their favorite poet.

SUPPLEMENTARY RESOURCES

Arp, Thomas R. (Editor), *Perrine's Literature: Structure, Sound and Sense.*
  An excellent resource on poetry.

Friedman, Norman. *e. e. cummings: The Art of His Poetry.*

Perrine, Laurence. *Perrine's Sound and Sense: An Introduction to Poetry.*
  Perrine set the standard for poetry interpretation.

Schwartz, Sanford. *The Matrix of Modernism: Pound, Eliot, and Early Twentieth-Century Thought.*

Notes:

CRITICAL THINKING

A. Ezra Pound was a notorious racist and supporter of the Nazi party in Germany. Do you see evidence of racism in his poems? Should we avoid reading his poetry because he is a racist?

ANSWER: *This answer will have to be an opinion. One does not find evidence of racism in his poems.*

B. Agree or disagree with each critic below:

At his best, of course, Frost does not philosophize. The anecdote is absorbed into symbol. The method of indirection operates fully: the senses of realistic detail, the air of casual comment, are employed to build up and intensify a serious effect. (Cleanth Brooks, *Modern Poetry,* p. 113)

Despite his great virtues, you cannot read a great deal of Frost without this effect of the *deja vu.* Sententiousness and a relative absence of formal daring are his main defects. Even in his finest work, the conventionality of rhythm and rhyme contributes a certain tedium, temporarily relegated to a dim corner of the reader's consciousness. (M.L. Rosenthal, *The Modern Poets,* pp. 112-113)

ANSWER: *Answers will vary but Cleanth Brooks correctly highlights Frost's powerful Realism and Naturalism. One needs to remember this when one reads Frost on the surface. Rosenthal argues that Frost's images are predictable and bland. I do not necessarily agree.*

C. Read "Home Burial" and "Death of a Hired Hand" by Robert Frost and compare the themes of these poems with *Ethan Frome,* Edith Wharton. Identify elements of Naturalism and Realism in these literary works. How does nature function in these two writer's prose/poetry? How does each author use irony? Why is irony a particularly effective literary device for naturalistic writers to use?

ANSWER: *Frost and Wharton use nature to emphasize the neutrality or malevolence of nature. Robert Frost's poems "Home Burial" and "Death of a Hired Hand" have similar themes to Edith Wharton's* Ethan Frome. *These themes are conflict, loneliness, and isolation. Both works focus on rocky, painful, relations, and the inability of the individuals involved to be friends. They display a naturalistic world view, which is evidenced by the use of irony, which is particularly suited to expressing the naturalistic worldview.*

D. Read as many of Langston Hughes' poems as you can. Do you find examples of anger in his poetry? Explain.

ANSWER: *This reader finds no evidence of anger. His rhetoric is rich and generous. His metaphors are powerful. He seems to have no axe to grind.*

E. Compare and contrast "Cassandra," "Richard Cory," and "Mr. Flood's Party" by Edwin Arlington Robinson.

ANSWER: *Inevitably, a Robinson poem portrays a naturalistic vision of hopelessness and loss of control. "Cassandra" laments the fast passage of hopeless time (akin to Emerson's "Day.") Ditto "Richard Cory" and "Mr. Flood's Party." Often the characters in a Robinson poem are full of hopelessness.*

F. Some scholars argue that Edna St. Vincent Millay is a second-rate poet. Support what you think.

ANSWER: *This is not a fair scholarly assessment. She may not be the best poet of the 20th century, but her poetry, especially "Renasance," is very good.*

G. In Robert Frost's poem *Fire and Ice,* what is the speaker's tone of voice in the first two lines? Is it surprising? How does his tone suit or contrast with the content of what he is saying? What gives this poem its power?

ANSWER: *Frost is evoking common images—fire and ice—to express an apocalyptic vision that is the heart of all Naturalism.*

ENRICHMENT

You are retained by a major publisher to put together an anthology of the best American poetry of the 20th century. What 5 American poets and poems would you include and why?

ANSWER: *Answers will be opinions.*

FINAL PROJECT

Students should correct and rewrite all essays and place them in their Final Portfolio.

LESSON 21 TEST

IDENTIFICATION (90 POINTS)

Identify the author of the following passages and explain why you made your choice. Choose from Ralph Waldo Emerson, Nathaniel Hawthorne, William Bradford, Mark Twain, Stephen Crane, Edgar Allan Poe, and Edith Wharton.

A. It was many and many a year ago,
In a kingdom by the sea,
That a maiden there lived whom you may know
By the name of Annabel Lee; And this maiden she lived with no other thought
Than to love and be loved by me.

I was a child and she was a child,
In this kingdom by the sea;
But we loved with a love that was more than love—
I and my Annabel Lee;
With a love that the winged seraphs of heaven
Coveted her and me.

B. There is a time in every man's education when he arrives at the conviction that envy is ignorance; that imitation is suicide; that he must take himself for better, for worse, as his portion; that though the wide universe is full of good, no kernel of nourishing corn can come to him but through his toil bestowed on that plot of ground which is given to him to till. The power which resides in him is new in nature, and none but he knows what that is which he can do, nor does he know until he has tried. Not for nothing one face, one character, one fact, makes much impression on him, and another none. This sculpture in the memory is not without preestablished harmony. The eye was placed where one ray should fall, that it might testify of that particular ray. We but half express ourselves, and are ashamed of that divine idea which each of us represents. It may be safely trusted as proportionate and of good issues, so it be faithfully imparted, but God will not have his work made manifest by cowards. A man is relieved and gay when he has put his heart into his work and done his best; but what he has said or done otherwise, shall give him no peace. It is a deliverance which does not deliver. In the attempt his genius deserts him; no muse befriends; no invention, no hope.

C. Being thus arrived in a good harbor and brought safe to land, they fell upon their knees and blessed the God of heaven, who had brought them over the vast and furious ocean, and delivered them from all the perils and miseries thereof, again to set their feet on the firm and stable earth, their proper element. And no marvel if they were thus joyful, seeing wise Seneca was so affected with sailing a few miles on the coast of his own Italy; as he affirmed, that he had rather remain twenty years on his way by land, then pass by sea to any place in a short time; so tedious and dreadful was the same unto him.

D. No expense had been spared on the setting, which was acknowledged to be very beautiful even by people who shared his acquaintance with the Opera houses of Paris and Vienna. The foreground, to the footlights, was covered with emerald green cloth. In the middle distance symmetrical mounds of woolly green moss bounded by croquet hoops formed the base of shrubs shaped like orange-trees but studded with large pink and red roses. Gigantic pansies, considerably larger than the roses, and closely resembling the floral pen-wipers made by female parishioners for fashionable clergymen, sprang from the moss beneath the rose-trees; and here and there a daisy grafted on a rose-branch flowered with a luxuriance prophetic of Mr. Luther Burbank's far-off prodigies. In the centre of this enchanted garden Madame Nilsson, in white cashmere slashed with pale blue satin, a reticule dangling from a blue girdle, and large yellow braids carefully disposed on each side of her muslin chemisette, listened with downcast eyes to M. Capoul's impassioned wooing, and affected a guileless incomprehension of his designs whenever, by word or glance, he persuasively indicated the ground floor window of the neat brick villa projecting obliquely from the right wing.

E. For the most wild, yet most homely narrative which I am about to pen, I neither expect nor solicit belief. Mad indeed would I be to expect it, in a case where my very senses reject their own evidence. Yet, mad am I not—and very surely do I not dream. But tomorrow I die, and to-day I would unburthen my soul. My immediate purpose is to place before the world, plainly, succinctly, and without comment, a series of mere household events. In their consequences, these events have terrified—have tortured—have destroyed me. Yet I will not attempt to expound them. To me, they have presented little but Horror—to many they will seem less terrible than *barroques*. Hereafter, perhaps, some intellect may be found which will reduce my phantasm to the common-place—some intellect more calm, more logical, and far less excitable than my own, which will perceive, in the circumstances I detail with awe, nothing more than an ordinary succession of very natural causes and effects.

F. The House of the Seven Gables, antique as it now looks, was not the first habitation erected by civilized man on precisely the same spot of ground. Pyncheon-street formerly bore the humbler appellation of Maule's-lane, from the name of the original occupant of the soil, before whose cottage-door it was a cow-path. A natural spring of soft and pleasant water—a rare treasure on the sea-girt peninsula, where the Puritan settlement was made—had early induced Matthew Maule to build a hut, shaggy with thatch, at this point, although somewhat too remote from what was then the centre of the village. In the growth of the town, however, after some thirty or forty years, the site covered by this rude hovel had become exceedingly desirable in the eyes of a prominent and powerful personage, who asserted plausible claims to the proprietorship of this, and a large adjacent tract of land, on the strength of a grant from the legislature. Colonel Pyncheon, the claimant, as we gather from whatever traits of him are preserved, was characterized by an iron energy of purpose. Matthew Maule, on the other hand, though an obscure man, was stubborn in the defence of what he considered his right; and, for several years, he succeeded in protecting the acre or two of earth, which, with his own toil, he had hewn out of the primeval forest, to be his garden-ground and homestead.

G. There was a feller here once by the name of *Jim* Smiley, in the winter of '49—or maybe it was the spring of '50—I don't recollect exactly, somehow, though what makes me think it was one or the other is because I remember the big flume wasn't finished when he first came to the camp; but any way, he was the curiosest man about always betting on any thing that turned up you ever see, if he could get any body to bet on the other side, and if he couldn't he'd change sides—any way that suited the other man would suit *him*—any way just so's he got a bet, *he* was satisfied. But still, he was lucky—uncom-

mon lucky; he most always come out winner. He was always ready and laying for a chance; there couldn't be no solitry thing mentioned but that feller'd offer to bet on it—and take any side you please, as I was just telling you. If there was a horse-race, you'd find him flush, or you'd find him busted at the end of it; if there was a dog-fight, he'd bet on it; if there was a cat-fight, he'd bet on it; if there was a chicken-fight, he'd bet on it; why, if there was two birds setting on a fence, he would bet you which one would fly first—or if there was a camp-meeting, he would be there reglar, to bet on Parson Walker, which he judged to be the best exhorter about here, and so he was, too, and a good man. If he even seen a straddle-bug start to go any wheres, he would bet you how long it would take him to get wherever he was going to, and if you took him up, he would foller that straddle-bug to Mexico but what he would find out where he was bound for and how long he was on the road. Lots of the boys here has seen that Smiley, and can tell you about him. Why, it never made no difference to *him*—he would bet on *anything*—the dangdest feller. Parson Walker's wife laid very sick, once, for a good while, and it seemed as if they warn't going to save her; but one morning he come in, and Smiley asked him how she was, and he said she was considerable better—thank the Lord for his inf'nit mercy—and coming on so smart that, with the blessing of Providence, she'd get well yet—and Smiley, before he thought, says, "Well, I'll resk two-and-a-half that she don't, anyway."

H. During the afternoon of the storm, the whirling snows acted as drivers, as men with whips, and at half-past three, the walk before the closed doors of the house was covered with wanderers of the street, waiting. For some distance on either side of the place they could be seen lurking in doorways and behind projecting parts of buildings, gathering in close bunches in an effort to get warm. A covered wagon drawn up near the curb sheltered a dozen of them. Under the stairs that led to the elevated railway station, there were six or eight, their hands stuffed deep in their pockets, their shoulders stooped, jiggling their feet. Others always could be seen coming, a strange procession, some slouching along with the characteristic hopeless gait of professional strays, some coming with hesitating steps wearing the air of men to whom this sort of thing was new. It was an afternoon of incredible length.

The snow, blowing in twisting clouds, sought out the men in their meagre hiding-places and skilfully beat in among them, drenching their persons with showers of fine, stinging flakes. They crowded together, muttering, and fumbling in their pockets to get their red, inflamed wrists covered by the cloth.

I. The cause of so much amazement may appear sufficiently slight. Mr. Hooper, a gentlemanly person, of about thirty, though still a bachelor, was dressed with due clerical neatness, as if a careful wife had starched his band, and brushed the weekly dust from his Sunday's garb. There was but one thing remarkable in his appearance. Swathed about his forehead, and hanging down over his face, so low as to be shaken by his breath, Mr. Hooper had on a black veil. On a nearer view it seemed to consist of two folds of crape, which entirely concealed his features, except the mouth and chin, but probably did not intercept his sight, further than to give a darkened aspect to all living and inanimate things. With this gloomy shade before him, good Mr. Hooper walked onward, at a slow and quiet pace, stooping somewhat, and looking on the ground, as is customary with abstracted men, yet nodding kindly to those of his parishioners who still waited on the meeting-house steps. But so wonder-struck were they that his greeting hardly met with a return.

J. His aunt Polly stood surprised a moment, and then broke into a gentle laugh.

"Hang the boy, can't I never learn anything? Ain't he played me tricks enough like that for me to be looking out for him by this time? But old fools is the biggest fools there is. Can't learn an old dog new tricks, as the saying is. But my goodness, he never plays them alike, two days, and how is a body to know what's coming? He 'pears to know just how long he can torment me before I get my dander up, and he knows if he can make out to put me off for a minute or make me laugh, it's all down again and I can't hit him a lick. I ain't doing my duty by that boy, and that's the Lord's truth, goodness knows. Spare the rod and spile the child, as the Good Book says. I'm a laying up sin and suffering for us both, *I* know. He's full of the Old Scratch, but laws-a-me! he's my own dead sister's boy, poor thing, and I ain't got the heart to lash him, somehow. Every time I let him off, my conscience does hurt me so, and every time I hit him my old heart most breaks. Well-a-well, man that is born of woman is of few days and full of trouble, as the Scripture says, and I reckon it's so. He'll play hookey this evening, and I'll just be obleeged to make him work, to-morrow, to punish him. It's mighty hard to make him work Saturdays, when all the boys is having holiday, but he hates work more than he hates anything else, and I've *got* to do some of my duty by him, or I'll be the ruination of the child."

CREATIVE WRITING. (10 POINTS)

Compose your own poem. A simplistic method of beginning poetry thinking is to write your name down the page and then to use adjectives or nouns that describe you—they should also begin with each of the letters listed down the page. For example:

Jolly
Athlete
Maudlin
Encounter
Simple

LESSON 21 TEST ANSWERS

IDENTIFICATION (90 POINTS)

Identify the author of the following passages and explain why you made your choice. Choose from Ralph Waldo Emerson, Nathaniel Hawthorne, William Bradford, Mark Twain, Stephen Crane, Edgar Allan Poe, and Edith Wharton.

A. **ANSWER:** *"Anabel Lee" by E. A. Poe. Notice the rime and style of this poem and the Romantic images. (i.e., immutability and death)*

B. **ANSWER:** *In "Self-Reliance" Ralph Waldo Emerson invites the reader to a subjective understanding of reality in line with Transcendentalism.*

C. **ANSWER:** *In Of Plimoth Plantation, William Bradford speaks as a Christian Theist.*

D. **ANSWER:** *In Age of Innocence, Edith Wharton exhibits her penchant to aristocratic images that exhibit presumption and superficiality.*

E. **ANSWER:** *Typically "The Black Cat," by E. A. Poe, uses first person narration and images of horror to advance a Romantic agenda.*

F. **ANSWER:** *In The House of Seven Gables, Nathaniel Hawthorne continues to explore his Puritan, Christian Theistic past.*

G. **ANSWER:** *Typically "The Celebrated Jumping Frog of Calaveras County," exhibits Mark Twain's colloquialism and humor.*

H. **ANSWER:** *In "Men in the Storm," Stephen Crane describes nature in malevolent terms.*

I. **ANSWER:** *"The Minister in the Black Veil," Nathaniel Hawthorne*

J. **ANSWER:** *The Adventures of Tom Sawyer, Mark Twain*

CREATIVE WRITING (10 POINTS)

Compose your own poem. A simplistic method of beginning poetry thinking is to write your name down the page and then to use adjectives or nouns that describe you—they should also begin with each of the letters listed down the page. For example:

ANSWER:
Merciful
Anxious
Real
Yawning

LESSON 22

THE MODERN AGE, 1915-1946: LATE ROMANTICISM/ NATURALISM *(Part 3)*

Readings Due For This Lesson: Students should review *A Farewell to Arms*, Ernest Hemingway.

Reading Ahead: Students should review *Their Eyes Were Watching God*, Zora Neale Hurston. How does Janie develop as a character?

Goal: Students will analyze the important work *A Farewell to Arms*, by Ernest Hemingway.

Goals/Objectives: What is the purpose of this lesson?	Strategies to meet these goals: How will I obtain these goals/objectives?	Evaluation: How will I know when I have met these goals/ objectives?
Students will understand this concept: narrator of *A Farewell to Arms*. (cognitive goal)	Students will write an essay on this topic: Who is the narrator of this story? What effect does this form of narration have on the story? (Critical Thinking A)	Students, with minimal errors, will clearly answer the assigned question in a 1-2 page essay.
Students will increase their vocabulary. (cognitive goal)	Students will collect at least five new vocabulary words from their reading and use these words in their essays. Note: the paucity of words in this book is reflective of Hemingway's cogent/ journalistic style.	Students will use five vocabulary words in conversation during the week as well as use the words in their essays and in conversation.
Students will understand this concept: journalistic style. (cognitive goal)	Students will write an essay on this topic: Hemingway writes in a journalistic *style*. Give examples of this style and contrast it to the style that we read in *The Scarlet Letter*. (Critical Thinking B)	Students, with minimal errors, will clearly answer the assigned question in a 1-2 page essay.
Students will consider the generalization that the Christian theistic worldview is superior to all other world views. (affective goal)	Students will write an essay on this topic: Hemingway's vision was deeply impacted by social Darwinism and by a lesser degree by the philosopher Frederick Nietzsche. In his book *The Meaning*	Students, with minimal errors, will clearly answer the assigned question in a 1-2 page essay.

Goals/Objectives: What is the purpose of this lesson?	Strategies to meet these goals: How will I obtain these goals/objectives?	Evaluation: How will I know when I have met these goals/ objectives?
	of Evolution, George Gaylord Simpson writes: "Man is the result of a purposeless and materialistic process that did not have him in mind. He was not planned ... discovery that the universe . . . lacked any purpose or plan has the inevitable corollary that the workings of the universe cannot provide any automatic, universal, eternal, or absolute criteria of Right and wrong." Find evidence of this worldview in this book. (Critical Thinking C)	
Students will exhibit higher-level thinking skills as they compare protagonists in these two novels. (cognitive goal)	Students will write an essay on this topic: Critics have suggested that Hemingway calls his character Henry because he wants to compare him with Henry Fleming in *The Red Badge of Courage.* Compare and contrast these two literary characters. (Critical Thinking D)	Students, with minimal errors, will clearly answer the assigned question in a 1-2 page essay.
Students will exhibit higher-level thinking as they discuss their vision of truth as contrasted with Hemingway's view of truth. (cognitive goal)	Students will write an essay on this topic: Many find Hemingway's vision of truth to be quite disturbing—in fact rather hopeless. What about you? Evidence your views from the text. (Critical Thinking E)	Students, with minimal errors, will clearly answer the assigned question in a 1-2 page essay.
Students will understand this concept: foil. (cognitive goal)	Students will write an essay on this topic: Hemingway uses several characters—e.g., Rinaldi and Ferguson—to develop his main characters. These characters are called *foils.* Tell how Hemingway uses these foils. (Critical Thinking F)	Students, with minimal errors, will clearly answer the assigned question in a 1-2 page essay.
Students will exhibit higher level thinking as they agree or disagree with this statement from Paul Johnson. (cognitive goal)	Students will write an essay on this topic: In his book *Modern Times,* Paul Johnson writes: "Among the advanced races, the decline and ultimately the collapse of the religious impulse would leave a huge vacuum. The history of modern times is in great part the history of how that vacuum is filled." Agree	Students, with minimal errors, will clearly answer the assigned question in a 1-2 page essay.

Goals/Objectives: What is the purpose of this lesson?	Strategies to meet these goals: How will I obtain these goals/objectives?	Evaluation: How will I know when I have met these goals/ objectives?
	or disagree with this statement and evidence your answer by referencing *A Farewell to Arms*. (Critical Thinking G)	
Students will consider the generalization that fornication under all circumstances is sinful. (affective goal)	Catherine and Henry openly, without apology, sin. What does the Bible say about fornication? Is there any justification for their actions? (Biblical Application)	Students, with minimal errors, will clearly answer the assigned question in a 1-2 page essay.
Students will understand this concept: World War I. (cognitive goal)	Students will write a *report* on World War I. (Enrichment A)	Students, with minimal errors, will clearly answer the assigned question in a 1-2 page *report*.
Students will understand this concept: *A Farewell to Arms* as an autobiography. (cognitive goal)	Students will write an essay on this topic: Research Hemingway's life. How autobiographical was this book. (Enrichment B)?	Students, with minimal errors, will clearly answer the assigned question in a 1-2 page essay.
Students will exhibit higher-level thinking as they discuss how American literature mirrors the same stages. (cognitive goal)	Students will write this essay: H. R. Rookmaaker—who was deeply influenced by Francis Shaeffer—in his book *Modern Art and the Death of Culture*, argues that art has experienced four stages. Based on what you have studied this year, in what ways does American literature mirror the same stages? (Enrichment C)	Students, with minimal errors, will clearly answer the assigned question in a 1-2 page essay.
Students will understand this concept: comparison/contrast essay the beginning of these two novels. (Enrichment D)	Students will compare and contrast the beginning of Stephen Crane's *A Red Badge of Courage* and the beginning of *A Farewell to Arms*. (Enrichment D)	Students, with minimal errors, will clearly answer the assigned question in a 1-2 page essay.
Students will exhibit higher-level thinking as they write alternative endings to this book. (cognitive goal)	Students will write this essay: Write an alternative ending to this book. (Enrichment E)	Students, with minimal errors, will clearly answer the assigned question in a 1-2 page *alternative ending to the book*.
Students will understand this concept: Hegelian thought. (cognitive goal)	Students will write an essay on this topic: Hemingway was a Hegelian. Find examples of Hegelian thought in Hemingway's writings. (Enrichment F)	Students, with minimal errors, will clearly answer the assigned question in a 1-2 page essay.

Goals/Objectives: What is the purpose of this lesson?	Strategies to meet these goals: How will I obtain these goals/objectives?	Evaluation: How will I know when I have met these goals/objectives?
Students will understand this concept: nihilism. (cognitive goal)	Students will write an essay on this topic: Gertrude Himmelfarb, in her book *On Looking Into the Abyss* argues that in the field of literature the great works are no longer read—or if they are, there are essentially no rules for interpreting them; in philosophy, truth and reality are considered non-existent. In historical studies the historian comes to any conclusions he chooses. Some philosophers call this view *nihilism*. In what way does Himmelfarb capture the world of Catherine and Henry? (Enrichment G)	Students, with minimal errors, will clearly answer the assigned question in a 1-2 page essay.
Students will review how to write a comparison essay. (cognitive goal)	Students will write an essay on this topic: Hemingway argued that no new novel had been written since Twain wrote *Huckleberry Finn*. In what ways are *A Farewell* and *Huckleberry Finn* similar? Explore the Realism is used in both novels. (Enrichment H)	Students, with minimal errors, will clearly answer the assigned question in a 1-2 page essay.
Students will understand this concept: the consequences of sin. (cognitive goal)	In his book *Not the Way it is Supposed to Be: A Breviary of Sin*, Cornelius Plantinga argues we need a healthy reminder of our sin and guilt. Not only do we need a healthy reminder of how sin affects us personally, we must remember that the truth of traditional Christianity saws against the grain of much in contemporary culture and therefore needs constant sharpening. In light of the sinful life that Catherine and Henry lived, and the results of that sin, what application does Plantinga's view have on this hapless couple? (Enrichment I)	Students, with minimal errors, will clearly answer the assigned question in a 1-2 page essay.
Students will work in a group setting. (behavioral goal)	In a class, in a co-op experience, or during a family discussion, students will answer this question: What might be a "Christian" ending to this novel?	Students will exhibit practical listening skills and will manifest understanding of opposing worldviews.

Goals/Objectives: What is the purpose of this lesson?	Strategies to meet these goals: How will I obtain these goals/objectives?	Evaluation: How will I know when I have met these goals/ objectives?
Students will be able to recall the information taught in the lesson. (cognitive goal)	Lesson 22 Test	Students will take the test at the end of this lesson and score at least 80%.
Students will experience reflective writing. (affective/spiritual goal)	Using the Journal Guide Questions in the Appendices, students will record at least three entries this week. Suggested Scriptures: John 21	Students will show evidence that they have reflected on this issue, including informed discussions and written responses.

SUGGESTED
Weekly *Implementation*

DAY 1	DAY 2	DAY 3	DAY 4	DAY 5
Prayer journal.	**Prayer journal.**	**Prayer journal.**	**Prayer journal.**	**Prayer journal.**
Students review the required reading(s) before the assigned lesson begins.	Student should review reading(s) from next lesson.	Students should write rough drafts of all assigned essays.	Student will re-write corrected copies of essays due tomorrow.	Essays are due.
Teacher may want to discuss assigned reading(s) with students.	Student should outline essays due at the end of the week.	The teacher or a peer evaluator may correct rough drafts.		Students should take the Lesson 22 test.
Teacher and students will decide on required essays for this lesson, choosing two or three essays.	Per teacher instructions, students may answer orally in a group setting some of the essays that are not assigned as formal essays.			Reading ahead: Students should review *Their Eyes Were Watching God*, Zora Neale Hurston.
The rest of the essays can be outlined, answered with shorter answers, or skipped.				Guide: How does Janie develop as a character?
Students will review all readings for Lesson 22				

Note: References to sources are in student edition.

ENRICHMENT ACTIVITIES/PROJECTS

The family could read *The Old Man and the Sea*, Ernest Hemingway, orally and compare it to *A Farewell to Arms*.

Students should watch the *World War I Collection* (1996) to learn more about the War.

SUPPLEMENTAL RESOURCES

Dodds, E.R. *Pagan and Christian in an Age of Anxiety.*

Fourth century way of dealing with hostile environment. Christianity triumphed over paganism because Christianity rejected all gods but accepted all people. They promised eternal life in heaven yet they showed love to all persons. In the face of Hemingway's Naturalism, Dodd argued that many Christians experienced a loss of nerve.

Gergen, Kenneth J. *The Saturated Self: Dilemmas of Identity in Contemporary Life.*

The whole concept of identity began with Freud, but Hemingway and other modernist writers explored the concept of self and invited the reader to unprecedented levels of self-centeredness.

Hatch, Nathan O. *Taking the Measure of the Evangelical Resurgence: 1942-1992.*

If there is such a huge resurgence of evangelicalism, why is there a disconnection problem? Hatch examines a time much like the time in which Hemingway lived—when culture was re-examining all presumptions.

Keegan, John. *An Illustrated History of World War I.*

Keegan, a British historian, writes the best overall survey of World War I that is on the market today.

Marsden, George. *The Soul of the American University.*

Marsden explains why American academic life excludes religion, and argues that since the reasons for this exclusion are not valid, there should be more room for the free exercise of religion in higher learning. Initially, the relegation of region to the periphery of American universities was justified on Enlightenment grounds. Today, however, few believe in pure scientific objectivity and understand that all intellectual inquiry takes place in a framework of presuppositions and moral commitments. We find today the university in a moral crisis. Tolerance and diversity are the preview values, but there is no longer any standard by which limits can be placed on tolerance. This movement gained momentum when Hemingway was alive.

Noll, Mark. *The Scandal of the Evangelical Mind.*

Given the "intellectual disaster" of some Christian groups, Noll aims to reconnect evangelicals to their pre-fundamentalist heritage. Noll is bold in asking evangelicals to soften their distinctive themes for the sake of intellectual engagement.

Oden, Thomas C. *Agenda for Theology: After Modernity...What?*

Oden issues a call to students and others to return to tradition and orthodoxy. Modernity is defined as "A Time, A Mentality, and a Malaise." Major revealing features of modern consciousness are an unrestrained, individual freedom, the goal of which is to liberate one from all restrictions, constraints, traditions, and all social patenting—all of which are self-evidently presumed to be humanizing (p.47). Modernity has contempt for other viewpoints. Modernity is reductionistic Naturalism.

Postman, Neil. *Amusing Ourselves to Death.*

Television is transforming our culture into one vast arena for show business (p. 80). TV is the highest order of abstract thinking that television consistently undermines (p.41). The early church was low tech but high commitment. Clear boundaries. Today we are high-tech and low commitment.

Schultze, Quentin. *Televangelism and American Culture.*

To examine how and why televanglists are helping to transform American Christianity from a church into a business, from a historic faith into a popular religion based at least in part on superstition. An examination of these trends indicates that marketing and ministry are now close partners. Each influences the other, and not usually for the good. (p.11)

Sweet, Leonard I. *The Modernization of Protestant Religion in America.*

Hemingway and his expatriate community in Paris turned their back on mainline religion and embraced a hedonistic Naturalism. Factors that contributed to the decline of the mainline churches are: the growth of individualism, high criticism professionalization of the clergy, unwise and unpopular decisions made by denominational bureaucrats, ecumenism, actionism, and pluralism. The end result of all this has been the decline of the mainline churches—both numerically and spiritually. Evangelicals, fundamentalists, and Pentecostals moved to center stage as modernism has been forced into retreat. In characterizing the mainline denominations during these five decades, Sweet notes: "With everything gone, there was little reason for people to stay." Sweet gives much attention to the relationship between the denominational leaders and the church members, who were growing increasingly distant. This led to the leadership taking stands without considering the beliefs and feelings of the people in the pews, which then resulted in a growing distrust by the members of their leaders. Sweet describes these developments as a loss of mastery and mandate—that is, the loss of mastery of the common touch and mandate of the common faith.

Wacker, Grant. *Uneasy in Zion: Evangelicals in Postmodern Society.*

To most of us, the desire to have cultural worldview alternatives is to look toward our faith. To understand the growth of Evangelicalism one must look at the big picture as seen in the social transformations (particularly since WWII) brought about by mass communication and high technology. Evangelicalism as we know it today is a cultural form which grew out of a developing America.

Wacker, Grant. *Searching for Norman Rockwell: Popular Evangelicalism in Contemporary America.*

Evangelicals thrived even when Hemingway wrote because they understood that godliness is not passed through the loins of godly parents but must be rekindled in the hearts and minds of each generation.

Wells, David F. *God in the Wasteland: The Reality of Truth in a World of Fading Dreams*

Wells in convinced that Modernity is now the Tempter seducing human pride to betray itself through a pawn-like participation in "an ironic recapitulation of the first dislocation in which God's creatures replaced their Creator and exiled Him from His own world" (p. 14).

Notes:

SUGGESTED VOCABULARY WORDS

Chapter VII feigned. (*imitate*)
Chapter XV felicitations. (*congratulations*)

CRITICAL THINKING

A. Who is the narrator of this story? What effect does this form of narration have on the story?

ANSWER: *Henry tells the story. This reader finds him to be a particularly immature and unreliable narrator. His naturalistic, self-centered view makes every interpretation suspect. What seems to him to be fatalistic bad luck seems to be divine retribution to this reader!*

B. Hemingway writes in a journalistic *style*. Give examples of this style and contrast it to the style that we read in *The Scarlet Letter*.

ANSWER: *Hemingway writes in an active voice, straightforward style. He uses very few adjectives and modifiers. This is naturalistic but more a realistic writing style. Form, therefore, follows function. Hawthorne, on the other hand, deliberately wrote with rich metaphors and language. He was trying to reach for reality beyond the sensual setting. Form, to Hawthorne, had nothing to do with function. One can see this in the first, verbose, and apparently superfluous chapter "The Custom House."*

C. Hemingway's vision was deeply impacted by social Darwinism and by a lesser degree by the philosopher Frederick Nietzsche. In his book *The Meaning of Evolution*, George Gaylord Simpson writes: "Man is the result of a purposeless and materialistic process that did not have him in mind. He was not planned . . . discovery that the universe . . . lacked any purpose or plan has the inevitable corollary that the workings of the universe cannot provide any automatic, universal, eternal, or absolute criteria of Right and wrong." Find evidence of this worldview in this book.

ANSWER: *Ironically, Henry is wounded for no reason in his dugout. With no purpose Catherine dies. This is pretty hopeless. It also reflects a "survival of the fittest" motif. On the other hand, one might argue that the philosopher Nietzsche—as pagan as he is—offers a fairly comprehensive picture of Frederick Henry and his creator, Ernest Hemingway. A contemporary of Darwin, he also advanced the cause of Naturalism. Nietzsche coined the phrase "God is dead." He says the only reality is this world of life and death, conflict and change, creation and destruction. For centuries, religious ideas have given meaning to life in the western world; but as they now collapse, Nietzsche observed, humanity faces a grave crisis of nihilism and despair. While I vociferously disagree with Nietzsche's vision, I like Nietzsche's honesty. His prophetic view is refreshing. Nietzsche took the hopeless vision of Naturalism and Social Darwinism to its natural conclusion. Nietzsche saw that a world where only power prevailed, a world without Christianity, would inevitably lead to totalitarianism and destruction. He saw, then, in the late 19th century that inevitably western culture would create an Adolf Hitler or*

Joseph Stalin. The basic character of life in this world is what Nietzsche called the "will to power." He admired those who were strong enough to face this reality, for they alone could live joyfully. But this "modern superman" lived without God and without any hope of salvation. Nietzsche is basically a Naturalist: fundamentally, man is only an animal who has developed in an unusual way. The "will to power" brings about new forms of competition and superiority and can lead to "superman" humanity. Here is a passage from Nietzsche that reflects this Naturalism: "When we hear the ancient bells growling on a Sunday morning we ask ourselves: Is it really possible! This, for a Jew, crucified two thousand years ago, who said he was God's son? The proof of such a claim is lacking. Certainly the Christian religion is an antiquity projected into our times from remote prehistory; and the fact that the claim is believed—whereas one is otherwise so strict in examining pretensions—is perhaps the most ancient piece of this heritage. A god who begets children with a mortal woman; a sage who bids men work no more, have no more courts, but look for the signs of the impending end of the world; a justice that accepts the innocent as a vicarious sacrifice; someone who orders his disciples to drink his blood; prayers for miraculous interventions; sins perpetrated against a god, atoned for by a god; fear of a beyond to which death is the portal; the form of the cross as a symbol in a time that no longer knows the function and ignominy of the cross—how ghoulishly all this touches us, as if from the tomb of a primeval past! Can one believe that such things are still believed?"—from Nietzsche's Human, all too Human. *Some philosophers and their theories are so bizarre that their theories can be easily rejected (e.g., Darwin and evolution). But Nietzsche unnerves me. While he is wrong in his assessment of Christianity, his discernment about the future of Western culture is uncanny. The British historian Paul Johnson (*Modern Times*, p. 48) writes: Among the advanced races, the decline and ultimately the collapse of the religious impulse would leave a huge vacuum. The history of modern times is in great part the history of how that vacuum is filled. Nietzsche rightly perceived that the most likely candidate would be what he called the 'Will to Power,' which offered a far more comprehensive and in the end more plausible explanation of human behavior than either Marx or Freud. In place of religious belief, there would be secular ideology. Those who once filled the ranks of the totalitarian clergy would become totalitarian politicians. And, above all, the Will to Power would produce a new kind of messiah, uninhibited by any religious sanctions whatever, and with an unappeasable appetite for controlling mankind. The end of the old order, with an unguided world adrift in a relativistic universe, was a summons to such gangster-statesmen to emerge. They were not slow to make their appearance.*

D. Critics have suggested that Hemingway calls his character Henry because he wants to compare him with Henry Fleming in *The Red Badge of Courage.* Compare and contrast these two literary characters.

ANSWER: *It is no coincidence that both characters have similar names. They are remarkably the same character: both are captured by fate. Both have a "farewell to arms" experience and then embrace a Naturalistic vision. Perhaps Henry Fleming does not experience the heartbreak that Frederick Henry does—but in a naturalistic world everything is happenstance anyway. By the way—it is fair to say that Henry Fleming, Frederick Henry, Ethan Frome, and later American literary figures share a lot of the same characteristics. They are a modern American literary archetype.*

E. Many find Hemingway's vision of truth to be quite disturbing—in fact rather hopeless. What about you? Evidence your views from the text.

ANSWER: *This reader finds Hemingway's vision to be pathetic, but very accurate to what I find in contemporary society. I do not wish to patronize other worldviews, but a worldview that embraces hopelessness so fervently certainly does appear to be very wholesome and life-giving. Os Guinness discusses this fact and postulates that Naturalism and other post-modern worldviews are insufficient to explain reality, and most Americans are getting tired of trying.*

F. Hemingway uses several characters—e.g., Rinaldi and Ferguson—to develop his main characters. These characters are called *foils.* Tell how Hemingway uses these foils.

ANSWER: *They develop Henry's lackluster character. They show that he is really a pretty good guy—although he appears to be pretty wimpy to many readers. Catherine Barkley develops Henry in several ways: she calls forth his "who really cares" naturalistic side. She is a monolithic character who barely changes. She dies the way she lives: with an "I'm going to die," she says. "I'm not afraid. It's just a dirty trick." The priest reminds me of the priest on the old television program M*A*S*H and likewise similar to the chaplain in* Billy Budd. *He is powerless in the face of life's dilemmas and never objects to Henry's nihilistic immortality. I like Helen Ferguson most of all. She represents conventional Judeo-Christian morality. So, to Hemingway, she is an antagonist.*

G. In his book *Modern Times,* Paul Johnson writes: "Among the advanced races, the decline and ultimately the collapse of the religious impulse would leave a huge vacuum. The history of modern times is in great part the history of how that vacuum is filled." Agree or disagree with this statement and evidence your answer by referencing *A Farewell to Arms.*

ANSWER: *The reader agrees with Johnson—observe what happened in Hemingway's generation (i.e., the rise of Totalitarianism). In* A Farewell to Arms *we observe two lost souls trying to make meaning out of tragedy in a godless world. This gives all Christian readers pause to pray for all unsaved people around us.*

BIBLICAL APPLICATION

Catherine and Henry openly, without apology, sin. What does the Bible say about fornication? Is there any justification for their actions?

ANSWER: *The wages of sin is death. There is no justification that excuses the infraction. Sin breaks us, ultimately. We do not break it. Many years ago my childhood friend and I, using an umbrella to soften our fall, decided to jump off a barn. We were hurting no one. We were sincere in our belief that we would float down harmlessly to the ground. However, when my friend jumped off the barn, he broke his ankle. Sin breaks us no matter how sincere it is or how harmless it seems.*

ENRICHMENT

A. Write a *report* on World War I.

ANSWER: *World War I began in Europe in 1914. America entered in 1917. The Central Powers included Germany, Austria-Hungary, and Turkey. The allies included the British Commonwealth, France, and Italy. Some Americans, like Hemingway, volunteered early and fought for the allies (in his case in Italy). World War I, 1914-1918, was initially a European War. Americans wanted nothing to do with it. Once committed to going to war, though, in 1917, America intended to make the world—using Woodrow Wilson's words—"safe for democracy." Virtually no one wanted to go to war in 1914, and it was not clear whose side to join anyway. Americans were sympathetic toward England and her allies, but millions of Americans were of German descent. Support for the allies was never a foregone conclusion. However, by 1917, unrestricted submarine warfare and German mistakes—like the Zimmerman Telegram incident—made American participation on the allied side inevitable. While casualties on the American side were relatively light when compared to other allied casualties—more Americans died in the 1919 flue epidemic—Americans nonetheless were horrified and resolved never again to be involved in foreign wars. This view was further cemented when Woodrow Wilson was humiliated at the infamous Treaty of Versailles. In fact, Congress refused to ratify the Treaty of Versailles and made its own peace with Germany. This movement toward isolationism ushered in the excesses and hedonism of the 1920's.*

B. Research Hemingway's life. How autobiographical was this book?

ANSWER: *Hemingway in fact was wounded in Italy and met, and fell in love with a British nurse. However, the nurse never returned his affections; the similarities to Hemingway's life end here.*

C. In his book *Modern Art and the Death of Culture*, H. R. Rookmaaker—who was deeply influenced by Francis Shaeffer—argues that art has experienced four stages:

1. **Pre-enlightenment. (Middle Ages to 18th Century)** Reflects a belief in an ordered universe, transcendent values, absolute morality.

2. **Enlightenment Art. (18th Century)** Reflects Naturalism. Art ceases to reflect transcendent convictions. The seeds of modern art are planted.

3. **Impressionism. (19th century)** Reflects the sense experience between painter and object. Feelings are important.

4. **Absurdism. (early 20th century)** Reflects an admission that there is no meaning.

Based on what you have studied this year, in what ways does Western literature mirror the same stages?

ANSWER: *The nihilism endemic to absurdism is evident everywhere in American culture. As one scholar observed, there is "a death of outrage" in American society. From the movies we watch, the books we read, and the politicians we elect, we can see that absurdism is alive and well. Unfortunately.*

D. Compare and contrast the beginning of Stephen Crane's *A Red Badge of Courage* and the beginning of *A Farewell to Arms*.

E. Write an alternative ending to this book.

ANSWER: *Answers will have to be opinions.*

F. Hemingway was a Hegelian. The philosopher Hegel believed strongly in the dialectic. He starts with a thesis (a position put forward for argument). Opposed to this is a contradictory statement or antithesis. Out of their opposition comes a synthesis which embraces both. But since the truth lies only in the whole system, this first synthesis is not yet the truth of the matter, but becomes a new thesis, with its corresponding antithesis and synthesis. And so on.

Truth, then, is not absolute and is always open to interpretation. Truth lies in the "search" in the "system." Find examples of Hegelian thought in Hemingway's writings.

ANSWER: *Frederick Henry does not hesitate to lie or to steal or to fornicate, if it suits his purposes. Truth, then, to him, is a subjective decision based on circumstances.*

G. In her book *On Looking into the Abyss*, Gertrude Himmelfarb argues that in the field of literature the great works are no longer read—or if they are, there are essentially no rules for interpreting them; in philosophy, truth and reality are considered non-existent. In historical studies the historian comes to any conclusions he chooses. Some philosophers call this view *nihilism*. In what way does Himmelfarb capture the world of Catherine and Henry?

ANSWER: *Again, Catherine and Frederick answer to no one but their desires. Their "love" is a mutually beneficial arrangement to sustain their subjective delusions. They are not under, and would not accept, a higher authority, power, or moral system. Absolute truth, then, to this couple, is an oxymoron.*

H. Hemingway argued that no new novel had been written since Twain wrote *Huckleberry Finn*. In what ways are *A Farewell* and *Huckleberry Finn* similar? Explore the Realism is used in both novels.

ANSWER: *The Arkansas feud in <u>The Adventures of Huckleberry Finn</u> and the death scene of Catherine in <u>A Farewell to Arms</u> both exhibit Realism. In fact both novels purport to be ordinary events in the lives of ordinary people. Both have journey motifs of a sort and both end on a realistic, sour note. Huckleberry wanders into romanticism with the Tom Sawyer scene, some claim, but that is debatable.*

I. In his book *Not the Way it is Supposed to Be: A Breviary of Sin*, Cornelius Plantinga argues we need a healthy reminder of our sin and guilt. Not only do we need a healthy reminder of how sin affects us personally, we must remember that the truth of traditional Christianity saws against the grain of much in contemporary culture and therefore needs constant sharpening. In light of the sinful life that Catherine and Henry lived, and the results of that sin, what application does Plantinga's view have on this hapless couple?

ANSWER: *Platinga's thesis would cut in two ways. First, in a literary sense, the fact that these two characters appear in American literature, and therefore they are appearing in American culture, reflects the disregard for sin that Americans tolerate. Next, these two characters do not appear to show any hesitation, any guilt for their sin, and, then, they feel no remorse for their sin. In fact, even when Frederick Henry is considering the tragedy that has befallen himself, he never repents of this bad choices. In fact, if he thinks of God at all, it is in a very negative way. Plantinga would argue that this couple has reaped the consequences of lives that ignore the consequences of sin.*

FINAL PROJECT

Students should correct and rewrite all essays and place them in their Final Portfolio.

245

LESSON 22 TEST

OBJECTIVE QUESTIONS (25 POINTS)

_____ 1. Henry was wounded (A) while attacking a German machine gun nest (B) while sitting in his fox hole enjoying a meal (C) while resting in the rear (D) while he visited an old girl friend.

_____ 2. Catherine was (A) a nurse (B) a teacher (C) an American journalist (D) another patient.

_____ 3. Who were fighting the Italian? (A) British and French (B) Austrians and Russians (C) Serbians and Americans (D) Austrians and Germany

_____ 4. Catherine and Henry (A) escaped to a lake resort (B) decided to return to America (C) felt bad about their behavior and married (D) never left the hospital.

_____ 5. At the end of the novel (A) Catherine and Henry escape to Hungary (B) Catherine dies in childbirth (C) Catherine and Henry are tragically killed in an auto accident (D) Catherine and Henry are arrested and shot for desertion.

DISCUSSION QUESTIONS. (50 POINTS)

A. What does Hemingway mean when he says, "Abstract words such as glory, honor, courage, or hallow were obscene beside the concrete names of villages, the numbers of roads, the names of rivers, the number of regiments and the dates"?

B. It is raining constantly in *A Farewell to Arms*. What effect does this have in the novel?

C. What narrative technique does Hemingway employ? Why?

D. Frederick Henry is not a hero, he is an anti-hero. Explain.

E. A foil is a character who resembles the main character in all respects except one—the one trait that the writer wants to highlight. Give an example of a foil.

DISCUSSION QUESTION. (25 POINTS)

The following is a diagram of Hegelian dialectics that deeply impacted Hemingway's worldview. Take 3 ethical issues and employ Hegelian dialectics to solve them. For example, discussions of homosexuality in the courts have evolved to something like this: one side argues that homosexuality is evil and wrong under all conditions (Theory A). Another party argues that homosexuality is no one's business and appropriate according to the will of the people involved (Theory B). A Hegelian compromise would be: homosexual behavior is appropriate as long as the individuals care for each other and are faithful to each other. Of course, the Bible states categorically that homosexuality always has been, and always will be, sinful! How has our culture justified other ethical issues by Hegelian compromise? Give at least 3 in a 75-150 word essay.

> Hegel believed strongly in the dialectic. He starts with a thesis (a position put forward for argument). Opposed to this is a contradictory statement or antithesis. Out of their opposition comes a synthesis which embraces both. Since the truth lies only in the whole system, this first synthesis is not yet the truth of the matter, but becomes a new thesis, with its corresponding antithesis and synthesis. And so on. Truth, then, is not absolute and is always open to interpretation. Truth lies in the "search" in the "system."

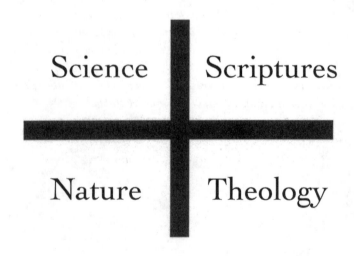

LESSON 22 TEST ANSWERS

OBJECTIVE QUESTIONS. (25 POINTS)

1. B
2. A
3. D
4. A
5. B

DISCUSSION QUESTIONS. (50 POINTS)

A. What does Hemingway mean when he says, "Abstract words such as glory, honor, courage, or hallow were obscene beside the concrete names of villages, the numbers of roads, the names of rivers, the number of regiments and the dates"?

ANSWER: *To the Realist writer, Hemingway hyperbole implies hypocrisy; to the taciturn Naturalist writer, Hemingway verbosity is a camouflage for the horror that is life.*

B. It is raining constantly in *A Farewell to Arms*. What effect does this have in the novel?

ANSWER: *Nature, like life, is malevolent. Notice how often Naturalist writers use dreary landscapes and weather.*

C. What narrative technique does Hemingway employ? Why?

ANSWER: *First person omniscient allows Hemingway to participate in the action without being obligated to tell what anything else thinks (not that it really matters to the self-centered Frederick Henry).*

D. Frederick Henry is not a hero, he is an anti-hero. Explain.

ANSWER: *Valor, courage, and nobility are insulting to Henry. He makes decisions out of his own need and subjectivity.*

E. A foil is a character who resembles the main character in all respects except one—the one trait that the writer wants to highlight. Give an example of a foil.

ANSWER: *Rinaldi (foil to Henry) and Ferguson (foil to Catherine) are two.*

DISCUSSION QUESTION. (25 POINTS)

ANSWER: *Justification of abortion, which is really murder, is one example. We "compromise" by stating that the woman's choice is most important. Euthanasia (i.e., mercy killing) is another example. We justify the killing of someone because he is in pain, or unhappy, or old, or so on. There are others. The point is that once we start climbing the slippery slop of dialectic ethics we go nowhere but down.*

LESSON 23

THE MODERN AGE, 1915-1946: LATE ROMANTICISM/ NATURALISM (Part 4)

Readings Due For This Lesson: Students should review *Their Eyes Were Watching God*, Zora Neale Hurston.

Reading Ahead: Students should read *The Unvanquished*, William Faulkner. Is Bayard a Romantic? Naturalist? Realist?

Goal: Students will analyze *Their Eyes Were Watching God*, Zora Neale Hurston.

Goals/Objectives: What is the purpose of this lesson?	Strategies to meet these goals: How will I obtain these goals/objectives?	Evaluation: How will I know when I have met these goals/ objectives?
Students will understand the concept: frame story. (cognitive goal)	Students will discuss the form that Hurston employs to tell her story. What are advantages and disadvantages of using this form? (Critical Thinking A)	Students, with minimal errors, will clearly answer the assigned question in a 1-2 page essay.
Students will increase their vocabulary. (cognitive goal)	Students will collect at least five new vocabulary words from their reading and use these words in their essays.	Students will use five vocabulary words in conversation during the week as well as use the words in their essays and in conversation.
Students will understand this concept: writing with colloquialisms. (cognitive goal)	Students will write an essay on this topic: Hurston was a highly educated African-American woman, yet she wrote in an African-American dialect. Why? (Critical Thinking B)	Students, with minimal errors, will clearly answer the assigned question in a 1-2 page essay.
Students will understand this concept: narrative technique. (cognitive goal)	Students will discuss Hurston's narrative technique. (Critical Thinking C)	Students, with minimal errors, will clearly answer the assigned question in a 1-2 page essay.
Students will understand this concept: 2 themes. (cognitive goal)	Students will write an essay on this topic: What are two themes in this book. How does Hurston develop them? (Critical Thinking D)	Students, with minimal errors, will clearly answer the assigned question in a 1-2 page essay.

Goals/Objectives: What is the purpose of this lesson?	Strategies to meet these goals: How will I obtain these goals/objectives?	Evaluation: How will I know when I have met these goals/objectives?
Students will understand this concept: parallels between Janie's life and Hannah's life. (cognitive goal)	Students will write an essay on this topic: Draw parallels between Janie's life and Hannah's life. (Biblical Application)	Students, with minimal errors, will clearly answer the assigned question in a 1-2 page essay.
Students will understand the concept: the way American authors have handled race interactions. (cognitive goal)	Students will write an essay on this topic: How have other American authors handled race interactions in American culture? (Enrichment A)	Students, with minimal errors, will clearly answer the assigned question in a 1-2 page essay.
Students will understand the concept: paternalism. (cognitive goal)	Students will write an essay on this topic: What is paternalism and what is disturbing about this view of race relations? (Enrichment B)	Students, with minimal errors, will clearly answer the assigned question in a 1-2 page essay.
Students will work in a group setting. (behavioral goal)	In a class, in a co-op experience, or during a family discussion, students will answer this question: When have you exhibited prejudice in relationships with other people of color?	Students will exhibit practical listening skills and will manifest understanding of opposing worldviews.
Students will be able to recall the information taught in the lesson. (cognitive goal)	Lesson 23 Test	Students will take the test at the end of this lesson and score at least 80%.
Students will experience reflective writing. (affective/spiritual goal)	Using the Journal Guide Questions in the Appendices, students will record at least three entries this week. Suggested Scriptures: Colossians	Students will show evidence that they have reflected on this issue, including informed discussions and written responses.

SUGGESTED
Weekly *Implementation*

DAY 1	DAY 2	DAY 3	DAY 4	DAY 5
Prayer journal.	**Prayer journal.**	**Prayer journal.**	**Prayer journal.**	**Prayer journal.**
Students review the required reading(s) before the assigned lesson begins.	Student should review reading(s) from next lesson.	Students should write rough drafts of all assigned essays.	Student will re-write corrected copies of essays due tomorrow.	Essays are due.
Teacher may want to discuss assigned reading(s) with students.	Student should outline essays due at the end of the week.	The teacher and/or a peer evaluator may correct rough drafts.		Students should take Lesson 23 test.
Teacher and students will decide on required essays for this lesson, choosing two or three essays.	Per teacher instructions, students may answer orally in a group setting some of the essays that are not assigned as formal essays.			Reading Ahead: Review *Their Eyes Were Watching God*, Zora Neale Hurston.
The rest of the essays can be outlined, answered with shorter answers, or skipped.				Guide: How does Janie develop as a character?
Students will review all readings for Lesson 23.				

Note: References to sources are in student edition.

ENRICHMENT ACTIVITIES/PROJECTS
Students should interview African-American family members or friends who lived during the 1930s.

SUPPLEMENTAL RESOURCES
Abrahams, Roger D., ed. *Afro-American Folktales*.

Adair, James A., *Racial Intermarriage and Christianity*.

Anderson, David C., *Children of Special Value*.

Bunin, Sherry and Catherine, *Is That Your Sister?*

Clauerbaut, David, *Urban Ministry*.

CRITICAL THINKING

A. Discuss the form that Hurston employs to tell her story. What are advantages and disadvantages of using this form?

   ANSWER: *Hurston tells her story in a frame. The whole story is a conversation/flashback between the same two people sitting on a porch. This strategy/form allows the author to suspend time and tell the reader the entire story in a relatively short* *period of time. It takes Janie about 2 hours to tell 40 years of history to her friend Phoebe. One disadvantage is that the reader might forget the "frame story." This was easily solved by Hurston keeping the flashback as the main story and offering very few details about the frame story.*

B. Hurston was a highly educated African-American woman, yet she wrote in an African-American dialect. Why?

ANSWER: *Hurston is writing from a literary realism bent. She wants her characters to appear real. While she is not in the least bit sermonic, she wishes her reader to understand and perhaps even to admire the specialties of African-American southern rural culture.*

C. Discuss Hurston's narrative technique.

ANSWER: *In spite of frequent dialogue, Hurston uses limited omniscient narration. This allows her to develop her protagonist through dialogue and commentary.*

D. What are two themes in this book? How does Hurston develop them?

ANSWER: *The first and by-far the most pervasive theme is the search for love. We see that emerging as she moves form marriage to marriage. Next, is the theme of sustaining community. The community, with all its faults, is the place of refuge in Janie's life. In fact, she returns home at the beginning of the novel to tell her story.*

BIBLICAL APPLICATION

Draw parallels between Janie's life and Hannah's life.

ANSWER: *Both were married to less than inspiring husbands and both had to have faith in something greater than themselves. Both found what they were looking for. Hannah, of course, was a follower of God. The reader is not sure about Janie's faith journey.*

ENRICHMENT

A. How have other American authors handled race interactions in American culture?

ANSWER: *Race interactions fascinated many white American writers. It has had a ubiquitous presence in American culture. For instance, it was common, in American literature written by whites, for a mixed-race person to be maladjusted,* *unstable person, a misfit. Many white American writers and social critics found the whole enterprise to be absurd—for example, witness the racially-mixed character named Joe Christmas in William Faulkner's* Light in August. *Joe was a freak. Doomed. Joe "lurked and crept among its secret places, yet he remained a foreigner to the very immutable laws which earth must obey." Finally, Joe moved in a straight line to his destiny—death. From the unhappy Joe Christmas in William Faulkner's* A Light in August *to Dick Peters in Edgar Allen Poe's "The Narrative of Arthur Gordon Pym" American literature has been ungenerous with racially-mixed people. In colonial days there were reports that "a white woman in North Carolina not only acquired a dark color, but several of the features of a Negro, by marrying and living with a black husband." It was unhealthy for a white person to fraternize with a black person. In light of this, Hurston's viewpoint is refreshing.*

B. William Faulkner, another southern author, describes race relations in this way:

> There are two of them . . . Uncle Buck and Uncle Buddy . . . They lived in a two-room log house with about a dozen dogs, and they kept the niggers in the manor house. It don't have any windows now and a child with a hairpin could unlock any lock in it, but every night when the niggers come up from the fields Uncle Buck or Uncle Buddy would drive them into the house and lock the door with a key almost as big as a horse pistol; probably they would still be locking the front door long after the last nigger has escaped out the back. And folks said that Uncle Buck and Uncle Buddy knew this and that the niggers knew that they knew it . . .. (*The Unvanquished*)

Faulkner saw race relations in what historians call "paternalism." What is paternalism and what is disturbing about this view of race relations?

ANSWER: *Paternalism is a way to describe race relations that assumes a superior white race benevolently taking care of the black race.*

FINAL PROJECT

Students should correct and rewrite all essays and place them in their Final Portfolio.

LESSON 23 TEST

OBJECTIVE TEST. (50 POINTS)

1._____ Janie's first husband is (A) Tea Cake (B) Logan (C) Joe (D) James

2._____ What kills Jamie's third husband? (A) a tornado (B) a flood (C) small pox (D) a hurricane

3._____ Janie is telling her story to (A) Pheoby (B) Nanny (C) Joe (D) Tea Cake

4._____ Tea Cake teaches Jamie to play (A) poker (B) chess (C) checkers (D) Monopoly

5._____ Janie's first husband is a (A) fisherman (B) carpenter (C) farmer (D) factory worker

DISCUSSION QUESTIONS (50 POINTS)

A. Discuss the way Hurston uses Janie's three husbands to mark her progress toward fulfillment in life.

B. Hurston uses one particular metaphor to describe Janie's life. What is it and how does she use it?

LESSON 23 TEST ANSWERS

OBJECTIVE TEST. (50 POINTS)

1. __B__
2. __D__
3. __A__
4. __C__
5. __C__

DISCUSSION QUESTIONS (50 POINTS)

A. Discuss the way Hurston uses Janie's three husbands to mark her progress toward fulfillment in life.

ANSWER: *Logan, husband #1, offers Janie protection as she begins her differentiation process as a young woman. Joe, husband #2, allows Janie to experience prestige and power. Tea Cake, husband #3, showed Janie the love she always wanted.*

B. Hurston uses one particular metaphor to describe Janie's life. What is it and how does she use it?

ANSWER: *Hurston compares Janie's life to a tree. The first time is in Ch. 2. In her search for true love Janie "had glossy leaves and bursting buds." Later, in Ch. 4, Joe, her second husband, stimulates her to new, bolder adventures—Hurston compares Joe to a pollinating bee. And so forth.*

LESSON 24
THE MODERN AGE, 1915-1946: LATE ROMANTICISM/ NATURALISM *(Part 5)*

Readings Due For This Lesson: Students should review *The Unvanquished*, William Faulkner.

Reading Ahead: Students should review *The Pearl*, John Steinbeck. What themes does Steinbeck develop in this short novel?

Goal: Students will analyze *The Unvanquished*, by William Faulkner.

Goals/Objectives: What is the purpose of this lesson?	Strategies to meet these goals: How will I obtain these goals/objectives?	Evaluation: How will I know when I have met these goals/ objectives?
Students will understand this concept of setting. (cognitive goal) Students will accept the generalization that the setting greatly impacts the meaning of a novel. (cognitive goal)	Students will write an essay on this topic: Why is the setting so important to this story? (Critical Thinking A)	Students, with minimal errors, will clearly answer the assigned question in a 1-2 page essay.
Students will increase their vocabulary and thereby increase their scores on standardized tests. (cognitive goal)	Students will collect at least five new vocabulary words from their reading and use these words in their essays.	Students will use five vocabulary words in conversation during the week as well as use the words in their essays and in conversation.
Students will understand the concept of point of view. (cognitive goal) Students will manifest higher thinking skills as they evaluate the point of view in this novel. (cognitive goal)	Students will write an essay on this topic: What is the point of view? Why does it make this book more effective? (Critical Thinking B)	Students, with minimal errors, will clearly answer the assigned question in a 1-2 page essay.
Students will understand the concept of imagery and will be able to identify it in literary works. (cognitive goal)	Students will write an essay on this topic: Faulkner's prose is so powerful that it seems like poetry. This technique is accomplished by his puissant (powerful, strong) imagery. Can you find examples of this in the text? (Critical Thinking C)	Students, with minimal errors, will clearly answer the assigned question in a 1-2 page essay.

Goals/Objectives: What is the purpose of this lesson?	Strategies to meet these goals: How will I obtain these goals/objectives?	Evaluation: How will I know when I have met these goals/objectives?
Students will understand the concept of colloquial language. (cognitive goal) Students will manifest higher thinking skills as they evaluate its necessity in a work of art or literature. (cognitive goal)	Students will write an essay on this topic: there is a great deal of colloquial language in the story. How important is the informal language? How important is the use of a Southern dialect? How do you feel about Faulkner's frequent use of the word *nigger*? (Critical Thinking D)	Students, with minimal errors, will clearly answer the assigned question in a 1-2 page essay.
Students will understand the concept of main character. (cognitive goal)	Students will write an essay on this topic: Who is the main character? Granny? Bayard? Colonel Sartoris? Defend your answer. (Critical Thinking E)	Students, with minimal errors, will clearly answer the assigned question in a 1-2 page essay.
Students will manifest higher thinking skills as they determine whether this chapter is necessary in this literary work. (cognitive goal)	Students will write this essay: The chapter "An Odor of Verbena" has been criticized as being an entirely different story, or a story within a story. Some critics wonder if it really belongs. What do you think? (Critical Thinking F)	Students, with minimal errors, will clearly answer the assigned question in a 1-2 page essay.
Students will understand the concept of family sin. (cognitive goal) Students will also learn how to write a comparison essay. (cognitive goal) Students will consider the generalization that, at salvation, God orchestrates the future of a new believer. (affective goal)	Students will write an essay on this topic: Faulkner discusses in great detail the whole issue of "family sin." Compare the results of David and Bathsheba's relationship with the experience of Faulkner's characters. (Biblical Application)	Students, with minimal errors, will clearly answer the assigned question in a 1-2 page essay.
Students will understand the theories behind the causes of the Civil War. (cognitive goal)	Students will write an essay on this topic: What do you think about the theories behind the causes of the Civil War? Research the causes of the Civil War. (Enrichment)	Students, with minimal errors, will clearly answer the assigned question in a 1-2 page essay.
Students will understand this concept: compare and contrast worldviews. (cognitive goal)	Students will write an essay on this topic: Compare and contrast the worldview of the state draft investigator and the marshal. (Critical Thinking A)	Students, with minimal errors, will clearly answer the assigned question in a 1-2 page essay.

Goals/Objectives: What is the purpose of this lesson?	Strategies to meet these goals: How will I obtain these goals/objectives?	Evaluation: How will I know when I have met these goals/objectives?
Students will manifest higher level thinking as they evaluate the title of this short story. (cognitive goal)	Students will write an essay on this topic: Why is Faulkner's title appropriate for this story. (Critical Thinking B)	Students, with minimal errors, will clearly answer the assigned question in a 1-2 page essay.
Students will understand the concept of narrative technique. (cognitive goal)	Students will write an essay on this topic: Describe Faulkner's narrative technique. How does it enhance his story? (Critical Thinking C)	Students, with minimal errors, will clearly answer the assigned question in a 1-2 page essay.
Students will understand the concept of plot development. (cognitive goal)	Students will write an essay on this topic: Even though very little real action occurs in this story, the plot develops very well. How does Faulkner accomplish this? (Critical Thinking D)	Students, with minimal errors, will clearly answer the assigned question in a 1-2 page essay.
Students will manifest higher level thinking (comparison/contrast) as they analyze this short story and compare it to another Faulkner literary work. (cognitive goal)	Students will write an essay on this topic: Compare and contrast this short story in style and substance with *Unvanquished*. (Critical Thinking E)	Students, with minimal errors, will clearly answer the assigned question in a 1-2 page essay.
Students will manifest higher level thinking (comparison/contrast) as they analyze this quote. (cognitive goal)	Students will write this essay: To Faulkner, and to most southerners, land, people, and history were vital. In that context, what does Faulkner mean in the following quote? (Enrichment A)	Students, with minimal errors, will clearly answer the assigned question in a 1-2 page essay.
Students will understand this concept: the effect Sherwood Anderson had on William Faulkner. (cognitive goal)	Students will write an essay on this topic: William Faulkner was deeply influenced by the American short story writer Sherwood Anderson. In a one to two page essay, discuss similarities between this short story and "The Tall Men." (Enrichment B)	Students, with minimal errors, will clearly answer the assigned question in a 1-2 page essay.
Students will work in a group setting. (behavioral goal)	In a class, in a co-op experience, or during a family discussion, students will answer this question: Students should discuss the effect corporate sin has on a society/nation	Students will exhibit practical listening skills and will manifest understanding of opposing worldviews.

Goals/Objectives: What is the purpose of this lesson?	Strategies to meet these goals: How will I obtain these goals/objectives?	Evaluation: How will I know when I have met these goals/objectives?
Students will be able to recall the information taught in the lesson. (cognitive goal)	Lesson 24 Test	Students will take the test at the end of this lesson and score at least 80%.
Students will experience reflective writing. (affective/spiritual goal)	Using the Journal Guide Questions in the Appendices, students will record at least three entries this week. Suggested Scriptures: Colossians	Students will show evidence that they have reflected on this issue, including informed discussions and written responses.

SUGGESTED

Weekly *Implementation*

DAY 1	DAY 2	DAY 3	DAY 4	DAY 5
Prayer journal.	**Prayer journal.**	**Prayer journal.**	**Prayer journal.**	**Prayer journal.**
Students review the required reading(s) before the assigned lesson begins.	Student should review reading(s) from next lesson.	Students should write rough drafts of all assigned essays.	Students will re-write corrected copies of essays due tomorrow.	Essays are due.
Teachers may want to discuss assigned reading(s) with students.	Student should outline essays due at the end of the week.	The teacher and/or a peer evaluator may correct rough drafts.		Students should take Lesson 24 test.
Teacher and students will decide on required essays for this lesson, choosing two or three essays.	Per teacher instructions, students may answer orally in a group setting some of the essays that are not assigned as formal essays.			Reading Ahead: Review *The Pearl*, John Steinbeck.
The rest of the essays can be outlined, answered with shorter answers, or skipped.				Guide: What themes does Steinbeck develop in this short novel?
Students will review all readings for Lesson 24.				

Note: References to sources are in student edition.

ENRICHMENT ACTIVITIES/PROJECTS

The student should read the Snopes' trilogy (*The Hamlet*, *The Town*, and *The Mansion*). They can complete a Book Checkup for each book.

Students should write more journal entries.

—You were part of the Johnstown Flood. Why is it such a distressing event in your life? Your son/daughter is born this year. What is his/her name?

—You reluctantly join the American army in France during World War I. What caused this war? Give at least six entries. As a survivor of the Civil War you are invited to visit the battlefields. You are killed in Belleau Woods. You will now pretend that you are your son/daughter.

—You lost all your money in the Great Depression. You vote for FDR, and he is elected. You then work in the WPA. What is happening?

—You join the American army in World War II. Give me ten entries about what happened in this war from beginning to end.

—You watch your TV and are upset with McCarthyism. Why are you upset?

—The Russians send Sputnik into space, Kennedy is elected, and you build a bomb shelter in your back yard. What is happening?

—You are horrified to see your son's hair growing below his ears. There are race riots in Newark. A neighbor's son is killed in Vietnam. What is happening?

—You observe the Berlin wall fall (even though you are one hundred years old). Your grandson asks you to tell him the most important ten events in American history. What do you tell him?

SUPPLEMENTAL RESOURCES

Anderson, Walter Truett. *Reality Isn't What It Used To Be.*

Faulkner was the quintessential modern writer who ushered into American culture the Postmodern era. Six stories competing in Postmodern era: 1. Western myth of progress; 2. Marxism and Revolution; 3. Christian Fundamentalism; 4. Islamic Fundamentalism; 5. Green; 6. New Age.

Bloom, Allan. *The Closing of the American Mind.*

As it now stands, students have a powerful image of what a perfect body is and pursue it incessantly. But deprived of guidance they no longer have any image of a perfect soul and hence do not long to have the eternal

conflict between good and evil has been replaced with 'I'm okay, you're okay.' Men and women once paid for difficult choices with their reputations, their sanity, and even their lives. But no more. America has no-fault automobile accidents, no fault insurance, and no consequence choices.

Gaede, S.D. *When Tolerance is No Virtue.*

In our culture, there is considerable confusion about how we ought to live with our differences and a cacophony of contradictory justifications for one approach as opposed to another. All appeal to the need of tolerance, but there is nothing like common argument on what that means. The question our culture raises by nature and development is what is truth and what can we believe? Our culture doesn't know the answers. In fact, we have lost confidence in truth and have come to the conclusion that truth is unattainable. Thus, tolerance moves to the forefront. G. K. Chesterton wrote: Toleration is the virtue of the man without convictions. The Christian Response: A. We need to understand the culture in which we live—one in which relativism is growing which leads to injustice. B. We must know what is right and do it. C. We must seek justice—we cannot turn a blind eye to the injustices related to multi-culturalism. D. We must affirm truth and not tolerate relativism. E. The church must be who it is—it must express its convictions about truth and justice and practice and express tolerance (i.e., love) to the multi-cultural body of Christ.

Minter, David L. *William Faulkner: His Life and Work.*

Novak, Michael. *Spirit of Democratic Capitalism.*

No political or economic system will survive without a cultural base (i.e., religion). Ergo, we are in deep trouble in America because no revival is occurring in the Church.

Plantinga, Cornelius. *Not the Way it is Supposed to Be: A Breviary of Sin.*

We need a healthy reminder of our sin and guilt. Not only do we need a healthy reminder of how sin affects us personally, we must remember that the truth of traditional Christianity saws against the grain of much in contemporary culture and therefore needs constant sharpening. Christianity's major doctrines need regular restatement so that people may believe them or believe them anew.

Willard, Dallas. *The Spirit of the Disciplines: How God Changes Lives.*

The disciplines for the spiritual life, rightly understood, are time tested activities consciously undertaken by us as new men or women to allow our spirit ever increasing sway over our embodied selves. They help by assisting the ways of God's Kingdom to take the place of the habits of sin embedded in our bodies.

Notes:

The Unvanquished
William Faulkner (1934)

VOCABULARY WORDS

Chapter	Word
I, 2	impunity (*immunity*)
	dispensation (*allocation*)
II, 2	cajoling (*coaxing*)
	Annihilation (*destruction*)
	Inviolate (*hallowed*)

CRITICAL THINKING

A. Why is the setting so important to this story?

ANSWER: *The "lost cause" drives this novel. Without the pathos that was the American Civil War, this novel would lose much of its energy. The realistic grandmother confronts the Union general, for instance. As the War progresses, the Colonel loses his romanticism—as Ahab in Moby Dick loses his—and replaces it with a raw realism, devoid of sentimentality. Bayard, too, has his disillusioning moments. The American Civil War is the vehicle that takes the reader to where Faulkner wishes him to go.*

B. What is the point of view? Why does it make this book more effective?

ANSWER: *First person—from Bayard. Does this form of narration make this book more effective? Absolutely. The whole experience of the Civil War through the eyes of a teenager is at the heart of this novel. Bayard is a remarkable interpreter and we all appreciate his candor. Also, his understatement (e.g., when his grandmother cons the union army) is especially appreciated and makes the entire novel more effective. This reader is not sure how reliable a narrator Bayard is. I would not expect his views about slavery to be too open-minded. On the other hand, he is young and unaffected by other events that unfold in this novel. In that sense he is somewhat neutral and somewhat reliable.*

C. Faulkner's prose is so powerful that it seems like poetry. This technique is accomplished by his puissant imagery. Can you find examples of this in the text?

ANSWER: *The chase scene at the end is powerful. Faulkner uses a great deal of stream of consciousness and complex adjectival constructions.*

D. There is a great deal of colloquial language. How important is the informal language? How important is the use of a Southern dialect? How do you feel about Faulkner's frequent use of the word *nigger*?

ANSWER: *The purpose of informal language in The Unvanquished is to make the novel more realistic. Faulkner uses pronunciation and grammatical form to create more fully developed characters which ultimately add to the effectiveness of the novel. At the same time, since the original copyright date was 1934, the reader should expect that Faulkner would be less sensitive to African-American readers than today's authors. However, the use of pejorative appellations for anyone is unfortunate. In any event, Faulkner creates very strong African-American characters (e.g., Lucas in Intruder in the Dust and Ringo in The Unvanquished, among others) despite his insensitive language.*

E. Who is the main character? Granny? Bayard? Colonel Sartoris? Defend your answer.

ANSWER: *While Colonel Sartoris and Granny are important characters and much of the action revolves around their behavior; in fact Bayard is the protagonist. It is from Bayard's viewpoint that the action in the novel unfolds. Faulkner often uses a boy as his protagonist/narrator to interpret reality (e.g., The Light in August and Intruder in the Dust).*

F. The chapter "An Odor of Verbena" has been criticized as being an entirely different story, or a story within a story. Some critics wonder if it really belongs. What do you think?

ANSWER: *This chapter is a story within a story, but it is important to the development of the plot. It also appropriately develops Bayard's further as a powerful character and the inheritor of the Sartoris reputation. It shows that the old South lives in the character of Bayard who avenged his family's demise.*

BIBLICAL APPLICATION

Faulkner discusses in great detail the whole issue of "family sin." In one novel, *Absalom, Absalom,* he blames the destruction of an entire family upon the sins of a father. The Snopes—an unprincipled, materialistic family—represent life in parts of the South (see *The Hamlet*, *The Town*, and *The Mansion*). Like rats in an empty house, they move in and take over as the moneyed, educated aristocracy self-destructs. In this book, Bayard and the Sartoris family are in a steady but definite decline. Compare the results of David and Bathsheba's relationship with the experience of Faulkner's characters.

ANSWER: *David commits adultery. One result of this sin is the heartache that Absalom brought him. In his writing Faulkner often discusses the consequences of sin on a section of country or a community of people. He does this in all his novels, but especially in his novel* Intruder in the Dust. *In other novels he introduces a family called the Snopes, a poor, utilitarian group of people who do not value the aristocratic South. Like a scourge of locusts, they destroy the South and the old way of life. The Snopes, like Absalom, represent a type of judgment. In this novel, Bayard watches the judgment unfold. His grandmother and father do not survive the judgment.*

ENRICHMENT

The writing of history is the selection of information and the synthesis of this information into a narrative that will stand the critical eye of time. However, history is never static. One never creates the definitive theory of an historical event. Some historians invite each generation to re-examine its own story and to reinterpret past events in light of present circumstances.

The creation of this story is more difficult than it seems. From the beginning the historian is forced to decide what sort of human motivations matter most: Economic? Political? Religious?

For instance, what causes the American Revolution? The historian Bernard Bailyn argues that ideology or the history of thought causes the American Revolution. Historian Oscar Handlin argues the Revolution is caused by social upheaval (i.e., the dislocation of groups and classes of people). Sydney Ahlstrom argues that religion is an important cause of the American Revolution. The historian will look at several theories of history and primary source material and then decide for himself what really happened, sometimes resulting in what is called "revisionist" history.

COMMENTARY:

The past, or at least the *interpretation* of the past, is constantly changing according to new scholarship. Therefore, as new sources are discovered, and old ones reexamined, the historian understands that *theories* of history may change. "Every true history is contemporary history," historians Gerald Grob and George Billias write. Students are asked to make the *theories* of historical events personal and contemporary.

While historians know that they can never be completely neutral about history, scholarly historical inquiry demands that they implement the following principles:

Historians must evaluate the veracity of sources. There must be a hierarchy of historical sources.

Historians must be committed to telling both sides of the historical story. They may choose to lobby for one view over the other, but historians must fairly present all theories.

Historians must avoid stereotypes and archetypes. They must overcome personal prejudices and dispassionately view history in ruthlessly objective terms.

Historians must be committed to the truth no matter where their scholarship leads them. At times historians will discover unflattering

> Only God can change history.

information about their nation/state. They must not hesitate to accept and then to tell the truth.

Finally, historians understand that real, abiding, and eternal history ultimately is made only by people who obey God at all costs.

After everything is said and done, historians are only *studying* the past. They cannot really *change* the past; they can, however, change understanding of and presentation about the past. Theories about the past come and go and change with each generation. Historians debate about history, but they can never change history—they can re-write history, but they cannot change it.

God alone can change history for the future. When a person is reborn, his present, future, and, yes, even his past is changed. History is literarily rewritten. He is a new creation. That bad choice, that sin, that catastrophe is placed under the blood of the Lamb through the grace of Jesus and everything starts fresh and new: a new history for a new person.

Let me illustrate. My great-great-great grandfather was a slave owner in Eastern Tennessee 139 years ago; his passion was to kill Yankees. From that inheritance I grew up to mistrust, even to hate African-Americans. Like so many people captured by their history and culture, my present and future came from my past. However, when I was a senior in high school, Jesus

Christ became my Lord and Savior. My attitudes changed. It took time and work and purposeful re-newing of my mind, but prejudices gradually disappeared. Ultimately, I married my New Jersey wife, and we have three African-American adopted children–whose ancestors, by the way, may have been owned by my great-great-great uncle! My children's children –African-American children–will be my grandchildren. Imagine! Quite literally, my legacy has been rewritten. It has been changed irrevocably by my decision to invite Jesus Christ to be Savior of my life. In a real sense, my family prejudice, existing for generations, ended in this generation. The destructive, historical cycle that was part of my history has ended. No one can accomplish that but the Lord Jesus. *History is being rewritten!* My prayer is that if you do not know this God who can change history—even your history—that these historical literary units may encourage you to listen to Jesus Christ who wants to come into your heart as Savior.

Most of us think that writing history is pretty simple: we merely find out what happened and write it down. But it isn't that simple. The reason that the Civil War occurred is open to great debate. To most Northern writers the war resulted from a conspiracy of slaveowners committed to an immoral institution; the North was defending the union. Southern writers, on the other hand, depicted an aggressive North determined to destroy the South. Slavery was not the cause of the war. Later, slavery expansion was seen as the cause; others argued for states' rights.

What do you think? Research the causes of the Civil War.

ANSWER: *Answers will have to be opinions: one opinion is that the Civil War was caused by the fear that southerners had that the cessation of slavery expansion would end their way of life. Some theorize that the inability of the American political system to assuage those fears in 1860 caused the American Civil War.*

The Tall Men

CRITICAL THINKING

A. Compare and contrast the worldview of the state draft investigator and the marshal.

ANSWER: *The state draft investigator is a "by the book" sort of man. The marshal is more flexible. Faulkner is satirizing the intransigent investigator.*

B. Why is Faulkner's title appropriate for this story?

ANSWER: *Once the boys understood their duty, they accomplished it with no dispute. They were so "tall" that they could even hug and kiss their parents good-bye.*

C. Describe Faulkner's narrative technique. How does it enhance his story?

ANSWER: *Omniscient narration is important to Faulkner's stream of consciousness characterization.*

D. Even though very little real action occurs in this story, the plot develops very well. How does Faulkner accomplish this development?

ANSWER: *Mostly by good writing and lengthy development of internal and external conflict among the characters.*

E. Compare and contrast this short story in style and substance with *Unvanquished*.

ANSWER: *The style of writing is very similar. Stream of consciousness is used to develop the characters. There is very little action. The action occurs in the minds of the characters. Themes are subtly but effectively presented. The setting is in the South. There are very few differences between these two works except that one is a short story and one is a novel. In a way, "Tall Men" could fit as a chapter in Unvanquished.*

ENRICHMENT

A. To Faulkner, and to most southerners, land, people, and history were vital. In that context, what does Faulkner mean in the following quote? "And I knew them too. I had seen them too, who had never been further . . . than I could return by night to sleep. It was these places . . . the places that men and women have lived in and loved whether they had anything to paint pictures of them or not, all the little places quiet enough to be lived in and loved and the names of them before they were quiet enough, and the names of the deeds that made them quiet enough and the names of the men and the women who did the deeds, who lasted and endured and fought the battles and lost them and fought again because they didn't even know they had been whipped, and tamed the wilderness and overpassed the mountains and deserts and died and still went on as the shape of the United States grew and went on. I knew them too: the men and women still powerful seventy-five years and twice that and twice that again afterward, still powerful and still dangerous and still coming, North and South and East and

West, until the name of what they did and what they died for became just one single word, louder than any thunder. It was America, and it covered all the western earth." ("Shall Not Perish," William Faulkner)

ANSWER: *Faulkner is expanding on the popular notion of Manifest Destiny—that Americans were destined to dominate the North American continent. A similar view was expressed in the late 19th century Turner Thesis (which posited that the American character was formed by the frontier)*

B. William Faulkner was deeply influenced by the American short story writer Sherwood Anderson. In a one to two page essay, discuss similarities between this short story and "The Tall Men."

ANSWER: *Anderson's writing is similar to Faulkner's; however, in this reader's opinion, Faulkner is a much superior writer. Faulkner liked Anderson's writings because Anderson develops his characters well and often uses streams of consciousness. Faulkner writes in very complicated, long prose, but Anderson writes in much smaller, simpler prose, but they both present well-developed, complicated characters. They also explore a similar them: individuals displaced from the land are without direction and hope. "The land" is important to both men. A sense of time, place, and situation permeate both men's writings.*

FINAL PROJECT

Students should correct and rewrite all essays and place them in their Final Portfolio.

LESSON 24 TEST

OBJECTIVE QUESTIONS (50 POINTS)

_____ 1. Ringo is (A) a slave (B) a Confederate soldier (C) a horse (D) a soldier in Colonel Sartoris' army.

_____ 2. Colonel Sartoris is (A) an artillery officer in the union army (B) a Confederate cavalry officer (C) a retired military friend (D) a friendly union officer.

_____ 3. A classic figure who could be compared to Granny would be (A) Robin Hood (B) Ivanhoe (C) Ulysses (D) Billy Pilgrim.

_____ 4. Ab Snopes is (A) an unprincipled Southern poor white man (B) a friendly Yankee lieutenant (C) a favorite house (D) a soldier in Colonel Sartoris' cavalry.

_____ 5. Druscilla was (B) a fragile Southern belle (b) Ringo's sister (C) a tomboy Southern woman (D) a wounded neighbor.

ESSAY (50 POINTS)

William Faulkner has retained you to be his ghost writer. You agree to write a short story, 3-5 pages, exhibiting the style, characterization, plot, and other literary elements that are similar to his own.

LESSON 24 TEST ANSWERS

OBJECTIVE QUESTIONS (50 POINTS)

1. __A__
2. __B__
3. __A__
4. __A__
5. __B__

ESSAY (50 POINTS)

William Faulkner has retained you to be his ghost writer. You agree to write a short story, 3-5 pages, exhibiting the style, characterization, plot, and other literary elements that are similar to his own.

Presumably the student's story occurs in the south and exhibits several Faulknerian themes: love, alienation, racism. In the following short story the narrator is an expatriate southerner living in the north who visits his mother in the delta:

SAMPLE FAULKNERIAN SHORT STORY:

Larry King was gently scolding Al Gore. CNN Larry King Live was blaring from my mother's opaque Panasonic twenty-five inch screen. Electrons danced across this colander of 21st century entertainment. Cable television munificence clashed with dancing electronic intruders. Bounteous contradictions were everywhere evident.

It didn't matter, though, because my mother only accessed one third of her available channels. The effort to bring in more varied offerings in the upper channels was pointless anyway. From Mom's perspective, she only needed CNN, the Weather Channel, and the History Channel. Even the local news didn't interest her now. This was all the entertainment she needed and, to her, news was entertainment. Mom was dying of pancreatic cancer.

Lying under a crocheted brightly-colored afghan knitted by her mother, affectionately called Big Momma by all other generations, mom was obviously defeated by the cancer interlopers who had completely subdued her body and were now warring with her spirit. With her blonde frosted wig slightly askew mom very much appeared the defeated warrior.

She needed the bright color in the afghan to tease vigor from her wasted frame and color from her pallid skin. Big Momma had shamelessly knit bright chartreuse, gold, and pinks into her afghan. Her clashing

choices doomed the afghan to family coffers or to the most destitute recipient who had no ardor for natural, appealing, subtle hues or had no affordable choice anyway. My mother's body, naturally big boned and pudgy until recently, now jutted unnaturally out from loose knitted perimeters. Her angular right knee was lassoed by a frayed portion of Big Momma's much used, little appreciated afghan. It looked like a reptile peeking through the burnished flora of a sticky jungle thicket.

It suited my mother just fine now, though. She felt frayed, tattered, and very old. She also felt used and useless. In the dim hue of Larry King Live the afghan and my mother had a bizarre, surrealistic appearance that accurately depicted the environs of her crumbling world.

It started with a stomach ache. Ordinary in scope and sequence this stomach ace nonetheless was an aberration in my mother's medical portfolio: Mom simply wasn't sick. Ever. Her delusion of immortality was so common to her personality that sickness was beyond the realm of her possibilities.

Unfortunately, the stomach ache ended and the anemia began. In most medical communities anemia is a sure sign that something is amiss in the gastrointestinal regions. In the Southern Arkansas universe, where my mother lived, medicine was more empathic than empirical and anemia was perceived as too much fried chicken or turnip greens. This diagnosis worked well enough, perhaps better, that conventional interventions, in colds, flu, and the occasional gall bladder attack. However, in the really big things—like pancreatic cancer—normal rural southern medical practice was hopelessly negligent and inevitably nugatory.

My mother, who walked three miles a day and regularly ate chicken gizzards fried in old lard, shrugged her shoulders and forgot about the whole thing. In fact, even after Geritol and BC Powders failed, she refused to visit her doctor. To question a doctor-friend's diagnosis was worse than cancer. With confident sanguineness, old Dr. E. P. Donahue, throat reflector protruding from his head, oversized Masonic ring protruding from his left middle finger, pronounced mom to be in remarkably good health. Dr. Donahue, who had delivered all Mom's three boys, was infallible—the medical "pope" as it were, whose edicts, once promulgated, were infallible.

Mom's malady, however, was already fatal. Her stamina and obstinacy propelled her forward for almost a year, but the carcinoma had already ambushed her. No one could tell, though, because she was in such great health. "My health," my mother ironically shrugged, "killed me."

By the time our family surgeon and good friend Dr. Johnny Joe Jones, one of Dr. Donahue's cardinals, called the hogs with mom one last time before she went into the operating room and opened her up with his scalpel, mom was mellifluent with metastatic carcinoma.

Dr. Johnny Joe was the best surgeon in Arkansas. There was one—Dr. Robert P. Howell—who was as good but it was rumored that he was a Unitarian. Besides, he enjoyed Jack Daniels too much. That was ok if one sought his services on a Wednesday. He was sober on Wednesdays out of respect for his Assembly of God mother who always went to church on Wednesdays. And it was Thursday.

Trained in Houston, TX—the medical school mecca of the South—everyone wanted a doctor trained in Houston—he must be good if he was from Houston—Dr. Johnny Joe was a brilliant, skilled surgeon. He had assisted in the first heart transplant attempt (the patient died) in Arkansas. He was also a Presbyterian. Everyone knew that the best doctors were Presbyterians who went to medical school in Houston. In spite of one nasty habit—Dr. Johnny Joe chewed Red Chief Tobacco during surgery—he was much sought after. "Wipe my mouth, nurse," Dr. Johnny Joe asked. Dr. Jones loved the Razorbacks. When he had to miss the game he nonetheless kept the radio blaring in the operating room. Once, while removing Mrs. Nickle's appendix, Texas intercepted a pass and ran back for a touchdown. Reacting to this tragedy, Dr. Jones' scalpel cut out Mrs. Nickle's appendix and spleen. No one blamed him.

No, my mother was fortunate to have him. He was pretty busy but since he was a good friend of my mother's old neighbor Josephine Mae Stuart, he agreed to take my mom's case.

Five minutes after Dr. Johnny Joe opened my mother up, he determined that the villainous corporeality had begun in the pancreas but it had progressed too far too quickly and it was not worth anyone's while for him to do anything but remove a particularly nefarious and ripe-with-cancer gall bladder. Deep inside my mother's liver, with his rubber clad left hand, Dr. Johnny Joe had rolled the marble-size tumors between his thumb and index finger. "Wipe my mouth, nurse," He sighed.

Mom's tumor-infected gall bladder was sent to Houston for tests but Dr. Johnny Joe had already announced my mother's death sentence. It was over just that quickly. With buck season in full swing, Dr. Johnny Joe was still able to kill a four point later that afternoon. Mom went home to die. Mom did not know that her gall bladder had been removed until she received her hospital bill. She thought it would be impolite to say anything. Dr. Johnny Joe could have taken out her heart, and she would have still been grateful.

Arkansas medicine was like that. Doctors politely did as they pleased. We Northerners want to know what our physicians do. We make them give us forms to sign and we ask for long lectures. We look at their diplomas on their walls and we want to know if they are board certified. All mom wanted was a smile, a nod, and a pat on her hand. "Johnny Joe is a good boy," mom said. "Josephine says he visits his mother every Saturday and he tithes."

For the first time my mother was hedged in. She could not fight this thing. Her chances of survival, Dr. T. J. Jackson, the oncologist, who was a Texas Longhorn fan—a grievous shortcoming only overcome by his obvious doctoring skills—adjudged, were zero. But she never wanted to hear the truth. Neither Dr. Johnny Joe nor Dr. Jackson told mom. She didn't want to know and they were too polite to tell her. My blood boiled. I smelled malpractice here. Mom only smelled okra gumbo stewing in the kitchen.

It turns out, however, she knew anyway and the okra gumbo probably did her more good anyway. Virginia Maria, her childhood Catholic friend who gambled with her on the grounded riverboats at Greenville, Mississippi, told her, "Nelle, I'm so sorry to hear you're going to die. And probably before the July Bonanza Night!"

"I'm sorry to hear that I'm going to miss the July Bonanza Night too," she calmly responded.

As if she was sipping a new brand of orange pekoe tea, to make her family happy, she tried a little chemotherapy. No one dared die of cancer in 1999 without having a little chemo-therapy. Hospice care was for colored folks, my mom said, who did not have insurance. She meant to have all the medical care Blue Cross and Blue Shield owed her. Unfortunately, it only succeeded in destroying what hair she had left and caused her to discard her last pack of Winston Lights.

"Do you have, Mr. Vice President," Larry King leaned across his desk, "anything else to add."

Although we didn't know it, this was the last few weeks of her life. Mom knew it. She had literally moved into her living room. She didn't want to die in the backwaters of a bedroom. She didn't want to die on the bed where she and my father had made love and dreamed dreams that neither lived. She didn't want to die on the periphery of life. She wanted to be in the middle of the action. Her living room controlled all accesses to her house. She was the gatekeeper and planned to man her station until she literally dropped dead. A captain at her helm. With her CB radio scanning for police gossip, with practically every light burning, with her television running day and night, mom wanted to feel the ebullience of life until the bitter end. She intended to watch Larry King Live until she dropped dead.

It was Christmas, and this was both the last Christmas I would be with my mother on this earth and the first one I had spent with her for two decades. The juxtaposition of these to portentous events seemed strangely ironical to me. I had lost my mother only to reclaim her in death.

I wasn't proud of the fact that I hadn't been home for Christmas in twenty-two years. I had too many kids, too many bills, and too little income to justify a two-day trip from my Pennsylvania farm to Southern Arkansas. Besides, who wanted to leave the postcard, snowy Pennsylvania Laurel Highlands to spend Christmas along the dirty black railroad ties of the Delta? Who wanted to replace the pristine Mennonite farms of Western PA with the cotton strewn roads of Southern Arkansas?

"I want to tell you a few things, Jimmy (my name), before I join your dad," she said. Mom never said that she was "dying" or even "passing away." She was always going to join dad who had died eighteen years previously.

My mother told me some stories that changed my history. Not that history changed—*my* history changed. Those hours, those days before she died changed the way I saw my past, and therefore my present and future, forever. I began to write this story about my mother. But, while she was an ever-present company in my life, I realized I was unqualified to write about her life. I could barely talk about my own. What I discovered really, was that this is a story about both our lives—lives that would be thrown together and torn apart in ancestral kinship, in hatred, and finally thrown together again in great love. It is also about a land, southern Arkansas, that we both loved and hated. (James P. Stobaugh, unpublished novel)

LESSON 25

THE MODERN AGE, 1915-1946: LATE ROMANTICISM/ NATURALISM *(Part 6)*

Readings Due For This Lesson: Students should review *The Pearl*, John Steinbeck.

Reading Ahead: Students will review *The Emperor Jones*, Eugene O'Neill. Is the Emperor Jones a victim or the perpetrator of his own destruction?

Goal: Students will analyze *The Pearl*, John Steinbeck.

Goals/Objectives: What is the purpose of this lesson?	Strategies to meet these goals: How will I obtain these goals/objectives?	Evaluation: How will I know when I have met these goals/ objectives?
Students will understand the concept: foreshadowing. (cognitive goal)	Students will write an essay on this topic: How does Steinbeck use foreshadowing in his book? (Critical Thinking A)	Students, with minimal errors, will clearly answer the assigned question in a 1-2 page essay.
Students will increase their vocabulary and thereby increase their scores on standardized tests. (cognitive goal)	Students will collect at least five new vocabulary words from their reading and use these words in their essays. They will also define the assigned words and use them in conversation and essays during the week.	Students will use five vocabulary words in conversation during the week as well as use the words in their essays and in conversation.
Students will understand the concept: symbolism. (cognitive goal)	Students will write an essay on this topic: How does Steinbeck use ants to make some points? (Critical Thinking B)	Students, with minimal errors, will clearly answer the assigned question in a 1-2 page essay.
Students will manifest higher thinking skills as they analyze the priest's role in this short novel. (cognitive goal)	Students will write an essay on this topic: How does Steinbeck present the priest in *The Pearl*? (Critical Thinking C)	Students, with minimal errors, will clearly answer the assigned question in a 1-2 page essay.
Students will understand the concept: theme. (cognitive goal)	Students will write an essay on this topic: List several themes in *The Pearl*. (Critical Thinking D)	Students, with minimal errors, will clearly answer the assigned question in a 1-2 page essay.

Goals/Objectives: What is the purpose of this lesson?	Strategies to meet these goals: How will I obtain these goals/objectives?	Evaluation: How will I know when I have met these goals/objectives?
Students will understand the concept: naturalism. (cognitive goal) Students will consider the generalization that naturalism is an inaccurate worldview for Christians. (affective goal)	Students will write an essay on this topic: What does this book tell you about the way the naturalist Steinbeck sees God? (Biblical Application A)	Students, with minimal errors, will clearly answer the assigned question in a 1-2 page essay.
Students will manifest higher thinking skills as they analyze this quote from the priest. (cognitive goal)	Students will write this essay: Respond to the Priest's sermon which stated "Each man and woman is like a soldier sent by God to guard some part of the castle of the Universe. (Biblical Application B)	Students, with minimal errors, will clearly answer the assigned question in a 1-2 page essay.
Students will exhibit higher thinking skills as they evaluate Juana's decision to return the pearl to her husband. (cognitive goal)	Students will write an essay on this topic: Even though Juana knows that the pearl will cause disaster, she returns it to her husband after it was lost. Why would she do this? (Enrichment)	Students, with minimal errors, will clearly answer the assigned question in a 1-2 page essay.
Students will consider the generalization that forgiveness is necessary for maturation in the Christian life. (affective/behavioral goal)	Parents/educators will discuss the necessity for students to forgive themselves if they make bad choices, to repent, and to purpose to do better next time.	Students and educators/parents will discuss forgiveness. Students will openly share in this discussion.
Students will work in a group setting. (behavioral goal)	In a class, in a co-op experience, or during a family discussion, students will answer this question: an alternative ending to this book.	Students will exhibit practical listening skills and will manifest understanding of opposing worldviews.
Students will be able to recall the information taught in the lesson. (cognitive goal)	Lesson 25 Test	Students will take the test at the end of this lesson and score at least 80%.
Students will experience reflective writing. (affective/spiritual goal)	Using the Journal Guide Questions in the Appendices, students will record at least three entries this week. Suggested Scriptures: John 3	Students will show evidence that they have reflected on this issue, including discussions and written responses.

SUGGESTED
Weekly *Implementation*

DAY 1	DAY 2	DAY 3	DAY 4	DAY 5
Prayer journal.	**Prayer journal.**	**Prayer journal.**	**Prayer journal.**	**Prayer journal.**
Students review the required reading (s) before the assigned lesson begins.	Student should review reading (s) from next lesson.	Students should write rough drafts of all assigned essays.	Students will re-write corrected copies of essays due tomorrow.	Essays are due.
Teacher may want to discuss assigned reading(s) with students.	Student should outline essays due at the end of the week.	The teacher and/or a peer evaluator may correct rough drafts.		Students should take Lesson 25 test.
Teacher and students will decide on required essays for this lesson, including two or three essays.	Per teacher instructions, students may answer orally in a group setting some of the essays that are not assigned as formal essays.			Reading Ahead: Students should review *The Emperor Jones*, Eugene O'Neill.
The rest of the essays can be outlined, answered with shorter answers, or skipped.				Guide: Is the Emperor Jones a victim of his circumstances or the perpetrator of his own destruction?
Students will review all readings for Lesson 25.				

Note: References to sources are in student edition.

ENRICHMENT ACTIVITIES/PROJECTS

With parental permission students should watch the movie *The Grapes of Wrath* (1940).
    Students should write alternate endings to the book.

VOCABULARY WORDS

Chapter	Word
Epilogue	parable *(a short, moral story)*
I	detachment *(separation)*
	frantically *(with desperation)*
III	fiercely *(with violent passion)*
	Prophecy *(inspired prediction)*
VI	lumbered *(encumbered)*

SUPPLEMENTAL RESOURCES

Astro, Richard. *Steinbeck as a Western American Author.*
    This critical response is an interesting overview of Steinbeck's writing.

French, Warren. *Steinbeck's Transcendentalism.*
    The naturalist Steinbeck and transcendentalism seem to be an oxymoron. French disagrees.

Minter, David. *Steinbeck's Depression-Era Writing.*

Minter develops the notion that Steinbeck's writings were deeply affected by the Depression.

Notes:

The Pearl

John Steinbeck

CRITICAL THINKING

A. How does Steinbeck use foreshadowing in his book?

ANSWER: *Juana suggests that the pearl is evil long before it has visited its full measure of evil upon them. Near the end of Chapter 3, Juana even suggests that the pearl will destroy their son, as it ultimately does. Ironically this was the very reason Kino prayed for the pearl.*

B. How does Steinbeck use ants to make some points?

ANSWER: *Men, like ants, work very hard to advance themselves but often to no avail. The reader may remember that Ernest Hemingway uses a similar image at the end of A Farewell to Arms.*

C. How does Steinbeck present/describe the priest in *The Pearl?*

ANSWER: *The priest is selfish, manipulative, and perhaps even dishonest. This gives the reader insight to Steinbeck's naturalist views. Steinbeck's priest is similar to Hemingway's priest (A Farewell To Arms) and Melville's priest (Billy Budd).*

D. List several themes in *The Pearl.*

ANSWER: *There are many: The oppression of Native Americans; Fate vs. Free Well; the price of being wealthy.*

BIBLICAL APPLICATION

A. What does this book tell you about the way the naturalist Steinbeck sees God?

ANSWER: *Steinbeck, like most naturalists, is an agnostic. The priest is presented in very negative ways. Nature is very impersonal and negative. There is a strong sense of fate—a malevolent power that is up to no good.*

B. Respond to the Priest's sermon which stated "Each man and woman is like a soldier sent by God to guard some part of the castle of the Universe."

ANSWER: *Steinbeck's priest is much worse than the priest we see in other naturalistic novels (e.g., A Farewell to Arms). He is not only ineffectual, he is malevolent. This statement betrays the selfishness of the priest: that the poor fisherman should give away the pearl—presumably to the priest—because the poor man should accept his station in life. The priest is manipulative and dishonest. The notion that "Each man and woman is like a soldier sent by God to guard some part of the castle of the Universe" invites the fisherman to accept the priest's own selfish agenda.*

ENRICHMENT

Even though Juana knows that the pearl will cause disaster, she returns it to her husband after it was lost. Why would she do this?

ANSWER: *Answers will vary, but, perhaps she loved him too much to see him suffer; perhaps she feared him or his reactions. Later, after her son is killed, no doubt, she wished she had not returned it to him.*

FINAL PROJECT

Students should correct and rewrite all essays and place them in their Final Portfolio.

LESSON 25 TEST

OBJECTIVE TEST (50 POINTS)

1. _____Kino is originally prompted to pray for a great pearl because (A) his son was bitten by a scorpion and he needed money for medicine (B) he needed money for the dentist (C) he was tired of living so poorly (D) his son had a chance to attend the university and he did not have enough money to send him

2. _____Who suggests that the pearl be abandoned? (A) Kino (B) the son (C) Juana (D) the doctor

3. _____While escaping from his pursuers (A) Juana is killed (B) Coyotito is killed (C) Kino loses the pearl (D) Kino falls and is drown

4. _____The only friends Kino seems to have are (A) Juan and Apolonia (B) the priest and his housekeeper (C) Jose and Maria (D) the doctor and his wife

5. _____This story is a(n) (A) epic (B) narrative poem (C) fable (D) parable

DISCUSSION QUESTION (50 POINTS)

In what sense is *The Pearl* a parable?

LESSON 25 TEST ANSWERS

OBJECTIVE TEST (50 POINTS)

ANSWER:

1. __A__
2. __C__
3. __B__
4. __A__
5. __D__

DISCUSSION QUESTION (50 POINTS)

In what sense is *The Pearl* a parable?

ANSWER: *The Pearl can be interpreted on many levels. On one hand the book is based upon an actual historical event. A poor Mexican Native did indeed find a pearl. The book, however, is also a parable—which is a type of allegory. An allegory is a story meant to teach a moral lesson, in which the characters symbolize something else. A parable is a short allegory. In the New Testament the Prodigal Son is a famous parable. On one level, The Pearl, like The Grapes of Wrath, is an allegory of economic injustice. Juan Tomas is a symbol of Native American common sense; Kino is a symbol of the poor's desire to advance themselves; and the doctor, priest, and pearl buyers are symbols of oppression.*

LESSON 26
THE MODERN AGE, 1946-1960: REALISM/ NATURALISM
(Part 1)

Readings Due For This Lesson: Students should review *Emperor Jones*, Eugene O'Neill.

Reading Ahead: Students should review *The Little Foxes*, Lillian Hellman. In what ways are the characters dysfunctional?

Goal: Students will analyze *The Emperor Jones*, Eugene O'Neill.

Goals/Objectives: What is the purpose of this lesson?	Strategies to meet these goals: How will I obtain these goals/objectives?	Evaluation: How will I know when I have met these goals/ objectives?
Students will understand this concept: suspense. (cognitive goal)	Students will write an essay on this topic: Discuss in detail how O'Neill builds suspense in this play. (Critical Thinking A)	Students, with minimal errors, will clearly answer the assigned question in a 1-2 page essay.
Students will increase their vocabulary and thereby increase their scores on standardized tests. (cognitive goal)	Students will collect at least five new vocabulary words from their reading and use these words in their essays. They will also define the assigned words and use them in conversation and essays during the week.	Students will use five vocabulary words in conversation during the week as well as use the words in their essays and in conversation.
Students will understand this concept: conflict in the play. (cognitive goal)	Students will write an essay on this topic: There are several layers of conflict in this play. Comment on the several kinds of conflict that arise in this play. (Critical Thinking B)	Students, with minimal errors, will clearly answer the assigned question in a 1-2 page essay.
Students will exhibit higher level thinking as they analyze this play and identify examples of naturalism. (cognitive goal)	Students will write an essay on this topic: Find several instances of Naturalism in this play. (Critical Thinking C)	Students, with minimal errors, will clearly answer the assigned question in a 1-2 page essay.
Students will understand this concept: setting. (cognitive goal)	Students will write an essay on this topic: What is the setting and how does it affect the outcome of this play? (Critical Thinking D)	Students, with minimal errors, will clearly answer the assigned question in a 1-2 page essay.

Goals/Objectives: What is the purpose of this lesson?	Strategies to meet these goals: How will I obtain these goals/objectives?	Evaluation: How will I know when I have met these goals/ objectives?
Students will manifest higher level thinking as they identify Smithers' purpose in this play. (cognitive goal)	Students will write an essay on this topic: Who is Smithers and what is his purpose in this play? (Critical Thinking E)	Students, with minimal errors, will clearly answer the assigned question in a 1-2 page essay.
Students will understand this concept: Freudian psychology as it applies to this play. (cognitive goal)	Students will write this essay: One scholar observed that O'Neill makes an "effort to interpret life in consonance with the findings of science, especially Freudian psychology, and at the same time a longing to find cosmic release in a mystical universe." (Enrichment)	Students, with minimal errors, will clearly answer the assigned question in a 1-2 page essay.
Students will understand the consequences of unforgiveness. (cognitive/affective goal)	Students will write an essay on this topic: The Emperor Jones was haunted by unforgiveness that had been visited on him by others. Tragically he was destroyed by that unforgiveness. . . Propose a reason for why this was so. (Biblical Application A)	Students, with minimal errors, will clearly answer the assigned question in a 1-2 page essay.
Students will remember and celebrate the way God used a person(s) in their lives. (affective goal) Students will exhibit the skill of writing a descriptive essay. (cognitive goal)	Students will write an essay on this topic: The following is a story of this author's call into the ministry. Do you have someone who deeply affected your life and encouraged you in your faith? Describe that person. (Biblical Application B)	Students, with minimal errors, will clearly answer the assigned question in a 1-2 page essay.
Students will work in a group setting. (behavioral goal)	In a class, in a co-op experience, or during a family discussion, students will answer this question: What is the net result of racial anger in your life?	Students will exhibit practical listening skills and will manifest understanding of opposing worldviews.
Students will be able to recall the information taught in the lesson. (cognitive goal)	Lesson 26 Test	Students will take the test at the end of this lesson and score at least 80%.
The student will experience reflective writing. (affective/spiritual goal)	Using the Journal Guide Questions in the Appendices, students will record at least three entries this week. Suggested Scriptures: Acts 6	Students will show evidence that they have reflected on this issue, including informed discussions and written responses.

SUGGESTED
Weekly *Implementation*

DAY 1	DAY 2	DAY 3	DAY 4	DAY 5
Prayer journal.	**Prayer journal.**	**Prayer journal.**	**Prayer journal.**	**Prayer journal.**
Students review the required reading(s) before the assigned lesson begins.	Student should review reading(s) from next lesson.	Students should write rough drafts of all assigned essays.	Student will re-write corrected copies of essays due tomorrow.	Essays are due.
Teacher may want to discuss assigned reading(s) with students.	Student should outline essays due at the end of the week.	The teacher and/or a peer evaluator may correct rough drafts.		Students should take Lesson 26 test.
Teacher and students will decide on required essays for this lesson, choosing two or three essays.	Per teacher instructions, students may answer orally in a group setting some of the essays that are not assigned as formal essays.			Reading Ahead: Review *The Little Foxes*, Lillian Hellman.
The rest of the essays can be outlined, answered with shorter answers, or skipped.				Guide: In what ways are the characters dysfunctional?
Students will review all readings for Lesson 26.				

Note: References to sources are in student edition.

ENRICHMENT ACTIVITIES/PROJECTS

Students should read Ashley Bryan, *Sing to the Sun; The Story of Lightning and Thunder;*

   Climbing Jacob's Ladder: Heroes of the Bible in African-American Spirituals;

   Turtle Knows Your Name; and

   All Night, All Day: A Child's First Book of African-American Spirituals.

Notes:

CRITICAL THINKING

A. Discuss in detail how O'Neill builds suspense in this play.

   ANSWER: *Brutus Jones is alone in his fears. Using the sound of drums and flashback O'Neill keeps us on the edge of our seat. From the moment Brutus enters the forest, he enters a surrealistic journey back in time to his own past.*

B. There are several layers of conflict in this play. Comment on the several kinds of conflict that arise in this play.

   ANSWER: *Jones vs. Jones, Jones vs. slaveholders, Jones vs. his subjects.*

C. Find several instances of Naturalism in this play.

   ANSWER: *The pervasive sense of nature and fate are powerful in this play. The forest is foreboding and evil. There is no moral structure that holds the world together. In fact, it is the abandonment of that faith structure that doomed Brutus.*

D. What is the setting and how does it affect the outcome of this play?

   ANSWER: *The small island represents a microcosm of the world. On this canvas O'Neill is able to paint a naturalistic world of unforgiveness and hopelessness. Brutus is unable to*

escape his world the same way Ethan Frome is unable to escape his. There is no moral vision in this world.

E. Who is Smithers and what is his purpose in this play?

   ANSWER: *Besides being a foil to develop Brutus, O'Neill is making a point that the "Smithers" are tailor-made for this naturalistic world. Pragmatic, amoral, self-centered Smithers thrive while Brutus is destroyed. O'Neill makes no comment but the fact is that one is better off being completely uncaring about his world if one wishes to prosper in this world.*

ENRICHMENT

One scholar observed that O'Neill makes an "effort to interpret life in consonance with the findings of science, especially Freudian psychology, and at the same time a longing to find cosmic release in a mystical universe." Discuss this observation with your educator.

   ANSWER: *The flashbacks to Brutus' past, the haunting dreams, all evidence a Freudian view of reality. Brutus can no more escape his past than he can escape his present—both will destroy him.*

BIBLICAL APPLICATION

A. The Emperor Jones was haunted by unforgiveness that had been visited on him by others. Tragically he was destroyed by that unforgiveness. Twenty years after World War II, A psychologist conducted a study of survivors of the Nazi concentration camps and their guards. To his horror, he discovered that the survivors had a higher suicide rate, divorce rate, and even higher rate of death by cancer than the concentration camp guards. In spite of the fact that the guards were guilty of heinous crimes and the former inmates were innocent victims, it was the innocent victims who fared much poorer. Propose a reason for why this was so.

   ANSWER: *As disconcerting as this may be, perhaps it could be that until the Jewish community could forgive its captors it would continue to be haunted by the past. There are physical as well as spiritual ramifications to unforgiveness.*

B. The following is a story of this author's call into the ministry. Do you have someone who deeply affected your life and encouraged you in your faith? Describe him/her.

ANSWER: *Answers will vary, but check the writing for style, grammar, usage, sentence structure, etc.*

FINAL PROJECT

Students should correct and rewrite all essays and place them in their Final Portfolio.

LESSON 26 TEST

ESSAY (100 POINTS)

In your essay state the central thesis of this essay and discuss how the author supports his argument. Then, agree or disagree with his conclusion.

By the time O'Neill, who was white, wrote *Emperor Jones*, the marriage of race and power was secure within the African-American community. Equality was no longer a goal—empowerment was. The movement now wanted more than a piece of the pie—it wanted to be in charge. After so much misery and given the failure of white America to address the needs of the African-American urban community, who could blame them? African-Americans wanted to be both away from whites and in charge. Brutus manifested this marriage of power and separatism, which encouraged a permanent state of rage.

"Anytime you make race a source of power," a Black Power leader wrote, "you are going to guarantee suffering, misery, and inequality. . . we are going to have power because we are black!" (Vincent Harding, *Hope and History*) Many African-Americans today, influenced by black nationalism, argue that the distribution of power in American society has become the single issue of overriding importance to the upward progress of African-Americans. From 1965 to the present every item on the black agenda has been judged by whether or not it added to the economic or political empowerment of black people. In effect, Martin Luther King's dialogue of justice for all—whites and blacks—has been cast into the conflagration of empowerment (Theodore Cross, *The Black Power Imperative*). The triumph of black nationalism made black anger an indelible part of the racial reconciliation quest. Thus, Brutus, on his island paradise finally felt he had it all: he was in charge and separated from whites.

Black nationalism was mostly nonviolent. However, some African-American leaders were very angry. To these people, gradualism was anathema. It suggested that races could coexist at the very time when many were suggesting that the races should remain separated. In *In The Fire Next Time* (1962) James Baldwin wrote, "rope, fire, torture, castration, infanticide, rape . . . fear by day and night, fear as deep as the marrow of the bone." By 1970, many African-American thinkers, religious leaders, social workers, and politicians were outraged. In fact, hatred and unforgiveness ran so deeply in African-American culture that the struggle became the end itself—instead of a means to an end.

The theme that O'Neill explored in his play is as alive today as it ever was. Today, the politic of difference has led to an establishment of "grievance identities." The African-American community has documented the grievance of their group, testifying to its abiding alienation.

Even though predominantly white colleges and universities now enroll a majority of the more than 1.3 million black college students, the fact is there is not much race-mixing (interracial marriage and adoption) really occurring. Racism still divides and conquers. One African-American student confessed, "We have a campus of 25,000 students and there is no mixing across cultural and racial lines . . . even during a campus rally for racial unity all the blacks cluster together and all the whites cluster together."

No one can deny that the Civil Rights initiatives in the 1960's brought substantial improvements to the African-American community. As a result of these encouraging developments, many black Americans developed what some historians call a "black revolution in expectations." African-Americans no longer felt that they had to put up with the humiliation of second-class citizenship. This progress was short lived and incomplete. White privilege—basic underpinnings that are based on the myth of racial homogeneity and white supremacy—mitigated all progress.

The real demon here, however, is unforgiveness. Clearly it destroyed Brutus; clearly it will destroy anyone in its path. (James P. Stobaugh)

LESSON 26 TEST ANSWERS

ESSAY (100 POINTS)

In your essay state the central thesis of this essay and discuss how the author supports his argument.

Then, agree or disagree with his conclusion.

ANSWER: *The author argues that Brutus and his contemporaries have every reason to be humanly angry and unforgiving, but ultimately this destroys the person exhibiting the unforgiveness. Some students will agree with the author and others will disagree.*

LESSON 27
THE MODERN AGE, 1946-1960: REALISM/NATURALISM
(Part 2)

Readings Due For This Lesson: Students should review *The Little Foxes*, Lillian Hellman.

Reading Ahead: Students should review *The Glass Menagerie*, Tennessee Williams. What is the worldview of the narrator and why does Williams use him to tell the story?

Goal: Students will analyze *The Little Foxes*, by Lillian Hellman.

Goals/Objectives: What is the purpose of this lesson?	Strategies to meet these goals: How will I obtain these goals/objectives?	Evaluation: How will I know when I have met these goals/objectives?
Students will understand this concept: the relationship between Horace and his wife Regina. (cognitive goal)	Students will write an essay on this topic: Describe in great detail the relationship of Horace and his wife Regina. This relationship is a key element of the play. (Critical Thinking A)	Students, with minimal errors, will clearly answer the assigned question in a 1-2 page essay.
Students will increase their vocabulary and thereby increase their scores on standardized tests. (cognitive goal)	Students will collect at least five new vocabulary words from their reading and use these words in their essays. They will also define the assigned words and use them in conversation and essays during the week.	Students will use five vocabulary words in conversation during the week as well as use the words in their essays and in conversation.
Students will understand these concepts: credible plot, setting, characterization, conflict, and resolution. (cognitive goal)	Students will write an essay on this topic: Why did (did not) you enjoy this play? Evaluate the play according to how well Hellman presented a credible plot, setting, characterization, conflict, and resolution. (Critical Thinking B)	Students, with minimal errors, will clearly answer the assigned question in a 1-2 page essay.
Students will understand this concept: realism. (cognitive goal)	Students will write an essay on this topic: Find several instances of realism in this play. (Critical Thinking C)	Students, with minimal errors, will clearly answer the assigned question in a 1-2 page essay.

Goals/Objectives: What is the purpose of this lesson?	Strategies to meet these goals: How will I obtain these goals/objectives?	Evaluation: How will I know when I have met these goals/objectives?
Students will exhibit higher-level thinking as they compare Regina Giddens to Jezebel. (cognitive goal) Students will consider the generalization that the "Jezebel" mentality is undesirable and even immoral. (affective goal)	Students will write an essay on this topic: Compare Regina Giddens to Jezebel. (Biblical Application)	Students, with minimal errors, will clearly answer the assigned question in a 1-2 page essay.
Students will manifest higher level thinking as they evaluate why the South has produced so many great writers. (cognitive goal)	Students will write an essay on this topic: Faulkner, Hellman, Williams, Welty, Ransom, O'Connor and other great writers came from the South. Why do you think so much great literature has come out of the South in this century? (Critical Thinking D)	Students, with minimal errors, will clearly answer the assigned question in a 1-2 page essay.
Students will manifest evaluation skills as they speculate upon the absence of good fathers in American literature. (cognitive goal) Students will value the biblical example of fatherhood. (affective goal)	Students will write this essay: What sort of fathers do we find in our plays? How do they measure up to the sort of father encouraged in Scripture? (Enrichment A)	Students, with minimal errors, will clearly answer the assigned question in a 1-2 page essay.
Students will understand the concepts: self-reflection and existential possibilities. (cognitive goal) Students will consider the generalization that our culture deifies self-reflection and existential possibilities. (affective goal)	Students will write an essay on this topic: React to this assessment of contemporary culture. Our culture deifies self-reflection and existential possibilities. (Enrichment B)	Students, with minimal errors, will clearly answer the assigned question in a 1-2 page essay.
Students will work in a group setting. (behavioral goal)	In a class, in a co-op experience, or during a family discussion, students will answer this question: What is the biblical model for fatherhood?	Students will exhibit practical listening skills and will manifest understanding of opposing worldviews.
Students will be able to recall the information taught in the lesson. (cognitive goal)	Lesson 27 Test	Students will take the test at the end of this lesson and score at least 80%.

Goals/Objectives: What is the purpose of this lesson?	Strategies to meet these goals: How will I obtain these goals/objectives?	Evaluation: How will I know when I have met these goals/objectives?
Students will experience reflective writing. (affective/spiritual goal)	Using the Journal Guide Questions in the Appendices, students will record at least three entries this week. Suggested Scriptures: Genesis 11-12	Students will show evidence that they have reflected on this issue, including informed discussions and written responses.

SUGGESTED
Weekly *Implementation*

DAY 1	DAY 2	DAY 3	DAY 4	DAY 5
Prayer journal.	**Prayer journal.**	**Prayer journal.**	**Prayer journal.**	**Prayer journal.**
Students review the required reading(s) before the assigned lesson begins.	Student should review reading(s) from next lesson.	Students should write rough drafts of all assigned essays.	Student will re-write corrected copies of essays due tomorrow.	Essays are due.
Teacher may want to discuss assigned reading(s) with students.	Student should outline essays due at the end of the week.	The teacher and/or a peer evaluator may correct rough drafts.		Students should take Lesson 27 test.
Teacher and students will decide on required essays for this lesson, choosing two or three essays.	Per teacher instructions, students may answer orally in a group setting some of the essays that are not assigned as formal essays.			Reading Ahead: Review *The Glass Menagerie*, Tennessee Williams.
The rest of the essays can be outlined, answered with shorter answers, or skipped.				Guide: What is the worldview of the narrator and why does Williams use him to tell the story?
Students will review all readings for Lesson 27.				

Note: References to sources are in student edition.

ENRICHMENT ACTIVITIES/PROJECTS

Students should cast parts for this play from their families.

Students should cast parts for this play from contemporary actors/actresses.

SUPPLEMENTAL RESOURCES

Bills, Steven H. *Lillian Hellman, an Annotated Bibliography.*

Estrin, Mark W. ed. *Critical Essays on Lillian Hellman.*

Falk, Doris V. *Lillian Hellman.*

Hellman, Lillian. *Pentimento: A Book of Portraits.*

Moody, Richard. *Lillian Hellman, Playwright.*

Rollyson, Carl. *Lillian Hellman: Her Legend and Her Legacy.*

Notes:

CRITICAL THINKING

A. Describe in great detail the relationship of Horace and his wife Regina. This relationship is a key element of the play.

ANSWER: *Horace represents the monied, educated, but steadily declining South. He embraces abstract, absolute truth. Regina, on the other hand, is a Philistine, strong woman who represents the New South.*

B. Did you enjoy this play? Why or why not? Evaluate this play according to how well Hellman presented a credible plot, setting, characterization, conflict, and resolution.

ANSWER: *Readers may relate to the feelings of lostness, failure, and hopelessness that pervade this play. While the characters are regional, they manifest universal characteristics. The setting is quite appropriate. The decaying south is a popular theme among mid-20th century authors. It is difficult to locate a climax in the play, but the conflict between the husband and wife is epic. There is no satisfactory resolution, but that is Hellman's whole point: life is not tied up nicely into neat packages.*

C. Find several instances of realism in this play.

ANSWER: *The best examples of Realism are reflected in dialogue and characterization. The feelings of confusion and animosity are abundantly clear in dialogues. Hellman makes no effort to romanticize any relationship, even the marriage relationship.*

D. Faulkner, Hellman, Williams, Welty, Ransom, and other great writers came from the South. Why do you think so much great literature has come out of the South in this century?

ANSWER: (See Introduction: Southern Renaissance, Student Edition, Lesson 32) *Some have argued that in the post-Reconstruction struggle, the South grew strong and educated. The authors had parents and grandparents who lost a major war—they were the only Americans in the 1930s who could say that. They lived in a conquered land, but they embraced their history and land with honor. However, the Southern Renaissance grew out of a reaction to northern progressivism: Characteristics of the Agrarian Movement in the Southern Renaissance include reaction against northern modernism which they saw as dehumanizing, against abstraction, and against the clock-punching mentality that was seen as coming at the expense of the value of human life. The Agrarian Movement was interested in the whole person—not in people as machines and producers. Associates of the movement valued religious sensibilities, especially Catholic, and celebrated and protected the south's agrarian past. The south traditionally valued a sense of place and traditions related to the Bible, excellent criteria for good literature growth. It is not surprising that the south produced such exceptional authors, poets, and playwrights with this strain of culture.*

Poetry from the Agrarian Movement had classical traits because the poets worked from the ancient Greek concepts of democracy and balance. The Agrarian Movement was inherently conservative in that the north was viewed as progressive and all about change and advancement; the south was about valuing past and what already existed. Southern Renaissance literature is against using utility as the measuring stick for worth. The book I'll take My Stand: The South and the Agrarian Tradition compiles twelve southern authors and critics who discuss and define these traits and views.

William Faulkner and other Southern authors grew out of these roots. Faulkner was pure literary genius, but his success was not necessarily related to the Agrarian Movement—he would have been a genius regardless of when he was born. Other writers after Faulkner have all had to reckon with his influence. Even though Flannery O'Connor was influenced by him and other Agrarians, she was a writer with her own staying power.

BIBLICAL APPLICATION

Compare Regina Giddens to Jezebel.

ANSWER: *Both are completely pragmatic (practical, realistic, hardheaded). Both manipulate their spouses and invite them to places of unbelief and immorality.*

ENRICHMENT

React to this assessment of contemporary culture. Our culture deifies self-reflection and existential possibilities. Without Christians standing to say, "Why?" we will lose the sense of irony. There will be no individual essence to which we remain true or committed. As the boundaries of definition give way, so does the assumption of self-identity. "Who am I?" is a teeming world of provisional possibilities—a question other generations dared not ask, a question that is asked all the time now. Who will answer that question for this generation . . .. (Kenneth J. Gergen, *The Saturated Self: Dilemmas of Identity in Contemporary Life*)

ANSWER: *Answers will vary.*

FINAL PROJECT

Students should correct and rewrite all essays and place them in their Final Portfolio.

LESSON 27 TEST

COMPLETE THE FOLLOWING CHECKLIST. (100 POINTS)

NAME OF PLAY:

NAME OF AUTHOR:

I. BRIEFLY DESCRIBE: (10 Points)

PROTAGONIST—

ANTAGONIST—

OTHER CHARACTERS USED TO DEVELOP PROTAGONIST—

DO ANY OF THE CHARACTERS REMIND ME OF A BIBLE CHARACTER? WHO? WHY?

II. SETTING: (10 Points)

III. TONE: (10 Points)

IV. BRIEF SUMMARY OF THE PLOT: (20 Points)

IDENTIFY THE CLIMAX OF THE PLAY.

V. THEME. (THE QUINTESSENTIAL MEANING/PURPOSE OF THE BOOK IN ONE OR TWO SENTENCES): (10 Points)

VI. AUTHOR'S WORLD VIEW: (20 Points)
HOW DO YOU KNOW THIS? WHAT BEHAVIORS DO(ES) THE CHARACTER(S) MANIFEST THAT LEAD YOU TO THIS CONCLUSION?

VII. WHY DID YOU LIKE/DISLIKE THIS PLAY? (10 Points)

LESSON 27 TEST ANSWERS

COMPLETE THE FOLLOWING CHECKLIST. (100 POINTS)

ANSWER:

NAME OF PLAY: *The Little Foxes*

NAME OF AUTHOR: Lillian Hellman

I. BRIEFLY DESCRIBE: (10 Points)

PROTAGONIST– *Horace*

ANTAGONIST– *Regina*

OTHER CHARACTERS USED TO DEVELOP PROTAGONIST– *Addie, Cal, Birdie.*

DO ANY OF THE CHARACTERS REMIND ME OF A BIBLE CHARACTER? WHO? WHY? *Regina = Jezebel*

II. SETTING: (10 Points) *Southern United States in the early 20th century*

III. TONE: (10 Points) *Serious*

IV. BRIEF SUMMARY OF THE PLOT: (20 Points) *Regina, represented the corrupted old south, destroys her gentile, but alcoholic husband Horace.*

IDENTIFY THE CLIMAX OF THE PLAY. *When Horace realizes that the "Reginas" of the world now control his world (at the end of the play).*

V. THEME. (THE QUINTESSENTIAL MEANING/PURPOSE OF THE BOOK IN ONE OR TWO SENTENCES): (10 Points) *The story of the decline of a family, of a worldview, of a civilization.*

VI. AUTHOR'S WORLDVIEW: (20 Points) HOW DO YOU KNOW THIS? WHAT BEHAVIORS DO(ES) THE CHARACTER(S) MANIFEST THAT LEAD YOU TO THIS CONCLUSION? *Both exhibit Naturalism (a sense that there is no control in the universe).*

VII. WHY DID YOU LIKE/DISLIKE THIS PLAY? (10 Points) *Answers will vary.*

LESSON 28

THE MODERN AGE, 1946-1960: REALISM/ NATURALISM
(Part 3)

Readings Due For This Lesson: Students will review *The Glass Menagerie*, Tennessee Williams.

Reading Ahead: Students will review *The Glass Menagerie*, Tennessee Williams.

Students should review *The Crucible*, Arthur Miller (Lesson 30). Should John Proctor pretend he is a witch in order to save his life?

Goal: Students will analyze *The Glass Menagerie*, Tennessee Williams.

Goals/Objectives: What is the purpose of this lesson?	Strategies to meet these goals: How will I obtain these goals/objectives?	Evaluation: How will I know when I have met these goals/ objectives?
Students will understand the concept of relationship. (cognitive goal)	Students will write an essay on the following topic: Describe in detail the characters in this play. (Critical Thinking A)	Students, with minimal errors, will clearly answer the assigned question in a 1-2 page essay.
Students will increase their vocabulary and thereby increase their scores on standardized tests. (cognitive goal)	Students will collect at least five new vocabulary words from their reading and use these words in their essays. They will also define the assigned words and use them in conversation and essays during the week.	Students will use five vocabulary words in conversation during the week as well as use the words in their essays and in conversation.
Students will understand the concepts of credible plot, setting, characterization, conflict, and resolution. (cognitive goal)	Students will write an essay on the following topic: What is the conflict? (Critical Thinking B)	Students, with minimal errors, will clearly answer the assigned question in a 1-2 page essay.
Students will understand the concept of realism. (cognitive goal)	Students will write an essay on the following topic: Why does Williams title his play "The Glass Menagerie"? (Critical Thinking C)	Students, with minimal errors, will clearly answer the assigned question in a 1-2 page essay.

Goals/Objectives: What is the purpose of this lesson?	Strategies to meet these goals: How will I obtain these goals/objectives?	Evaluation: How will I know when I have met these goals/ objectives?
Students will exhibit higher-level thinking as they compare characters. (cognitive goal)	Students will write an essay on the following topic: Describe the dreams of Laura, Amanda, and Jim. Do any of them fully attain their dreams? (Critical Thinking D)	Students, with minimal errors, will clearly answer the assigned question in a 1-2 page essay.
Students will manifest higher level thinking as they evaluate why the South has produced so many great writers. (cognitive goal)	Students will write an essay on the following topic: Compare the way Amanda handles disappointment with the way biblical Joseph handles disappointment. (Biblical Application)	Students, with minimal errors, will clearly answer the assigned question in a 1-2 page essay.
Students will be able to recall the information taught in the lesson. (cognitive goal)	Lesson 28 Test	Students will take the test at the end of this lesson and score at least 80%.
Students will experience reflective writing. (affective/spiritual goal)	Using the Journal Guide Questions in the Appendices, students will record at least three entries this week. Suggested Scriptures: Genesis 45-50	Students will show evidence that they have reflected on this issue, including informed discussions and written responses.

SUGGESTED
Weekly *Implementation*

DAY 1	DAY 2	DAY 3	DAY 4	DAY 5
Prayer journal.	**Prayer journal.**	**Prayer journal.**	**Prayer journal.**	**Prayer journal.**
Students review the required reading(s) before the assigned lesson begins.	Students should review reading(s) from next lesson.	Students should write rough drafts of all assigned essays.	Students will re-write corrected copies of essays due tomorrow.	Essays are due.
Teacher may want to discuss assigned reading(s) with students.	Students should outline essays due at the end of the week.	The teacher and/or a peer evaluator may correct rough drafts.		Students should take Lesson 28 test.
Teacher and student will decide on required essays for this lesson, choosing two or three essays. The rest of the essays can be outlined, answered with shorter answers, or skipped.	Per teacher instructions, students may answer orally in a group setting some of the essays that are not assigned as formal essays.			Reading Ahead: Students should review *The Crucible*, Arthur Miller (Lesson 30).
Students will review all readings for Lesson 28.				Guide: Should John Proctor pretend he is a witch in order to save his life?

ENRICHMENT ACTIVITIES/PROJECTS

Many Christians are worried about the effect movies are having on American culture. As a *Newsweek* reporter wrote:

People can croak, "Entertainment, Entertainment," until they are blue in the face. The fact remains that films like "Close Encounters of the Third Kind," "Superman," and even "Star Wars" have become jerry-built substitutes for the great myths and rituals of belief, hope and redemption that cultures used to shape before mass secular society took over.

Students should give examples from their own lives and American culture that evidence this statement.

Students should discuss why Williams uses the quote from E. E. Cummings on his title page for *The Glass Menagerie*.

SUPPLEMENTAL RESOURCES

Barron's Booknotes, *The Glass Menagerie*.
    Excellent student and teacher guide to this play.

Beaurline, L. A. "TGM: From Story to Play" *Modern Drama 8.*

The Glass Menagerie. (1987) Video
    A wonderful video version of William's most famous play.

Presley, Delma E. *The Glass Menagerie: An American Memory*

Siebold, Thomas. ed., *Readings on the Glass Menagerie.*

Spoto, Donald. *The Kindness of Strangers: The Life of TW.*

Notes:

CRITICAL THINKING

A. Describe in detail the characters in this play.

ANSWER: *Amanda is a fading Southern Belle. Laura is the poor spinster. Tom is the harried brother/son. Jim is the "gentleman caller."*

B. What is the conflict?

ANSWER: *In Amanda's world to be unmarried is to be without valuable identity. Amanda wants to turn back the clock. She can't. Tom values wealth and personal freedom from responsibility. He has neither. Laura is the most satisfied of the characters.*

C. Why does Williams title his play "The Glass Menagerie"?

ANSWER: *The characters of this play are similar to Laura's fragile glass menagerie collection. They are injured, vulnerable people who are easily damaged further and quick to damage each other.*

D. Describe the dreams of Laura, Amanda, Tom, and Jim. Do any of them fully attain their dreams?

ANSWER: *Laura wishes to stay safely at home. She is the most contented character. Amanda wishes her daughter to be married to her "beau." Tom wants to escape his past and this present. Jim wants the American dream. No one really gets his dreams.*

BIBLICAL APPLICATION

Compare the way that Amanda handles disappointment with the way the biblical Joseph handles disappointment.

ANSWER: *Amanda does not believe in a benevolent, omnipotent God. Therefore, she languishes in hopelessness. Joseph, in spite of bad things happening with regularity, remains hopeful because of his faith in God.*

FINAL PROJECT

Students should correct and rewrite all essays and place them in their Final Portfolio.

LESSON 28 TEST

COMPLETE THE FOLLOWING CHECKLIST: (100 POINTS)

NAME OF PLAY:

NAME OF AUTHOR:

I. BRIEFLY DESCRIBE: (10 Points)

PROTAGONIST—

ANTAGONIST—

OTHER CHARACTERS USED TO DEVELOP PROTAGONIST—

DO ANY OF THE CHARACTERS REMIND ME OF A BIBLE CHARACTER? WHO? WHY?

II. SETTING: (10 Points)

III. TONE: (10 Points)

IV. BRIEF SUMMARY OF THE PLOT: (20 Points)

IDENTIFY THE CLIMAX OF THE PLAY.

V. THEME (THE QUINTESSENTIAL MEANING/PURPOSE OF THE BOOK IN ONE OR TWO SENTENCES): (10 Points)

VI. AUTHOR'S WORLD VIEW: (20 Points)

HOW DO YOU KNOW THIS? WHAT BEHAVIORS DO(ES) THE CHARACTER(S) MANIFEST THAT LEAD YOU TO THIS CONCLUSION?

VII. WHY DID YOU LIKE/DISLIKE THIS PLAY? (10 Points)

LESSON 28 TEST ANSWERS

COMPLETE THE FOLLOWING CHECKLIST: (100 POINTS)

NAME OF PLAY: *The Glass Menagerie*
NAME OF AUTHOR: *Tennessee Williams*

I. BRIEFLY DESCRIBE: (10 Points)
PROTAGONIST– *Tom*
ANTAGONIST— *Amanda*
OTHER CHARACTERS USED TO DEVELOP PROTAGONIST– *Jim, Laura*
DO ANY OF THE CHARACTERS REMIND ME OF A BIBLE CHARACTER? WHO? WHY?
Answers will vary.

II. SETTING: (10 Points) *Urban South*

III. TONE: *Serious*

IV. BRIEF SUMMARY OF THE PLOT: (20 Points)
Amanda, her daughter Laura, and her son Tom languish in a Depression era apartment in a southern city. Laura, who is obsessed with a glass menagerie, is content to live her days in safe reticence. Amanda, however, wants much more. She is thrilled, then, when she hears Tom will be bringing to dinner a "gentleman caller." However, again, her hopes are to be dashed.

IDENTIFY THE CLIMAX OF THE PLAY. *When Jim shares his good news.*

V. THEME (THE QUINTESSENTIAL MEANING/PURPOSE OF THE BOOK IN ONE OR TWO SENTENCES): (10 Points) *This story is about broken promises and dreams.*

VI. AUTHOR'S WORLD VIEW: (20 Points)
HOW DO YOU KNOW THIS? WHAT BEHAVIORS DO(ES) THE CHARACTER(S) MANIFEST THAT LEAD YOU TO THIS CONCLUSION?
Naturalism. By his abiding pessimism and fatalism, the narrator reminds us that God is absent or innocuous.

VII. WHY DID YOU LIKE/DISLIKE THIS PLAY? (10 Points)

THE MODERN AGE, 1946-1960: REALISM/ NATURALISM
(Part 4)

Readings Due For This Lesson: Review *The Glass Menagerie*, Tennessee Williams.

Reading Ahead: *The Crucible*, Arthur Miller. Should John Proctor pretend he is a witch in order to save his life?

Goal: Students will analyze *The Glass Menagerie*, Tennessee Williams.

Goals/Objectives: What is the purpose of this lesson?	Strategies to meet these goals: How will I obtain these goals/objectives?	Evaluation: How will I know when I have met these goals/objectives?
Students will exhibit higher thinking skills as they compare Amanda to Regina Giddens and Horace Giddens. (cognitive goal)	Students will write an essay on the following topic: Is Amanda Wingfield more like Regina Giddens or Horace Giddens? Why? (Critical Thinking A)	Students, with minimal errors, will clearly answer the assigned question in a 1-2 page essay.
Students will increase their vocabulary and thereby increase their scores on standardized tests. (cognitive goal)	Students will collect at least five new vocabulary words from their reading and use these words in their essays. They will also define the assigned words and use them in conversation and essays during the week.	Students will use five vocabulary words in conversation during the week as well as use the words in their essays and in conversation.
Students will understand the concept of theme. (cognitive goal)	Students will write an essay on the following topic: Quoting C.S. Lewis, we "are half-hearted creatures, fooling about with drink and sex and ambition when infinite joy is offered us, like an ignorant child who wants to go on making mud pies in a slum because he cannot imagine what is meant by the offer of a holiday at the sea." Explore the theme of this play in light of this quote. (Critical Thinking B)	Students, with minimal errors, will clearly answer the assigned question in a 1-2 page essay.

Goals/Objectives: What is the purpose of this lesson?	Strategies to meet these goals: How will I obtain these goals/objectives?	Evaluation: How will I know when I have met these goals/objectives?
Students will exhibit higher level thinking as they evaluate the veracity of attending movies whose actors are immoral. (cognitive goal)	Students will write an essay on the following topic: Should Christians support movies that help non-Christian persons prosper? (Critical Thinking C)	Students, with minimal errors, will clearly answer the assigned question in a 1-2 page essay.
Students will exhibit higher-level thinking as they compare world-views of several American authors. (cognitive goal)	Students will write an essay on the following topic: Pretend that Anne Bradstreet, Ralph Waldo Emerson, Nathaniel Hawthorne, Stephen Crane, Ernest Hemingway, and Tennessee Williams have a conversation about the following topics: God, the Bible, Salvation, Nature, and Fate. (Critical Thinking D)	Students, with minimal errors, will clearly answer the assigned question by filling in the chart.
Students will manifest higher level thinking as they define and then evaluate what the American dream is and if it is attainable. (cognitive goal)	Students will write an essay on the following topic: What is the American dream at the beginning of the 21st century? Is it attainable? (Critical Thinking E)	Students, with minimal errors, will clearly answer the assigned question in a 1-2 page essay.
Students will exhibit higher level thinking as they compare two Tennessee Williams' plays.	Students will write an essay on the following topic: Read another Tennessee Williams' play and compare it to this one. (Enrichment)	Students, with minimal errors, will clearly answer the assigned question in a 1-2 page essay.
Students will work in a group setting. (behavioral goal)	In a class, in a co-op experience, or during a family discussion, students will answer the following question: What constitutes a good movie, play, or television program? What criteria do you use in deciding when to turn off the television?	Students will exhibit practical listening skills and will manifest understanding of opposing world-views.
Students will be able to recall the information taught in the lesson. (cognitive goal)	Lesson 29 Test	Students will take the test at the end of this lesson and score at least 80%.
Students will experience reflective writing. (affective/spiritual goal)	Using the Journal Guide Questions in the Appendices, students will record at least three entries this week. Suggested Scriptures: Genesis 45-50	Students will show evidence that they have reflected on this issue, including informed discussions and written responses.

SUGGESTED
Weekly *Implementation*

DAY 1	DAY 2	DAY 3	DAY 4	DAY 5
Prayer journal. Students review the required reading(s) before the assigned lesson begins. Teacher may want to discuss assigned reading(s) with students. Teacher and students will decide on required essays for this lesson, choosing two or three essays. The rest of the essays can be outlined, answered with shorter answers, or skipped. Students will review all readings for Lesson 29.	**Prayer journal.** Students should review reading(s) from next lesson. Students should outline essays due at the end of the week. Per teacher instructions, students may answer orally in a group setting some of the essays that are not assigned as formal essays.	**Prayer journal.** Students should write rough drafts of all assigned essays. The teacher and/or a peer evaluator may correct rough drafts.	**Prayer journal.** Students will re-write corrected copies of essays due tomorrow.	**Prayer journal.** Essays are due. Students should take Lesson 29 test. Reading Ahead: Review *The Crucible*, Arthur Miller. Guide: Should John Proctor pretend he is a witch in order to save his life?

Note: References to sources are in student edition.

ENRICHMENT ACTIVITIES/PROJECTS

Americans fiercely defend the right to privacy, yet we open our homes, our lives, and our minds to a constant barrage of messages from television, plays, and film. Students should discuss what constitutes a good movie, play, or television program. What criteria do they use in deciding to turn off the television?

Students should rewrite *The Glass Menagerie* as if it were a Christian moral drama. Keep the same setting and characters, but present them, and the plot, in appropriate roles.

SUPPLEMENTAL RESOURCES

Barron's Booknotes, *The Glass Menagerie*.
   Excellent student and teacher guide to this play.

Beaurline, L. A. "TGM: From Story to Play." *Modern Drama 8.*

The Glass Menagerie. (1987) Video
   A wonderful video version of William's most famous play.

Presley, Delma E. *The Glass Menagerie: An American Memory*

Siebold, Thomas ed., *Readings on the Glass Menagerie.*

Spoto, Donald. *The Kindness of Strangers: The Life of TW.*

Notes:

CRITICAL THINKING

A. Is Amanda Wingfield more like Regina Giddens or Horace Giddens? Why?

ANSWER: *Amanda is more like Horace. Like Horace, she is harmless but tragic. Both are motivated by history and tradition. Both deeply feel their past. Both are injured by spouses.*

B. *Chariots of Fire*, a famous and popular movie, by most accounts, has a Christian message, and most pastors recommend it to their congregations during its heyday. However, this movie includes actors who obviously are not Christians, and it is owned by Hollywood studios who care nothing about Judeo-Christian values. Should Christians support movies that help non-Christian people prosper? How about Mel Gibson's *The Passion of Christ*?

ANSWER: *Answers will have to be opinions.*

C. Pretend that Anne Bradstreet, Ralph Waldo Emerson, Nathaniel Hawthorne, Stephen Crane, Ernest Hemingway, and Tennessee Williams have a conversation about the following topics: God, the Bible, Salvation, Nature, and Fate. Complete the following chart with phrases they might use in their conversation.

ANSWER:

	Anne Bradstreet	Ralph Waldo Emerson	Nathaniel Hawthorne	Stephen Crane	Ernest Hemingway	Tennessee Williams
God	God is alive, all powerful and very interested in human affairs.	Nature is God. The Holy Spirit is Human intuition.	Same as Anne Bradstreet although he embraced nature. (small letter n)	If there is a God, He cares nothing about people.	See Crane.	See Crane.
Bible	The Bible is the inspired Word of God.	Good stories.	Same as Bradstreet	Bad stories that are for fools.	See Crane.	See Crane.
Salvation	Salvation comes through faith in Jesus Christ.	Within Nature's fold one will find salvation (a sort of Nirvana)	Same as Bradstreet	There is no salvation.	See Crane.	See Crane.
Nature	Nature is neutral.	Nature is god.	Nature is important because it represents God's work	It is neutral.	It is malevolent.	It is evil.
Fate	A loving God controls our futures.	Nature and human will control the future.	God is in control.	Fate is like rolling dice. No one is in control.	See Crane.	See Crane.

D. Amanda believes in several common myths about success and hard work. She thinks that if she had only married one of those rich gentlemen callers she would be successful. She admires the imaginary groups in her magazines. Likewise, she believes in the American dream—if one works hard enough, he will prosper. Ironically, the "gentleman caller" Jim O'Connor agrees with Amanda. He also has big plans. Only Laura and Tom seem to face reality squarely.

The personal failure of all the characters in the play in some ways parallels the larger failure of Depression era America. The Depression turned millions of American dreams into nightmares.

The New Deal failed to stop the Great Depression. Only World War II with full employment could end the Depression. Unfortunately, however, there was no solution to the dilemma facing Jim, Laura, Tom and Amanda, at least not in this world.

What is the American dream at the beginning of the 21st century? Is it attainable?

ANSWER: *Answers will have to be opinions, but it appears that most Americans are seeking the same things represented in a Tennessee Williams' play.*

ENRICHMENT

Read another Tennessee Williams' play and compare it to this one.

ANSWER: *One play with which to compare The Glass Menagerie could be A Streetcar Named Desire. Blanche Dubois, the protagonist in the play, is a fading Southern belle. She has just lost her ancestral home, Belle Reve, and her teaching position as a result of promiscuity. However, she reluctantly participated in this behavior in order to survive. Blanche was described by Tennessee Williams as moth-like. She is a refined, cultured, intelligent woman who is never willing to hurt someone, but she is at the mercy of the brutal, realistic, Naturalistic world. Stanley Kowalski is a common, working man who is simple, straight forward and tolerates nothing but the unembellished truth and lives in a world without refinements. He is common, crude and vulgar. He is the opposing force to Blanche's struggles and her world of illusion. Stella Kowalski is Blanche's younger, married sister who lives in the French Quarter of New Orleans. She has turned her back to her aristocratic upbringing to enjoy common marriage with a brute. She has abandoned any Romantic notions. Stella is caught between the two opposing worlds of Blanche and Stanley.*

FINAL PROJECT

Students should correct and rewrite all essays and place them in their Final Portfolio.

LESSON 29 TEST

DISCUSSION QUESTIONS (100 POINTS)

A. Some critics argue that *The Glass Menagerie* is a savage attack on 20th Century American culture. Agree or disagree and support your argument from the text.

B. Some critics argue that Williams is no Naturalist—in fact, they argue, he is a Theist (not necessarily Christian)—or at least a "moralist"—in the same tradition of Hawthorne. Agree or disagree and support your argument from the text.

C. The play has seven scenes. The first four take place over a few days' time during the winter season. The remaining scenes occur on two successive evenings during the following spring. Since the play contains no formal "acts," a director can prescribe an intermission at any time. How would you divide the play if you were directing a performance? Why?

D. Laura is one of the most pathetic figures in American literature. Is she really that physically crippled or is she more emotionally crippled?

E. How credible is Tom as a narrator? As a character in the play?

LESSON 29 TEST ANSWERS

DISCUSSION QUESTIONS (100 POINTS)

A. Some critics argue that *The Glass Menagerie* is a savage attack on 20th Century American culture. Agree or disagree and support your argument from the text.

ANSWER: *Williams felt that our superficial culture enslaved Americans to dreams that could never occur. Everyone—Tom, Jim, Amanda, and Laura (to a lesser degree)—were motivated by visions of reality that were not real at all.*

B. Some critics argue that Williams is no Naturalist—in fact, they argue, he is a Theist (not necessarily Christian)—or at least a "moralist"—in the same tradition of Hawthorne. Agree or disagree and support your argument from the text.

ANSWER: *Williams is a sentimental Naturalist, but I see no evidence he holds to any higher moral structure.*

C. The play has seven scenes, and the first four take place during the winter. The remaining scenes occur on two successive evenings during the following spring. Since there are no formal "acts," a director can prescribe an intermission at any time. How would you divide the play if you were directing a performance? Why?

ANSWER: *Answers will vary.*

D. Laura is one of the most pathetic figures in American literature. Is she really that physically crippled, or is she more emotionally crippled?

ANSWER: *She is more emotionally than physically crippled.*

E. How credible is Tom as a narrator? As a character in the play?

ANSWER: *Both as a narrator and a character in the place he exhibits self-centeredness that fractures his credibility as a narrator and character.*

LESSON 30

THE MODERN AGE, 1946-1960: REALISM/ NATURALISM
(Part 5)

Readings Due For This Lesson: Students should review *The Crucible*, Arthur Miller.

Reading Ahead: Students will review *A Separate Peace*, John Knowles. Did Gene purposely hurt Finny?

Goal: Students will analyze *The Crucible*, Arthur Miller.

Goals/Objectives: What is the purpose of this lesson?	Strategies to meet these goals: How will I obtain these goals/objectives?	Evaluation: How will I know when I have met these goals/ objectives?
Students will exhibit higher thinking skills as they discuss whether or not John Proctor is a realistic character. (cognitive goal)	Students will write an essay on the following topic: Is John Proctor a realistic character? Does he seem more a product of the 1950s than a character living in the 17th century? (Critical Thinking A)	Students, with minimal errors, will clearly answer the assigned question in a 1-2 page essay.
Students will increase their vocabulary and thereby increase their scores on standardized tests. (cognitive goal)	Students will collect at least five new vocabulary words from their reading and use these words in their essays. They will also define the assigned words and use them in conversation and essays during the week.	Students will use five vocabulary words in conversation during the week as well as use the words in their essays and in conversation.
Students will exhibit higher-level thinking as they react to this quote by Arthur Miller. (cognitive goal)	Students will write an essay on the following topic: Later, after the play was written, Arthur Miller said: "In my play, Danforth seems about to conceive of the truth, and surely there is a disposition in him at least to listen to arguments that go counter to the line of the prosecution. There is no such swerving in the record, and I think now, almost four years after writing it, that I was wrong in mitigating the evil of this man and the judges he	Students, with minimal errors, will clearly answer the assigned question in a 1-2 page essay.

Goals/Objectives: What is the purpose of this lesson?	Strategies to meet these goals: How will I obtain these goals/objectives?	Evaluation: How will I know when I have met these goals/ objectives?
	represents. Instead, I would perfect his evil to its utmost and make an open issue, a thematic consideration of it, in the play." Why do you agree or disagree with Miller? (Critical Thinking B)	
Students will exhibit higher level thinking as they discuss how a 17th century court could justify executing people accused of being witches. (cognitive goal)	Students will write an essay on the following topic: How could a 17th century court justify executing people accused of being witches? (Critical Thinking C)	Students, with minimal errors, will clearly answer the assigned question in a 1-2 page essay.
Students will understand Elizabeth Proctor's role. (cognitive goal)	Students will write an essay on the following topic: What is Elizabeth Proctor's role? (Critical Thinking D)	Students, with minimal errors, will clearly answer the assigned question in a 1-2 page essay.
Students will manifest higher level thinking as they discuss how the government can protect its people without resorting to excesses. (cognitive goal)	Students will write an essay on the following topic: How can the government protect its people without resorting to excesses? (Enrichment) (Critical Thinking B)	Students, with minimal errors, will clearly answer the assigned question in a 1-2 page essay.
Students will work in a group setting. (behavioral goal)	In a class, in a co-op experience, or during a family discussion, students will answer the following question: Should John Proctor pretend that he is a witch in order to save his life?	Students will exhibit practical listening skills and will manifest understanding of opposing world-views.
Students will be able to recall the information taught in the lesson. (cognitive goal)	Lesson 30 Test	Students will take the test at the end of this lesson and score at least 80%.
Students will experience reflective writing. (affective/spiritual goal)	Using the Journal Guide Questions in the Appendices, students will record at least three entries this week. Suggested Scriptures: Ezekiel	Students will show evidence that they have reflected on this issue, including informed discussions and written responses.

SUGGESTED
Weekly Implementation

DAY 1	DAY 2	DAY 3	DAY 4	DAY 5
Prayer journal.	**Prayer journal.**	**Prayer journal.**	**Prayer journal.**	**Prayer journal.**
Students review the required reading(s) before the assigned lesson begins.	Students should review reading(s) from next lesson.	Students should write rough drafts of all assigned essays.	Student will re-write corrected copies of essays due tomorrow.	Essays are due.
Teacher may want to discuss assigned reading(s) with students.	Students should outline essays due at the end of the week.	The teacher and/or a peer evaluator may correct rough drafts.		Students should take Lesson 30 test.
Teacher and students will decide on required essays for this lesson, choosing two or three essays.	Per teacher instructions, students may answer orally in a group setting some of the essays that are not assigned as formal essays.			Reading Ahead: Students should review *A Separate Peace*, John Knowles.
The rest of the essays can be outlined, answered with shorter answers, or skipped.				Guide: Did Gene purposely hurt Finny?
Students will review all readings for Lesson 30.				

Note: References to sources are in student edition.

ENRICHMENT ACTIVITIES/PROJECTS

Students should research the McCarthy Senate hearings of the 1950s.

Students should read another Arthur Miller play and compare it to this one.

SUPPLEMENTAL RESOURCES

Bigsby, Christopher (Editor). *The Cambridge Companion to Arthur Miller.*

Gottfried, Martin. *Arthur Miller: His Life and Work.*

Notes:

CRITICAL THINKING

A. Is John Proctor a realistic character? Does he seem more a product of the 1950s than a character living in the 17th century?

ANSWER: *A strong case could be made that John Proctor is much more of a 20th century character than a 17th century character. For one thing, he does not appear to be the least bit religious and that would certainly take him out of the "Puritan" category altogether.*

B. How could a 17th century court justify executing people accused of being witches?

ANSWER: *As Danforth says in Act III, "a person is either with this court or he must be counted against it." The public officials honestly believed that there were witches. In their view, they were merely obeying Scripture and thereby cleansing the community of the Devil.*

C. What is Elizabeth Proctor's role?

ANSWER: *Elizabeth exists to develop John Proctor. She is the perfect foil.*

ENRICHMENT

Arthur Miller wrote *The Crucible* as a criticism of the excesses of the 1950 McCarthy Hearings. These were a series of congressional hearings to reveal Communist spies and sympathizers in the United States government. No doubt there were excesses, and some innocent people had their reputations ruined. On the other hand, there really was some illegal, very harmful espionage occurring in high places in the United States government. In light of September 11, 2001, how can the government protect its people without resorting to excesses?

ANSWER: *Answers will vary. Students should discuss issue like profiling, tolerance, politically correct speech and actions, and other forms of identifying potential terrorists.*

FINAL PROJECT

Students should correct and rewrite all essays and place them in their Final Portfolio.

LESSON 30 TEST

OBJECTIVE TEST (T OR F) (50 POINTS)

1. _____ The play begins with women dancing in the forest with the slave Tituba.

2. _____ The Rev. Parris sees them doing this.

3. _____ The leader of the girls is Abigail.

4. _____ John Proctor believes the girls and asks for a witch trial.

5. _____ Rev. Parris oversees a trial.

DISCUSSION QUESTION (50 POINTS)

Agree or disagree with this statement: "A critic said, 'I speak of sin.' It is an unfashionable word nowadays and Miller rarely uses it. He is... sufficiently imbued with the skepticism of modern thought to shy away from the presumptions implicit in it. But that Miller is willy-nilly a moralist—one who believes he knows what sin and evil are—is inescapable."

LESSON 30 TEST ANSWERS

OBJECTIVE TEST (T OR F) (50 POINTS)

1. __T__
2. __T__
3. __T__
4. __F__
5. __T__

DISCUSSION QUESTION (50 POINTS)

Agree or disagree with this statement: "A critic said, 'I speak of sin.' It is an unfashionable word nowadays and Miller rarely uses it. He is... sufficiently imbued with the skepticism of modern thought to shy away from the presumptions implicit in it. But that Miller is willy-nilly a moralist—one who believes he knows what sin and evil are—is inescapable."

ANSWER: *In agreeing, I see no evidence that Miller has any problem with Proctor's infidelity. This opinion does not justify Abigail's action or sanction burning witches. However, I see no evidence, like this critic, that Miller even believes there is sin or that he knows what it means. In short, Miller has written a modernist, Naturalistic drama, not a moral play as T. S. Eliot did around the same time (i.e., <u>Murder in the Cathedral</u>).*

LESSON 31
CONTEMPORARY WRITERS, 1960-PRESENT (*Part 1*)

Readings Due For This Lesson: Students will review *A Separate Peace*, John Knowles.

Reading Ahead: Students should review "Everything That Rises Must Converge," Flannery O'Connor; "A Worn Path," Eudora Welty; "The Jilting of Granny Weatherall," Katherine Anne Porter.

What themes emerge in Southern literature?

Goal: Students will analyze *A Separate Peace*, John Knowles.

Goals/Objectives: What is the purpose of this lesson?	Strategies to meet these goals: How will I obtain these goals/objectives?	Evaluation: How will I know when I have met these goals/objectives?
Students will understand the concept of internal conflict. (cognitive goal)	Students will write an essay on the following topic: Gene feels challenged and stiffled by the Devon School. He enjoys the community but finds it debilitating too. In the same way, many of John Knowles' major characters fight to achieve an understanding with where they are, testing themselves constantly against their current situations. Give examples of these internal conflicts from the text. (Critical Thinking A)	Students, with minimal errors, will clearly answer the assigned question in a 1-2 page essay.
Students will increase their vocabulary and thereby increase their scores on standardized tests. (cognitive goal)	Students will collect at least five new vocabulary words from their reading and use these words in their essays. They will also define the assigned words and use them in conversation and essays during the week.	Students will use five vocabulary words in conversation during the week as well as use the words in their essays and in conversation.

Goals/Objectives: What is the purpose of this lesson?	Strategies to meet these goals: How will I obtain these goals/objectives?	Evaluation: How will I know when I have met these goals/objectives?
Students will understand the concept of reliable narration. (cognitive goal)	Students will write an essay on the following topic: Gene is the narrator of the story. He tells us what is going on; we see everything through his eyes. How reliable a narrator is Gene? Would Finny (until his death) be a better narrator? Why not have a teacher or a parent relate the story? Would it matter? (Critical Thinking B)	Students, with minimal errors, will clearly answer the assigned question in a 1-2 page essay.
Students will exhibit higher level thinking as they evaluate whether Gene caused Finny to fall from the tree. (cognitive goal)	Students will write an essay on the following topic: Did Gene cause Finny to fall from the tree? (Critical Thinking C)	Students, with minimal errors, will clearly answer the assigned question in a 1-2 page essay.
Students will understand the concept of setting. (cognitive goal)	Students will write an essay on the following topic: How important is the setting? (Critical Thinking D)	Students, with minimal errors, will clearly answer the assigned question in a 1-2 page essay.
Students will understand the concept of theme. (cognitive goal)	Students will write an essay on the following topic: Give one or two themes of this novel. (Critical Thinking E)	Students, with minimal errors, will clearly answer the assigned question in a 1-2 page essay.
Students will exhibit higher level thinking as they predict what themes, characters, and plots will emerge in 20 years. (cognitive goal)	Students will write an essay on the following topic: Predict what themes, characters, and plots will emerge in 20 years. (Enrichment)	Students, with minimal errors, will clearly answer the assigned question in a 1-2 page essay.
Students will work in a group setting. (behavioral goal)	In a class, in a co-op experience, or during a family discussion, students will answer the following question: What trends in literature do you see emerging?	Students will exhibit practical listening skills and will manifest understanding of opposing world-views.
Students will be able to recall the information taught in the lesson. (cognitive goal)	Lesson 31 Test	Students will take the test at the end of this lesson and score at least 80%.
Students will experience reflective writing. (affective/spiritual goal)	Using the Journal Guide Questions in the Appendices, students will record at least three entries this week. Suggested Scriptures: Joshua	Students will show evidence that they have reflected on this issue, including informed discussions and written responses.

SUGGESTED
Weekly *Implementation*

DAY 1	DAY 2	DAY 3	DAY 4	DAY 5
Prayer journal. Students review the required reading(s) before the assigned lesson begins. Teacher may want to discuss assigned reading(s) with students. Teacher and students will decide on required essays for this lesson, choosing two or three essays. The rest of the essays can be outlined, answered with shorter answers, or skipped. Students will review all readings for Lesson 31.	**Prayer journal.** Students should review reading(s) from next lesson. Student should outline essays due at the end of the week. Per teacher instructions, students may answer orally in a group setting some of the essays that are not assigned as formal essays.	**Prayer journal.** Students should write rough drafts of all assigned essays. The teacher and/or a peer evaluator may correct rough drafts.	**Prayer journal.** Students will re-write corrected copies of essays due tomorrow.	**Prayer journal.** Essays are due. Students should take Lesson 31 test. Reading Ahead: Review "Everything That Rises Must Converge," Flannery O'Connor; "A Worn Path," Eudora Welty; "The Jilting of Granny Weatherall," Katherine Anne Porter. Guide: What themes emerge in Southern literature?

Note: References to sources are in student edition.

Notes:

ENRICHMENT ACTIVITIES/PROJECTS

Students should examine the best-seller list. What trends in literature do you see emerging?

SUPPLEMENTAL RESOURCES

Knowles, John. *Indian Summer.*
    Out of print, this book by Knowles exhibits the same moral dilemmas and strong characterizations.

Knowles, John. *Peace Breaks Out.*
    The Sequel to *A Separate Peace.*

Post-World War II Literature

The period after World War II ushered in a period of confusion and, then, optimism. There was no profound disillusionment that followed World War I. However, by the 1960s this self-assured buoyancy had deteriorated into selfish individualism and unchecked egalitarianism. This narcissism spawned a literary and artistic movement called Absurdism. The central premise of Absurdism is that there was no meaning, no structure to life. Absurdism argued that we live in veiled chaos unencumbered by any scientific or sociological law or system. Champions of this movement were/are John Barth and Kurt Vonnegut, Jr. A similar artistic/literary movement in Europe was the Existentialism of Jean Paul Sartre and Albert Camus.

> While a cold war raged overseas, a culture war broke out at home.

The Separate Peace was set during World War II, but it was a product of the 1950s. During the 1950s, Americans experienced unprecedented prosperity. This prosperity invited most Americans to a new form of conservatism that posited the view point that "if it works, don't fix it." Therefore, conformity and uniformity were watchmen on the walls of early 1950 American culture. One social historian explains, "Everyone preferred group norms and cultural icons rather than experiencing the uncomfortableness of non-conformity." The camaraderie and community engendered in World War II invited Americans to embrace the security of group conformity. Most Americans craved the security of a simpler world of the 1930s rather than the uncomfortable, risky, unknown world that was to come.

Post-war Americans preferred to maintain old, traditional values, not to invent new ones. This included job choices and home life. Though men and women had been forced into new employment patterns during World War II, once the war was over, traditional roles were reaffirmed. As soon as the War ended, women basically went home to be housewives. Again, returning soldiers expected to be the breadwinners; women, even when they worked, assumed their proper place was at home. Now they could return home. Sociologist David Riesman observed the importance of peer-group expectations in his influential book, *The Lonely Crowd*. He called this new society "other-directed," and maintained that such societies led to stability as well as conformity. Television contributed to the homogenizing trend by providing young and old with a shared experience reflecting accepted social patterns. Radio and then television created an American culture that competed with local culture. This new culture invited conformity.

However, not all Americans conformed to such cultural norms. A number of writers and other artists rebelled against conventional values. Stressing spontaneity and spirituality, they asserted intuition over reason, Existentialism and Mysticism over denominational faith. This new worldview was reminiscent of the Transcendental movement of the previous century.

These new cultural rebels went out of their way to challenge the patterns of respectability and shock the rest of the culture.

Their literary work displayed their penchant for non-conformity. Jack Kerouac typed his best-selling novel *On the Road* on a 75-meter roll of paper. Lacking accepted punctuation and paragraph structure, the book glorified the possibilities of the free life. Poet Allen Ginsberg gained similar notoriety for his poetry. John Lennon and *The Beatles* broke new ground. The movie *The Blob* established new patterns when Steve McQueen and his teenage friends, unable to rely on adult superiors, took matters into their own hands, broke the law, and ultimately figured out themselves how to kill this monster. The viewer knew without any doubt that youth unencumbered by adult supervision was the hope for America's future.

This was only the beginning. More iconoclastic, artistic movements quickly followed. Elvis Presley, who seems fairly tame to later generations, in fact revolutionized non-conformity music. Born in Tupelo, Mississippi, Elvis Presley popularized African American soul music and took it a step further. In effect he created a new music genre: rock and roll. Presley shocked Americans with his long hair, seductive lyrics, and undulating hips.

Other artists followed. Painter Jackson Pollock discarded easels and laid out gigantic canvases on the floor and then applied paint, sand and other materials in wild splashes of color. Akin to Dadaism and Surrealism, this new abstract, called "modern art" invited the participant to new levels of subjectivity, individualism, and narcissism. Meaning now resided in the viewer, not in the artists. Americans could now find meaning in their own experience rather than in socially accepted norms and rituals. These artists and authors, whatever their medium, provided fertile ground for the more radical social revolutions of the 1960s.

What makes *A Separate Peace* so important is that within its pages a moral vision, albeit a fractured one, returns to American literature. Perhaps literature is headed back in the direction of the Puritans!

A Separate Peace
John Knowles

CRITICAL THINKING

A. Gene feels challenged and stiffled by the Devon School. He enjoys the community but finds it debilitating too. In the same way, many of John Knowles' major characters fight to achieve an understanding with where they are, testing themselves constantly against their current situations. Give examples of these internal conflicts from the text.

ANSWER: *Throughout the novel Gene struggles with his jealousy towards Finny. Later, he feels guilty (after he injures Finny). This is the source of much internal conflict for Gene. Finny begins almost too late to admire the friend he has in Gene, evidenced through his internal conflict—the primary internal conflict that Finny exhibits. Finny, however, as a character, is not as developed as Gene. There are other examples of internal conflict in every character—especially as the characters (foils) relate to the mock trial at the end of the novel.*

B. Gene is the narrator of the story. He tells us what is going on; we see everything through his eyes. How reliable a narrator is Gene? Would Finny (until his death) be a better narrator? Why not have a teacher or a parent relate the story? Would it matter?

ANSWER: *The reliability of the narrator, particularly in this novel is critical. One wonders, at times, if Gene is reliable. The philosopher Kant warns us that we can create a moral imperative to do almost anything. One wonders, after the fact, if Gene has not created a reality that suits his own moral imperative. The notion that he could have injured his best friend is unthinkable! On the other hand, Gene's winsome personality, sincerity, and intelligence disarm the reader and invite him to believe Finny. It is your call!*

C. Did Gene cause Finny to fall from the tree?

ANSWER: *That is the million dollar question! In this reader's opinion: absolutely! Did he mean to do so? Well, I'm not sure . . . but he did it.*

D. How important is the setting?

ANSWER: *The setting of a novel is, quite simply, where and when the story takes place. Another way of describing it is "spirit of place," the atmosphere generated by descriptions of the environment and the characters' relationship to it. In Devon School, John Knowles has created a setting rich in evocative detail. And, of course, the time of the novel is also very important: World War II.*

E. Give one or two themes of this novel.

ANSWER: *Honesty, Mutability.*

ENRICHMENT

Predict what themes, characters, and plots will emerge in 20 years.

ANSWERS: *Answers will have to be opinions. One opinion is literature that appeals to the affective realm will be most desirable.*

FINAL PROJECT

Students should correct and rewrite all essays and place them in their Final Portfolio.

LESSON 31 TEST

OBJECTIVE QUESTIONS (T OR F) (50 POINTS)

1. _____ Gene is a good student and a great athlete.

2. _____ This novel occurs during World War II.

3. _____ Devon is an exclusive prep school.

4. _____ Gene and Phineas fall out of the tree, but only Phineas is hurt.

5. _____ Phineas ultimately dies June 6, 1944, on the beach at Normandy.

ESSAY (50 POINTS)

In a 200-300 word essay create a sequel to *A Separate Peace* being careful to keep in place the integrity of the story and characters.

LESSON 31 TEST ANSWER

OBJECTIVE QUESTIONS (T OR F) (50 POINTS)

1. __F__
2. __T__
3. __T__
4. __F__
5. __F__

ESSAY (50 POINTS)

In a 200-300 word essay create a sequel to *A Separate Peace* being careful to keep in place the integrity of the story and characters.

ANSWER: *Answers will vary.*

LESSON 32
CONTEMPORARY WRITERS, 1960–PRESENT: THE SOUTHERN RENAISSANCE *(Part 2)*

Readings Due For This Lesson: Students will review "Everything That Rises Must Converge," Flannery O'Connor; "A Worn Path," Eudora Welty; "The Jilting of Granny Weatherall," Katherine Anne Porter.

Reading Ahead: Students should review *Cold Sassy Tree*, Olive Ann Burns. How does the protagonist mature both physically and spiritually?

Goal: Students will analyze "Everything That Rises Must Converge," Flannery O'Connor; "A Worn Path," Eudora Welty; "The Jilting of Granny Weatherall," Katherine Anne Porter.

Goals/Objectives: What is the purpose of this lesson?	Strategies to meet these goals: How will I obtain these goals/objectives?	Evaluation: How will I know when I have met these goals/objectives?
Students will understand the concept: similarities between Julian and his mother. (cognitive goal)	Students will write an essay on the following topic: In what ways are Julian and his mother similar? Different? How does O'Connor communicate these differences to the reader? (Critical Thinking A)	Students, with minimal errors, will clearly answer the assigned question in a 1-2 page essay.
Students will increase their vocabulary and thereby increase their scores on standardized tests. (cognitive goal)	Students will collect at least five new vocabulary words from their reading and use these words in their essays. They will also define the assigned words and use them in conversation and essays during the week.	Students will use five vocabulary words in conversation during the week as well as use the words in their essays and in conversation.
Students will understand the concept of irony. (cognitive goal)	Students will write an essay on the following topic: Why is it ironic that both Julian and his mother focus their dreams on the same things? (Critical Thinking B)	Students, with minimal errors, will clearly answer the assigned question in a 1-2 page essay.

Goals/Objectives: What is the purpose of this lesson?	Strategies to meet these goals: How will I obtain these goals/objectives?	Evaluation: How will I know when I have met these goals/objectives?
Students will manifest higher thinking skills as they analyze what the title means. (cognitive goal)	Students will write an essay on this topic: What does the title mean? (Critical Thinking C)	Students, with minimal errors, will clearly answer the assigned question in a 1-2 page essay.
Students will consider the concept: unforgiveness. (cognitive goal)	Students will write an essay on the following topic: Julian is sure that he is captured by unforgiveness for the rest of his life. Write another ending to this story: It is five years later; Julian comes to your church. You engage him in conversation and discover that he is unhappy because he cannot forgive himself. What will you say to him? Use the Bible to support your statements. (Biblical Application A)	Students, with minimal errors, will clearly answer the assigned question in a 1-2 page essay.
Students will understand the concept of naturalism. (cognitive goal) Students will consider the generalization that salvation is not connected to behavior. (affective goal)	Students will write an essay on the following topic: In my small 1950s church there was a very kind, godly man who faithfully attended church every Sunday morning and even taught Sunday school. In fact, he was an officer on our administrative board. I remember him fondly. All the children called him Uncle George. He also was the Grand Wizard of the state Ku Klux Klan. Should he have been allowed to hold important offices in the church? Should he have been allowed to attend church at all? Was he saved? (Biblical Application B)	Students, with minimal errors, will clearly answer the assigned question in a 1-2 page essay.
Students will manifest higher thinking skills as they analyze their own racial views. (cognitive goal)	Students will compose the following essay: Race affects where we live, the jobs we hold, the person we marry. Do you struggle with race issues? How do they affect you? (Enrichment A)	Students, with minimal errors, will clearly answer the assigned question in a 1-2 page essay.
Students will understand the concept of point of view. (cognitive goal)	Students will write an essay on the following topic: Henry James, William Faulkner, and many other American writers experimented with fictional points of view (some	Students, with minimal errors, will clearly answer the assigned question in a 1-2 page essay.

Goals/Objectives: What is the purpose of this lesson?	Strategies to meet these goals: How will I obtain these goals/objectives?	Evaluation: How will I know when I have met these goals/objectives?
	are still doing so). James often restricted the information in the novel to what a single character would have known. In his novel *The Sound and the Fury* Faulkner breaks up the narrative into four sections, each giving the viewpoint of a different character (including a mentally retarded boy). *As I Lay Dying* employs a similar approach. In "Everything That Rises Must Converge" Flannery O'Connor also employs a fairly sophisticated point of view. What is it? (Enrichment B)	
Students will manifest higher level thinking as they evaluate this short story. (cognitive goal)	Students will write an essay on the following topic: What kills Julian's mother: her shock at seeing an African-American wearing the same dress as she is wearing or the way Julian is treating her? (Enrichment C)	Students, with minimal errors, will clearly answer the assigned question in a 1-2 page essay.
Students will understand the concept of journey motif. (cognitive goal)	Students will write an essay on the following topic: how Welty uses the journey motif in "A Worn Path" to advance the action. (Critical Thinking A)	Students, with minimal errors, will clearly answer the assigned question in a 1-2 page essay.
Students will understand this concept: Welty's purpose for introducing the hunter and clinic attendant. (cognitive goal)	Students will write an essay on the following topic: What is the purpose of Welty's introducing the hunter and clinic attendant? (Critical Thinking A)	Students, with minimal errors, will clearly answer the assigned question in a 1-2 page essay.
Students will exhibit higher-level thinking as they discuss what universal truth is revealed in "A Worn Path." (cognitive goal)	Students will write an essay on the following topic: universal truth revealed in "A Worn Path." (Enrichment)	Students, with minimal errors, will clearly answer the assigned question in a 1-2 page essay.
Students will exhibit higher-level thinking as they discuss the qualities that Granny owned which helped her live successfully. (cognitive goal)	Students will write an essay on the following topic: qualities that Granny owned which helped her live successfully. (Critical Thinking A)	Students, with minimal errors, will clearly answer the assigned question in a 1-2 page essay.

Goals/Objectives: What is the purpose of this lesson?	Strategies to meet these goals: How will I obtain these goals/objectives?	Evaluation: How will I know when I have met these goals/objectives?
Students will understand the concept of stream of consciousness. (cognitive goal)	Students will write an essay on the following topic: how Porter uses steam of consciousness. (Critical Thinking B)	Students, with minimal errors, will clearly answer the assigned question in a 1-2 page essay.
Students will work in a group setting. (behavioral goal)	In a class, in a co-op experience, or during a family discussion, students will answer the following question: How do people adjust to painful life experiences?	Students will exhibit practical listening skills and will manifest understanding of opposing world-views.
Students will be able to recall the information taught in the lesson. (cognitive goal)	Lesson 32 Test	Students will take the test at the end of this lesson and score at least 80%.
Students will experience reflective writing. (affective/spiritual goal)	Using the Journal Guide Questions in the Appendices, students will record at least three entries this week. Suggested Scriptures: John 3	Students will show evidence that they have reflected on this issue, including informed discussions and written responses.

SUGGESTED
Weekly *Implementation*

DAY 1	DAY 2	DAY 3	DAY 4	DAY 5
Prayer journal.	**Prayer journal.**	**Prayer journal.**	**Prayer journal.**	**Prayer journal.**
Students review the required reading(s) before the assigned lesson begins.	Students should review reading(s) from next lesson.	Students should write rough drafts of all assigned essays.	Students will re-write corrected copies of essays due tomorrow.	Essays are due.
Teacher may want to discuss assigned reading(s) with students.	Students should outline essays due at the end of the week.	The teacher and/or a peer evaluator may correct rough drafts.		Students should take Lesson 32 test.
Teacher and students will decide on required essays for this lesson, two or three essays.	Per teacher instructions, students may answer orally in a group setting some of the essays that are not assigned as formal essays.			Reading Ahead: *Cold Sassy Tree*, Olive Ann Burns.
The rest of the essays can be outlined, answered with shorter answers, or skipped.				Guide: How does the protagonist mature both physically and spiritually?
Students will review all readings for Lesson 32.				

Note: References to sources are in student edition.

ENRICHMENT ACTIVITIES/PROJECTS

Students should write a report on the rise of the New South at the end of the Civil War.

Students should write a report on the Southern agrarian movement centered at Vanderbilt University in the thirties.

Students should memorize the "I Have a Dream," by Martin Luther King, Jr.

I Have a Dream
Martin Luther King, Jr.

I say to you today, my friends, so even though we face the difficulties of today and tomorrow, I still have a dream. It is a dream deeply rooted in the American dream.

I have a dream that one day this nation will rise up and live out the true meaning of its creed: "We hold these truths to be self-evident; that all men are created equal."

I have a dream that one day on the red hills of Georgia the sons of former slaves and the sons of former slave owners will be able to sit down together at the table of brotherhood.

I have a dream that one day even the state of Mississippi, a state sweltering with the heat of injustice, sweltering with the heat of oppression, will be transformed into an oasis of freedom and justice.

I have a dream that my four little children will one day live in a nation where they will not be judged by the color of their skin but by the content of their character.

I have a dream today.

I have a dream that one day down in Alabama, with its vicious racists, with its governor having his lips dripping with the words of interposition and nullification, that one day right down in Alabama little black boys and black girls will be able to join hands with little white boys and white girls as sisters and brothers.

I have a dream today.

I have a dream that one day every valley shall be exalted, every hill and mountain shall be made low, the rough places will be made plain, and the crooked places will be made straight, and the glory of the Lord shall be revealed, and all flesh shall see it together.

This is our hope. This is the faith that I will go back to the South with. With this faith we will be able to hew out of the mountain of despair a stone of hope. With this faith we will be able to transform the jangling discords of our nation into a beautiful symphony of brotherhood.

With this faith we will be able to work together, to pray together, to struggle together, to go to jail together, to stand up for freedom together, knowing that we will be free one day.

This will be the day when all of God's children will be able to sing with new meaning, "My country 'tis of thee, sweet land of liberty, of thee I sing. Land where my fathers died, land of the Pilgrims' pride, from every mountainside, let freedom ring."

And if America is to be a great nation, this must become true. So let freedom ring from the prodigious hilltops of New Hampshire. Let freedom ring from the mighty mountains of New York. Let freedom ring from the heightening Alleghenies of Pennsylvania.

Let freedom ring from the snow-capped Rockies of Colorado. Let freedom ring from the curvaceous slopes of California. But not only that; let freedom ring from the Stone Mountain of Georgia. Let freedom ring from Lookout Mountain of Tennessee.

Let freedom ring from every hill and molehill of Mississippi. From every mountainside, let freedom ring.

And when this happens, and when we allow freedom to ring, when we let it ring from every village and every hamlet, from every state and every city, we will

be able to speed up that day when all of God's children, black men and white men, Jews and gentiles, Protestants and Catholics, will be able to join hands and sing in the words of the old Negro spiritual, "Free at last! Free at last! Thank God Almighty, we are free at last!"

Supplementary Resources

Bellah, Robert N. and Frederick E. Greenspahn, *Uncivil Religion: Interreligious Hostility in America.*

Bloom, Harold ed., *Modern Critical Views: Flannery O'Connor.*

Fairlie, Henry. *The Seven Deadly Sins Today.*

Himmelfarb, Gertrude. *On Looking Into the Abyss.*
The first essay, with the same title as the book, describes how in the field of literature the great works are no longer read—or if they are, there are essentially no rules for interpreting them; how in philosophy, truth and reality are considered non-existent. And how in history deconstruction allows the historian to come to any conclusions he chooses. The second essay continues this line of thought, focusing especially on the freedom taken by authors or professors in recreating events and biographies to suit their ends, which often involves watering down the great individual accomplishments and events of history. This then allows them to place themselves above the people or events they are describing.

MacMullen, Ramsy. *Christianizing the Roman Empire A.D. 100-400.*
MacMullen gives us insights on how to do evangelism in a hostile environment.

Ragen, Brian A. *A Wreck on the Road to Damascus: Innocence, Guilt, & Conversion in Flannery O'Connor.*

Rookmaaker, H. R. *Modern Art and the Death of Culture.*

Tanquerey, A. *The Spiritual Life.*

Woodward, C. Vann. "Why the Southern Renaissance?" *Virginia Quarterly Review.*

Notes:

Flannery O'Connor

CRITICAL THINKING

A. In what ways are Julian and his mother similar? Different? How does O'Connor communicate these differences to the reader?

ANSWER: *They are both prejudiced. Julian's mother is prejudiced against people of another color. Julian is prejudiced against prejudiced people. Are they different? Julian claims to be open-minded; His mother makes no claim. On the other hand, Julian's open-mindedness is a sort of tyranny—as long as his mother agrees to be like him, she is ok. G. K. Chesterton wrote: "Toleration is the virtue of the man without convictions." The only conviction Julian has is that everyone who agrees with him is right and everyone who does not is wrong. Julian claims to be intolerant but he is also immoral—he is not committed to any corpus of authority, much less the Christian Bible, and therefore he has nothing on which to base his good works. It is difficult to be intolerant and immoral at the same time. As bigoted as Julian's mom is, she still is more principled than Julian. In her sincerity, in her consistent worldview, she is more tolerant of differences than is Julian.*

B. Why is it ironic that both Julian and his mother focus their dreams on the same things?

ANSWER: *They both want to be loved, to be accepted, and affirmed.*

C. What does the title mean?

ANSWER: *In the heat of the moment both personalities appear the same. They converge. At the same time, they are very much apart.*

D. Henry James, William Faulkner, and many other American writers experimented with fictional points of view (some are still doing so). James often restricted the information in the novel to what a single character would have known. In *The Sound and the Fury* Faulkner breaks up the narrative into four sections, each giving the viewpoint of a different character (including a mentally retarded boy). *As I Lay Dying* employs a similar approach. In "Everything That Rises Must Converge," Flannery O'Connor also employs a fairly sophisticated point of view. What is it?

ANSWER: *O'Connor tells the story of Julian's mom through Julian, who is the narrator. While the reader knows what Julian is thinking—limited omniscience—he also knows what Julian's mom is thinking. O'Connor uses Julian's impressions of his mother, as well as dialogue, to give the insights of Julian's mother. In fact, the reader may feel he knows Julian's mother better than he knows Julian!*

E. What kills Julian's mother: her shock at seeing an African-American wearing the same dress she is wearing or the way Julian is treating her?

ANSWER: *The cumulative effect of all these incidences killed Julian's mother. Perhaps the shock of living in a new age where races where treated equally killed her!*

BIBLICAL APPLICATION

A. Julian is sure that he is captured by unforgiveness for the rest of his life. Write another ending to this story: It is five years later and Julian comes to your church. You engage him in conversation and discover that he is unhappy because he cannot forgive himself. What will you say to him? Use the Bible to support your statements.

ANSWER: *Answers will have to be opinions. Presumably, you might begin a relationship with him, eventually share Christ with him, and hopefully in the process he would experience forgiveness.*

B. In my small 1950s church there was a very kind, godly man who faithfully attended church every Sunday morning and even taught Sunday school. In fact, he was an officer on our administrative board. All the children called him Uncle George. He also was the Grand Wizard of the state Ku Klux Klan. Should he have been allowed to hold important offices in the church? Should he have been allowed to attend church at all? Was he saved?

ANSWER: *Answers will have to be opinions.*

ENRICHMENT

Race affects where we live, the jobs we hold, the person we marry. No matter where we are or who we are, in one way or another our lives are affected by racial issues. To suggest in 1997 that racial difficulties are no longer a reality in American culture is to ignore reality. Americans inherit a history—good and bad—of racial interaction that profoundly affects individual and corporate worldviews. Race as a category in politics, social welfare policy, and religion became significant for the first time in open discussions in the 1960's and 1970's. These discussions continue today. Whether in a conversation on the edge of an indigo field outside

Columbia, South Carolina, in 1730 or in inner-city Philadelphia in 1997, racial discussions inevitably generated controversy. Racial anger is a reaction to the perceived failure of these discussions and their inability to bring expected results. In her own way Flannery O'Connor captures some of this struggle in the lives her two protagonists in "Everything That Rises Must Converge."

Do you struggle with race issues? How do they affect you?

ANSWER: *Answers will vary.*

Eudora Welty

CRITICAL THINKING

A. Discuss how Welty uses the journey motif to advance the action in "A Worn Path."

ANSWER: *Phoenix, the protagonist, makes a regular journey into a local, small town to obtain medicine for her little grandson, who is permanently injured because he swallowed lye. Phoenix has made this journey so often that her mind is free to wander. The reader, then, is treated to the delicious insights that Phoenix's mind offers. Phoenix is on a trip to town and on a trip in her mind while she is on the road to the town.*

B. What is the purpose of Welty's introducing the hunter and clinic?

ANSWER: *The hunter is the perfect foil. Phoenix, who stoically responds to the hunter, reveals the strength of character that propels this short story into greatness. Inside Phoenix is a lifetime of hardship perpetrated by poverty and racism. She may be poor, but her mind and experience are rich, and they enrich all around her if the participant will only notice. She is perceived as an insignificant person, but the reader knows better. With her decades of endurance, she is the rock of Gibraltar! Thus, the reader is not bothered, because Phoenix is not bothered, when the hunter patronizes Phoenix by calling her "Granny" and assuming that she, like a child, is going to town to see Santa Claus. Likewise, the lady who ties her shoes for her and the first attendant at the clinic call her "Grandma." The attendant rudely asks whether she is deaf and treats Phoenix as if she is stupid.*

ENRICHMENT

What universal truth is revealed in "A Worn Path"?

ANSWER: *Phoenix demonstrates a miraculous ability to accept and to triumph over the harsh circumstances of her life and to go on. Phoenix's life symbolizes the path traveled by poor and oppressed people everywhere.*

Katherine Anne Porter

CRITICAL THINKING

A. What internal qualities in Granny help her live successfully?

ANSWER:
She is resourceful and creative. She is quick to change when necessary. Adversity is an opportunity to solve problems.

B. How does Porter use steam of consciousness and dialogue to advance the action in "The Jilting of Granny Weatherall"?

ANSWER: *Porter uses stream-of-consciousness narration which communicates to the reader the thoughts, memories, and associations of Granny's mind. This technique is especially important to the story because it shows Granny's alternating confused and clear thoughts during her final moments as she moves from lucid consciousness to confusion during dying. Also, it allows the narrator to illuminate meaning by moving back and forth from the past to the present. Porter is not bound by time in her narration. The dialogue functions as a sort of interlude, almost comic relief to the somber tone of the short story. Both stream of consciousness and dialogue (some of which are spoken thoughts in Granny's mind) give a sense of urgency to Granny's thoughts, feelings, memories, and volition.*

FINAL PROJECT

Students should correct and rewrite all essays and place them in their Final Portfolio.

LESSON 32 TEST

ESSAYS. (100 POINTS)

A. Write an evaluation of one of the short stories in this lesson ("Everything That Rises Must Converge," Flannery O'Connor; "A Worn Path," Eudora Welty; "The Jilting of Granny Weatherall," Katherine Anne Porter).

Be candid in expressing your reactions to the work. Why did you like or not like the story? Support your arguments with specific references to the work. In your essay consider the theme, characters, plot, and other literary elements.

B. Contrast the character presented in the following short prose piece with the women presented in this lesson's short stories: "Everything That Rises Must Converge," Flannery O'Connor; "A Worn Path," Eudora Welty; "The Jilting of Granny Weatherall," Katherine Anne Porter.

Southern Arkansas was a generous but exhausted land. Cotton grew to bountiful heights. Southwest winds permanently bent rice plants pregnant with pounds and pounds of offspring. Pecan trees cradled whole acres of antediluvian loam with their gigantic arms. Every spring, bayous and rivers deposited a rich delta gift along the banks of grateful farm land. It was a gift from Minnesota and Ohio—freely given by the omnipresent Mississippi River. This was really an unselfish land, a land that seemed to give more than it took.

The house in which I now lived was a natural addition to this magnificent land. Built during the depression years of cheap labor, the House—so named by Mammaw—reflected my grandparent's unbounded optimism. They had built it with a profitable business and Depression-priced labor. They shamelessly flaunted their prosperity in a culture that was painfully impoverished. No one seemed to mind. The South has always been kind to its elitists. They were a chosen people, or so they claimed with every offering of ebullience. No one questioned their credentials—especially when my grandmother imported bricks from New Orleans streets, painted wicker chairs from replete Havana shops, and crystal chandeliers from abandoned Liverpool mansions. I remember that the bricks surrounding our fireplace evoked a faint smell of horse manure every winter as we enjoyed our winter fires.

The House was a testimony both to my grandmother's generosity and to her eccentricities. Five thousand square feet, six bedrooms and five full baths, and a full basement—the only full basement in my below sea level community—the house appeared in *Southern Living* in 1931 and 1932. The servant's quarters were above the kennel, and they were better than many of our neighbor's houses. The kitchen was built of cool New Orleans bricks and attached to the house by a closed walkway.

Our neighbors were mostly black. Mammaw was a determined racist. Her racism was a blue-blooded paternalistic variety that supposed the whole world must know and accept that African-Americans were inferior to the white race.

My mother's racism was much different. My mother was victimized *by* racism but was not a victim *of* racism. Racism was a fad to her. It was her ticket into southern respectability. Born into abject poor white trash poverty, mom was only too glad to gain prestige through racism. Racism was held sincerely, and it resolutely brought acceptance—in a word, pedigree. It tied ones blood lines to Arkansas ethos as surely as belonging to the Daughters of the Confederacy. In fact, she grasped it with gusto and vigor. Her manifestations of racism were particularly insidious and full of vigor. She hated blacks but loved the intrigue that they brought to her world. They made her life, her country, and her land nonpareil. It was not the fear or the anger that drew her. It was the anger and the intrigue that so much nonplused emotion brought her. Her racism was her own. Like a woman preparing for a debutante party. She nurtured it, refined it, savored it. It was her gentleman caller for whom she had waited all her life.

My grandmother had begged old man Parker to loan her money to build it. No bank would loan her money to build her house. Or at least no banker would loan it to my grandfather. He had only solvency and prosperity to offer. My grandmother had other things to offer.

The problem for those who believe in the existence of races, particularly the superiority of one over another, is to demonstrate that real differences can be demonstrated objectively. White Arkansans in the 1950s were fascinated by race. There existed a paradox of pluralism: a land of ambivalent diversity. Everyone celebrated our diversity, but no one knew how to live with it. Or at least no one knew how to live with it in a just way, although justice never really was a topic of anyone's conversation. We had created a language to describe American people groups. "White trash"were poor white people. "Niggers" were African-Americans who "misbehaved," and "Nigras" were African-Americans who conformed to what we considered a proper African-American to be. Of course, back then they weren't called African-Americans. In the minds of my mother, my grandmother, and countless other community members the idea of race, then, emerged from the ways that social meaning becomes attached to physical differences. "Black" meant subservient; "White" meant dominant.

My white community pursued power, already convinced they were entitled to it.

Racial discussions were complicated by the myth of homogeneity—as if there were a pure white and a pure black race. Ironically, American racial homogeneity was an illusion. Very few white southerners in my community were 100% black or 100% white. Miscegenation had been epidemic for over a century.

Nonetheless, most of my white neighbors normally described their racial identity in homogeneous terms. The reality was that individuals and their racial communities were not homogeneous. When one was classified white, one enjoyed the privileges of the dominant caste. Non-whites did not enjoy these privileges. So, the whole discussion of American racism was made even more complicated by the ambiguous defining apparatus of Arkansas racial language, which my white community needed—a language that was homogeneous and antiseptic.

The problem was, as I intimated, my grandparents wanted to build their mansion too close to what my community called "Nigger Town." At least my Mammaw wanted to built it there; my grandfather most assuredly did not. He wanted to build his house in the new Wolf Project where all sensible, prosperous, blue-blooded white southerners lived. However, he lacked imagination and he knew it, so he dutifully submitted the decision to Mammaw—not that he could do anything else. No one ever denied Mammaw anything that she really wanted.

Mammaw was no Civil Rights activist, nor did she pretend that she had any high moral standards. Mammaw was no hypocrite. She was a cold realist, and she cared for no one more than herself. Her egotism was unalloyed with any idealism. She loved us, her family, dearly, but she loved herself more. She knew a propitious place to build a house and was not going to let the absence of money or the pretension of Southern society stop her.

Old man John John Parker at the bank at first denied her request, but Mammaw walked into his business, the Fitzgerald County stock exchange, sat on his lap, kissed him on the mouth (not the cheek!), and asked in her most polished and sophisticated Southern accent, "please, Mr. John John, will you loan me the money to build my house?" Whether from warm enticement of further benefits, or from cold fear that she would do something else to embarrass him, Old Man Parker loaned her the money at no interest. The deal was sealed when Mammaw promised to bake him a Christmas pecan pie for the rest of his life. And she did. Parker ate pecan pie every Christmas until he died (in fact it may have killed him—when he died he weighed a whopping 330 pounds). Only once did Mammaw fail to live up to her bargain—one season the pecan crop was abysmally bad, and she had to substitute Vermont walnuts. Old Man Parker hardly noticed because Mammaw compensated the loss with her 100 proof rum cake! Mammaw did not like to cook—nor did she have to cook—she always had servants, but when she did anything, cooking, building a house, playing hide and seek with her grandchildren, she played and cooked to win.

Married to her first husband when she was fifteen and divorced from her second one when she was sixteen, Mammaw was truly an iconoclast. She was the first unrepentant divorced woman my small Southern railroad town had ever known. Her first husband abused her once, and she nearly killed him. In fact she would have killed him, but the shot gun she used was loaded with number eight shot and only blistered his backside. Buck shot would have killed him, and he knew it.

Mammaw merely walked away from the marriage and the man. It was beneath her to file for divorce—but Judge Johnstown knew what she wanted, everyone did, so he filed and granted divorce within the week. Her first husband never remarried and suffered in ebullient regret for the rest of his life. For penance, he became a United Pentecostal pastor. As far as I know, Mammaw never spoke or thought of the man again.

Mammaw was an enigma that greatly bothered our arcane Southern society. Again, Mammaw was an iconoclast. She cared nothing about what others thought—except to irritate potential critics. For instance, Mammaw, a fourth generation Methodist, loved to visit the Presbyterian Church because the pastor's wife wore stylist dresses. Mammaw wore scandalous short dresses, and while she refused to inhale, she carried a lit cigarette in her right hand to pique scurrilous busybodies.

Her unrepentant divorce had to be punished. Banished from the Country Club, most felt that she was sufficiently castigated. Once excoriated, Mammaw was supposed to repent, but Mammaw was not penitent. In fact, when she married my grandfather—the wealthiest and most eligible bachelor in town—the town was only too happy to invite my grandmother back into the country club. She refused, and all her offspring and generations following grew-up without the benefit of Southern country club amenities. Mammaw never again set a foot in the Fitzgerald County Country Club.

Mammaw had three sons. My dad was the youngest. Uncle Jimbo, the oldest sibling, was one of the most prosperous landowners in the area. Uncle Ricky went to Harvard and later became a Harvard Business School professor. My dad, who loved The House and Mammaw and black-eyed peas on New Year's Day, stayed at The House and married my mother when he was 17.

(James P. Stobaugh, unpublished novel)

LESSON 32 TEST ANSWERS

ESSAYS. (100 POINTS)

A. Write an evaluation of one of the short stories in this lesson ("Everything That Rises Must Converge," Flannery O'Connor; "A Worn Path," Eudora Welty; "The Jilting of Granny Weatherall," Katherine Anne Porter).

Be candid in expressing your reactions to the work. Why did you like or not like the story? Support your arguments with specific references to the work. In your essay consider the theme, characters, plot, and other literary elements.

ANSWER: *O'Connor's short story is superb, almost flawless. The characters are economically and precisely created.*

The plot is well-considered; the action flows quickly to a powerful climax. One theme—love and hate are very close emotions—is subtly developed.

B. Contrast the character presented in the following short prose piece with the women presented in this lesson's short stories: "Everything That Rises Must Converge," Flannery O'Connor; "A Worn Path," Eudora Welty; "The Jilting of Granny Weatherall," Katherine Anne Porter.

ANSWER: *All the women in these stories were strong-willed, well-developed protagonists.*

LESSON 33
CONTEMPORARY WRITERS, 1960–PRESENT (*Part 5*)

Readings Due For This Lesson: Students should review *Cold Sassy Tree*, Olive Ann Burns.

Reading Ahead: Students should review *The Chosen*, Chiam Potok. Did Danny make the right choice?

Goal: Students will analyze *Cold Sassy Tree*, Olive Ann Burns.

Goals/Objectives: What is the purpose of this lesson?	Strategies to meet these goals: How will I obtain these goals/objectives?	Evaluation: How will I know when I have met these goals/ objectives?
Students will understand the concept of central conflict in this novel. (cognitive goal)	Students will write an essay on the following topic: the central conflict in this novel. (Critical Thinking A)	Students, with minimal errors, will clearly answer the assigned question in a 1-2 page essay.
Students will increase their vocabulary and thereby increase their scores on standardized tests. (cognitive goal)	Students will collect at least five new vocabulary words from their reading and use these words in their essays. They will also define the assigned words and use them in conversation and essays during the week.	Students will use five vocabulary words in conversation during the week as well as use the words in their essays and in conversation.
Students will understand the concept of narration. (cognitive goal)	Students will write an essay on the following topic: the reliability of the young narrator in this novel. (Critical Thinking B)	Students, with minimal errors, will clearly answer the assigned question in a 1-2 page essay.
Students will manifest higher thinking skills as they analyze how Will matures as a character. (cognitive goal)	Students will write an essay on the following topic: In what ways has the narrator matured? What objects does Burns use to show this? (Critical Thinking C)	Students, with minimal errors, will clearly answer the assigned question in a 1-2 page essay.
Students will understand the concept of female characters in the novel. (cognitive goal)	Students will write an essay on the following topic: real versus archetypal female characters in *Cold Sassy Tree.* (Critical Thinking D)	Students, with minimal errors, will clearly answer the assigned question in a 1-2 page essay.

Goals/Objectives: What is the purpose of this lesson?	Strategies to meet these goals: How will I obtain these goals/objectives?	Evaluation: How will I know when I have met these goals/objectives?
Students will understand the concept of Will's faith journey. (cognitive goal)	Students will write an essay on the following topic: Will's faith journey. (Enrichment)	Students, with minimal errors, will clearly answer the assigned question in a 1-2 page essay.
Students will understand the concept of the rise of the New South.	Students will write a *report* on the rise of the New South at the end of the Civil War.	Students, with minimal errors will write a report on the New South and another report on the Southern agrarian movement—total of 3 pages.
Students will understand the concept of the Southern agrarian movement at Vanderbilt University in the thirties.	Students will write a *report* on the Southern agrarian movement centered at Vanderbilt University in the thirties.	
Students will work in a group setting. (behavioral goal)	In a class, in a co-op experience, or during a family discussion, students will answer the following question: Did Rucker do the right thing in marrying a woman only weeks after his first wife died?	Students will exhibit practical listening skills and will manifest understanding of opposing worldviews.
Students will be able to recall the information taught in the lesson. (cognitive goal)	Lesson 33 Test	Students will take the test at the end of this lesson and score at least 80%.
Students will experience reflective writing. (affective/spiritual goal)	Using the Journal Guide Questions in the Appendices, students will record at least three entries this week. Suggested Scriptures: Psalm 23	Student will show evidence that they have reflected on this issue, including informed discussions and written responses.

SUGGESTED
Weekly *Implementation*

DAY 1	DAY 2	DAY 3	DAY 4	DAY 5
Prayer journal. Students review the required reading(s) before the assigned lesson begins. Teacher may want to discuss assigned reading(s) with students. Teacher and students will decide on required essays for this lesson, choosing two or three essays. The rest of the essays can be outlined, answered with shorter answers, or skipped. Students will review all readings for Lesson 33.	**Prayer journal.** Students should review reading(s) from next lesson. Students should outline essays due at the end of the week. Per teacher instructions, students may answer orally in a group setting some of the essays that are not assigned as formal essays.	**Prayer journal.** Students should write rough drafts of all assigned essays. The teacher and/or a peer evaluator may correct rough drafts.	**Prayer journal.** Students will re-write corrected copies of essays due tomorrow.	**Prayer journal.** Essays are due. Students should take Lesson 33 test.

Note: References to sources are in student edition.

ENRICHMENT ACTIVITIES/PROJECTS

Students should write a *report* on the rise of the New South at the end of the Civil War.

Students should write a *report* on the Southern agrarian movement centered at Vanderbilt University in the thirties.

After parental permission, students and parents may want to see the movie *Cold Sassy Tree* (1989).

SUPPLEMENTAL RESOURCES

Inge, Tonnette Bond. *Southern Women Writers: The New Generation.*

Manning, Carol S. *The Female Tradition in Southern Literature.*

Tate, Linda. *A Southern Weave of Women.*

Notes:

CRITICAL THINKING

A. What is the central conflict in this novel?

ANSWER: *The central conflict is that of the rugged individualist taken to task and then being broken through small town bigotry.*

B. The narrator in this novel is a young boy. How reliable is he?

ANSWER: *He is the ideal narrator. He is both a participant invested in the story and a neutral observer. Intelligent beyond his years, Will offers insights that greatly enhance the story and make him a reliable narrator.*

C. In what ways has the narrator matured? What objects does Burns use to show this maturity or lack of maturity?

ANSWER: *The accident on the train trestle causes Will to think about life and death. The photograph of Will, Rucker, and Miss Love is a token of all the lessons about love that Will learns from that relationship. The root of the sassafras tree reminds Will of old Cold Sassy. The agricultural college diploma evidences that Will has followed his dream of becoming a farmer.*

D. Are the female characters in *Cold Sassy Tree* real or archetypal?

ANSWER: *This novel presents some of the most realistic, strong women in 20th century literature.*

BIBLICAL APPLICATION

Discuss Will's faith journey.

ANSWER: *Burns uses death to refine her protagonist's faith journey. Death is a major theme. It frames the story. It begins with Mattie Lou's death and closes with Rucker's death. This causes Will to question the meaning of life and the mercy of God. Will himself almost dies, a brush with mortality that intensifies his desire to understand God. He wonders but never really discovers if God is actually involved in the everyday affairs of people.*

FINAL PROJECT

Students should correct and rewrite all essays and place them in their Final Portfolio.

LESSON 33 TEST

OBJECTIVE TEST (T OR F) (50 POINTS)

1. _____ Miss Love and Rucker marry because they deeply love each other.

2. _____ Miss Love works at Rucker's store.

3. _____ Miss Love is perceived as a Yankee.

4. _____ Lightfoot is Will's best friend in church.

5. _____ Rucker dies at the end of the novel.

ESSAY (50 POINTS)

What does the Cold Sassy Tree symbolize?

LESSON 33 TEST ANSWER

OBJECTIVE TEST (T OR F) (50 POINTS)

1. F
2. T
3. T
4. F
5. T

ESSAY (50 POINTS)

What does the Cold Sassy Tree symbolize?

ANSWER: *The Cold Sassy tree gives the novel its title and the town its name; it stands for Rucker's and Miss Love's strength and composure in the face of adverse community opinion. One critic observed, too, that the town takes its name from the trees; the shrinking sassafras grove parallels the town's bittersweet progress. With the eradication of the sassafras trees over time, the town grows more modern and distances itself more from its heritage.*

LESSON 34
CONTEMPORARY WRITERS, 1960-PRESENT *(Part 4)*

Readings Due For This Lesson: Students should review *The Chosen*, Chiam Potok.
Goal: Students will analyze *The Chosen*, Chiam Potok.
Reading Ahead: Students will present Portfolio.

Goals/Objectives: What is the purpose of this lesson?	Strategies to meet these goals: How will I obtain these goals/objectives?	Evaluation: How will I know when I have met these goals/objectives?
Students will understand the concept of central conflict in this novel. (cognitive goal)	Students will write an essay on the following topic: Should Danny have become a psychotherapist even though it violated his father's wishes? (Critical Thinking A)	Students, with minimal errors, will clearly answer the assigned question in a 1-2 page essay.
Students will increase their vocabulary and thereby increase their scores on standardized tests. (cognitive goal)	Students will collect at least five new vocabulary words from their reading and use these words in their essays. They will also define the assigned words and use them in conversation and essays during the week.	Students will use five vocabulary words in conversation during the week as well as use the words in their essays and in conversation.
Students will understand the concept of narration. (cognitive goal)	Students will write an essay on the following topic: Do you like the ending of the book? Why? (Critical Thinking B)	Students, with minimal errors, will clearly answer the assigned question in a 1-2 page essay.
Students will manifest higher thinking skills as they analyze how Will matures as a character. (cognitive goal)	Students will write an essay on this topic: Potok is a master story-teller. In some ways "what he does not write" is important as "what he does write." Explain. (Critical Thinking C)	Students, with minimal errors, will clearly answer the assigned question in a 1-2 page essay.
Students will understand the concept of female characters in the novel. (cognitive goal)	Students will write an essay on the following topic: the role of women in this novel. (Critical Thinking D)	Students, with minimal errors, will clearly answer the assigned question in a 1-2 page essay.

Goals/Objectives: What is the purpose of this lesson?	Strategies to meet these goals: How will I obtain these goals/objectives?	Evaluation: How will I know when I have met these goals/objectives?
Students will understand the concept of Will's faith journey. (cognitive goal)	Students will write an essay on the following topic: why Potok tells the story from Reuven's point of view rather than Danny's. (Critical Thinking E)	Students, with minimal errors, will clearly answer the assigned question in a 1-2 page essay.
Students will work in a group setting. (behavioral goal)	In a class, in a co-op experience, or during a family discussion, students will answer the following question: Did Rucker do the right thing marrying a woman only weeks after his first wife died?	Students will exhibit practical listening skills and will manifest understanding of opposing worldviews.
Students will be able to recall the information taught in the lesson. (cognitive goal)	Lesson 34 Test	Students will take the test at the end of this lesson and score at least 80%.
Students will experience reflective writing. (affective/spiritual goal)	Using the Journal Guide Questions in the Appendices, students will record at least three entries this week. Suggested Scriptures: Acts 1-6	Students will show evidence that they have reflected on this issue, including informed discussions and written responses.

SUGGESTED
Weekly Implementation

DAY 1	DAY 2	DAY 3	DAY 4	DAY 5
Prayer journal.	**Prayer journal.**	**Prayer journal.**	**Prayer journal.**	**Prayer journal.**
Students review the required reading(s) before the assigned lesson begins. Teacher may want to discuss assigned reading(s) with students. Teacher and students will decide on required essays for this lesson, choosing two or three essays. The rest of the essays can be outlined, answered with shorter answers, or skipped. Students will review all readings for Lesson 34.	Students should review reading(s) from next lesson. Students should outline essays due at the end of the week. Per teacher instructions, students may answer orally in a group setting some of the essays that are not assigned as formal essays.	Students should write rough drafts of all assigned essays. The teacher and/or a peer evaluator may correct rough drafts.	Students will re-write corrected copies of essays due tomorrow.	Essays are due. Students should take Lesson 34 test. Complete Portfolio for next week.

Note: References to sources are in student edition.

Notes:

ENRICHMENT ACTIVITIES/PROJECTS

After parental permission, students should see the movie *The Chosen* (1982).

Students should read the sequel *The Promise*.

SUPPLEMENTAL RESOURCES

Levi, Primo. *Survival in Auschwitz.*

Falcon, Ted. *Judaism for Dummies.*

Potok, Chiam. *All other works.*

CRITICAL THINKING

A. Should Danny have become a psychotherapist even though it violated his father's wishes?

   ANSWER: *Answers will vary, but discussions could include autonomy in decision-making, submission to authority, mutuality in relationships, etc.*

B. Do you like the ending of the book? Why?

ANSWER: *Answers will vary. Students should discuss whether Reuven's decision to break with his father is credible.*

C. Potok is a master story-teller. In some ways *what he does not write* is important as *what he does write.* Explain.

ANSWER: *Potok skillfully flatters his readers by trusting them to pick-up subtle signals between Reuven and Danny. He shows more than tells the reader how these two young men grow to be such close friends.*

D. What role to women have in this novel? Why?

ANSWER: *Very little. They are weak characters and exist only as foils.*

E. Why does Potok tell the story from Reuven's rather than Danny's point of view?

ANSWER: *One suspects that Potok can identify with Reuven more than Danny. Reuven, also, is a more modern interpreter.*

FINAL PROJECT

Complete your final project and prepare it for presentation to peers, parents, and/or co-op groups.

LESSON 34 TEST

OBJECTIVE TEST (T OR F) (50 POINTS)

1. _____ Reuven and David are the two main characters.

2. _____ Reuven is a Hasidic Jew.

3. _____ Danny and Reuven meet when Danny hits Reuven with a baseball.

4. _____ Danny's father wishes Danny to take his place as leader of the Hasidim.

5. _____ Ironically, Reuven becomes a Rabbi.

DISCUSSION QUESTION (50 POINTS)

A. Discuss the way Potok develops his most fascinating character, Reb Saunders.

B. What is the central thematic conflict that occurs between Reuven and Danny?

LESSON 34 TEST ANSWER

OBJECTIVE TEST (T OR F) (50 POINTS)

1. __T__
2. __F__
3. __T__
4. __T__
5. __T__

DISCUSSION QUESTION (50 POINTS)

A. Discuss the way Potok develops his most fascinating character, Reb Saunders.

ANSWER: *Reb Saunders is a bundle of contradictions. He is a fanatic Hasidic Jew, but he does not oppose Danny's decision to become a psychotherapist. He loves Danny but practices a form of mental torture by never speaking to him. He is a man full of profundity that transcends this novel and makes him one of the most fascinating characters in American literature.*

B. What is the central thematic conflict that occurs between Reuven and Danny?

ANSWER: *Reuven and his family support the founding of the Jewish state of Israel (they are Zionists), but Danny and his family strongly oppose the founding of the Jewish state of Israel.*

LESSON 35

AMERICAN LITERATURE PORTFOLIO: SUBMIT THIS WEEK.

This Final Portfolio is composed of what you have accomplished this year through *American Literature: Encouraging Thoughtful Christians to be World Changers.*

Consider this project a portfolio of your academic progress for this academic year. You should arrange to have an exhibition for peers, parents, and other academicians. You should keep your American Literature Portfolio as a record of your development as a writer, as a critical thinker, and as an American Literature scholar. It could also serve as a Biblical Application Journal if you have opted to complete the biblical application questions.

The **American Literature Portfolio** should contain the following in an attractive binder, clearly labeled with title, academic year, and your name:

AMERICAN LITERATURE PORTFOLIO

Table of Contents
Corrected Literary Essays
Literary Checkups
Writing Journals
Pictures (or paraphernalia, or travel journals) from field trips
Supplemental Material (or other pertinent information)
Vocabulary cards (in a separate pocket-type folder)

AMERICAN LITERATURE

ENCOURAGING THOUGHTFUL CHRISTIANS TO BE WORLD CHANGERS

APPENDICES

APPENDIX A

Writing Tips

How do students produce concise, well-written essays?

GENERAL STATEMENTS

• Essays should be written in the context of the other social sciences. This means that essays should be written on all topics: science topics, history topics, social science topics, etc.

• Some essays should be rewritten, depending on the assignment and the purpose of the writing; definitely those essays which are to be presented to various readers or a public audience should be rewritten for their best presentation. Parents and other educators should discuss with their students which and how many essays will be rewritten. Generally speaking, I suggest that students rewrite at least one essay per week.

• Students should write something every day and read something every day. Students will be prompted to read assigned whole books before they are due. It is imperative that students read ahead as they write present essays or they will not be able to read all the material. Remember this too: students tend to write what they read. Poor material—material that is too juvenile—will be echoed in the vocabulary and syntax of student essays.

• Students should begin writing assignments immediately after they are assigned. A suggested implementation schedule is provided. Generally speaking, students will write about one hour per day to accomplish the writing component of this course.

• Students should revise their papers as soon as they are evaluated. Follow the implementation schedule at the end of each course.

Every essay includes a *prewriting phase, an outlining phase,* a *writing phase,* a *revision phase,* and for the purposes of this course, *a publishing phase.*

PRE-WRITING THINKING CHALLENGE

ISSUE

State problem/issue in five sentences.

State problem/issue in two sentences.

State problem/issue in one sentence.

NAME THREE OR MORE SUBTOPICS OF THE PROBLEM.

NAME THREE OR MORE SUBTOPICS OF THE SUBTOPICS.

WHAT INFORMATION MUST BE KNOWN TO SOLVE THE PROBLEM OR TO ANSWER THE QUESTION?

STATE THE ANSWER TO THE QUESTION/
PROBLEM
—In five sentences.

—In two sentences.

—In one sentence.

STATED IN TERMS OF OUTCOMES, WHAT
EVIDENCES DO I SEE THAT CONFIRM THAT I
HAVE MADE THE RIGHT DECISION?

ONCE THE PROBLEM/QUESTION IS
ANSWERED/SOLVED, WHAT ONE OR TWO
NEW PROBLEMS/ANSWERS MAY ARISE?

ABBREVIATED PRE-WRITING THINKING CHALLENGE

What is the issue?
State problem/issue in five sentences.
State problem/issue in two sentences.
State problem/issue in one sentence.
Name three or more subtopics of problem.
Name three or more subtopics of the subtopics.
What information must be known to solve the problem
or to answer the question?
State the answer to the question/problem
—in five sentences —in two sentences —in one sen-
tence.
Stated in terms of outcomes, what evidences do I see
that confirm that I have made the right decision?

Once the problem or question is answered or solved,
what are one or two new problems or answers that
could arise?

PRE-WRITING PHASE

Often called the brainstorming phase, the pre-writing
phase is the time you decide on exactly what your topic

is. What questions must you answer? You should articulate a thesis (a one sentence statement of purpose for
why you are writing about this topic. The thesis typically has two to four specific points contained within
it). You should decide what sort of essay this is—for
instance, a definition, an exposition, a persuasive argument—and then design a strategy. For example, a
clearly persuasive essay will demand that you state the
issue and give your opinion in the opening paragraph.

Next, after a thesis statement, you will write an outline. *No matter what length the essay may be, 20 pages or one
paragraph, you should create an outline.*

Outline
Thesis: In his poem *The Raven*, Edgar Allan Poe
uses literary devices to describe such weighty topics as
death and *unrequited love*, which draw the reader to an
insightful and many times emotional moment. (Note
that this thesis informs the reader that the author will
be exploring *death* and *unrequited love*.)

I.   Introduction (Opens to the reader the explo-
      ration of the writing and tells the reader what
      to expect.)
II.   Body (This particular essay will include two
      main points developed in two main para-
      graphs, one paragraph about death and one
      paragraph about emotions. The second para-
      graph will be introduced by means of a transi-
      tion word or phrase or sentence.)
      A. Imagining Death
      B. Feeling Emotions
III. Conclusions (A paragraph which draws con-
      clusions or solves the problem mentioned in
      the thesis statement.)

One of the best ways to organize your thoughts is
to spend time in concentrated thinking, what some call
brainstorming. Thinking through what you want to
write is a way to narrow your topic.

Sample Outline:
Persuasive Paper with Three Major Points (Arguments)

I. Introduction: <u>Thesis statement</u> includes a listing or a summary of the three supportive arguments and introduces the paper.

II. Body
A. Argument 1
   Evidence
   (transition words or phrases or sentences to the next topic)
B. Argument 2
   Evidence
   (transition words or phrases or sentences to the next topic)
C. Argument 3
   Evidence
   (transition words or phrases or sentences to the conclusion)

III. Conclusion: Restatement of arguments and evidence used throughout the paper (do not use the words *in conclusion*—just conclude).

NOTE: For greater detail and explanation of outlining, refer to a composition handbook. Careful attention should be paid to parallel structure with words or phrases, to correct form with headings and subheadings, to punctuation, and to pairing of information. Correct outline structure will greatly enhance the writing of any paper.

Sample Outline:
Expository Essay with Four Major Points

I. Introduction: <u>Thesis statement</u> includes a listing or mention of four examples or supports and introduces the paper; use transitional words or phrases at the end of the paragraph.

II. Body
A. Example 1
   Application
   (transition words or phrases or sentences to the next topic)
B. Example 2
   Application
   (transition words or phrases or sentences to the next topic)
C. Example 3
   Application
   (transition words or phrases or sentences to the next topic)
D. Example 4
   Application
   (transition words or phrases or sentences to the conclusion)

III. Conclusion: Restatement of thesis, drawing from the evidence or applications used in the paper (do not use the words *in conclusion*—just conclude).

NOTE: For greater detail and explanation of outlining, refer to a composition handbook. Careful attention should be paid to parallel structure with words or phrases, to correct form with headings and subheadings, to punctuation, and to pairing of information. Correct outline structure will greatly enhance the writing of any paper.

The Thinking Challenge

The following is an example of a Thinking Challenge approach to Mark Twain's *The Adventures of Huckleberry Finn:*

The Problem or The Issue or The Question:

Should Huck turn in his escaped slave-friend Jim to the authorities?

State problem/issue in five sentences, then in two sentences, and, finally, in one sentence.

Five Sentences:
Huck runs away with Jim. He does so knowing that he is breaking the law. However, the lure of friendship overrides the perfidy he knows he is committing. As he floats down the Mississippi River, he finds it increasingly difficult to hide his friend from the authorities and to hide his feelings of ambivalence. Finally he manages to satisfy both ambiguities.

Two Sentences:
Huck intentionally helps his slave friend Jim escape from servitude. As Huck floats down the Mississippi River, he finds it increasingly difficult to hide his friend from the authorities and at the same time to hide his own feelings of ambivalence.

One Sentence:
After escaping with his slave-friend Jim and floating down the Mississippi River, Huck finds it increasingly difficult to hide his friend from the authorities and at the same time to hide his own feelings of ambivalence.

Name three or more subtopics of problem.
Are there times when we should disobey the law?
What responsibilities does Huck have to his family?
What should Huck do?

Name three or more subtopics of the subtopics.
Are there times when we should disobey the law?
Who determines what laws are unjust?
Should the law be disobeyed publicly?
Who is injured when we disobey the law?
What responsibilities does Huck have to his family?
Who is his family? Jim? His dad?
Is allegiance to them secondary to Jim's needs?
Should his family support his civil disobedience?

What should Huck do?
Turn in Jim?
Escape with Jim?
Both?

What information must be known?
Laws? Jim's character? If he is bad, then should Huck save him?

State the answer to the question/problem in five, two, and one sentence(s).

Five Sentences:
Huck can escape with Jim with profound feelings of guilt. After all, he is helping a slave escape. This is important because it shows that Huck is still a moral, if flawed, character. Jim's freedom does outweigh any other consideration—including the laws of the land and his family's wishes. As the story unfolds the reader sees that Huck is indeed a reluctant criminal, and the reader takes comfort in that fact.

Two Sentences:
Showing reluctance and ambivalence, Huck embarks on an arduous but moral adventure. Jim's freedom outweighs any other need or consideration.

One Sentence:
Putting Jim's freedom above all other considerations, Huck, the reluctant criminal, embarks on an arduous but moral adventure.

Once the Problem or Issue or Question is solved, what are one or two new problems that may arise? What if Huck is wrong? What consequences could Huck face?

Every essay has a beginning (introduction), a middle part (body), and an ending (conclusion). The introduction must draw the reader into the topic and usually presents the thesis to the reader. The body organizes the material and expounds on the thesis (a one sentence statement of purpose) in a cogent and inspiring way. The conclusion generally is a solution to the problem or issue or question or is sometimes a summary. Paragraphs in the body are connected with transitional words or phrases: *furthermore, therefore, in spite of.* Another effective transition technique is to mention in the first sentence of a new paragraph a thought or word that occurs in the last sentence of the previous paragraph. In any event, the body should be intentionally organized to advance the purposes of the paper. A disciplined writer *always* writes a rough draft. Using the well-thought out outline composed during the pre-writing phase is an excellent way to begin the actual writing. The paper has already been processed mentally and only lacks the writing.

WRITING PHASE

The writer must make the first paragraph grab the reader's attention enough that the reader will want to continue reading.

The writer should write naturally, but not colloquially. In other words, the writer should not use clichés and everyday coded language. *The football players blew it* is too colloquial.

The writer should use as much visual imagery and precise detail as possible, should assume nothing, and should explain everything.

REWRITING PHASE

Despite however many rewrites are necessary, when the writer has effectively communicated the subject and corrected grammar and usage problems, she is ready to write the final copy.

Top Ten Most Frequent Essay Problems

Agreement between the Subject and Verb: Use singular forms of verbs with singular subjects and use plural forms of verbs with plural subjects.

WRONG: Everyone finished their homework.

RIGHT: Everyone finished his homework (*Everyone* is an indefinite singular pronoun).

Using the Second Person Pronoun—"you," "your" should rarely, if ever, be used in a formal essay.

WRONG: You know what I mean (Too informal).

Redundancy: Never use "I think" or "It seems to me"

WRONG: I think that is true.

RIGHT: That is true (We know you think it, or you would not write it!).

Tense consistency: Use the same tense (usually present) throughout the paper.

WRONG: I was ready to go, but my friend is tired.

RIGHT: I am ready to go but my friend is tired.

Misplaced Modifiers: Place the phrase or clause close to its modifier.

WRONG: The man drove the car with a bright smile into the garage.

RIGHT: The man with a bright smile drove the car into the garage.

Antecedent Pronoun Problems: Make sure pronouns match (agree) in number and gender with their antecedents.

WRONG: Mary and Susan both enjoyed her dinner.

RIGHT: Mary and Susan both enjoyed their dinners.

Parallelism: Make certain that your list/sentence includes similar phrase types.

WRONG: I like to take a walk and swimming.

RIGHT: I like walking and swimming

345

<u>Affect vs. Effect:</u> Affect is a verb; Effect is a noun unless it means to achieve.

WRONG: His mood effects me negatively.

RIGHT: His mood affects me negatively.

RIGHT: The effects of his mood are devastating.

<u>Dangling Prepositions:</u> Rarely end a sentence with an unmodified preposition.

WRONG: Who were you speaking to?

RIGHT: To whom were you speaking?

<u>Transitions:</u> Make certain that paragraphs are connected with transitions (e.g., furthermore, therefore, in spite of).

RIGHT: Furthermore, Jack London loves to describe animal behavior.

APPENDIX B

COMPOSITION EVALUATION EVALUATION TECHNIQUE #1

Based on 100 points: 85/B-

I. Grammar and Syntax: Is the composition grammatically correct?

(25 points) 15/25

Comments: See Corrections. Look up "Subject/Verb Agreement," "Run-on Sentences," "Verb Tense," "Parallel Structure," and "Use of the Possessive" in your grammar test; read about them, write the grammar rules on the back of your essay, and then correct these parts of your essay.

II. Organization: Does this composition exhibit well considered organization? Does it flow? Transitions? Introduction and a conclusion?

(25 points) 20/25

Comments: Good job with transitional phrases and with having a strong introduction. Your thesis statement gives me a clear idea about the content of your paper. Your conclusion explains your thesis very thoroughly. If you want to sermonize in your essay, be sure to mention that in the introduction.

III. Content: Does this composition answer the question, argue the point well, and/or persuade the reader?

(50 points) 50/50

Comments: Nice insights. You have used solid quotes from the poem to support your argument that Taylor uses nature elements to teach a moral view.

COMPOSITION EVALUATION TECHNIQUE 2

I. Organization
____ Is the writer's purpose stated clearly in the introduction? Is there a thesis sentence? What is it?
____ Does the writer answer the assignment?
____ Does the introduction grab the reader's attention?
____ Is the purpose advanced by each sentence and paragraph?
____ Does the body (middle) of the paper advance the purpose?
____ Does the conclusion accomplish its purpose?
Other helpful comments for the writer:

II. Mechanics
____ Does the writer use active voice?
____ Does the writer use the appropriate verb tense throughout the paper?
____ Is there agreement between all pronouns and antecedents?
____ Is there appropriately subject/verb agreement?
____ Are the transitions effective and appropriate?
Other mechanical trouble spots:

III. Argument
____ Are you persuaded by the arguments?
Other helpful comments for the writer:

COMPOSITION EVALUATION TECHNIQUE THREE

Peer Checklist
(May Prefer to Use Evaluation Technique Forms One or Two)

I. Organization
___ Is the writer's purpose clearly introduced? What is it?
___ Does the organization of the paper coincide with the outline?
___ Does the writer answer the assignment?
___ Does the introduction grab the reader's attention?
___ Is the purpose advanced by each sentence and paragraph? (Are there sentences which don't seem to belong in the paragraphs?)
___ Does the body (middle) of the paper advance the purpose?
___ Does the conclusion solve the purpose of the paper?

Comments regarding organization:

II. Mechanics
___ Does the writer use active voice?
___ Does the writer use the appropriate verb tense throughout the paper?
___ Is there agreement between all pronouns and antecedents?
___ Are there effective and appropriately used transitions?

Comments regarding other mechanical problems:

III. Argument

___ Are you persuaded by the arguments?
___ Does the author need stronger arguments? More arguments?

Other helpful comments:

APPENDIX C

NOVEL REVIEW

BOOK _____ STUDENT _____

AUTHOR _____ DATE OF READING _____

I. BRIEFLY DESCRIBE:
PROTAGONIST—

ANTAGONIST—

OTHER CHARACTERS USED TO DEVELOP PROTAGONIST—

IF APPLICABLE, STATE WHY ANY OF THE BOOK'S CHARACTERS REMIND YOU OF SPECIFIC BIBLE CHARACTERS.

II. SETTING:

III. POINT OF VIEW: (CIRCLE ONE) FIRST PERSON, THIRD PERSON, THIRD PERSON OMNISCIENT

IV. BRIEF SUMMARY OF THE PLOT:

V. THEME (THE QUINTESSENTIAL MEANING/PURPOSE OF THE BOOK IN ONE OR TWO SENTENCES):

VI. AUTHOR'S WORLDVIEW: HOW DO YOU KNOW? WHAT BEHAVIORS DO(ES) THE CHARACTER(S) MANIFEST THAT LEAD YOU TO THIS CONCLUSION?

VII. WHY DID YOU LIKE/DISLIKE THIS BOOK?

VIII. THE NEXT LITERARY WORK I READ WILL BE . . .

SHORT STORY REVIEW

SHORT STORY _____ STUDENT _____

AUTHOR _____ DATE OF READING _____

I. BRIEFLY DESCRIBE
PROTAGONIST—

ANTAGONIST—

OTHER CHARACTERS USED TO DEVELOP PROTAGONIST—

IF APPLICABLE, STATE WHY ANY OF THE STORY'S CHARACTERS REMIND YOU OF SPECIFIC BIBLE CHARACTERS.

II. SETTING

III. POINT OF VIEW: (CIRCLE ONE) FIRST PERSON, THIRD PERSON, THIRD PERSON OMNISCIENT

IV. BRIEF SUMMARY OF THE PLOT

IDENTIFY THE CLIMAX OF THE SHORT STORY.

V. THEME (THE QUINTESSENTIAL MEANING/PURPOSE OF THE STORY IN ONE OR TWO SENTENCES):

VI. AUTHOR'S WORLDVIEW:
HOW DO YOU KNOW THIS? WHAT BEHAVIORS DO(ES) THE CHARACTER(S) MANIFEST THAT LEAD YOU TO THIS CONCLUSION?

VII. WHY DID YOU LIKE/DISLIKE THIS SHORT STORY?

VIII. THE NEXT LITERARY WORK I READ WILL BE . . .

DRAMA REVIEW

PLAY _____ STUDENT _____

AUTHOR _____ DATE OF READING _____

I. BRIEFLY DESCRIBE
PROTAGONIST—

ANTAGONIST—

IF APPLICABLE, STATE WHY ANY OF THE PLAY'S CHARACTERS REMIND YOU OF SPECIFIC BIBLE
CHARACTERS.

II. SETTING

III. POINT OF VIEW: (CIRCLE ONE) FIRST PERSON, THIRD PERSON, THIRD PERSON OMNISCIENT

IV. BRIEF SUMMARY OF THE PLOT

IDENTIFY THE CLIMAX OF THE PLAY.

V. THEME (THE QUINTESSENTIAL MEANING/PURPOSE OF THE PLAY IN ONE OR TWO SENTENCES)

VI. AUTHOR'S WORLDVIEW
HOW DO YOU KNOW THIS? WHAT BEHAVIORS DO(ES) THE CHARACTER(S) MANIFEST THAT LEAD YOU TO THIS CONCLUSION?

VII. WHY DID YOU LIKE/DISLIKE THIS PLAY?

VIII. THE NEXT LITERARY WORK I WILL READ WILL BE . . .

NON-FICTION REVIEW

LITERARY WORK _____ STUDENT _____

AUTHOR _____ DATE OF READING _____

I. WRITE A PRÉCIS OF THIS BOOK. IN YOUR PRÉCIS, CLEARLY STATE THE AUTHOR'S THESIS AND SUPPORTING ARGUMENTS.

II. ARE YOU PERSUADED? WHY OR WHY NOT?

III. WHY DID YOU LIKE/DISLIKE THIS BOOK?

IV. THE NEXT LITERARY WORK I READ WILL BE . . .

APPENDIX D

PRAYER JOURNAL GUIDE

Journal Guide Questions

Bible Passage(s): _____

_____

_____

1. Centering Time (a list of those things that I must do later):

3. Reading Scripture Passage (with notes on text):

4. Living in Scripture:

A. How does the passage affect the person mentioned in the passage? How does he/she feel?

2. Discipline of Silence (remain absolutely still and quiet).

B. How does the passage affect my life? What is the Lord saying to me through this passage?

6. Discipline of Silence

5. Prayers of Adoration and Thanksgiving, Intercession, and Future Prayer Targets:

APPENDIX E

BOOK LIST FOR SUPPLEMENTAL READING

Note:
Not all literature is suitable for all students; educators and students should choose literature appropriate to students' age, maturity, interests, and abilities.

Jane Austen, EMMA

Charlotte Brontë, JANE EYRE

Thomas Bulfinch, THE AGE OF FABLE

Pearl S. Buck, THE GOOD EARTH

John Bunyan, PILGRIM'S PROGRESS

Agatha Christie, AND THEN THERE WERE NONE

Samuel T. Coleridge, RIME OF THE ANCIENT MARINER

Jospeh Conrad, HEART OF DARKNESS, LORD JIM

James F. Cooper, THE LAST OF THE MOHICANS, DEERSLAYER

Stephen Crane, THE RED BADGE OF COURAGE

Clarence Day, LIFE WITH FATHER

Daniel Defoe, ROBINSON CRUSOE

Charles Dickens, GREAT EXPECTATIONS, A CHRISTMAS CAROL, A TALE OF TWO CITIES, OLIVER TWIST, NICHOLAS NICKLEBY

Arthur C. Doyle, THE ADVENTURES OF SHERLOCK HOLMES

Alexander Dumas, THE THREE MUSKETEERS

George Eliot, SILAS MARNER

T.S. Eliot, MURDER IN THE CATHEDRAL, SILAS MARNER

Anne Frank, THE DIARY OF ANNE FRANK

Oliver Goldsmith, THE VICAR OF WAKEFIELD

Edith Hamilton, MYTHOLOGY

Nathaniel Hawthorne, THE SCARLET LETTER, THE HOUSE OF THE SEVEN GABLES

Thor Heyerdahl, KON-TIKI

J. Hilton, LOST HORIZON, GOODBYE, MR. CHIPS

Homer, THE ODYSSEY, THE ILIAD

W. H. Hudson, GREEN MANSIONS

Victor Hugo, LES MISERABLES, THE HUNCHBACK OF NOTRE DAME

Zora Neale Hurston, THEIR EYES WERE WATCHING GOD

Washington Irving, THE SKETCH BOOK

Rudyard Kipling, CAPTAINS COURAGEOUS

Harper Lee, TO KILL A MOCKINGBIRD

Madeline L'Engle, A CIRCLE OF QUIET, THE SUMMER OF THE GREAT GRANDMOTHER, A WRINKLE IN TIME

C. S. Lewis, THE SCREWTAPE LETTERS, MERE CHRISTIANITY, CHRONICLES OF NARNIA

Jack London, THE CALL OF THE WILD, WHITE FANG

George MacDonald, CURATE'S AWAKENING, ETC.

Sir Thomas Malory, LE MORTE D'ARTHUR

Guy de Maupassant, SHORT STORIES

Herman Melville, BILLY BUDD, MOBY DICK

Monsarrat, THE CRUEL SEA

C. Nordhoff & Hall, MUTINY ON THE BOUNTY

Edgar Allen Poe, POEMS & SHORT STORIES

E. M. Remarque, ALL QUIET ON THE WESTERN FRONT

Anne Rinaldi, A BREAK WITH CHARITY: STORY OF THE SALEM WITCH TRIALS

Carl Sanburg, ABRAHAM LINCOLN

William Saroyan, THE HUMAN COMEDY

Sir Walter Scott, IVANHOE

William Shakespeare, HAMLET, MACBETH, JULIUS CAESAR, AS YOU LIKE IT, ROMEO AND JULIET, A MIDSUMMER NIGHT'S DREAM, ETC.

George Bernard Shaw, PYGMALION

Sophocles, ANTIGONE

Harriet Beecher Stowe, UNCLE TOM'S CABIN

John Steinbeck, OF MICE AND MEN, GRAPES OF WRATH

R. L. Stevenson, DR. JEKYLL AND MR. HYDE, TREASURE ISLAND, KIDNAPPED

Irving Stone, LUST FOR LIFE

Jonathan Swift, GULLIVER'S TRAVELS
Booth Tarkington, PENROD
J.R.R. Tolkien, THE LORD OF THE RINGS TRILOGY
Mark Twain, ADVENTURES OF HUCKLEBERRY FINN, THE ADVENTURES OF TOM SAWYER
Jules Verne, MASTER OF THE WORLD
Booker T. Washington, UP FROM SLAVERY
H. G. Wells, COLLECTED WORKS
Tennessee Williams, THE GLASS MENAGERIE

FOR OLDER STUDENTS

Chinua Achebe, THINGS FALL APART
Aristotle, POETICUS
Edward Bellamy, LOOKING BACKWARD
Jorge Luis Borges, VARIOUS SHORT STORIES
Stephen V. Benet, JOHN BROWN'S BODY
Charlotte Brontë, WUTHERING HEIGHTS
Camus, THE STRANGER
Chaucer, THE CANTERBURY TALES, BEOWULF
Willa Cather, MY ANTONIA
Miguel de Cervantes, DON QUIXOTE
Fyodor Dostovesky, CRIME AND PUNISHMENT, THE IDIOT, THE BROTHERS KARAMAZOV
William Faulkner, THE HAMLET TRIOLOGY
F. Scott Fitzgerald, THE GREAT GATSBY
John Galsworthy, THE FORSYTHE SAGA
Lorraine Hansberry, RAISIN IN THE SUN
Thomas Hardy, THE RETURN OF THE NATIVE, THE MAYOR OF CASTERBRIDGE

A. E. Housman, A SHROPSHIRE LAD
Henrik Ibsen, A DOLL'S HOUSE
Charles Lamb THE ESSAYS OF ELIA
Sinclair Lewis, BABBITT, ARROWSMITH
Kamala Markandaya, NECTAR IN A SIEVE
Gabriel Barcia Marquez, 100 YEARS OF SOLITUDE
John P. Marquand, THE LATE GEORGE APLEY
E. Lee Masters, A SPOON RIVER ANTHOLOGY
Somerset Maugham, OF HUMAN BONDAGE
Arthur Miller, THE CRUCIBLE, DEATH OF A SALESMAN
Eugene O'Neill, THE EMPEROR JONES
George Orwell, ANIMAL FARM, 1984
Thomas Paine, THE RIGHTS OF MAN
Alan Paton, CRY THE BELOVED COUNTRY
Plato, THE REPUBLIC
Plutarch, LIVES
O. E. Rolvaag, GIANTS IN THE EARTH
Edmund Rostand, CYRANO DE BERGERAC
Mary Shelley, FRANKENSTEIN
Sophocles, OEDIPUS REX
John Steinbeck, THE PEARL
Ivan Turgenev, FATHERS AND SONS
William Thackeray, VANITY FAIR
Leo Tolstoy, WAR AND PEACE
Edith Wharton, ETHAN FROME
Walt Whitman, LEAVES OF GRASS
Thornton Wilder, OUR TOWN
Thomas Wolfe, LOOK HOMEWARD ANGEL

APPENDIX F

GLOSSARY OF LITERARY TERMS

Allegory A story or tale with two or more levels of meaning—a literal level and one or more symbolic levels. The events, setting, and characters in an allegory are symbols for ideas or qualities.

Alliteration The repetition of initial consonant sounds. The repetition can be juxtaposed (side by side; e.g., simply sad). An example:

I conceive therefore, as to the business of being profound, that it is with writers, as with wells; a person with good eyes may see to the bottom of the deepest, provided any water be there; and that often, when there is nothing in the world at the bottom, besides dryness and dirt, though it be but a yard and a half under ground, it shall pass, however, for wondrous deep, upon no wiser a reason than because it is wondrous dark. (Jonathan Swift)

Allusion A casual and brief reference to a famous historical or literary figure or event:

You must borrow me Gargantua's mouth first. 'Tis a word too great for any mouth of this age's size. (Shakespeare)

Analogy The process by which new or less familiar words, constructions, or pronunciations conform to the pattern of older or more familiar (and often unrelated) ones; a comparison between two unlike things. The purpose of an analogy is to describe something unfamiliar by pointing out its similarities to something that is familiar.

Antagonist In a narrative, the character with whom the main character has the most conflict. In Jack London's "To Build a Fire" the antagonist is the extreme cold of the Yukon rather than a person or animal.

Archetype The original pattern or model from which all other things of the same kind are made; a perfect example of a type or group. (e.g. The biblical character Joseph is often considered an archetype of Jesus Christ)

Argumentation The discourse in which the writer presents and logically supports a particular view or opinion; sometimes used interchangeably with *persuasion*.

Aside In a play an aside is a speech delivered by an actor in such a way that other characters on the stage are presumed not to hear it; an aside generally reveals a character's inner thoughts.

Autobiography A form of nonfiction in which a person tells his/her own life story. Notable examples of autobiography include those by Benjamin Franklin and Frederick Douglass.

Ballad A song or poem that tells a story in short stanzas and simple words with repetition, refrain, etc.

Biography A form of nonfiction in which a writer tells the life story of another person.

Character A person or an animal who takes part in the action of a literary work. The *main character* is the one on whom the work focuses. The person with whom the main character has the most conflict is the *antagonist*. He is the enemy of the main character (*protagonist*). For instance, in *The Scarlet Letter*, by Nathaniel Hawthorne, Chillingsworth is the antagonist. Hester is the protagonist. Characters who appear in the story may perform actions, speak to other characters, be described by the narrator, or be remembered. Characters introduced whose sole purpose is to develop the main character are called *foils*.

Classicism An approach to literature and the other arts that stresses reason, balance, clarity, ideal beauty, and orderly form in imitation of the arts of Greece and Rome.

Conflict A struggle between opposing forces; can be internal or external; when occurring within a character is called *internal conflict*. An example of this occurs in Mark Twain's *Adventures of Huckleberry Finn*. In this novel Huck is struggling in his mind about whether to return an escaped slave, his good friend Jim, to the authorities. An *external conflict* is normally an obvious conflict between the protagonist and antagonist(s). London's "To Build a Fire" illustrates conflict between a character and an outside force. Most plots develop from conflict, making conflict one of the primary elements of narrative literature.

Crisis or *Climax* The moment or event in the *plot* in which the conflict is most directly addressed: the main character "wins" or "loses"; the secret is revealed. After the climax, the *denouement* or falling action occurs.

Dialectic Examining opinions or ideas logically, often by the method of question and answer

Discourse, Forms of Various modes into which writing can be classified; traditionally, writing has been divided into the following modes:
Exposition Writing which presents information
Narration Writing which tells a story
Description Writing which portrays people, places, or things
Persuasion (sometimes also called *Argumentation*) Writing which attempts to convince people to think or act in a certain way

Drama A story written to be performed by actors; the playwright supplies dialogue for the characters to speak and stage directions that give information about costumes, lighting, scenery, properties, the setting, and the character's movements and ways of speaking.

Dramatic monologue A poem or speech in which an imaginary character speaks to a silent listener. Eliot's "The Love Song of J. Alfred Prufrock" is a dramatic monologue.

Elegy A solemn and formal lyric poem about death, often one that mourns the passing of some particular person; Whitman's "When Lilacs Last in the Dooryard Bloom'd" is an elegy lamenting the death of President Lincoln.

Essay A short, nonfiction work about a particular subject; *essay* comes from the Old French word *essai*, meaning "a trial or attempt"; meant to be explanatory, an essay is not meant to be an exhaustive treatment of a subject; can be classified as formal or informal, personal or impersonal; can also be classified according to purpose as either expository, argumentative, descriptive, persuasive, or narrative.

Figurative Language See *metaphor, simile, analogy*

Foil A character who provides a contrast to another character and whose purpose is to develop the main character.

Genre A division or type of literature; commonly divided into three major divisions, literature is either poetry, prose, or drama; each major genre can then be divided into smaller genres: poetry can be divided into lyric, concrete, dramatic, narrative, and epic poetry; prose can be divided into fiction (novels and short stories) and nonfiction (biography, autobiography, letters, essays, and reports); drama can be divided into serious drama, tragedy, comic drama, melodrama, and farce.

Gothic The use of primitive, medieval, wild, or mysterious elements in literature; Gothic elements offended 18th century classical writers but appealed to the Romantic writers who followed them. Gothic novels feature writers who use places like mysterious castles where horrifying supernatural events take place; Poe's "The Fall of the House of Usher" illustrates the influence of Gothic elements.

Harlem Renaissance Occurring during the 1920s, a time of African American artistic creativity centered in Harlem in New York City; Langston Hughes was a Harlem Renaissance writer.

Hyperbole A deliberate exaggeration or overstatement; in Mark Twain's "The Notorious Jumping From of Calaveras County," the claim that Jim Smiley would follow a bug as far as Mexico to win a bet is hyperbolic.

Idyll A poem or part of a poem that describes and idealizes country life; Whittier's "Snowbound" is an idyll.

Irony A method of humorous or subtly sarcastic expression in which the intended meanings of the words used is the direct opposite of their usual sense.

Journal A daily autobiographical account of events and personal reactions.

Kenning Indirect way of naming people or things; knowledge or recognition; in Old English poetry, a metaphorical name for something.

Literature All writings in prose or verse, especially those of an imaginative or critical character, without regard to their excellence and/or writings considered as having permanent value, excellence of form, great emotional effect, etc.

Metaphor (Figure of speech) A comparison which creatively identifies one thing with another dissimilar thing and transfers or ascribes to the first thing some of the qualities of the second. Unlike a *simile* or *analogy*, metaphor asserts that one thing is another thing—not just that one is like another. Very frequently a metaphor is invoked by the verb *to be*:

Affliction then is ours;
We are the trees whom shaking fastens more. (George Herbert)
Then Jesus declared, "I am the bread of life." (John 6:35)
Jesus answered, "I am the Way and the truth and the life." (John 14:6)

Meter A poem's rhythmical pattern, determined by the number and types of stresses, or beats, in each line; a certain number of *metrical feet* make up a *line* of verse; (pentameter denotes a line containing five metrical feet); the act of describing the meter of a poem is called *scanning* which involves marking the stressed and unstressed syllables, as follows:
iamb A foot with one unstressed syllable followed by one stressed syllable, as in the word *abound*.
trochee A foot with one stressed syllable followed by one unstressed syllable, as in the word *spoken*.
anapest A foot with two unstressed syllables followed by one stressed syllable, as in the word *interrupt*.

dactyl A foot with a stressed syllable followed by two unstressed syllables, as in the word *accident*.
spondee Two stressed feet: *quicksand*, *heartbeat*; occurs only occasionally in English.

Motif A main idea element, feature; a main theme or subject to be elaborated on.

Narration The way the author chooses to tell the story.
First Person Narration: A character and refers to himself or herself, using "I." Example: Huck Finn in *The Adventures of Huckleberry Finn* tells the story from his perspective. This is a creative way to bring humor into the plot.
Second Person Narration: Addresses the reader and/or the main character as "you" (and may also use first person narration, but not necessarily). One example is the opening of each of Rudyard Kipling's *Just So Stories*, in which the narrator refers to the child listener as "O Best Beloved."
Third Person Narration: Not a character in the story; refers to the story's characters as "he" and "she." This is probably the most common form of narration.
Limited Narration: Only able to tell what one person is thinking or feeling. Example: in *A Separate Peace*, by John Knowles, we only see the story from Gene's perspective.
Omniscient Narration: Charles Dickens employs this narration in most of his novels.
Reliable Narration: Everything this Narration says is true, and the Narrator knows everything that is necessary to the story.
Unreliable Narrator: May not know all the relevant information; may be intoxicated or mentally ill; may lie to the audience. Example: Edgar Allan Poe's narrators are frequently unreliable. Think of the delusions that the narrator of "The Tell-Tale Heart" has about the old man.

Narrative In story form.

Onomatopoeia. Use of words which, in their pronunciation, suggest their meaning. "Hiss," for example, when spoken is intended to resemble the sound of steam or of a snake. Other examples include these: *slam, buzz, screech, whirr, crush, sizzle, crunch, wring, wrench, gouge, grind, mangle, bang, blam, pow, zap, fizz, urp, roar, growl, blip, click, whimper,* and, of course, *snap, crackle, and pop.*

Parallelism Two or more balancing statements with phrases, clauses, or paragraphs of similar length and grammatical structure.

Plot Arrangement of the action in fiction or drama— events of the story in the order the story gives them. A typical plot has five parts: *Exposition, Rising Action, Crisis* or *Climax, Falling Action,* and *Resolution* (sometimes called *Denouement).*

Précis Summary of the plot of a literary piece.

Protagonist The enemy of the main character (*antagonist*).

Rhetoric Using words effectively in writing and speaking.

Setting The place(s) and time(s) of a story, including the historical period, social milieu of the characters, geographical location, descriptions of indoor and outdoor locales.

Scop An Old English poet or bard.

Simile A figure of speech in which one thing is likened to another dissimilar thing by the use of *like, as,* etc.

Sonnet A poem normally of fourteen lines in any of several fixed verse and rhyme schemes, typically in rhymed iambic pentameter; sonnets characteristically express a single theme or idea.

Structure The arrangement of details and scenes that make up a literary work.

Style An author's characteristic arrangement of words. A style may be colloquial, formal, terse, wordy, theoretical, subdued, colorful, poetic, or highly individual. Style is the arrangement of words in groups and sentences; *diction* on the other hand refers to the choice of individual words; the arrangement of details and scenes make up the *structure* of a literary work; all combine to influence the tone of the work; thus, diction, style, and structure make up the *form* of the literary work.

Theme The one-sentence, major meaning of a literary piece, rarely stated but implied. The theme is not a moral, which is a statement of the author's didactic purpose of his literary piece. A thesis statement is very similar to the theme.

Tone The attitude the author takes toward his subject; author's attitude is revealed through choice of details, through diction and style, and through the emphasis and comments that are made; like theme and style, tone is sometimes difficult to describe with a single word or phrase; often it varies in the same literary piece to suit the moods of the characters and the situations. For instance, the tone or mood of Poe's "Annabel Lee" is very somber.

Credits, Permissions, and Sources

Efforts have been made to conform to US Copyright Law. Any infringement is unintentional, and any file which infringes copyright, and about which the copyright claimant informs me, will be removed pending resolution.

All graphics are copyrighted by Clipart.com unless otherwise noted.

Most of the literature cited in this book is in the public domain. Much of it is available on the Internet through the following sites:

Bartleby.com, Great Books Online
Aeschylus, *Oresteia*
Budda, *The Bhagavad-Gûtââ*
Confucius, *The Sayings of Confucius*
Epictetus, *The golden sayings of Epictetus*, with the Hymn of Cleanthes; translated and arranged by Hastings Crossley
Mohammed, *Koran*
Plato, *Apology*
Unknown, *The Song of Roland*

Susan Wise Bauer, *Writing The Short Story* (Charles City, VA)

Classical Short Stories: The Best of the Genre (http://www.geocities.com/short_stories_page/index.html)
Leo Tolstoy, The Death of Ivan Ilych, Translated by Louise and Aylmer Maude.

Early Christian Writings (http://www.earlychristianwritings.com/justin.html)
Writings, by Polycarp, Justin Martyr, and Clement

Enuma Elish translated by N. K. Sanders (http://www.piney.com/Enuma.html)

Everypoet.com
Dante, *Inferno*

Gilgamesh Epic, translated by E. A. Speiser, in *Ancient Near Eastern Texts* (Princeton, 1950), pp. 60-72, as reprinted in Isaac Mendelsohn (ed.), *Religions of the Ancient Near East*, Library of Religion paperbook series (New York, 1955). PP. 100-6; notes by Mendolenson (http://www-relg-studies.scu.edu/netcours/rs011/restrict/gilflood.htm).

Herodotus, *Histories*. Translated by Rawlinson. (http://www.concordance.com/)

Herodotus and the Bible, Wayne Jackson (http://www.christiancourier.com/archives/)

http://www.cyberhymnal.org/htm/m/i/mightyfo.htm
Martin Luther, *A Mighty Fortress is Our God*

Infomotions, Inc. The Alex Catalogue of Electronic Texts (http://www.infomotions.com/alex/).

Infoplease.com. 2002 Family Education Network. (http://aolsvc.aol.infoplease.com/ipa/A0874987.html)

The Internet Classics Archive (http://classics.mit.edu/Aristotle/poetics.1.1.html)

Aristotle, *Poetics*

Internet Applications Laboratory at the University of Evansville
Plato, *Symposium*

The Library of Congress Collection (http://www.loc.gov/exhibits/gadd/)

Lecture on Sor Juana Ines de la Cruz (http://www.latin_american.cam.ac.uk/SorJuana/)
Sor Juana Ines de la Cruz, "May Heaven Serve as Plate for the Engraving" and "Yet if, for Singing your Praise."

National Park Service (http://www.nps.gov/edal/index.htm)

The Pachomius Library (http://www.ocf.org/OrthodoxPage/reading/St.Pachomius/Liturgical/didache.html)
Unknown, *The Didache*, edited by Friar Martin Fontenot Gonzalez

Shinto Creation Stories (http://www.wsu.edu/~dee/ANCJAPAN/CREAT2.HTM)
The Creation of the gods (Translated by W.G. Aston, Nihongi (London: Kegan, Paul, Trench, Trüübner, 1896), 1-2

Stephane Theroux. Classic Reader (http://classicreader.com/)
Anton Chekov, *The Sea Gull*
Andrew Barton Paterson, *The Man From Snowy River*

University of Oregon. (http://www.uoregon.edu)
Iliad, Homer. Translated by Samuel Butler.

University of Pennsylvania (www.sas.upenn.edu/)
Author Unknown, *Ani Papyrus: Book of the Dead*

University of Virginia. Browse E-Books by Author (http://etext.lib.virginia.edu/ebooks/Wlist.html).

University of Wisconsin, Milwaukee. The Classic Text: Traditions and Interpretations (http://www.uwm.edu/Library/special/exhibits/clastext/clshome.htm)

NOTES

NOTES

NOTES

NOTES

NOTES

NOTES

NOTES

NOTES

NOTES

NOTES

NOTES

NOTES

NOTES